PRAISE FOR **FLYING THROUGH MIDNIGHT**

"A no-holds-barred account of the secret air war over Laos. John Halliday paints a compelling cockpit view of the action, but he also immerses his readers in layer upon layer of sensations and emotions associated with those dangerous nighttime missions. He takes us on a hell of a ride!"

—Col. Tom Yarborough, author of
*Da Nang Diary: A Forward Air Controller's
Gunsight View of Combat in Vietnam*

"A riveting first-person account of a pilot and his crew flying night missions in a C-123 over Laos during the Vietnam War."
—Bob Kerrey, Medal of Honor recipient
and former U.S. senator

"In 1970 a twenty-four-year-old pilot flies over Laos with no identifying papers or patches. His commander in chief—Richard Nixon—denies his existence. Now for the first time, John Halliday takes you into the cockpit as he flies his dangerous top-secret mission."

—James Bradley, author of
Flags of Our Fathers and *Flyboys*

"This book goes right to the heart of how a pilot takes responsibility for an aircrew flying secret night missions…and it describes the catch-22 craziness of that war. This book is destined to become one of the great books about the Vietnam War."

—Frederick Downs, author of
The Killing Zone: My Life in the Vietnam War

"Halliday s̶̶̶̶̶̶̶̶̶̶̶̶̶ ̶̶̶̶̶̶̶̶̶̶plex thoughts experienced by comba̶̶̶̶̶̶ ̶̶̶̶̶̶̶̶̶̶̶̶̶̶̶̶at flying over Laos."

of *Cleared Hot!:*
Pilot in Vietnam

FLYING
THROUGH
MIDNIGHT

A Pilot's Dramatic Story of His
Secret Missions Over Laos
During the Vietnam War

JOHN T. HALLIDAY

St. Martin's Paperbacks

This is a true story. To honor the privacy of my former comrades, I changed some names and physical descriptions. We shared this crisis together, so writing this book was like talking with old friends. I would love to continue that conversation and post our correspondence on www.flyingthroughmidnight.com.

FLYING THROUGH MIDNIGHT

Copyright © 2005 by John Halliday.

Cover photo © Ted Carlson/Check Six.

Library of Congress Catalog Card Number: 2005044068

ISBN: 0-312-94203-6
EAN: 9780312-94203-8

Pages 467-468 constitute an extension of the copyright page.

Printed in the United States of America

Scribner hardcover edition / October 2005
St. Martin's Paperbacks edition / February 2007

St. Martin's Paperbacks are published by St. Martin's Press, 175 Fifth Avenue, New York, NY 10010.

10 9 8 7 6 5 4 3 2 1

For my darling wife, Sharon, and my father

The most important element in human life is Faith.
If God were to take away all his blessings and leave
me with but one gift, I would ask for Faith.

— ROSE FITZGERALD KENNEDY
ON THE FOUNTAIN AT BOSTON HARBOR

To understand today, you have to search through yesterday.

—PEARL S. BUCK

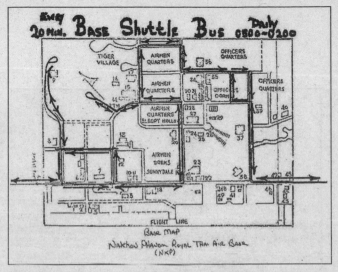

Base Map
Nakhon Phanom Royal Thai Air Base
(NKP)

1. Base Operations
2. Control Tower
3. Fire Station
4. Hq, 56th Special Operations Wing
5. TUOC
6. Supply, BEMO Complex
7. C.E.
8. Service Station
9. TFA
10. Photo Lab
11. Telephone Exchange
12. MARS Station
13. Dispensary
14. USO
15. Special Services
16. Hobby Shops
17. Library-Education Center
18. Life Support Section
19. AFTN
20. Skyraider INN (dining hall)
21. Base Finance
22. CBPO
23. NCO Open Mess
24. Outdoor Sports Facilities
25. Chapel
26. Amphitheater
27. Outdoor Sports Facilities
28. Bank of America
29. Theater
30. BX
31. Airmen's Open Mess
32. BX Concession Center
33. BX Cafeteria-Foodland
34. Bowling Center
35. Post Office
36. Gymnasium
37. Officers' Open Mess
38. Hq, 56th Combat Support Group
39. Housing Office
40. Sawadee Inn (VIP Quarters)
41. Swimming Pool
42. Civilian Personnel Office
43. BX Barber Shop-Snack Bar
44. Thai Restaurant
45. Main Gate
46. Thai Base Headquarters
47. Aerial Port
48. Motor Pool
49. Security Office

C-123K aircraft.
Photo taken at an unknown airfield in 1971.
Background aircraft is a USAF C-7A Caribou.

Photo Credit:
Copyright © 1971, Peter A. Bird

CHAPTER ONE

June 8, 1970

Wiley waved to me from across the ramp as I stepped off the C-130 shuttle plane from Bangkok. I lifted my hand in response, then raised it to my brow, shading my eyes against the Thai sun, merciless still at midafternoon. The hop from Bangkok was the final leg in my journey to Nakhon Phanom Air Base, where I was to begin my assignment with the 606th Special Operations Squadron, flying C-123 cargo missions around Thailand. Wiley's presence heartened me. I'd heard that most guys who arrived in Vietnam were unceremoniously dumped on the ramp in Saigon or Da Nang and left to find their own way to their unit.

Welcome to the war, buddy, such a callous reception announced.

Maybe *my* war would be different.

Wiley leaned against a blue Air Force pickup truck parked before a large billboard that shouted:

FLIGHTLINE PHOTOGRAPHY
STRICTLY PROHIBITED
VIOLATORS PUNISHABLE UNDER UCMJ

All I could think was, why would anybody care if I snapped a few pictures of cargo transports to send back home to Sharon?

Other than that puzzling note, my arrival at NKP was wholly different from what I'd heard of most Vietnam receptions. I felt I was being welcomed to some country club. Wiley ambled toward me wearing a big smile. "Hi, I'm Wiley. Welcome to the Candlesticks and NKP. I'm your sponsor. Let me help you with those bags," he boomed cheerfully. Relaxed smile. Happy eyes. An easygoing way about him. Definite Midwestern accent. Maybe Rockford or Madison. Huge, calloused farmer's hands. Probably grew up playing high school football and driving his grandfather's tractor during the summers.

Wiley looked much older than me, but I figured we must actually be about the same age. After all, every pilot assigned to the Candlestick squadron was probably in his early twenties like me. But Wiley seemed years older.

I wondered if something about this place had caused him to age more quickly, but I forced a smile to make a good first impression. "Hi, I'm John Halliday. Thanks for coming to meet me."

"C'mon, let's get you out of here and into someplace cool. Nobody here wears that flightsuit during the day. It's too damn hot."

He was right. My flightsuit was about to melt into my skin. The northeastern Thailand heat was a blast furnace. A real inferno. I took a breath, but the heat singed my nostrils. I shifted to mouth breathing, but the heat boiled down my windpipe.

Wiley helped me with my bags and then dropped them into the back of the six-pack. I tried to open the passenger door, but pulled back when the handle scorched my hand. "Use your sleeve," he suggested. We jumped in the air-conditioned truck and drove down the flightline. Impressive.

My own driver. I thought I was going to like this place better than Vietnam.

"How hot *is* it?" I complained as we passed rows of parked planes.

"It's one hundred and eight, with the humidity a pleasant ninety-five percent. We run from air-conditioned spot to air-conditioned spot," Wiley explained as he did a series of double takes at me, staring far too long and then looking away when I noticed him sizing me up.

"I thought you guys called this place Naked Fanny," I said, an attempt to break the ice, which failed.

"We *hate* that," he scolded. "Bob Hope pinned that on us when he came for Christmas last year. The name is Nakhon Phanom, but we call it NKP."

I thought, so much for my good-first-impression idea.

There! He did it again . . . the *long* look . . . checking me out.

As we drove down the flightline, the scene seemed caught in a 1940s time warp. The Andrews Sisters should have been singing in the background about the "Boogie Woogie Bugle Boy from Company B." There wasn't a modern jet aircraft in sight. The ramp was littered with propeller-driven aviation relics that belonged in someone's garage sale, not out here fighting a war. I could see A-1s, A-26s, C-123s, OV-10s, and Jolly Green Giant helicopters. Hand-me-down, cast-off airplanes no one else wanted. I figured the Air Force sent them way out here under the title "special operations" to make people feel good about having to fly these old rattletraps.

I realized I'd landed in aviation's backwater.

I noticed the ramp we were driving across—no, the sensation was more like riding a boat over small waves—wasn't even concrete. Instead, it was corrugated-metal sheeting, in which dead star-thistle weeds poked up through six-inch-round holes. Even the ramp was a castoff nobody wanted. I thought, ought to be slicker than owlshit taxiing on it when it rains.

Wiley pointed to a building. The sign over the door proclaimed:

606TH SPECIAL OPERATIONS SQUADRON

Wiley said proudly, "That's us." Beside the front door hung a six-foot oval wood sign, emblazoned with a winged candle burning bright above a black, mountainous background. The abbreviation "606 SOS" wreathed across the logo's top. "Our squadron patch," Wiley explained, handing me a stiff, new Candlestick patch.

I ripped my existing "Military Airlift Command" patch off its Velcro strips and replaced it with the golden-winged candlestick.

Wiley smiled, patted me on the back, and said, "Welcome to the Candlesticks. Now you're official."

Since I knew squadron names and patches attempt to capture a unit's mission, this name and patch seemed inconsistent with transporting boxes. I made a mental note to ask Wiley about it later.

As we made a right turn off the flightline, headed toward the officers' quarters, I said, "I noticed the razor-sharp security fence all around the base as we flew in and the guard towers manned with automatic weapons. I thought these Thai bases were secure."

"Well, the place is *pretty* safe," he chuckled. "There've been a few local skirmishes. But if you're a runner, I wouldn't recommend jogging along the perimeter fence."

"Oh, thanks," I answered weakly.

That too-long look came again. I knew what was coming. He asked, "Say, did anybody ever tell you that you look like a young version of Pat Boone, the boyish-looking crooner? You know, 'Love Letters in the Sand' . . . the white shoes . . . the clean-cut image . . . all that crap?"

"Yes," I groaned. "*All the time*. I had to live with that sappy image all the way through high school and college. I'd rather not start that here if you don't mind."

Wiley was perfect. "Sure. No problem, John."

As we drove down the block, I noticed the place seemed deserted. Where was everybody? The base should have been hopping with activity. Strange. An eerie feeling came over me. I should have asked Wiley what the big deal was, but kept my mouth shut. No sense asking more dumb questions, *confirming* my ignorance.

After three blocks of driving past rows of shed-type buildings typical of Thai bases, Wiley parked. I picked up my gear and we walked across a wide grass front lawn to the quarters I'd been assigned.

Grass? The dead, brown grass blades crunched under my boots like broken glass. "The rainy season doesn't start till November," Wiley explained.

I saw maids along the long front porch, cleaning rooms as if the place were a resort. This assignment is going to be okay, I reassured myself. My unease over what to expect from NKP and the fatigue from the long flight both began to fade.

I asked Wiley how much the maid service cost, because I didn't have a lot of money to spare and I would rather clean up after myself to save the fee. But he said not to worry . . . the Air Force paid the maids as part of the deal with the Thai government in Bangkok for letting us fly out of their country.

A man our age resembling Robert Redford was sitting on the porch drinking a beer under the mercilessly hot sun. Waves of sweat sheeted down his face. Why was he outside in this blast furnace?

Wiley introduced me. "Mark, this is your new roommate, John Halliday."

I offered a handshake, but Mark did not look up from what he was doing. I could see by his blank, distant expression he was off in some private world all his own. He had the plastic rings from a six-pack of *something* in his hands and was s-l-o-w-l-y pulling them apart. Mark took each ring and carefully stretched it until it was about to break. Just before the plastic failed, he held it up within a fraction of an inch of his eyes to focus on something I didn't understand.

"Nice to meet you, Mark. How are you doing?" I asked.

"Ninety-six down and two hundred and sixty-nine to go," he mumbled slowly.

I didn't understand. "What are you doing there?" I tried again.

"Watching . . . the . . . bubbles." Mark stumbled over each word.

I tried again. *"What?"*

"Watching the bubbles. Just before the plastic breaks, a whole bunch of little bubbles form. I stretch them out to see how big and long I can make them before the plastic fails. It's really neat to watch the bubbles pop." He did it again. Snap!

Mark smiled.

"Where'd you get all those plastic . . . holes, Mark?" I didn't know what to call those . . . things. They don't have a name. Back home, they're trash, but they seemed important to Mark.

"Drank it," he said proudly. "I *drank* it."

I stared at him, then climbed the rest of the wooden steps and walked into the room.

The room was a dungeon. Gray, chipped paint peeled from the walls. One lightbulb hanging from an ugly ceiling fixture cast a harsh light in the windowless room. Filthy, gray linoleum floors. No wonder Mark was out in the hot sun.

An old 1950s window air-conditioner, about to jump out of its crudely cut hole in the front wall, was trying unsuccessfully to beat back the wall of heat. I was getting a sinking feeling.

"The open-bay shower and johns are in the middle of the building, about seven doors down." Wiley pointed down the porch to continue the tour. "The Thai maids will walk in on you in the middle of a shower, put their hand over a smile, and giggle while they *pretend* to be on their way to clean out a toilet. But, don't worry . . . you'll get used to it. It's harmless sport for them."

More sinking feeling. So much for any shred of privacy.

Mark's bed was closest to the door. He had crudely taped a large monthly calendar on the wall beside his bed. My new roommate had scratched big, black *X* marks through all the previous days. He had scrawled large red numbers inside each remaining block to tally the number of days left before he returned to the States. Yesterday's number was 269. That meant Mark had been here only three months and his afternoons' entertainment was exploding plastic bubbles . . . Great.

That's not going to happen to me, I promised myself. I'm stronger than that. I am *not* going to change.

My bed was at the back of the dungeon. One beat-up, small metal desk completed the decor, except for a military-gray, portable metal closet whose doors I tried to open, only to discover them jammed shut. More sinking feeling. The place was a sewer. This could be a *long* year.

There was no chest of drawers for my stuff, so I threw my gear on my bed. Bad idea. The thin mattress sagged like a hammock clear down to the dusty floor. An explosion of fine dust flew up in my face. I coughed and rubbed my eyes. "Red Thai dust," Wiley explained. "You can't get rid of it . . . it's everywhere."

Any self-respecting homeless shelter would have thrown out the disgusting excuse for a mattress. I told Wiley, "Let's get out of here as soon as I can get out of this hot flightsuit. This place is depressing." I changed into the standard Southeast Asia off-duty outfit of shorts, T-shirt, and tennies. No socks. Then I asked Wiley, "Where's the club? I could use a cold beer." We turned and went back outside into the blast furnace.

Crazy Mark was still breaking bubbles, and in a neat pile beside him stood a stack of the same plastic rings. He'd been drinking a lot of *something*. It looked as if he was going to make an afternoon's entertainment of his sport. As Wiley walked me toward the officers' club, I hollered back at Mark, "See you later."

Mark did not look up, but he shouted as we walked away, "Don't look at everything in the BX the first day! Only look at one corner of a shelf to start. Save something for a month from now." I couldn't imagine what he meant.

"And can labels . . . read labels! The vegetable soup can is the best," Mark hollered.

"Okay, Mark, I will. See you later," I yelled back.

Mark needs to see a shrink fast, I thought. His contact with reality was slipping away. But that wasn't going to happen to me . . . I'm stronger than that, I again reassured myself.

"Is he always like *that*?" I asked Wiley.

Wiley looked confused. "Like *what*?"

"Well . . . you know . . . sort of . . . disconnected."

"Oh, that's just Mark. He's one of our best captains."

"You mean you let him fly *in command* like that?" I asked incredulously.

Wiley shrugged and answered matter-of-factly, "Oh, sure. He'd fly every night if we let him. We have to force him to take his CTO every month. If I remember right, he's leaving on a CTO tomorrow morning, so you'll have the place to yourself for a few days to get settled in."

"What's a CTO?"

"Oh, sorry, it's 'combat time off.' We get four days a month in Bangkok, and before you go thinking that's a good deal, don't worry; you'll earn it."

Earn it? Earn it? I thought to myself, what the hell have I gotten into? When they changed my assignment to NKP from Vietnam at the last minute, all they told me was this was an easy mission, hauling cargo around Thailand. A piece-of-cake assignment. I was thrilled at my good fortune.

Still confused, I asked, "What's the deal with the soup labels?"

"Actually, that's good advice," Wiley explained. "There isn't much to do around here, and reading canned-foods ingredients is good entertainment. I prefer the chili can myself . . . you'll see. And a trip to the BX trailer is something you'll have to plan and execute carefully, too. And Mark's right . . . don't look at everything the first day. Take one small corner of one shelf and *really* spend time looking at what's there."

We stepped off the curb and crossed the empty street.

"Force yourself not to look at the things on the shelf below or above or around the corner, or you'll be sorry later. You should probably have an experienced person go with you to stop you from looking at everything the first few times before you get the hang of it, or you won't have anything to look forward to. If you want, I'll take you the first time."

I stared at him, bewildered. Was he kidding?

"Don't worry . . . you'll see soon enough," he finished.

Out of the corner of my eye I caught Wiley shaking his head at my ignorance. He had that wry Vincent Price smile that seemed to say, "You'll be the next one. You can't stop it. Don't even try."

Stop *what*? No, I won't *see*. I won't be *next*. You're *wrong*. I'm stronger than that, I promised myself. The day *I* started reading labels would never come.

I thought we were going to the officers' club for a beer, but Wiley said, "Say, you want to stop by my trailer for a cold one? I've got a refrigerator and you can see the quarters you can move up to in about five months."

Five months? The sinking feeling grew. Five months locked in that dungeon with Crazy Mark? "Sure, thanks," I answered, trying to fight off a wave of depression.

Maybe I can find a way out of here before they get used to having me around, I thought to myself. I had heard of pilots talking their way into a different assignment right at the last minute. Maybe they needed some C-123 pilots over in Vietnam. I would keep quiet about my idea, go over to personnel the next morning, and see if I could get reassigned. I would be gone before they knew it. Good plan. I wouldn't even unpack my stuff. Knowing I would soon be away from NKP lifted my spirits and I began feeling better.

We climbed up tipsy concrete steps to Wiley's trailer. He opened the door, went inside, and I was hit by a blast of polar air. Wonderful!

"Hurry up, come in and close the damned door," he yelled. I jumped inside, slammed the door, and looked around . . . stunned.

Wiley's trailer half had the same space I would be sharing with Crazy Mark. He opened a door and proudly showed off his semiprivate bath. I looked around in awe. Built-in closets. Fake wood paneling on the walls and a chest of drawers.

Brass coach-light fixtures brightened the place so he could *read*. Blackout curtains covered the one small window—evidently for daytime naps. Air-conditioning from an exterior compressor. Wall-to-wall carpeting. A refrigerator! Two mattresses stacked on the twin bed for true comfort.

The place was a palace.

The room was stuffed floor to ceiling with every imaginable piece of state-of-the-art 1970 stereo equipment. It looked more like a sound studio than a place someone lived. Wiley had the newest equipment: a Sansui 5000 amplifier, an AKAI crossfield head reel-to-reel tape deck, the top-of-the-line Garrard English turntable, and four Pioneer CS99 speakers with fifteen-inch woofers. There was enough power to throb brooms marching out of the closet.

The stuff must have cost a fortune. I figured he must be rich.

Wiley opened the small Sanyo refrigerator stuffed with San Miguel beer and handed one to me. Then he jumped up and sat on his two mattresses, so trampoline-tight they didn't sink an inch. While mine sagged like a hammock? I looked around the cramped room and saw no chair, so I leaned back uncomfortably against the door.

Wiley noticed my discomfort and sprang off his trampoline-bed. "Sorry . . . you'll have to excuse my lack of manners. I'm not used to having guests over yet. I only moved in a couple days ago." Then he reached between a built-in closet and the wall and produced a garishly painted red folding chair from its niche. "Ain't she a beauty?" he said proudly. "I rescued her rummaging around the base junk pile, sanded her down, got a can of candy-apple red spray paint, and suddenly . . . I've got furniture. I can have company over!"

He unfolded the chair and said, "Here you go. Have a seat." Wiley pointed to the fridge and told me, "Help yourself to another cold one when you finish that one," and hopped back up on his trampoline mattress I eyed with envy.

"How come your mattress is so firm and mine sags to the floor?" I asked.

"Plywood," he answered seriously. "Three-quarter-inch all-American plywood."

I asked where I could get a sheet for myself.

"I'm not sure . . . it's in short supply. You have to *know* somebody or scrounge around for yourself to find a piece." I must have looked worried because he quickly added, "But I may know somebody who's leaving back for the States in a couple days. Maybe I can talk him out of his plywood for you . . . unless he's already promised it to someone else."

I smiled, thanked him, and sat down gingerly on his red relic. Then I waited for my sponsor to guide the rest of the conversation. After a few gulps of beer he finally asked, "So, how'd you get here?"

"Well, after jungle school in the Philippines, they put me on a C-141 to Bangkok . . ." I stopped when I saw Wiley start chuckling.

"No, no, no . . . I mean how'd you wind up in the military as a pilot in the first place?"

"Sorry . . . guess I'm nervous." I laughed uneasily with him. "I'd graduated from the University of Miami in Florida and was in graduate school in Washington, D.C., when I got a letter from my draft board saying my educational deferment had been canceled. They gave me thirty days from receipt to join some other service, or it looked like I'd be headed for Vietnam rice paddies with an M16 in my hands."

Wiley smiled and nodded as if he'd heard the story before.

"That same day a headline in the *Washington Post* described that the Air Force was short of pilots. So I ripped out the headline, went down to the recruiter's office, took a flight physical, and raised my hand. After that, I spent a year in pilot training, got married, spent eighteen months in California at Travis flying a big cargo plane in and out of Southeast Asia, and then got orders to Phan Rang over in Vietnam."

"You look awful young for this. Just how old *are* you?"

"Twenty-four," I said apologetically. "But I turn twenty-five next month," I rushed to add, realizing our talk was turning into a job interview.

"So how long you been out of pilot training?" he asked suspiciously.

"Two years," I answered proudly.

Wiley looked disappointed. "Ever been an aircraft commander before?"

"Nope." Wiley shook his head in disappointment. I hurried to explain so he wouldn't think me a weak pilot my old outfit bypassed for command. "My last unit wouldn't let lieutenants upgrade to AC. They mostly had us inventorying safety equipment, counting crew meals, and figuring takeoff data. Most of the ACs were old-fart majors and colonels old enough to be our fathers who wouldn't let us fly much."

Wiley seemed shocked. "You mean you've *never* been in charge of an airplane and crew before?"

"Nope . . . sorry," I answered sheepishly.

"Oh, jeeeez! We keep asking personnel to send us pilots with command experience and guys like you keep showing up."

I apologized again, but defended myself, explaining there was nothing I could have done.

Wiley let me off the hook. "It's all right. We'll make it work somehow."

I changed the subject. "So tell me what routes we fly. Are they scheduled cargo runs around the Thai bases, or random stuff?"

"Nobody told you?"

"Nobody's told me squat. I don't have a clue what goes on here. After jungle school I thought I was headed for Phan Rang, but at the last second got orders here. I got on a C-141 headed to Bangkok, spent last night at the military hotel, and here I am."

"That's the way it happened for all of us," Wiley said conspiratorially. "Nobody knows they're coming here until the last second. And our mission is more complicated than hauling cargo." He chuckled to himself.

I stumbled ahead. "So exactly what is it you guys do? Nobody could answer my questions."

"They're not *supposed* to be able to. Nobody's supposed to know this place even exists."

"Oh" was all I could manage.

"To be assigned here, you had to pass a security check above top secret—"

I jumped in, "Gee, I didn't know there was anything above top secret."

"*Everything* here is top secret or above, and later tonight I'll show you one of the reasons why. But as to what we do, it's one of my jobs as your sponsor to warn you right off the bat what can happen to you if you tell anyone—I mean *anyone*—what we do here."

I didn't know how to respond, but began feeling frightened.

He offered, "You can tell your wife . . . what's her name?"

"Sharon."

"Well, you can tell Sharon where you are, but you are not permitted to tell her what you're doing and especially not *where* we fly. You can't tell her in phone calls, letters, tapes, nor when you see her for R and R in Hawaii and you're strolling along some moonlit beach. Not even when you're back home a year from now . . . not until this war is long since over. If 'they' find out you've violated these rules, you can be expected to be prosecuted and punished to the maximum extent possible under the Uniform Code of Military Justice. Do I make myself clear?"

I thought he must be pulling my chain. "You've got to be kidding, Wiley. What could be going on at this godforsaken place anybody could possibly care that much about?"

He looked insulted and his face turned dark. "I'm dead serious. As far as anyone back home knows, this place doesn't exist. You can expect your letters to be opened and sampled at random, your phone calls to be monitored, and any voice tapes you send to Sharon to be opened, checked for divulging secrets, and be undetectably resealed."

"But what happens if I make an honest mistake and blurt something out?"

"Same thing. This is serious shit we're talking about, John. Oh, I almost forgot . . . you are especially *not* to talk about our mission at the O club in front of the Thai waitresses. That's an easy place to slip up and get caught. Let me tell you a story."

I nodded and grabbed another beer, deciding to humor him.

"Sometime after last Christmas 'they' opened up one of those family Christmas letters from this guy's parents in which his folks had published exactly what we do . . . blow by blow. He was in deep shit."

"So what's the big deal about writing about hauling cargo around Thailand? And what could they do worse than sending him *here*? What happened?"

"Nobody knows. In the middle of the day while we were all sleeping, his trailer-mate heard some commotion coming from this guy's side, but rolled over and went back to sleep, thinking the guy was just rearranging furniture."

"So what happened?"

"His trailer-mate found the guy's room stripped bare that evening. Everything was gone . . . his bed, dresser, stereo, all his tapes, photos of his girlfriend . . . his cans of food and beer . . . the place had been completely sanitized."

I began feeling frightened. "So what happened to him, Wiley? People can't just disappear."

"Well, *he* did. Nobody knows what happened to him. He was never seen again. But the point is . . . make sure you keep your mouth shut."

I reached for another beer. "How come all the secrecy about hauling cargo around Thailand?"

"I can't tell you here. We'll have to wait till we get to a secure area."

"When will that be?"

"Tomorrow night." Wiley looked around and whispered, "When we get behind the secure walls up at TUOC—the Tactical Unit Operations Center."

"Tomorrow night! I won't be able to sleep tonight the way you've built this up."

Wiley shook his head. "I can't say any more than that. I could get in lots of trouble."

"What? *Please* . . . surely you can tell me *something*."

Wiley thought hard for a while. "Okay, I'll give you the basics . . . but remember . . . you didn't hear it from me."

I told him I promised and crossed my heart. Gawd, what a jerk I was.

Wiley scooted forward on his trampoline and lowered his voice to a whisper. "We have two missions. The first is a simple night-flare-dropping mission, but it's only twenty percent of what we do these days. Dropping flares was the first job the C-123s had up here, and it's why our call sign became Candlestick. What we do is fly above friendly forces across the border in Laos and drop air burning flares suspended under parachutes. The light they give can be the difference between the good guys on the ground living through the night or being overrun by overwhelming numbers of bad guys."

I was surprised to learn we would be flying over Laos. Despite all the secret briefings I'd had the past two years, I didn't know the United States was involved in Laos. But not wanting to appear any more naïve than I already had, I answered, "Sounds simple enough. I could do that."

"I'm sure you could."

"So what's the main mission?"

"Killing trucks at night out on the Ho Chi Minh Trail."

"What!" I exploded. "How the hell can you possibly do that? The C-123 is just an old cargo plane."

He chuckled. "That's what everybody *thinks* and we want it to stay that way. But anyway, we cruise up and down the trail looking for supply trucks to destroy that TFA has already spotted for us."

"What a minute. What's TFA?"

"Task Force Alpha . . . that's one of the reasons I didn't want to start this discussion in a nonsecure location, but I'll come back to TFA later."

"Okay." I slid forward on his red chair and gulped my San Miguel.

"So when we spot a truck convoy, we drop three ground-burning markers off to one side of the road into the heavy jungle to mark the convoy's position. The jungle is so thick, the drivers can't see them burning. Then we'll set up a left-hand orbit over the target, call in some fighter aircraft, and give them bombing directions in reference to our ground marks. Then we sit back and watch the fighters blow the crap out of everything. It sounds simple, but it's effective."

I was stunned. "Oh, my God, Wiley. I had no idea this was a combat mission. The bad guys can't be too happy you're trying to blow them up. Do they shoot back?"

"Oh, absolutely," he answered matter-of-factly. "Every night. Sometimes we'll spend the whole night dodging shells. Some nights the whole sky is alive with red tracers coming up at us . . . it's a blast. You're gonna love it."

I shook my head. "Jesuzz, Wiley . . . I don't think so. I don't know if I'll be able to do that. But how in the world do you find trucks in the dark?"

"You gotta see this thing to believe it. We've got this new top-secret thing called a starlight scope that magnifies available moonlight something like a thousand times. It looks like your average backyard telescope. Each plane has one on board. Our 'scope navigator' uses it to look down through a hatch in the belly of the plane and spot truck headlights."

"There must be a long checkout program. A couple months, I suppose?" I was trying to digest all this.

"Well, we'll go out on the trail tomorrow night. We have a ten P.M. briefing. You're gonna be my copilot. I'll show you what it's like, but there's no formal training program. You're on the schedule a week from tomorrow night to fly in command." He slugged down more beer.

I felt nauseous. "Wiley, you gotta be shitting me. I can't be ready that fast."

"You don't have much choice. We're way short of pilots, so you'll be flying that mission in command next week ready or not."

"What else is there?" I asked dejectedly.

"You'd better force yourself to stay up all night tonight so you can sleep during the day tomorrow. Then tomorrow night we'll take off just before midnight and fly for about five hours. To help get your body clock reset, sometime around midnight tonight I'll take you over to Task Force Alpha and get you the tour. You'll have to have above a top-secret clearance to get in, but—"

"Wiley, top secret's all I've got."

"If you're *here,* you already have it. You just don't know it yet. They wouldn't have let you come here without a deep background check, though that takes months."

I let his news settle in while I gulped some beer. Finally I asked, "So how do you know where to look for trucks? Even with this fancy starlight scope, Laos is a big country."

"That's the best part," he answered enthusiastically. "Remember those huge electronic boards from the movie *Dr. Strangelove* that showed all those Russian bombers headed for the U.S. and ours headed at them?"

"Sure."

"Well, Task Force Alpha is a lot like that except with real-time displays in full color, three stories tall . . . it's the whole goddamned Ho Chi Minh Trail in full, living color."

"Wow, Wiley. So where is this TFA?"

"Maybe three hundred yards over off the north end of the base; it's carved right out of the jungle. I'll escort you over with my security badge until you get your own. We'll have to go through three sets of barbed wire, with whirring surveillance cameras and electronic gates we'll have to be buzzed through. Then we'll come upon this dark, monolithic building hiding in the jungle . . . the damned thing's *huge.*"

I sat and listened, stunned.

"Step out of the jungle and inside the building, you step back into America—but an America fifteen years from now . . . maybe 1984. It's beautiful . . . gleaming tile floors . . . glass walls everywhere. They have a full cafeteria where you can get anything you want. They even have real milk, not that powdered crap we get at the mess hall. And air-conditioning? The whole damned place is air-conditioned. There's even a bowling alley and a movie theater . . . and a whole bunch of civilians who look like IBM guys running around in three-piece suits all wearing glasses . . . it's 'Geek Central.' We never see them over on our part of the base, so I guess they have everything they need in there."

He went on, "Then there's this main control room that looks like the one we saw on TV during the Apollo moon shots, or maybe something out of a James Bond movie. There's computer terminals *everywhere*. But the main feature is this huge, three-story-tall Lucite . . . or maybe it's plastic, I don't know . . . full-color depiction of the whole Ho Chi Minh Trail with a real-time depiction of trucks coming down the trail. It's wild, man."

I felt dazzled. "How the hell can they pull that off?"

"Well, we've got these RF-4s they call wild weasels . . . I think . . . this is all on rumor . . . but I think they fly down the trail at a couple hundred feet at six hundred knots, dropping a series of electronic eavesdropping sensors alongside the road. You'll see one of the sensors tonight over at TFA. They're designed to bury themselves in the dirt while leaving their camouflaged antenna sticking out above ground level . . . looking like just another jungle plant."

"That's brilliant. But how does that information get to those Lucite boards?"

"Easy. The sensors are battery-powered and are set to pick up noise or ground vibrations of trucks driving by. They send those signals up to one of our own NKP planes called a mini-bat that relays the signals over to the Lucite screens at TFA."

"So what you're seeing is a *live* depiction of truck convoys coming down the trail?"

"Exactly."

"So when you fly out looking for trucks, you know where they are?"

"Sort of . . . They don't have the whole trail covered and

the sensors break down a lot and some get blown up; but it helps to know where to begin to look. Pretty cool, huh?"

"Wiley, I had no idea our country had this kind of technology. Sharon and I just bought a basic four-function, handheld calculator for a hundred bucks and thought that was high-tech. This level of technology never got into the news back home."

"It's not supposed to. The whole point is, you can sit back and watch all the sensors automatically fire off along the whole trail and see where the trucks are running any given night. Tonight we'll ask one of the geeks to point this handheld red-light gun they have to activate one of the sensors and we'll listen in. Sometimes you can hear the drivers bullshitting when they stop for dinner. If we're lucky, we might hear an airstrike. You can listen in on the fighter pilots' frequency and hear the explosions. It's a front-row, armchair-quarterback seat on the whole air war."

I was getting pumped up. "Incredible."

"The worst part of the TFA visit is coming back out to this part of the base. You step back in time forty years. It's depressing."

His story over, a silence grew between us. I looked around the room for something lighter to talk about. It was hard to miss his tall stacks of reel-to-reel audiotapes. Finally I said, "What are all these tapes? Where'd you get all of them? They must have cost a fortune. I couldn't afford all this stuff."

He shook his head. "I'm not rich . . . just single. The tapes are cheap and you'll need them because the only music they play on Armed Forces WNKP is our fathers' music. You know, Lawrence Welk, Mitch Miller, Andy Williams . . . that kind of crap . . . nothing any good. I got most of the tapes from Cheapskate Charlie up in Hong Kong. He makes pirated knockoff tapes of record albums you can't find here and sells them for a buck a tape . . . four tapes for three dollars. He'll make a special tape of anything you want."

"Isn't that illegal?"

"Hey!" Wiley answered sharply. "Music is the only thing that keeps us going . . . that and beer. Besides . . . we're on the other side of the planet getting our asses shot off every night at a place no one knows or gives a shit about. So who's gonna say anything?"

I stared at the mountain of equipment and tapes. "All I've got is a small clock radio, so I guess I'm stuck with Andy Williams."

"Well, you can come over anytime you want and listen to some good stuff. I know what it's like to be in that hellhole with Crazy Mark. I was his roommate until two days ago."

I suddenly realized where he'd gotten his plywood . . . *my* bed.

Then he bounced off his trampoline and said, "Let me show you my new sound system. I just finished dubbing this tape." He threw on a series of power switches along a whole wall of electronic equipment and the trailer began to hum like an electrical substation. The lights in Cleveland must have dimmed at the power draw as Marmalade whispered softly:

> *The changing . . . of sunlight . . . to moonlight*
> *Reflections of my life*
> *Ohhh, how they fill my eyes*
>
> *The greetings . . . of people . . . in trouble*
> *Reflections of my life*
> *Ohhh, how they fill my mind*

Wiley closed his eyes and mouthed the chorus with the band:

> *All my sorrows, sad tomorrows*
> *Take me . . . back . . . to my own home*
> *All my cryings; all my cryings*
> *Feel I'm dying, dying*
> *Take me back . . . to my own home . . .*

Soon he grabbed a mike, threw the "on" switch, and started belting out a karaoke routine. He closed his eyes, rocked back on his heels, leaned back, and howled off-key with the tape. Over and over and over and over.

> *All my cryings; all my cryings,*
> *Feel I'm dying, dying . . .*

It looked to be a two-hour tape containing nothing but the same song, "Reflections of My Life." I thought, what the hell have I gotten myself into? I had only met two guys and they were both certifiable . . . Crazy Mark and Weird Wiley.

After howling awhile, Wiley shoved a mike into my hand and said, "C'mon, John, you've got to get into this music. Give it a try."

"No thanks," I said quietly. "Maybe later," you crazy bastard. He shrugged it was my loss and whispered the next verse while I told myself, this is *not* going to happen to *me*. Not *me*. *I* can stay above it all. I'm stronger than they are. I'm going to stay just the way I am.

Wiley shook his head, rocked back, and screamed the chorus at the top of his lungs.

CHAPTER *TWO*

Wiley and I walked over to the club about 6 P.M. Beautifully carved teakwood double doors led to an interior that resembled a converted horse barn. The plywood floor buckled up and down in a series of waves, covered by a carpet new thirty years ago. At least the air-conditioning was working.

"There's not much in here." Wiley pointed around the facility. "There's the lobby here, one large dining area with a main bar and the quiet bar around to the right. There are a couple of pool tables beyond, around back. They did this project mostly on self-help, but it's the only place around to get you out of your room."

We were standing in a standard-looking restaurant lobby, with room for people to wait for a reservation if this were the States, but I couldn't imagine anyone needing a reservation in this place. No one manned the register. Glass display cases that back home would have been stuffed with Milky Ways, Mounds, and Snickers were empty.

Behind the register stood a large wooden display case labeled "Top Guns." Inside were posted color pictures of pilots my age. Labels below their photos identified them as "Shooter," "Lightning," and "Trigger." Even the heroes didn't have their real names anymore. I thought I recognized Shooter.

I turned to Wiley and asked, "Isn't that Bill Miller, the Miami Hurricanes quarterback? When I graduated from Miami, he was a year behind me and the newspapers expected him to go on to the NFL."

"Yeah, that's Miller, all right," Wiley said disgustedly. "He's one of the top A-1 squadron fighter pilots. I've seen him be so aggressive, it's scary. The man has no fear."

I thought, Wow! *Bill Miller!* The draft sure is a great equalizer. If *he* couldn't avoid the draft with *his* connections . . .

Wiley took me into the cavernous main dining room. The sea of tables was broken only by a raised stage along the left-hand wall, near the middle of the room. Every club in Southeast Asia boasts a local band that plays today's hits: "Proud Mary," "Yellow River," and "We Gotta Get Outta This Place."

We went into the dining room and Wiley explained, "The Candlestick tables are over there. The A-1 'Sandy' area is over in the center in front of the bandstand, the 'Vampire' tables are beyond that, the OV-10s are over near the kitchen . . . well, you get the idea." I saw an army of Thai waitresses standing against the wall waiting for customers.

The room was as deserted as the rest of the base.

"So where is everybody?" I asked.

"Oh . . . NKP doesn't get cranked up for another hour or so. Most of us fly at night, so most of the crews have been sleeping all day and will be here around eight o'clock. They've got a live Thai rock-and-roll band that comes in every night, except they won't be playing tonight. Come on, I'll show you where the Candlestick tables are and introduce you to a couple more FNGs."

I wondered why the band wouldn't be playing, but I didn't ask. I had already spent the afternoon parading my ignorance and didn't need to do it again. Better to be quiet for a while.

Wiley walked me over to the Candlestick tables where two men our age stood up, looked me in the eye, and smiled. Handshakes. Manners. Normal people. I was hoping Crazy Mark might be one of a kind.

Wiley made the introductions. "John, I want you to meet two more FNGs. This is Dick Eastwood and Rod Verano. They came up on the morning shuttle."

"Don't call me Dick," the ostrich-looking pilot scolded Wiley. "It's *Rich* or *Richard*. And everybody says Eastwood. My name has an *s* . . . it's Eastwood*s*."

I thought, pretty nervy, Rich-don't-call-me-Dick. The man was acting like a new dog in the neighborhood, raising his leg to mark his territory.

I didn't think his strategy would work with these combat veterans.

Rod's eyes got big at Rich's attitude, but he said nothing. Rod and Dick were still in their flightsuits and I noticed Rod's name tag showed a *B—Berano*—not *Verano* as Wiley had introduced him. Rod let Wiley's mistake slip by . . . smarter than Rich.

"Sure, no problem, Dick," Wiley mocked.

You just knew everyone was going to call Rich "Dick" . . . too good a target to pass up.

"I'm starving. Can we get something to eat?" I jumped in to smooth things over before Wiley could call Rich "Dick" again.

We took a table in the Candlestick area. A beautiful Thai waitress approached, bent over at the waist, beamed a pleasant smile, and cooed, "*Sawadee kap.* May I suggest 'The Special' . . . aged Kobe beef, baked potato, soup, and salad for a dollar fifty-five. Your beverage is complimentary. May I recommend our excellent sweetened iced tea?"

We ordered the special and the food was surprisingly good. I figured the food might compensate for the dungeon. It looked as if the club was the only place to hang out or get anything to eat.

After a while, the place began to fill with long-faced pilots and navigators, but nobody said boo. The only sound was two hundred knives and forks clanking on cheap china plates.

In the tone people reserve for whispering in church, Wiley told Rich and Rod about the flying schedule and how fast they'd be expected to check out as captain. Then he explained that they could bring their wives over from the States and how much time the women could spend at NKP visiting from Bangkok apartments without turning their husbands' assignment into an "accompanied tour"—stretching this twelve-month sentence into eighteen.

I was only half-listening . . . when I caught an odd movement out of the corner of my eye. A fiftysomething guy—old enough to be my father— in blue janitor's coveralls lurched through the middle of the crowded dining room. He was in sore need of a shave and his hair was a tattered Brillo pad. He looked like a homeless person seeking a handout and a bottle of Thunderbird. Must be the janitor, I figured, sent here by the DOD on civilian contract. But I couldn't understand why they allowed him in the club in a drunken stupor.

The old janitor stumbled around the room, slamming into dinner tables filled with young pilots and navigators, but no one said anything. No one even looked up. The old guy seemed headed for the john to relieve himself, though he looked more likely to simply topple as he spun his way along a wall of heavy curtains drawn closed against the picture windows.

A bend in the wall stopped him cold in midlurch, and I guessed he had lost his bearings. Someone should help him find the men's room, I thought. Next he leaned his head deep into the velvet curtains. It looked as if he were going to stand there and fall asleep.

I remember thinking, What's he *doing*? Oh, my God! He's *peeing*. He's peeing on the curtains! He's so damned drunk, he must think he made it to the men's room, or maybe he gave up and decided to simply cut loose. In a room full of people!

I grabbed Wiley's arm. "Wiley, the janitor over there is *peeing* on the curtains. You gotta stop him."

Wiley turned to look, then slowly turned back, looking exasperated. He shook his head. "John, that's not the janitor. That's the *wing commander*. He runs this whole damned place. We call him the Hawk. And on top of being the commander, he's probably the best damned fighter pilot we've got. I've seen him do things in combat you wouldn't believe. He's been a fighter pilot since Korea and knows more about flying than both of us ever will."

Embarrassed! My face flushed beet red. I'd managed to make Rich Eastwoods look good. I tried to recover with a question to show my concern. "But shouldn't someone help him? I mean, you can't just pee in public here, can you?"

"He can go anywhere he wants tonight," Wiley contradicted. "It's his way of dealing with the loss. I didn't want to tell you guys your first night here, but a plane from an A-1 squadron got shot down today. The guy was the Hawk's wingman. He watched him go down. There was no rescue. He had a clear view and watched the bad guys on the ground charge over to his buddy and blast away."

"They *killed* him!" Rod exclaimed. "Why'd they kill him? Aren't they supposed to take prisoners and send them to the Hanoi Hilton?"

"They don't take prisoners in northern Laos. Those people have never heard of the Geneva Convention. They kill you outright in terrible, violent ways," Wiley answered gravely.

I swallowed hard. Rod and Rich's eyes were white cue balls. Fear surged through my body. I thought to myself, Maybe I can still find a way out.

Wiley explained nervously, "So you guys know, the Hawk does this every time *anybody* is shot down . . . not just for his squadron like you might think. He'd be peeing on the curtains even if it was one of our Candlestick planes. I'm surprised you guys didn't pick up on the situation when the band wasn't playing. The band plays every night except after we 'lose one.' And what you thought was a janitor's outfit is his formal dress flightsuit. He just finished attending the memorial ceremony for his wingman. The reason the base was empty this afternoon was because everyone who wasn't sleeping to get ready to fly was at the memorial service."

Rich asked, "That's awfully quick grieving, isn't it?"

Wiley shook his head. "Better to grieve quick and put it behind you. You have to fly again soon and you can't afford that on your mind . . . you'll see."

Rod cleared his throat. Then his cracking voice asked, "How often does somebody get shot down?"

"Oh, not too often. The base loses only one every week or so . . . not too bad. The Candlesticks have taken hits over the years, but we've only lost one C-123."

Not too bad! Not too bad? Sounded bad to *me* . . . like the Candlesticks were due for a *second*.

Again I told myself, there must be a way out of this trap. I asked Wiley, "Has anyone ever gotten a transfer out of here? I mean, maybe they need pilots over in Vietnam."

He took a deep breath. "There was one guy three weeks ago who got off the C-130 in the morning, saw what you guys did, and claimed he developed a fear of flying. He was right back out on the afternoon shuttle. They made him disappear fast."

"What happened to him?" Rod asked, breathing heavily.

"Nobody knows. But I'm sure they took away his pilot wings. They prob'ly sent him to Vietnam, put an M16 in his hands, and threw him into the rice paddies with Special Forces as air liaison."

"That's a death sentence. He could get killed his first day," Rod protested.

"Yep," Wiley confirmed. "He could."

Rich and Rod looked stunned.

An hour went by and more Candle pilots and navigators showed up. As we listened to their astonishing combat stories, it felt good to know other victims had found a way to survive.

We peppered Wiley with questions. When he explained that club dues were twenty bucks a month, I asked if membership was mandatory since my pay had been screwed up for months. He told me it was and if I did not pay, they would post my name on a "nonmembers" shit list.

I had no idea where to come up with that much money.

After five hours of my listening to war stories, around midnight Wiley kept his promise to tour Task Force Alpha—that secret listening post. He escorted Rich, Rod, and me down a winding jungle path at the northeast corner of the base until we came upon the shadowy shape of TFA hiding in heavy foliage. I turned back to look for the base, but it was gone.

Wiley flashed his security badge to a guard, who buzzed us through a series of electronic gates that buzzed closed as we passed. Our escort, a spectacled geek in a white, button-down shirt and tie, met us at a vaultlike door.

Wiley had not lied. It *was* beautiful . . . gleaming tile floors . . . glass partitions . . . chrome furniture . . . air-conditioning . . . a cafeteria with every delight. As we entered the main control room jammed with geeks and computers, I was flabbergasted by the three-story, full-color, Lucite displays of trucks charging down the Ho Chi Minh Trail.

Until well after 3 A.M. we listened to trucks the sensors picked up. When I asked Wiley how the government arm-twisted these civilians into spending a year away from their families, he said the rumor was they were all volunteers. They'd only stay for ninety days and then go home. They could leave anytime, but never did because they were on *triple* pay.

As we were leaving, Wiley weaseled our escort out of a quart of milk. Cradling the milk in his arms like a newborn infant as we walked back down the jungle path, he explained he would freeze it into cubes, melt each one in an equal amount of water, and have real milk for a couple of months.

I think our tour into TFA was chiefly aimed to get Wiley that milk.

We got back to the club about 4 A.M. and stayed until sunrise and listened to more war stories whenever the Thai waitresses weren't around.

At first light, Wiley escorted me three blocks over to the squadron to get me signed in so I wouldn't be listed as AWOL. He pointed out the TUOC building across the parking lot, then said something about not being late for our 10 P.M. mission briefing. I mumbled that I'd been up over twenty-four hours, felt buzzy, and needed some rack time. We said our good-byes and I found my own way back to the dungeon.

I was relieved to find the place empty. Figuring Crazy Mark had left for Bangkok, I pulled my twin mattress off the rickety metal frame, plopped it on the floor, and planned to sleep the entire day.

With the door closed, I must have lost track of time. Because when I finally rolled over and looked through blurry eyes to check the time . . .

Nine twenty-nine? It couldn't be! I rubbed my eyes . . . still 9:29! I jumped up and ripped open the dungeon door. Dark! Had I slept the whole day? Fifteen hours? How? Wiley had warned me not to be late for our 10 P.M. briefing! Crap!

I raced down the porch, took a quick shower, and ran back to the room. No towels! I grabbed a T-shirt to dry. No outlet for my razor! I underweared my hair dry, slicked it straight back, and hoped nobody would notice my thirty-six-hour stubble. Hungry. I checked my watch . . . 9:41.

Out of time! I'd have to depend on the box meal Wiley had warned us about. TUOC was four long blocks away. Late!

There was no time to dig for a clean flightsuit and put the Velcro patches in their proper places, so I threw on yesterday's, splashed on English Leather, hoped nobody would notice my barnyard aroma, and raced toward TUOC.

Approaching the operations center, I checked my watch . . . 9:48.

Whew! I'd made it! I slowed to a walk, caught my breath, made as if everything were normal to the guard, showed my ID, and he checked me off an access list. Then I went inside, asked an NCO where the briefing room was, wandered down the hallway, found the room, and went inside.

They say it's the recoveries that count. Nice moves, I told myself. I'd covered my tracks. No one would ever know.

This was my first wartime top-secret, official USAF, look-behind-the-curtain combat briefing, so I had wanted extra time by myself to study the charts and pictures. So much for that idea. My pulse was still racing from charging across the base.

But this was *it*. Put up or shut up. All the training was behind me. Trying to beat the clock before the 10 P.M. briefing, I looked around the horse-stall-size room.

The walls were plastered with maps, charts, battle lines, the Ho Chi Minh Trail route structure, truck symbols, truck parks, enemy and friendly positions, known triple-A positions, as well as selected escape and evasion (SAFE) areas. A map of northern Laos, here dubbed Barrel Roll, covered one whole wall, while another wall was a map of southern Laos, labeled Steel Tiger.

Wow, I thought, just like in those old WWII movies, except now I'm *in* the movie. Excitement began to overwhelm my fears.

One black-and-white, eight-by-ten, daylight aerial photograph caught my eye. It pictured a short, dirt airstrip down at the bottom of a narrow, deep box canyon surrounded by mile-high stalagmites. The title read:

"EMERGENCY AIRFIELD—TOP SECRET—
NOFORN—LONG TIEN"

I figured this Long Tien must be our emergency airfield, but couldn't imagine how anyone could possibly get in there at night. It looked like trying to land inside Yosemite National Park at night . . . impossible. I figured there must be some secret plan they would cover in the briefing. Otherwise, they wouldn't have posted it as an alternate. I made a mental note to ask, if no one else did.

I checked my watch: 10:09.

Where was everybody? Had I screwed up again? Maybe I

was in the wrong room. I bolted for the hall and crashed into Wiley coming through the doorway. I backed up and apologized. Wiley looked angry.

Wiley introduced me to our navigators, Majors George Keene and Jack Ward. The majors and I took three of the four open seats at the briefing table, but then instead of taking the open chair beside me, Wiley sat way over in the far corner, crossed his arms, and scowled at the floor.

I was about to ask what was bothering him, but a ramrod-stiff briefing officer marched in, slammed the door, opened a three-inch-thick binder, and warned us, "Gentlemen, I remind you, this briefing is top secret—NoForn—no foreign dissemination. You may discuss the contents only with those who have a 'need to know.'"

After a half hour, the intelligence officer concluded, "To remind you, there is no night search-and-rescue capability. You'd have to find a way to survive to first light, but few have. Your escape and evasion letter of the day is *foxtrot,* and the letter of the week is *uniform*. Stomp one of them out in the snow to alert the Jolly Green choppers that it's not an enemy trap." No one laughed at his joke about jungle snow he'd probably told a hundred times, showing no sensitivity for the previous day's A-1 loss.

"Now, someone will be along soon to sanitize you. And, as always, Long Tien is your emergency alternate." The briefing officer chuckled to himself, reading from his guide to conclude his presentation. "Are there any questions?" He started to leave the podium.

"Yes," I said, stopping him. "This is my first mission. How do we get into Long Tien if we take a hit or lose an engine?"

"You don't. It's impossible. Nobody could possibly survive an approach into Long Tien," he answered bluntly, and continued to leave.

"But, sir, you briefed it as our emergency alternate," I reminded him.

He stopped midstride and glared at me. "That's just a square-filler, Lieutenant. The briefing rules require me to

give you an emergency airfield, so I do." He shook his head
in disgust at my insolence. How *dare* a mere lieutenant question a field-grade major.

"Then where do we divert into if we're forced down?" I
persisted.

"There isn't anyplace else," he fired back, and started to
leave again.

I knew we were going to get into it, but I was not going to
back down. My father taught me never to be afraid of rank.
This jerk didn't have to fly this mission. *We did.* I knew he
would probably head back to his air-conditioned trailer to
listen to Andy Williams.

So I went right back at him. "Then why do you brief a
field we can't possibly get into? That doesn't make any
sense. You briefed we're probably going to be shot at the
whole night. If we take a hit and are forced down, there must
be a way into Long Tien if 'they' decided it's our emergency
airfield. It looks impossible, but there must be a way. So how
would we get in there?"

He stopped with his hand on the doorknob, wheeled
around, glared at me, and chuckled. "You don't get it, do
you, *Lieutenant* . . . whatever your name is . . . it's goddamned impossible! Nobody could possibly get into Long
Tien at night. You'd have to be *crazy* to try it." His chuckle
turned to the ridicule of outright laughter.

He jabbed his finger at me and continued his attack. "The
runway's more than a mile down inside a narrow, blind box
canyon. There's only one way in and one way out through an
offset keyhole-size opening so tight you could barely
squeeze an airplane through in daylight. On top of that, there
aren't any navigation aids to guide you. You'd only have
your eyeballs to find your way around in the dark. Only the
CIA's Air America is authorized in there during the day, and
their expert pilots *refuse* to try it at night. You . . . you
wouldn't stand a prayer. At night, you'd smash against the
narrow canyon walls. It would be suicide. The canyon is
ringed by lethal limestone karst formations that boom
straight up more than eight thousand feet above sea level,

and even if you landed, you wouldn't be able to stop before you smashed into the mile-high karst wall at the end of the runway. And if that isn't enough to convince you, *Lieutenant,* we don't even know who owns the goddamn thing night to night; our intelligence reports are so bad. Some night we own the damned thing and some nights the bad guys own it. We never know."

I sat there, stunned. I involuntarily tried backing away, but my chair hit the wall.

I looked over at Wiley to rescue me, but he had suddenly found a spider spinning a web in a ceiling corner the most fascinating thing he'd ever seen.

No help there.

The major continued his attack. "Nobody could possibly get into Long Tien at night, so don't even *think* about trying. You'd kill yourself And if you somehow got lucky and managed to land, the welcoming party would kill you immediately . . . so don't go thinking about being captured and having some goddamned party for a few years up at the Hanoi Hilton. When Air America goes into places like Long Tien, they haul in security troops to hold off the bad guys. At night, control of those strips reverts to being a no-man's-land . . . up for grabs by whoever wants it. But what the hell do *you know,* you're just an FNG."

Then he slammed out of the room.

There it was again. *FNG.* I had to ask someone.

My voice was shaking when I asked Major Barton, "What's an FNG?"

"Fucking new guy," he explained.

When we had the room to ourselves, Wiley stood up and demanded to know where I was at pickup time.

I stammered I didn't know what he was talking about.

He said sternly, *remember,* he briefed me a crew van would pick up the enlisted crewmembers at the barracks and then swing by the dungeon for me at 21:45 sharp. The driver then stops by the trailers and *together* the crew drives out to the aircraft. They drop off the enlisted to start the preflight and finally drop the pilots and navs over here at TUOC.

So where *was* I? Wiley wanted to know.

The two navigators stared at the floor and were quiet.

Wiley told me when the van had honked outside the dungeon and I hadn't appeared, the enlisted guys thought I might have skipped out.

I apologized and explained I was falling asleep at sunrise when he'd detailed the night's agenda. Wiley assured me it was okay, but I could see from his expression it wasn't.

I guess they figured if they couldn't rely on me for something as simple as catching a bus, how could they depend on me when the shooting started?

With my tail tucked between my legs, the four of us walked in silence along the hallways to the armory and parachute shop.

First we checked out Smith & Wesson P-38 revolvers, six bullets, holsters, and gun belts at the armory window. I slung the whole thing around my waist and felt like an Old West gunfighter. I asked the technician for extra bullets in case we got into a firefight on the ground, but he quoted a regulation that authorized no more than six.

Why only six? I wondered. Six wouldn't last long against a bunch of bad guys armed with AK-47s. I was about to ask, but Wiley said, "We're late," so we quickly moved on to the chute shop to suit up.

The survival technicians handed me a jungle-camouflaged, nylon-webbed vest and helped me strap it on. One tech briefed me, "Sir, since I see you're an FNG, I'm going to review everything you have in the vest. Now the most important thing to your rescue is your survival radio, located in this pocket." He pulled out the palm-size radio and extended the antenna, turning it on.

"It's preset to frequency 243.0 and here's how to select the secret backup frequency in case 'Charlie' is eavesdropping. Now right across from the radio in this pouch here"— he pointed—"you've got one each fully charged backup battery. Up from that—"

I interrupted him, "How come we only get one spare battery? Guys over in Vietnam get two."

"Sir, I couldn't answer that. Up from your spare battery, you've got your signal mirror here . . . now remember . . . we've had more rescues from the signal mirror than any other signaling device. And if it breaks, you've then got two signaling devices that don't require any batteries."

I nodded.

"This next pouch"—his finger moved along my vest—"has your survival instructions book. Don't lose it. Moving along, sir, on these two pouches by your waist, one on each side, you've got your basic signal flares." He tugged on the pockets to make sure they were secure.

"Moving along, over here we have your bowie knife." He pulled it out and ran his finger down the gleaming blade. "Extremely sharp, sir. It'll cut jungle vines, chute cord tangled around you, bone, or anything else you can think of." He placed the blade back in its sheath.

"And over in this pouch we have your new jungle-penetrator pen-gun flare. Before these beauties, we lost several pickups when the pilot couldn't signal the Jolly Greens his location under the thick jungle canopy. These babies rip right up through the foliage so the choppers can locate you.

"And don't ever lose your compass, here." He pointed at yet another pouch.

I was losing track of pouches.

"Make sure you relay to the chopper the heading at the *bottom* of the compass, *not* the one at the *top* like you pilots always do. We've lost lots of guys when they gave the heading at the *top* of the compass that directed the choppers *away* from their location. By the time the choppers turned back around, it was too late."

I told him that would be a normal pilot mistake since we fly the heading at the *top*. It seemed to me a person afraid for his life would revert to everyday habits. I told him to fix the problem, all they had to do was put the compass face on *backward* during manufacture and we might be able to reduce the number of losses.

He shook his head sadly. "That makes a lot of sense, sir, but they've been makin' this compass the same way since WWII. They'll never change it."

And a lot more guys will die unnecessarily, I thought silently.

He finished my vest tour. "And rounding out this evening's ensemble, we have your sea-dye marker over here. Now don't ask me what the hell that's for, sir. It comes standard in every vest. Now, do you have any questions?"

I answered no.

"Oh, I almost forgot the most important thing. Here's your blood chit." He handed me a folded piece of colorful silk. "You'll have to sign for this and your weapon on this here hand receipt. They're accountable items. I'll need them both returned to me as soon as you get down, or there'll be a formal investigation with charges filed against you."

With that comforting thought in mind, I signed the receipt.

"Too many blood chits have found their way sewn onto the backs of souvenir leather jackets coming out of Okinawa, so they're cracking down," he explained. "Now tuck your chit away in a safe place. It might save your life one night."

I had no idea what a blood chit was or how the handkerchief-size piece of silk might save me, but not wanting to look more ignorant, I nodded.

"To give you something to look forward to when you get back down, sir, the first beer's on us." He displayed an ice chest stuffed with San Miguel.

I smiled. "Thanks."

Finally the technicians helped us don our parachutes, and then, looking like a family of hunched-over armadillos crossing a Texas blacktop, we waddled out to the airplane. By that time the engineer and rampers had completed the preflight, so we jumped in the seats, I read the checklist for Wiley, then we started the engines and took off headed for northern Laos, aka Barrel Roll.

CHAPTER THREE

June 10, 1970
Over Northern Thailand
12:06 a.m.

I am in the copilot seat. Wiley is in the left seat. Major Barton is seated behind us at the nav table through the open doorway, suspended midair on a movie director's boom. Major Ward is down below at the scope hole lying prone on an old mattress. He is staring straight down two miles and adjusting his starlight scope.

The flight engineer is twenty-five yards behind us in the cargo compartment scanning out the left-side portholes for trouble. Some kid clerk-typist is peering out the right-side portholes. Two "rampers" are arming our two pallets of high-explosive flares and ground markers ready for action.

I watch with surprise as Wiley levels off at *12,000 feet*. I remind him that regulation AFR 60-16 states our max altitude without supplemental oxygen in an unpressurized airplane is 10,000. I tell him diplomatically, "Maybe we should go back down to ten."

I look at Wiley and he looks back at me. His expression is blank.

Finally he says, "We'll stay here at twelve."

I repeat the oxygen requirement they beat into us at pilot training.

Wiley stares ahead and says nothing.

Now he reaches overhead, shuts down the jets, and begins cruising along at a whopping two miles a minute compared to modern jets' four times faster.

Everybody seems busy doing something but me. I ask Wiley if he wants me to give him a break and fly awhile.

He answers no.

With nothing to do but kill time, I lean forward against my shoulder straps and peer out the top of my front window . . . the North Star. No moon.

Time passes while the crew makes chitchat about issues I don't understand. Finally Major Barton announces, "Heads up, crew. We're crossing the Mekong. Let's keep the chatter down."

I watch Wiley reach for the overhead panel and turn off all our exterior lights . . . AFR 60-16 violation *number two*. Since there's no radar coverage way out here, the lights were our sole protection against a midair collision. I remind him of this.

No answer back from him.

I try again, "Maybe you didn't hear me, Wiley, but—"

He says bluntly, "We'll see." He is quiet and leaves the lights off.

We'll see? We'll see? What the hell kind of answer is *that*?

Wiley tells the rampers, "Cleared to open the ramp."

They acknowledge and I feel the airframe shudder as the giant door on the plane's rearmost floor drawbridges down. I turn, look back through the open door, and see the back end yawn open to the night. The two enlisted rampers tightrope-walk along the knife-edged ramp, poised to drop flares or ground-burning markers. One of them flicks a flashlight on to check his partner's safety-harness connections. The wind tries to rip the hair from their heads.

The ramper flicks his light off and I lose them in the dark. My mandatory fire-resistant gloves are drenched in sweat . . . useless. I take them off and hang them on my window rail to dry like laundry.

I see Wiley is bare-handed.

I am losing track of his flagrant violations.

Time passes in silence. Finally Major George Keene announces, "Okay, guys. We're over the PDJ. It could happen any minute. Jack, you should be picking up the trail."

Tension hits. My stomach somersaults.

Major Ward responds, "Got the route structure in sight. I'll take over heading control."

I ask Major Barton over interphone, "What's the PDJ?"

"The Plain de Jars," he explains. "It's the only flat spot in northern Laos. They named it after some French guy named Jars when they were fighting this war back in the fifties. The rest of the country is nothing but mountain range after mountain range occasionally broken up by towers of karst."

"What's karst?" I ask.

He explains, "Karst is—"

Wiley cuts in, "Knock it off, guys. We need to be quiet now."

I glare at him.

Egomaniac.

The only noise louder than the rolling thunder of our two Pratt & Whitney reciprocating engines are the air-ripping sawmill screams from the twin Hamilton Standard props. I can barely hear my own thoughts. Normal conversation off interphone is impossible.

I stare in disbelief as Wiley lights up a Chesterfield. I didn't even know he smoked! I watch his face ghoulishly illuminated by the occasional red glow from the burning tip. He has the sinister, focused look of a professional assassin studying his prey before squeezing off the fatal round.

I remind him now that AFR 60-16 states no one is permitted to smoke with the high explosives we have onboard.

He replies, "Thanks for reminding me," and lights another from the red tip of the first. "You want one?"

"I don't smoke."

He shrugs. "Suit yourself."

I fault myself. I glimpsed his Jekyll/Hyde nature yesterday. I guess I chose to look the other way.

No one says a word. The silence is getting hard to bear.
On top of that, this place stinks like a combined gym locker
room and auto-service bay.

I am just sitting in the dark with nothing to do. I feel like
the batboy for a major-league baseball game. I don't even
rate a map. If everybody else gets shot up, I couldn't find my
own way back to NKP.

I'm wondering what's ahead in the dark and how I'll react when the shooting starts. As this old battle-ax wallows
through the midnight sky, I lose sense of time. We seem suspended inside a giant ink bottle, going nowhere.

The atmosphere aboard is like a lit powder keg.

Wiley's Chesterfield burns down to his fingertips.

He lights another.

If Wiley offers a cigarette again . . . I think I'll take it.

Miles go by and all remains quiet . . . only the occasional
"Come right five degrees, Wiley" from Major Ward and the
muffled fears from my own heavy breathing echoing in my
headset.

In my imagination I see a mile-high neon sign ahead
flashing:

                          DEAD END
                          DEAD END

It's quiet out there. Maybe the gunners took the night
off . . .

"BREAK RIGHT, BREAK RIGHT, BREAK RIGHT!"

Wiley yanks this old machine up on the right wing.

Heavy g's slam me down in my seat.

Thirty-seven-millimeter tracers headed for the right wing!

My mind's eye sees a direct hit on the wing fuel tank. It
explodes in a ball of fire. The fire blossoms and burns
through the engine mounts. The engine starts shaking. Then
the prop vibrates like a worn-out house fan. It jumps off its
shaft and ripsaws through the fuselage, cutting Major Ward

in half. Unstable, the fuselage rips apart. Stringers and ribs spring apart like overtightened violin strings. Finally the cockpit separates as it did in the C-133 crash that killed my friend Duane.

Did Duane have minutes, smashed against the sides of the tumbling cockpit, to think about death?

I watch red tracers race by where the wing was *just a second* ago. I could've reached out and grabbed one! Had just *one* hit, we'd have turned into one of those smoking WWII B-17s.

A second round of tracers headed for us look like Fourth of July fireworks.

They rip by and bomb-burst explode a hundred feet overhead.

"Pilot, Scope," Major Ward snaps angrily. "I just spotted a huge convoy. How the *hell* do you expect me to count how many trucks they're running if you don't stay over the god-damned trail?"

"Scope, Pilot. I'll get us back right now," Wiley answers calmly. "Charles, gimme a heading."

"Pilot, Nav. Pick up a heading of zero four five . . . Jack, you should pick up the route structure again in a sec," Major Barton advises the scope navigator coolly.

"Nav, Scope. Got 'em again . . . monster convoy," Major Ward reports. "Must be a hundred trucks. Charles, I'll count 'em off in groups of ten. Never seen anything this big. They must be getting ready to make a major push. Ten trucks . . . another ten . . . and *another ten* . . . this is huge!"

"Break left. Break left. Break left," the left scanner yells.

Wiley stands this albatross up on its left wing and turns directly *into* the tracers!

I look out his side window *straight down to the ground*!

Multiple red streams headed *right for us*!

We're gonna get hit!

At the last second, Wiley jams in left rudder, firewalls the throttles, and whipsaws us through the middle of the barrage.

He's dancing with death.

I'm about to wet my pants.

I think to myself, This stupid bastard is *trying* to get us shot down!

Half the deadly streams rip by above our heads, but the other half disappear underneath the wing—headed for the bottom of the fuselage.

This is *it*!

My heart booms. My ass cheeks grab the seat cushion. I squeeze my armrests, slam shut my eyes, hold my breath, tense my body, and wait for the rumbles and vibrations from the explosion . . .

Nothing.

I stare *straight up* out my right window. The tracers zip up two thousand feet and explode in a deadly starburst.

Close!

I feel a migraine coming on.

"Wiley, how . . . how'd you learn to do *that*?" I holler off interphone.

Wiley shrugs and yells back, "I don't know, you pick it up as you go. You get a feel for it. It has a natural rhythm. Watch for the *patterns*. Don't worry . . . you'll get it," he assures me.

"But . . . why'd you turn *into* the flak? Shouldn't we be turning *away*?"

Wiley thinks about it. Then he shakes his head and hollers, "That would be the natural reaction, but that would get you killed. Turning *into* the flak narrows their effective angle and range."

I shake my head.

"And on top of that," he continues, "if I turned *away*, we'd be belly up, blind. By turning *into* their fire, I keep it in sight to make those last-second adjustments you saw. Not only that, by breaking *into* the shells, we're a narrower target. If I turned *away*, I'd present the entire underside of the fuselage and wing as a target, give them extra time to track us, plus more angles, *increasing* the odds of getting hit."

I feel depressed. I shake my head. "I don't think I'll ever be able to do that, Wiley."

Jack Ward breaks in angrily, "Pilot, Scope. Do you think you guys can shut up so I can keep us over the goddamn trail? Cut the crap."

"Roger, Scope. Returning to heading zero four five," Wiley answers.

We dodge more deadly red streams. The g's shove my headset down my sweat-soaked forehead. The headband covers my eyes and blinds me.

I shove it back up into place.

I ask, "Wiley, can they *see* us?" and wait for another blast from Major Ward.

Nothing comes.

Wiley explains with irritation, "Nope, they're just shooting at the noise from the props and recips, trying to get lucky." He's losing patience with me. "It would be different with a full moon. We have to be quiet now, John."

The skies turn mercifully dark and quiet. Thank God.

The quiet is short-lived.

"BREAK LEFT. BREAK LEFT. HARD *NOW*. Six clips."

"Break right. Break right! Seven clips on the right."

Thirty-seven-millimeter tracers race by both side windows.

I expect Wiley to break one way or the other, but he flies ahead.

What the *hell* can he be thinking?

I figure maybe his headset cord is disconnected. Or maybe he's preoccupied. So I yell, "They said, 'Break,' Wiley. Didn't you *hear* them?"

"Break left. Break left. Break left."

"No! No! No! *Not left*. Break *right*, break *right now*."

Wiley starts rolling left, then begins rolling right, then back left, and finally does nothing. He flies us *straight ahead* into the heavy line of tracers dead ahead!

We're trapped. No way out of this one.

We're gonna take a hit.

I squeeze my right hand under my tight-fitting parachute

harness, weave it under my survival vest, and wedge into my flightsuit against my bare chest. My heart is a runaway freight train increasing in speed with every salvo. The muscle feels about to launch itself out of my chest. Involuntarily, I press down hard to hold it in.

How stupid can you get?

Wiley hits a lever and bottoms out his seat—I guess so he can't *see* the tracers—and flies us straight ahead into the artillery barrage.

I think to myself, he's lost his mind. Like Crazy Mark. I'm going to die at the hands of a nutcase. Wiley seems disconnected from reality, oblivious to danger. I watch him stare at his instruments, blindly following Major Ward's headings over the trail as it meanders like the Mississippi.

I yell, "Wiley, if you don't start breaking soon, they're gonna shoot us down!"

No answer.

I glare at him. Stupid bastard!

"Break left."

"Break right."

"Break left."

Still nothing from Wiley. I shout again, "Wiley, you gotta start breaking or we'll be shot down."

I see he heard me, but he doesn't answer. As if what I'd said fell into a black hole.

Major Ward calls, "I've got ten . . . no . . . *twenty* trucks . . . big ones, too. Now another ten."

Charles answers calmly, "Got it, Jack."

Wiley finally answers me, "No, we won't."

I fire back, "What do you *mean,* we won't? You can't possibly—"

Wiley says solemnly, "They're *not* gonna shoot us down. You don't understand, John." His expression says his patience is gone. We are close to a split. "This old plane could take a hit and we'd still get home okay."

"You mean you're *planning* on taking a hit?" I ask incredulously.

"Well . . . sort of . . . I guess . . . I never thought about it that way," he answers with a sense of wonder. Then he turns back to his instruments and lights another Chesterfield.

"Break right, break right, break right."

Wiley flies on. "But that's *crazy*," I shout. "I may be the new guy, but letting guys shoot at you and *expecting* to get hit is *nuts*."

"No, it's not," he says calmly. "Actually, the C-123 has a good record of taking hits. It's a tank with wings."

I stare at him in disbelief. I can't think of anything to say to *that* nonsense.

He continues, "One of these airplanes based in Nam has so many bullet holes they call it Patches. One of our NKP planes flew back with a hole back by the ramp big enough for a refrigerator. I saw that one myself and stood up through the hole. This old machine is tough, John. It would take a direct hit from one of the rare fifty-seven-millimeter guns out here to take us out. The Candlesticks have been doing this for years and no one's ever been shot down . . . so . . . I'm going with the odds. On top of that, you've got that flak-resistant material under and around your seat to protect you. We'll be okay . . . you'll see."

I give up. There's no getting through to him. We're only halfway through this ride up the trail. There's still another hour of shelling ahead.

We're not gonna make it.

Sharon's going to be a widow.

I try to remember if I signed my will before I left home.

"Nav, Scope. I've got ten trucks and another ten . . . Pilot, give me four degrees to the right and keep her *steady*, dammit."

Multiple tracers of lethal flak encircle us again. For every tracer we can see, five or six explosive shells lie hidden in between. We become surrounded.

Finally, I realize Wiley is right. There's nowhere to break *to*. I'm going to die my first night over the trail. What a waste. Sharon and I don't have kids yet. I hope they don't tell her I died *counting*.

It would be different if we had fighters available to shoot

back. But they briefed us all the fighters were assigned to "higher priority targets."

Higher priority, my ass. They didn't ask *me*.

"BREAK RIGHT, BREAK RIGHT, BREAK RIGHT."

Tracers continue to envelop us, but Wiley flies on ahead. But what's that new sound over the props? Somebody's humming? What the . . . ?

It's Wiley! We're getting blasted and the stupid bastard is *singing* that Marmalade song . . .

I think to myself, This man is out to commit suicide. He's broken every rule in the book, flying like an out-of-control renegade.

Wait a minute! Maybe he's *hypoxic*. Maybe he's suffering from a lack of oxygen. Maybe I can remind him of the oxygen rule, build on that base, and coax him back to his senses. I feel woozy myself, so now is a good time to bring it up. I tell him, "Wiley, I'm getting hypoxic. Correct me if I'm wrong, but doesn't 60-16 require us to be on oxygen?"

I wait for an answer, but he stares at his instruments. Maybe he didn't hear . . . it's so fuckin' loud. I holler again, "Wiley, maybe you didn't hear me, isn't it mandatory we be on oxygen? Or maybe we should go down to ten thousand . . . ?"

"Well," he says slowly and deliberately, "that would normally be the case, but what you can't see is that the mountaintops are *above* ten thousand. So if we did it your way, we'd slam into them. On top of that, if we were down at ten, we'd be two thousand feet closer to those triple-A sites and we *would* get our asses shot off. That extra two thousand feet gives me the extra time I need to dodge the shells. Now you listen to me . . . all that crap they filled your head with back in pilot training will get you killed over here, John. Now if you feel light-headed, take a couple hits of oxygen and you'll feel better. In a few days, your blood will thin out and create extra red blood cells to compensate. If you're gonna make it this year, JT, you're gonna have to break some rules."

I give up, sit back in silence, and watch as we zip through multiple sheets of flak.

"Is it *always* this bad, Wiley?" I yell, my voice cracking.

"Well, this is pretty normal. The average night we'll dodge about eleven hundred rounds. One night last week I took sixteen hundred," he boasts as he continues to fly northeast, high above convoy after convoy.

"Nav, Scope. I've got ten more trucks and another ten . . . this convoy is *enormous*. Pilot, gimme twenty degrees left."

"Scope, Pilot. Roger. Twenty degrees left to a new heading of zero two five."

At least I can't hear the shells "Boom!" over the howling props and recips . . . some small blessing in that.

But we're the sole aircraft stupid enough to venture this far north.

That also makes us the only target.

Why are they wasting so much lead on this old garbage truck?

My heart jackhammers. That trapped-in-an-ink-bottle sensation returns. There's no sense of moving forward . . . only the neon strings of triple-A fire we whiz by give any sense of movement.

This is going to end in disaster unless I do something . . . have to keep trying to get to Wiley . . . no matter what . . .

I raise my left earcup to shout at him privately. "Wiley, maybe we could pull off the trail, parallel it north for ten miles, and come back to it down the road so they can't figure out where we are. How does that sound?"

His cigarette has burned out, so it's too dark to see his reaction. Wiley's voice says solemnly, "We'll see."

We'll see! We'll see? What the hell kind of answer is *that*?

"Nav, Scope. I've got ten more trucks . . . now another ten. Gimme ten degrees left."

"Scope, Pilot. Roger. Coming ten left to new heading of zero three five." Wiley lights another Chesterfield.

We're not gonna make it.

CHAPTER *FOUR*

Suddenly the skies turn quiet.

With a sense of relief I ask, "Wiley, do you think that's *it*? Have they given up?"

"Nah, this happens all the time," he explains. "All they're doing is radioing ahead to their buddies to let 'em know we're coming. They can't hear us while they're shooting, so there's more guns waiting for us down the road a ways until they hear us come into range and then they'll start up again."

Still trying to bring sanity to this situation, I keep my voice composed and try again. "Then why don't we fool them and pull off the trail and come back onto it ten miles later? How would—"

He raises his hand and cuts me off. "No, we'll stay *right here*. We're gonna be okay. You need to get used to this pretty soon, JT," he scolds me. "Remember, you're going to be on your own next week. There'll be crewmembers who'll be depending on you to take care of them, so now's a good time for you to get comfortable with this chaos. Now *be quiet* and pay attention."

My migraine blasts off from its launching pad, turning my headset into a vise someone seems intent on squeezing down tighter and tighter.

Streams of shells form a solid wall dead ahead again. They can't possibly miss and we don't have a goddamned emergency airfield to limp into when we *do* get hit. We're toast.

KA-BOOM!!!

One giant white starburst explodes in front of my window. I try to jump out of my seat to get away, but my shoulder harness pins me down. I *heard* that one, but there were no tracers to warn us.

The flash from the huge explosion lights the cockpit like a strobe light, and I spin around to look for Wiley's reaction. His face contorts like those gargoyles on European buildings. He's terrified, but I'm the only one who seen it.

The cockpit returns to dark, but Wiley remains silent.

How does he do *that*?

"What the hell was *that*?" I yell.

"That was your first look at a fifty-seven-millimeter," he explains calmly.

"Why couldn't we see it, like the thirty-sevens? Where were the tracers?" I ask, lowering my voice an octave to disguise my fears.

"Fifty-sevens don't have tracers, so they're always a surprise. It's a good thing the bad guys don't have many of 'em. One fifty-seven could take out the whole aircraft."

"Then how do we know when to break around them?"

"We don't."

"Then *please* . . . let's get the hell out of here," I beg.

"Nav, Scope. I just picked up another large convoy headed south. Nav, how many trucks are we up to now?"

"I count one hundred seventy so far," Charles answers. "This is big, guys. *Really* big. Something major's going on. I've never seen this many trucks before. Wiley, we've got to keep going," Charles urges.

Wiley looks at me, shrugs, looks back at his instruments, and flies ahead.

◆ ◆ ◆

After more than two hours avoiding flak and counting trucks, the shelling mercifully stops. The skies turn quiet and a sense of calm comes over me.

Whew! I've made it through the first night.

We've counted all the damned trucks Saigon could ever want, and now we can parallel the route structure safely south and get back to NKP in one piece. Maybe tonight's shelling will be the worst I'll see.

Wiley says, "Good job, everybody. Take five and then we'll fly back home." He turns and asks Charles, "You and Jack gonna swap out now?"

Charles answers yes and I watch him unbuckle and shinny down off his director's chair.

Good, I tell myself. We made it through safe and sound. We're going to make it back home safely, after all. It's over, thank God.

I loosen my chest strap to breathe easier and feel my heart begin to slow. This one's over. We've made it. Relief!

"Okay, JT, you've got the airplane," Wiley tells me because this old jalopy doesn't have an autopilot. Somebody has to hand-fly it all the time.

I rock the wings gently to let him know I've got the controls and watch him release his control column. "Okay, I've got the airplane. What do you want me to do?" I ask, looking for guidance since this is the first time he's let me fly.

"Whatever you want . . . make something up. Do circles or lazy eights, whatever. I don't care. I just need a break to eat my box lunch."

I fly circles for a while, but I keep seeing flashes out of the corner of my eye that look like city lights off to the east a ways. Maybe ten miles away at the most. But that doesn't make any sense. I don't remember the Barrel Roll map back at Intell showing any cities in northern Laos. Wiley probably knows.

"Wiley, what are those lights? Is that a city?"

"Oh, yeah, that's Vinh," he answers calmly.

"*Vinh? Vinh!* As in *North Vietnam, Vinh*?" I ask with rising fear.

"Well, yeah. So . . . what's your point?" he answers casually, taking another bite of peanut-butter-and-jelly sandwich.

I can't stand his nonsense any longer. I rip my headset off to get his attention and yell at him privately. "Wiley, the Intell briefing said there were fighters on strip alert at Vinh. They *must know* we're up here at their front door. If we circle around, taunting them this way, they're gonna get pissed off and launch their fighters. They'll race up here and shoot us down. We wouldn't stand a chance. C'mon now, let's get the hell out of here."

Wiley shakes his head. "You're wrong, JT. They're not gonna come up and get us. They're asleep and won't get out of bed for just one C-123. We're not worth their time," he says calmly, and chomps another bite of sandwich.

"But you don't *know* that," I holler. "At one hundred thirty knots against their six hundred knots, we'd be the turkey in a fuckin' turkey shoot. Let's get the hell outta here . . . *please*."

Wiley tells me, "Just keep on orbiting. After I finish my box lunch, we'll go back and do it again."

Nothing I've said all night has gotten to him, but I can't believe what he just said. I ask apprehensively, "What do you mean 'do it *again*'?"

"Well, we're only halfway done, JT. We gotta go back and look for more trucks," he says without emotion.

Do it again? Do it *again*? Go back through all that all over again? No way, I tell myself.

It's my responsibility to continue to try to get through to him. They taught us to repeat your concerns as copilot time after time. But I've followed their seven-step formula to the letter:

1. **Get the captain's attention.**
2. **State the nature of the problem.**

3. State how you *feel* about it.
4. State the negative consequences that will happen if
   the current course of action continues.
5. Offer your proposed solution.
6. Get a new decision from the captain: "Is that
   okay with you?"
7. Repeat the process until you get the desired
   results.

But the strategy has failed and I have nothing left in my
copilot bag of tricks. My repeated pleadings the Air Force
promised us would work seem to be having the opposite effect. They're pushing Wiley into a corner . . . less likely to
change his decision.

So it's over. He's in command and all I can do is sit here
and watch him kill us. Mutiny in combat is out of the question. I give it one last try. "Wiley, those gunners will just be
waiting for us. We're gonna take a hit. We're alone and
hours from home. No one's gonna come to our rescue.
Now . . . *please* . . . let's get off the trail and go home.
Please."

Wiley is silent.

After a while he says harshly, "Okay, I've got the airplane
back," and yanks the controls out of my hands.

"You've got the airplane," I confirm.

Uh-oh.

Wiley scolds me like a father. "Look, JT . . . I want you to
pay close attention to what I'm going to say. You've got to
get hold of yourself. This is how we make our living every
night, and you'd better get used to it or you'll never make it
through the year. You need to get control of your fears or you
won't be able to function and you'll be no good to me or
anybody else."

He continues, "In less than a week, the squadron's gonna
put you in command of a mission just like this, so you'd better get ready for it *right now*. Now, when we go through this
time, watch for the natural patterns and rhythm in the shells.

They're there, but you've just been *looking*. You're not *seeing*. The tracers have a natural rhythm you can move with, but you'll have to learn to deal with your own fears and set them aside on a shelf before you can see the patterns. Otherwise, your own fears will kill you well before any of the flak."

I shrink smaller and smaller down into my seat as he continues, "JT, I won't be here to take care of you next week. You'll be on your own. Whether you're ready or not, the squadron is gonna put you in this left seat. The navigators and enlisted people on that airplane are gonna depend on your cool reactions to keep them alive. So you need to grow up and grow up fast. Now pull yourself together, because we're going back in."

My mind forms the words *Wiley, you crazy bastard! Take this old tub off the trail and get us out of here before you kill us all!* but nothing comes out.

Coward.

I feel I'm in the scene from *Spartacus* with Kirk Douglas and Woody Strode: two slave gladiator friends waiting inside that cramped tunnel before entering the Roman Colosseum for deadly combat. One would die at the hands of the other, or the crowd would kill both of them. I cinch down my parachute chest straps to return to the arena where gunners await us, like bloodthirsty Colosseum crowds. Someone's going to die. There is nothing left to say. My heart pounding like a pile driver, we head back down the trail.

I look ahead on the dark horizon and see an upside-down waterfall of tracers across the width of the trail. Like Niagara Falls, but flowing uphill. The ominous red mass blocks our path home. The bad guys *know* we're coming. It won't be long now until we take a hit. Where and when it will come is the only question. All I can do is watch as we approach the wall of up-flowing lead. If anything goes wrong way out here, Thailand is hours away.

I bite back stomach bile as we head back in . . . this is it. Wiley, disconcertingly, looks as if he were talking to a friend on the phone . . . zero fear.

Zero brains.

We fly west over the trail for a while and then it *really* gets bad. My headset fills with nonstop "Break left!" and "Now back *right*!"

But I finally begin to see the patterns Wiley talked about. I begin to think, maybe I *can* do this, when I hear an electronic hummmm.

Ziiiiiiiip . . . ziiiiiiiip . . . ziiiiiiiip . . .

What's *that*?

I turn to ask Wiley, thinking it must be radio interference, but see his gargoyle mask has reappeared.

Ziiiiiiiip . . . ziiiiiiiip . . . ziiiiiiiip . . . ziiiiiiiip . . . ziiiiiiiip . . .

"Wiley, what's—"

"Shut up, JT," he snaps. "Charles, gimme your best heading north and get us the hell out of here . . . now!"

"Come right to heading three four five," Charles yells.

"Roger, coming to heading three four five." Wiley jerks the plane over on the right wing and jams in full right rudder. Now he firewalls the throttles up to max power, and this old tub starts to accelerate s-l-o-w-l-y . . . 135 . . . 140 . . . 143 . . .

Ziiiiiiiip . . . ziiiiiiiip . . . ziiiiiiiip . . . ziiiiiiiip . . . ziiiiiiiip . . .

Wiley commands, "Ramp, Pilot . . . close up the back of the airplane *now* and let me know as soon as it's closed."

"Pilot, Ramp . . . yes, sir, closing the ramp now."

Ziiiiiiiip . . . ziiiiiiiip . . . ziiiiiiiip . . . ziiiiiiiip . . . ziiiiiiiip . . . ziiiiiiiip . . .

Wiley keeps barking. "Engineer, start both jets! As soon as they're running, let me know. Hurry!"

"Roger, sir. Starting both jets."

I watch the engineer reach up to the overhead panel and throw the electric rotary jet controls to START, held there by a holding coil.

I can see by Wiley's expression that he's frightened. But

what's going on? Why are we starting the jets *now*? We're *never* supposed to start them at cruise unless a recip quits. We must be in a lot of trouble, but I don't even know what's happening!

Ziiiiiiip . . . ziiiiiiip . . . ziiiiiiip . . . ziiiiiiip . . . ziiiiiiip . . .

I remember the max speed with the ramp open is 150 knots, but Wiley blasts through that limit. One hundred and fifty-five knots now . . . the ramp could jam dead in its tracks. *What the hell is going on?*

Ziiiiiip . . . ziiiiiip . . . ziiiiiip . . . ziiiiiip . . . ziiiiiip . . . ziiiiiip . . .

Louder and faster zips every second now.

At 160 knots I hear, "Pilot, Ramp . . . the ramp's closed. Cleared to accelerate! Get the flock outta here!"

I think to myself, this crazy bastard has intentionally oversped the ramp and damaged the aircraft. He's damned lucky it closed. He'll be in *big trouble* back at NKP if we get out of this mess, at least I hope so . . . he deserves it.

Wiley demands, "Engineer, where the *fuck* are those jets? I need them *now,* not later!"

"Yes, sir . . . almost there. Remember, the design makes them slow to come up to speed. I'll advise when they're ready. Stand by."

Ziiiiip . . . ziiiiip . . . ziiiiip . . . ziiiiip . . . ziiiiip . . .

The zips come faster and shorter, more and more every second.

I'm about to jump out of my skin.

Ziiiiip . . . ziiiiip . . . ziiiiip . . . ziiiiip . . . ziiiiip . . . ziiiiip . . .

Faster and faster and louder and louder.

"Pilot, Engineer. The jets are ready!"

"Gimme max power. Hurry!" Wiley yells.

I watch the engineer hit both small electrical toggles at the base of the throttle quadrant to max, but the jet rpms stay at idle.

Come on! Come on! Accelerate, you goddamn pieces of shit!

Ziiiiip . . . ziiiiip . . . ziiiiip . . . ziiiiip . . . ziiiiip . . . ziiiiip . . . ziiiiip . . .

More, faster and faster zips.

What the *hell*?

By design, these two jets *never* accelerate at equal rates. This time, the left jet hits max power first and shoves the nose wildly right, fishtailing us like a dragster off the starting line. Suddenly the right jet reaches max, swerving the nose wildly back left.

We've lost control of the situation.

My heart pile-drives faster as I watch the airspeed climb through 160 to 170 and finally to 180 knots, our max cruise speed. I didn't know this old boat could go this fast.

Ziiip . . . ziiip . . . ziiip . . . ziiip . . . ziiip . . . ziiip . . . ziiip . . . ziiip . . . come louder and louder and faster and faster zips.

Wiley breaks left hard, holds that for a few seconds, then violently throws us back right and left and right and left. The g's slam me down in my seat. Now transverse g's hit me sideways, throwing me like a rag doll. My heart is in my mouth.

"Wiley . . . what's happening? What's that noise?" I yell.

"JT, that's a *radar-guided fifty-seven-millimeter gun* trying to get a lock on us," he yells back. "When those zips get this close together, that means he's almost got a radar lock on us and then he'll fire. He can't miss if he gets a lock."

Ziiip . . . ziiip . . . ziiip . . . ziiip . . . ziiip . . . ziiip . . .

"Ramp, Pilot. Deploy the chaff! Deploy the chaff! Hurry!"

"Roger, sir. Deploying chaff now!"

Wiley continues the violent serpentine maneuvers. "Wiley, what're you doing?" I shout.

"I'm trying to make it harder on him to get a lock."

"What's chaff?" I yell.

"We've got two containers of aluminum foil I didn't tell you about strapped to the outside of the aircraft."

"Aluminum foil against a radar-guided gun, Wiley? You've gotta be shitting me."

Zip . . . zip . . . zip . . . zip . . . zip . . . zip . . .

"It's the only defense we have. The foil's *supposed* to interrupt the radar and make it harder to lock onto us," Wiley explains.

"Pilot, Ramp . . . chaff deployed. That's all we have. We're out."

Zip—zip—zip—zip—zip—zip—zip—zip—zip—

"Have you ever used chaff before, Wiley? Does it work?" I yell.

"Nope . . . I don't know . . . this is the first time . . ."

Zip-zip-zip-zip-zip-zip-zip-

Great. We're fighting a modern weapon with bits of trash from my mother's kitchen.

Zip-zip-zip-zip-zip-zip-zip-zip-zip-

We're not gonna make it.

I'm not Catholic, but spontaneously cross myself.

Sweet Mary, Mother of God.

Zip . . . ziip . . . . ziiiip . . . . ziiiiip . . . . . ziiiiiip . . . . ziiii . . . . zi . . . . . z . . .

The zips fade.

"Okay, everybody, that's it," Wiley says, relaxes back in his seat, and throws off his shoulder harnesses. "We got him. Engineer . . . shut down the jets. Charles . . . mark that spot so they can take out that gun in the morning. That's it, guys. Good job. I'm buying the beer tonight. Charles, gimme a heading that will take us twenty miles north way off the trail and then take us home."

I can't believe what I just heard. "Wiley, are you telling me our *real* mission was to fly back and forth without any fighter coverage to make ourselves an easy target just to piss off the enemy so bad that they'd expose that gun so we could mark it so somebody else can come back and destroy it tomorrow?"

"Well, yeah . . . sort of . . . I guess. They asked us to smoke out that new gun. The bad guys have never had radar-guided artillery up here before, and we wanted to make sure they don't make it a habit. We're going to teach them a lesson in the morning that we won't tolerate it."

"So we were the slow-moving target in a *real* shooting gallery?"

"Well, yeah . . . I never thought of it that way, but I guess so."

"But why didn't you *tell* me? Why didn't I hear anything about this at the Intell briefing?"

"Well, you didn't have a need to know. This was a top-secret mission, so they only briefed me and Charles and Jack before we met up with you. Besides, I wasn't sure you'd come along if you knew what was going to happen."

I admit to myself, He's probably right, but I keep this to myself. I ask, "So how'd our squadron get so lucky to draw this stupid mission?"

"Oh, that's simple. The planners in Saigon know the Candlesticks are about the only outfit who'd accept a mission like this, and we're all damned proud of that reputation. Probably the only other units who'll take missions where they make themselves a live target are the A-1s and the Jolly Greens. The A-1s intentionally fly in low and get shot up while the Jolly Greens try to pick up a downed pilot, but neither of those guys have the range or endurance for a mission this far out. So it fell to the Candles."

I shake my head. These people are nuts. I'll never make it through the year. That's one down . . . only 364 more to go.

Good luck.

Guess I'll ask Crazy Mark where I can get one of those calendars.

As we fly back toward NKP, Wiley starts humming again . . .

> *All my cryings; all my cryings,*
> *Feel I'm dying, dying . . .*

CHAPTER *FIVE*

Five months later—November 6, 1970
Northern Laos—the Barrel Roll
Plain de Jars
Twelve thousand feet
10:32 P.M.

P ilot, Scope. Gimme two degrees right . . . that's it . . . steady . . . drop flare . . . drop flare . . . drop flare," Major Scott relays from his scope-hole mattress on our C-123's cargo compartment floor.

I am in command in the left seat, on my half-hour break from tedious hand-flying.

Rich (don't call me Dick), my copilot, turns the plane to begin *another* boring racetrack pattern over the Plain de Jars.

We have been orbiting this spot in far-northern Laos deep behind enemy lines since 8 P.M., dropping air-burning flares over a small patrol of good guys. Our candlelight is the difference between life and death for them. Their call sign is Tonto. Should we ever let the light go out, overwhelming numbers of bad guys would quickly overrun Tonto.

"Flares *away*!" Sergeant Bennett confirms from the cargo ramp, dropped wide-open against the night sky.

I wait to hear "Flares away" every time. The cargo compartment is again stuffed with those two pallets of high explosives. If just one of those flares or ground markers would stick in the deployment chute and ignite *inside* the aircraft, it could be the end. Our lives would depend on our rampers to clear the jam, or we would ignite in a supernova that would light up all northern Laos. Instant Crispy Critters.

I can see by the two overhead left- and right-wing fuel-tank gauges we have about an hour and a half's fuel remaining before we'll hit "bingo fuel" and need to head back to NKP from our position over the Plain de Jars. My Seiko Worldtimer shows 10:32. I can't afford many luxuries on what they pay us, but my new watch helps me think of Sharon and what normal people back home do during the day. I think this little link with the real world has helped me from turning into Crazy Mark or Weird Wiley; at least I hope so. The Worldtimer has two time zones, so I keep one on NKP local time and the other on West Coast time. Sharon is probably headed out the door now for her volunteer job at the Travis Air Force Base hospital. I hope it keeps her mind off how long this year is lasting.

Idle in the pilot seat, I note my wrist and forearm glisten in sweat below my rolled-up sleeves, even this late at night. Up here at twelve thousand feet, the jungle air is still so humid it feels like we're wearing divers' wet suits four sizes too small that *squeeze* the water out of us. One of our main problems is staying hydrated, so we drink tons of water. Air Force rules require us to fly with our sleeves rolled *down* and to wear our fire-retardant gloves in case of an onboard fire; but I just can't do it. Whoever came up with those stupid rules doesn't have to fly these missions. It was probably somebody like Desktop. Jack Ward taught me that I'm going to have to break lots of rules to avoid going home to Sharon in a body bag.

While Major Jack was "just" a navigator to most pilots, he remains my Zen master. The insights he shared with me have saved what now masquerades as my sanity and opened my mind to new forms of thought.

Anyways, the glove rule conflicts with my need to stay hydrated and still be able to *think*. I carry my gloves, but leave them in the zippered pocket on my right thigh. I've tried wearing them, but there was none of the subtle feedback you need to know what's going on. With bare hands, I can *feel* the airplane and anticipate problems before they slip out of control.

I look over at Rich at the controls and see his sleeves *rolled all the way down*. And he's wearing his damn gloves again.

Idiot.

I see his Nomex gloves are not only soaked with perspiration, but they're also stained with the white salts from five months of sweat. His old gloves have become useless against the onboard fire he fears, but new ones take too long to break in. Old gloves feel so good after they mold to your hand.

I think to myself, not too bright, Dick. The heat you're building up and the loss of water to your brain will make you unable to help me if something *does* go wrong.

I suggest, "Rich, one of the important things I learned from Jack Ward was not to dehydrate. I think you'd be better off if you took off those gloves and rolled up your sleeves."

Rich glares at me self-righteously. "John, the rules *clearly* state we're supposed to wear gloves at all times and have our sleeves rolled down in case of fire or bailout, so that's what I'm doing." Another lecture about *rules*.

I shake my head. I've been trying to be Wiley or Jack for Rich, but so far he's not listening. Now he thinks *I'm* the renegade; so I just let it go. I've been trying to get through to him on a whole host of issues these past few nights to no avail.

Maybe Rich isn't listening because although he's captain-qualified, the squadron keeps scheduling him only as copilot. So maybe he's insulted. I've heard that many of the enlisted guys refuse to fly with him in command. Maybe he's concerned about Peggy's pregnancy. Maybe he didn't get the benefits of Jack's lesson. Maybe his mother dropped him on his head as a baby.

Maybe he's just an ass.

Rich is like a sole spectator in the bleachers watching this closely fought football game. The game has been nip and tuck for months. Sometimes they win. Sometimes we win. When *we* win, I do so by cheating, and that drives Rich *crazy*. Jack taught me how important it is to cheat, and his strategy has worked wonders.

You *have* to play outside the rules to win, but Rich's commitment to the Air Force rulebook keeps him mentally locked in a losing strategy. He's watching the battle from the stadium upper stands through field glasses, and his only contribution is to occasionally pick up an electric bullhorn to announce, "You're *cheating*. You're not following the rules."

Jack explained Rich to me. "Rich's what we used to call a cookbook pilot. He's only good so long as he follows a published recipe: 'Add a quarter cup of flour, then a tablespoon of baking soda, *then* a quarter teaspoon of salt.' God help him if one night step three has to come first . . . he'll be lost, unable to function."

I'll bet the smarmy bastard had perfect attendance in public school.

We're scheduled to go home about midnight, when Candlestick 25 is scheduled to replace us for this flare-support mission.

I key the radio. "Tonto, Candle 23."

"Candle 23, Tonto. Go ahead."

"Tonto, Candle 23. Just want to make sure light okay."

"Roger, light okay . . . Tonto sleep now."

"Roger, we'll be right here if you need us," I answer.

I've been working with Tonto on and off for months and we've become friends. I want to make sure our flares make "light okay" to keep him safe from the bad guys down there. He's the only English-speaking person in a group of friendly Laotians under the command of General Bang-Pow. His real name is Vang Pao, but Bang-Pow sounds better. Our flares light the area below for Bang-Pow's good guys, our Laotian allies fighting the Pathet Lao bad guys. The light we provide Tonto and his men is their only security against being overrun in the dark by overwhelming enemy forces.

It's been a quiet night compared with most.

We navigate by dead reckoning, more like the explorers Lewis and Clark than fliers. We've been flying four-minute racetrack holding patterns, making random turns for the past three hours, dropping air-burning flares that drift down beneath parachutes. As one set of flares burn out, we reach the drop point again and drop another group of three or four. Easy money.

On slow nights like this, I constantly have to find ways to remind myself of the danger. Going around and around again and again this way, your mind can turn into old, cold oatmeal. Mush. When that happens, you're vulnerable. You can't sense the early warning signs of danger. To compensate, I do mental gymnastics.

I think about the natural risks below. Northern Laos defies Darwin. The place is *de*volving to a more primitive state. There are Komodo dragons and monitor lizards that can outrun a man and knock him down. Fifty-foot-long pythons that can swallow a man whole. Boas that can squeeze the breath out of a person and save the results for breakfast. Insects the size of your hand armed with inchlong scissor mandibles that can chew a finger off overnight.

Really. I'm not kidding. Look them up yourself.

We're all wearing chutes, of course, but I'm not sure they'd do us much good. This territory is nothing but mountain range after mountain range with occasional shafts of deadly karst. If we ever had to bail out, some tree limb would probably puncture a thigh or put out an eye.

Landing on the karst would be worse. I didn't believe what they said about karst when I first heard the stories—it's right out of Edgar Allan Poe. Karst formations look like eight-thousand-foot-tall Italian cypress trees made of limestone, zooming straight up off the surface. They stand stacked together in a grove of towering death, the sides of each shaft razor-sharp. To slide down the side would be a horrible end.

We don't look out the windows much because the scene gives you vertigo. Looking outside through the flickering flare light is like looking through a wall of dripping, oozing orange Jell-O. Nothing is real. The flickering candlelight from our slowly descending flares casts eerie shadows that create mountains from valleys and makes valleys out of mountains. The whole scene seems to be *moving*, as though it were *alive*. Look away for a moment and look back and what you thought was a mountain is really a valley, and that safe valley you thought you might duck into during an emergency is actually a mountain. The scene is a large-scale, constantly shifting Rorschach test. You can see anything you want to see and then it changes right before your eyes.

Looking directly into the flares is like looking into the sun. They'll quickly blind you. Our main skill is to keep from becoming disoriented. So we fly mostly by our cockpit instruments, even on clear nights like tonight.

Our ancient C-123 "Provider" is vibrating all over, like one of those Relax-A-Massage Magic Fingers vibrating beds you'd find in those mom-and-pop motels before Holiday Inns came along. You could pop in a quarter for a ten-minute joyride. Sharon and I used them on our honeymoon. Nice memory there. *We* continued to vibrate long after the quarter ran out, and I get the same feeling over here. I'm vibrating an hour after landing.

The airframe vibrations let me know the engines and props are okay. I only get concerned if the vibrations *stop*.

Our two R-2800 Pratt & Whitney reciprocating engines are turning those Hamilton Standard hydraulic propellers, keeping us safe above the enemy forces. The props are reliable, but these old engines have a history of failures. So I guess I worry about an engine failure more than anything else. The aircraft is way too heavy with explosives to clear the ten-thousand-foot mountaintops on a single recip, but then we could easily fire up the jet on the dead recip side to regain the lost power and limp safely home. No problem.

I've developed a deep respect for this old machine. At first I thought the stories were a joke. You see, the airplane was originally designed as a *wooden* glider toward the end of World War Two.

Back then the military had a shortage of transport aircraft to deliver troops to the European battlefields, so they dreamed up a wooden glider to be built cheap and fast, towed in, released, and landed in open fields. The infantrymen inside would pour out, leaving the aircraft behind. They never built the wooden version because the war ended.

When Korea came around, they urgently needed a troop transport that could fly into and out of dirt strips Army bulldozers could create in a couple of hours. Someone dusted off the old wooden-airplane blueprints, hung a couple of recip engines on it, and . . . voilà! C-123. Instant airplane with the nature of a glider.

For Vietnam, they added these two jet engines after a series of fatal crashes right after takeoff when one of the recips would eat itself. The planes were too heavy in the jungle heat to stay airborne with only a single engine and augured in. Several crews had to pay the price before the Air Force finally learned the lesson and added the jets.

At least they did one thing right . . . someone had the foresight to paint our Candlestick planes *all black* so we blend into the night sky.

The C-123 has the heart and soul of a "Hog." If Harley-Davidson had built just one airplane, this would be it. Tough-looking. Durable. Raw power. Kick-ass reputation. A brawler that can take a beating and win. Works great with half the parts missing. Slow as hell off the starting line, but great top-end performance. A tank with wings. "Electra Glide in Black."

Thailand seems a million miles away on nights like this. It's more than a one-hour flight south back across the Mekong into friendly territory.

I try not to think about it.

Since there's no autopilot, Rich and I swap flying duties every half hour. It's my turn to fly again, but I'm going to take a break.

Time to break another rule. I reach back and whack

George Keene on the bottom of his boot. "Charles, yo
ready to take your turn?"

"Sure," he answers without hesitation.

I look over at Rich and see his eyes grow wide wit
alarm. Letting our *navigator* Charles fly the airplane drive
him crazy, but I'm not going to stop trying to teach him wha
Wiley and Jack have taught me. For example, during th
taxi-out at NKP tonight, I briefed the crew that in an emer
gency we could always land back on the small, skinny, diml
lit parallel taxiway if the single runway was closed from
crash-landed A-1. Rich whipped his head around and sho
me a wild look.

Though not in the rulebook, if that taxiway was my onl
backup . . . I'd land on it in a heartbeat.

Rich hasn't gone through the metamorphosis most pilot
have by this time in their tour. I think it's because his wife
Peggy, is here. Maybe Rich's biggest priority is to simpl
survive each night and let Peggy know he's still alive. The
spend eight days a month together. She flies in fron
Bangkok on the shuttle for four, and he flies down to he
Bangkok apartment for four days a couple weeks later.
think his constant contact with her has prevented him from
changing over. Rod Berano hasn't changed over, either.
guess his wife Ginger's presence is also a constant reminde
of what he could lose any night.

All of us are more than close friends; we're family. Whe
we take our CTOs in Bangkok, most guys will visit Peggy
and Ginger, or a couple of the handful of other wives, t
check on their well-being and enjoy some semblance of fam
ily life. I think the occasional home-cooked meal and con
versations about family help keep me grounded in reality.

I can tolerate Rich on the ground. I just can't stand flying
with him because of his dedication to published rules. He'
not *thinking*. He's *complying*. A chimpanzee *complies*.

Anyways, I've been giving Charles flying lessons an
he's really good.

To a lot of pilots, Charles is "just a navigator." He's neve been a pilot. In fact, he flunked out of pilot training eighteen years ago. I don't think it was his fault. He doesn't *look* the part. Charles looks more like a middle-aged Clark Kent accountant type, while the Air Force seems to graduate pilots who look more like Superman. I think Charles was just the wrong package.

I intend to right some of that wrong. I want Charles to be able to tell his grandchildren he piloted an aircraft over the Ho Chi Minh Trail during this war. And teaching Charles to fly gives me an extra layer of protection. The prevailing theory is one pilot would still be functional to fly us back after we took a hit. I'm not so sure. If the bad guys got off a lucky shot, the armor plate around and under both pilot seats is supposed to absorb the shrapnel before it gets to Rich or me. But I can see a situation where both of us become incapacitated. I want somebody left aboard who can point this Hog back toward NKP and crash-land.

So Charles is my emergency backup plan. Strictly illegal, of course, having any navigator touch the controls. *Way, way, way* outside the rules, and it drives Rich ape shit.

Good.

Colonel Desktop would crucify me if he found out, and I'm worried Rich might snitch. I've been training Charles for several months and not one crewmember has objected. They all *know* some night their lives might depend on his rudimentary flying skills.

I depend on Charles to fill Rich's gaps. I should be able to turn to Rich for advice during tight situations, but all I get back is a blast of rules from his bullhorn. Charles has an open mind; so I depend on his advice before breaking the rules so completely that I get us into deep trouble I could never fly out of.

"Pilot, Scope. Gimme four degrees left . . . right there . . . hold her steady . . . drop flare . . . drop flare . . . drop flare."

"Flares *away*!"

Good. Everything's normal.

• • •

Getting up out of my left seat is a struggle. I push my left hand against the steel armor plate. The armor plate was a good idea. Sharon and I don't have kids yet and they may owe their future existence to the material.

As I stand up to change places with Charles, I see those little white stars in my eyes you get from too little oxygen reaching the brain . . . not enough red blood cells. Wiley was wrong about that one getting better.

Charles and I struggle to move out of each other's way in the tight space. He plops down in my left seat and I help him strap in. Then I step back and stand on the wide wooden platform that looks like the small back porches on those postwar houses. After the porch, it's two more steps down to the cargo floor. I loosen my parachute leg straps and do stretching exercises against the bulkhead to get some circulation back in my legs so they don't cramp. I feel the warm blood flow return.

I like this spot on the back porch. I can keep track of everything from here. Down to my right, I can see our "Scope" lying prone on that old mattress, peering out that three-foot-square open hatch in the cargo floor. Looks as if he's okay.

Now I turn all the way around to look out the back of the aircraft, completely open to the night sky. Our two rampers are silhouetted against the huge opening . . . an enormous picture window someone put there for us to watch the war. As Charles rolls us into the right turn, I can see our latest flares ignite and burn just below us. Glimmering, shimmering, twinkling candlelight . . . beautiful from this angle.

I turn back around, grab hold of the cockpit bulkhead for balance, and do deep knee bends to get the juices flowing . . . one . . . two . . . you feel things completely differently in an aircraft like this compared to the high-speed fighters we direct during airstrikes. A fighter pilot is co-cooned inside a pressurized compartment and looks at the war through electronic fire-control panels. During an attack, their voices rise an octave and they start talking fast.

I'm always afraid they're going to run smack into us.

They start their steep bomb runs way above our altitude, dive *right through our altitude* at over six hundred knots, drop their bombs below us, pull back up, going *through* our altitude a second time, jinking violently left and right to avoid enemy fire . . . and then they go away. For them, it's all over in a matter of seconds. Like watching TV. The war at arm's length.

Unpressurized here at 12,000 feet, with the entire back of our aircraft open to the night sky, the sense of presence is overwhelming. No electronic TV screens here. We're not flying through the sky—we're *part of the sky* for more than five hours. That open night sky *outside* flows all the way up to me *inside* on the back porch, so it's hard to tell where it stops and we begin. Like the sensation you get on a dark beach at night as the tide comes in to lap at your toes, then slowly covers your feet, then is up to your knees, and you aren't quite sure how that happened . . . .

That's nine . . . one more squat . . . ten. Whew! Better.

After a while I jump backward onto Charles's director's chair suspended in midair and lash on the wide leather lap belt so I don't fall out. With its nearly 360-degree swivel, this chair is a good place to keep track of everything. Charles's "desk" is a neat spread of maps and charts of the battleground and route structure of the Ho Chi Minh Trail. Pencils. Compass. Calipers. Ruler. He has things so well organized someone could take a picture for a recruiting poster.

I'm not sure if I mentioned it, but all our maps are unreliable. They're not off a bit—they can be *way off*. As a result, we're always a little lost. Our best map is inside Charles's head. We rely entirely on his experience and memory.

They've only recently started throwing up satellites to map the globe. Until this new technology, all earth maps have been approximations. Best guesses. Estimates. Our Laos maps are based on French guesstimates from the 1950s . . . so they're all wrong. They're close, but just wrong enough to kill you.

We've asked the DOD to route one of the earth-mapping satellites over Laos to produce better maps for us so we can know where the hell we really are and where the hell we're going, but they told us our request was a low priority. They've decided to map the United States first.

Low priority, my ass. They didn't ask *me*. Thanks for your support.

Our box lunches are stacked across the back corner of Charles's desk. I reach for mine—the one marked *JT*. I have no idea where the guys came up with *JT*. No one's ever called me that before. Puzzling.

I open my box and choke at the sight. Maybe somebody else is hungry. "Anybody want part of my box lunch?" I ask over interphone.

Our engineer, Tyrone, asks, "Which one'd you order, JT?"

I'm not sure why he asks because the insides are all the same. "I've got the standard peanut-butter-and-jelly sandwich on stale white bread with the hard ball of peanut butter right in the middle with a whisper of gray jelly. Tonight's epicurean delights also include the mandatory 'mystery meat' on dry, stale 'white.' No mayo, of course. You can also choke on the package of too salty peanuts or let your taste buds fly across the sample size of raisins. You can wash all that down with the required child's-size can of sour Donald Duck orange juice, and if that doesn't suit your fancy, you could try the small carton of warm, reconstituted milk."

Tyrone laughs. "I think I'll wait to eat back at the NCO club. Isn't it Mongolian barbecue night at both clubs?"

"I think so . . . good idea. I'll wait, too. We should be eating by two A.M.," I answer.

I'm too embarrassed to let them see I can't afford to throw away anything remotely edible, so later when no one's looking, I'll tuck most of my lunch into my helmet bag.

My Worldtimer's alternative time zone shows 10:37 A.M. in California. By now Sharon should be arriving at the hospital for her volunteer job as an ob-gyn chaperone. I wonder if she'll be waiting for me if I get home. We've been married two years, but we're basically newlyweds. The Air Force has kept me out flying since we got married, so we never got a chance to settle in with each other. The house may be empty if I get back. No one should have to start a marriage separated this long, so I'm afraid she may go back home to Rockford for good. I wouldn't blame her.

We get to talk *live* every couple of days thanks to the efforts of ham radio operators across the Pacific who bounce the signal from island to island and eavesdrop on the intimate details. Voyeurs.

We crewmembers wait in line in a small, cramped room along with fifty other guys for the six to eight hours it can take for your turn. Most guys have to stand, and the limited seating works like a reverse musical chairs. After several hours of sitting on the floor or standing, you finally work your way up to the torn cushion Salvation Army couches. The television in the corner no one watches plays day-old *CBS Evening News with Walter Cronkite,* black-and-white videos flown in from Honolulu, or *I Love Lucy* episodes we've all seen a dozen times.

When the radio operator blessedly shouts, *"Halliday,"* I go into a small, soundproof booth like the ones from grade-school hearing tests so we can talk privately. The one-way radio conversations work like a police radio. Only one person can talk at a time, and there's a five-second delay from transmission in California to receiving it in Thailand. The transmissions are weak and full of static, so for most of our talks we wind up shouting over each other and have to repeat the whole thing, wasting precious seconds of the five-minute time limit.

"John! The car broke down *again* . . . over!"

"I'm sorry, Sharon . . . over."

"And . . . paycheck didn't come *again*. What . . . I supposed to *do*? I . . . you said you fixed . . . problem . . . over."

"They *promised* the check would come to the house on time this time . . . over!"

"Well . . . didn't! How . . . expect . . . house payment? . . .

Can't keep asking my father . . . wiring . . . money . . .
time! . . ."

Precious seconds pass while I wait for her to say "over"
or continue, so I can answer her.

"Are you still there, Sharon? You have to say 'over' so I
know when I can answer. Try calling my old squadron out at
Travis. Maybe they can help you with the red tape . . . over."

"I did. They said . . . couldn't help me. What do you expect
me to do? Bank called . . . over!" Furious voice; ready to cry.

The operator breaks in, "Your five minutes are up, sir."

I plead with him, "Please, operator, I need more time. I
could lose my house if this keeps up."

"I'm sorry, sir. Your time is up. Say good-bye now."

"I LOVE YOU . . . over," I yell.

"WHAT?" she screams, and forgets to say "over" so the
timing gets screwed up and we yell over each other.

"WHAT?" I try to fit in.

". . . YOU!" *Click* is all I hear as they cut the connection.

Not very romantic, and difficult to sustain a marriage. Our
wives mainly talk about problems at home: the plumbing
leaks or they're threatening to shut off the phone or the backyard is flooded or the car broke down—*again*. Sharon's
mother is in the hospital with what looks like terminal cancer. I should be there. I've asked the new squadron commander to approve an emergency leave. That way we could
qualify for emergency airline fares so Sharon and I could
visit her mother in Rockford before the end comes. But he
told me Air Force policy is that I can go only after her mother
passes away. Something about not being a blood relative.

I can't say much during our calls because everything
we're doing is top secret and I don't have anything else to
talk about. Being at NKP is like one of those sensory-
deprivation tanks people come screaming out of in the middle of the experiment. There's a total absence of *everything,*
except for our flying, which I can't tell her about. But when I
don't have anything to say, she thinks I'm hiding something

or don't love her anymore. It's just there's nothing here *to* hide. I wish there were.

And those are the *good* nights in the isolation booth.

The bad nights are when I wait in line for eight hours only to hear the phone ring and ring and ring—unanswered. The operator says mournfully, "I'm sorry, sir, that's your authorized fifteen rings. I'll have to move on to the next person. Better luck tomorrow night."

I beg, "*Please.* I've waited in line eight hours. Try a couple more rings. *Please*. It's so import—"

Click.

After one of those, I'll stagger around the base in the dark for an hour or two. Then I'll remember the audiotapes Sharon and I mail back and forth. I pop a couple of those in and I begin to calm down when I hear her voice. The two tape machines were the best $50 investment I've ever made. I've saved every tape and play them again and again and again. When a tape snaps apart from overuse, I Scotch-tape the pieces together. The tapes are gold. Even the tough ones.

Sharon's having trouble with money. She wants to work, but the Air Force highly discourages officers' wives from working at salaried jobs. They feel their husband's pay should suffice. So rather than bite the only hand feeding us, she took the volunteer route.

But even if my paycheck came on time with the extra combat pay and $100 income tax exemption, only $450 comes into the house each month, $225 every two weeks. Not good. People on welfare get as much. She's having trouble putting food on the table. The house payment *alone* is $225. We used to rent, but when the apartment owner raised our rent to $195—up by the exact amount of the last year's military pay raise—and when we later caught the manager sneaking around inside our place when she thought we were still out shopping, we packed it in. For a dollar a day more, we could have our own house. We budgeted enough money, but the Air Force keeps losing the damned checks.

I can't believe someone in my old squadron hasn't offered to help Sharon through the red tape. The Travis finance office told her snidely, "Sorry, *ma'am*."

Sharon wasted precious gas last week driving up to the Sacramento Red Cross to ask for emergency funds to tide her over until the Air Force gets its act together. They looked at her suspiciously and demanded to know why an officer's wife needed money. When they made it clear any money wouldn't be a grant, but a loan they'd expect to be repaid starting next month, she told them to forget the whole damned thing and drove home disappointed and empty-handed.

As a result, she's missed a couple of house payments and the bank is threatening to take action. I flew for that squadron back at Travis for nearly two years, yet they're treating Sharon like a stranger looking for a handout. I shouldn't be surprised. The whole unit was filled with pilots like Lieutenant Colonel Desktop. So much for the Air Force "family" they keep selling us. It's hogwash. Sharon and her friend June *share* a head of lettuce and a can of Campbell's tomato soup for *two* dinners back-to-back. No salad dressing. They can't afford it. Just sugar on lettuce.

We moved into the new house right before I left for overseas. The down payment came from her matured insurance policy Sharon's dad bought when she was a baby. There's not one stick of furniture in the house, not even a bed. We can't afford one. Sharon sleeps on the living room floor on three quilts her grandmother made. She tells me she has to keep the heat turned off these cold nights so she can pay the gas and electric bill. Our three cats and the Afghan hound cuddle up with her to share body heat. She joked recently it was a "three-kitty" night.

I should be there.

The builders promised us under the contract to return the topsoil they ripped off from the backyard when their bulldozer stripped it down to the adobe hardpan and to completely sod the whole thing. They lied. After I left for overseas, they gave Sharon fifty bucks and a five-pound box of grass seed. When she protested to the owners they were breaking the contract we signed, they said they simply weren't going to comply.

A family moved in across the circle into an identical new house two months after I left. That family's husband was there to oversee the construction and growl at the appropriate time. He got his lawn put in.

I should be there.

Sharon bought a hoe for a quarter at a garage sale, and now she whacks away at the adobe hardpan every day. Whack, whack, whack for *hours*. She can only afford to buy one small five-pound box of grass seed with each paycheck. She'll work away on a six-foot-square section of the hardpan at a time. Whack. Whack. Whack. Seed, water, and hope that little green grass fuzz appears. Then stake out another six-foot hardpan section and whack away at that.

I should be there.

I'll be surprised if she lasts to my R & R in Hawaii next spring.

"Drop flare . . . drop flare . . . drop flare."

"Flares away!"

Good. No problems.

The bad guys know we're up here, of course, but they can't see us. We hide behind our own powerful candlelight. From the enemy's standpoint, it's like not being able to see the portrait photographer behind his bright studio lights. So our light is our own protective shield, giving us a small sense of security.

Lately, I've had this feeling of impending doom I can't shake. I feel something terrible is going to happen, but there's nothing I can put my finger on. I've told a few people about some recent weird coincidences that I fear will continue, and their eyes widen with disbelief.

I've had to stop talking about it.

I've tried to shake it off, but I can't ignore the feeling that something deadly monstrous is around the next corner. I watch for warning signs, but can't find any.

Maybe it's the engines.

I unbuckle from Charles's chair, jump down on the back porch, reach forward, and fingertip the throttles and prop levers to check for any signs of excessive vibrations that could warn of an impending failure . . . but they're okay. No problem there.

To get the kinks out, I stretch backward as far as my chute will permit.

Still, I feel some*thing* is hiding in the shadows, *watching*. *Waiting*.

CHAPTER *SIX*

I can see Rich's hands poised over the throttles and controls, as though Charles might suddenly spin the aircraft out of control. Poor Rich is ready to spring into action. If he'd open his eyes and *see*, he might relax, conserve his energy, and discover Charles flies these racetrack patterns better than we can.

I watch Rich's feet chattering against his rudder pedals, then look overhead and see the rudder cables dancing like hammered piano wires.

Rich, Rich, Rich. How am I going to get through to you?

I hop backward onto Charles's chair and buckle in. It's a good place to think.

The memories of the past five months now churn together in a giant blender. I want to tear my thoughts apart—slowly—to get a grip on what the hell is going on.

Maybe I can go about this musing the way I waded in the stream behind our house as a kid. I spent hours in the clear, shallow water picking up rocks looking for tadpoles.

When I first started looking for the little pre-frogs, I made a mess of things. I picked rocks up too quickly, stirring clouds of silt. I had to wait for the silt to flow downstream before I could see and try again.

I would try another rock, find no tadpoles, and hurl the rock downstream in frustration. Then I'd stomp over to another part of the stream, but my footsteps so muddied the water again that I couldn't see. Sometimes I rushed to grab a slippery rock, only to have it squirt out of my hands, plunge into the water, splash water up in my face, and stir up even more silt.

Only when I learned to remain still and concentrate on one area of submerged rocks did I begin to find any tadpoles. I picked up each rock slowly and held on carefully. If I didn't find anything, I *carefully* replaced the rock to keep the water clear.

Patience and concentration were the hallmarks . . . you have to look for small clues to larger issues.

So that's the way I think I'll go about this now: one rock at a time . . . a few tadpoles here and there . . . in no particular order . . . and try to understand how the events of these past five months seem to have taken on a life of their own. Events have been getting unsettling; a monster tsunami is building strength offshore in the dark waters—out of sight— that will soon overwhelm us without warning.

It's *coming*. I can *feel* it.

The first rock I spot as I reflect on the past five months is labeled *Colonel Desktop*. The rock is old, ugly, heavy, and riddled with knife-sharp edges.

I pick it up carefully so I don't cut my child-size hands.

They scheduled me as Desktop's copilot that first week, on a simple flare mission like tonight's. For hours we flew around the same racetrack pattern, which can produce a mild hypnosis if you're not careful.

Did I say simple? Not that night. Desktop turned the mundane into something bizarre.

We were *supposed* to orbit at 11,000 feet. Before I get started, you need to understand there's nothing more basic to flying than maintaining altitude. Nothing. If you have altitude, you have energy stored in your machine to make up for airspeed or heading mistakes . . . like going up that first roller-coaster hill where the cars store enough energy to last the whole ride.

Desktop and I started at 11,000 feet, but rapidly fell off an invisible cliff down to 10,500. As soon as we bottomed out, old Desktop madly trimmed nose *up*. The g-forces slammed me into my seat as we zoomed up *through* 11,000 on our way up to *11,500*. At the top of this roller coaster, Desktop shoved the controls full forward, trimmed nose *down,* and I levitated off my seat like Apollo astronauts on those 707 weightless flights.

I was baffled.

He bellowed, "Dammit, this plane's *still* screwed up! Something's wrong with the controls. This pitch trim's *still* out of whack. I wrote up the *same* problem on this *same* plane last month, and those jerks in maintenance signed it off without doing a goddamned thing! Here, you try it, Lieutenant."

He only calls us by rank. He's never bothered learning our names . . . proper military protocol for the fifties, but a bad idea in 1970.

His time has passed, but he doesn't know it. Or maybe he *does know* and this drives his rage.

"Okay, sir, I've got the airplane," I answered. I hoped if I humored him, he might settle down.

I took the controls as we ripped down to 11,000 and *nailed* the altitude. The indicator froze at 11,000 . . . plus or minus nothing.

I smiled inside, looked over at Desktop chomping his cigar, building dome pressure like Vesuvius before an eruption.

You have to understand, our pitch trim wheel looks like a car steering wheel mounted sideways along each side of the throttle quadrant. Whenever we roll into a turn, the wing loses lift. To compensate so we don't lose altitude, we manually roll in three handfuls of "nose-up" to "trim" the tail elevator *up*. Then when we roll out, the wing regains lift, so we have to trim *forward,* or the plane will climb. An irritating, yet simple task.

We spend all night trimming. Roll into a turn; trim up. Roll out; trim down. It's like working a stick shift compared to an automatic transmission. New planes like the C-141 have *electric* trim—the automatic version. Most of us don't even think about trimming; it's as natural as breathing.

Not Desktop. It gives him something to focus his anger on about being here.

I made a couple of faultless, easy turns while Desktop watched and built up more pressure under his lava dome. I couldn't find anything wrong with the flight controls, but I was still concerned the symptom he'd wrestled might be an early warning of a serious problem. Could an elevator cable be slipping off the overhead pulleys, which might lead to complete loss of control? Should we head back right away?

To let him save face before he became even more abusive, I told him, "Sir, it feels okay to me. Maybe it's an intermittent problem." ·

"Dammit! I've got the plane back. Let me see," he snarled.

I watched his efforts to see how to help. He trimmed the same way I did, but we still fell another thousand feet. He bellowed, "Dammit! There it goes *again*! See! I told you!"

It didn't make any sense.

Even Desktop was feeling the pressure. He was looking stupid in public, and our flight crew he'd been kicking all night couldn't have been happier. I held back a growing smirk. I thought, just deserts, you angry old bastard.

Even so, could there be a real problem? Should we head back?

Then I *felt* it in my feet . . . the cockpit floor was vibrating at odd intervals more than normal. If Desktop had stopped ranting, he'd have felt it, too.

Next I *heard* a herd of buffalo running up and down the cargo compartment.

What the . . . ?

Suddenly I knew.

I spun around and saw the *whole crew* listening on inter-phone just behind the cockpit, packed together like a foot-ball huddle. Whenever Desktop got the trim set, their huddle raced to the back. The six of them weighed over a thousand pounds, so their combined mass changed the cen-ter of gravity so dramatically Desktop had to trim the *oppo-site* direction.

"Dammit!" he bellowed, and then the huddle charged for-ward, putting Desktop in another pickle.

I saw the crew doubled over in laughter . . . even the nav-igators, his fellow officers. Whenever he gave the airplane back to me, they stopped and I nailed the altitude.

He'd erupt, *"Goddammit!"*

We spent hours roller-coastering. Desktop never caught on and he never got the critical message they were sending. While at first I thought their action seemed cruel, it was the only way he'd left open for them to communicate.

I first thought their message was aimed at Desktop. I was wrong. He was a lost cause.

Their message was aimed at *me*—the FNG soon to be their captain. It came through loud and clear: "You need to listen to us. If you isolate yourself, you put all of us at risk. No one can do this job alone. Let us help. We can either make you or break you. The choice is yours."

These days Desktop flies only over the time change that straddles two months—making him eligible for combat pay and the tax exemption in both. As a senior officer with office duties, he can order the schedulers to schedule him solely for flights that take off at 11 P.M. the *last* day of one month to "get his ticket punched." He'll fly *just across* the imaginary line into the combat zone a few minutes before midnight and then circle around doing nothing. Then a couple minutes af-ter midnight into the *next* month, he'll find "Something's wrong with the goddamned plane" and scurry back to NKP. Bingo! Two months' tax-exempt combat pay and take sixty days off.

Air Force leadership in action. The rest of us fly five combat missions a *week*. He'll fly six missions the *whole year,* paid seven times what we make. And while he's flying a desk? The rest of us have to pick up the slack, dodging shells with *his name* on them.

Desktop spends his days calling the States on military phone lines, politicking for his next job. We've heard him: "Hi, General Nuisance! Richard Desktop here . . . Yeah, Dick. You remember, General Smith's aide . . . Right. Yeah, I'm stuck over here at NKP. They made me third-in-command of a combat squadron . . . Medals? Oh, yes sir, they're putting me in for a Distinguished Flying Cross . . . Yes sir, combat missions over the Ho Chi Minh Trail . . . Hope you're saving a spot for me when I get back from this hellhole . . . In the spring? Great!

"Anything you need from the BX, General? . . . China for your better half? No problem, sir. I'll pack it up tomorrow. Anything else? . . . Oh, yes sir, I know the rule you imposed against GIs shipping Japanese motorcycles on federally funded military aircraft . . . damned congressmen . . . but there's a way around that . . . How? Easy. I'll have the bike shipped direct to you as *parts* in with someone's personal goods . . . you can have it reassembled there . . . Glad to help, sir. Give the missus my regards."

He calls his wife every day for a half hour: "Did you speak with General Confusion about an assignment for me? . . . Good girl."

No waiting in line. Just pick up the phone. No static. No Salvation Army couch. No five-minute timer. No voyeurs. Talk as long as you want. Real phone lines. Great connections. Taxpayer-funded.

A real morale-buster.

They've promised us they're going to lay another transpacific cable so the rest of us can talk with our families more often. Now imagine laying a brand-new cable the length of the Pacific Ocean, up and down all those underwater mountains. Surrounded by fish. This war will be long over before that happens, or the communication satellites they're starting to hurl up will overwhelm cable technology.

The second-cable story is a lie.

But the real problem facing our country is that Southeast Asia is filled with *thousands* of Desktops. They're one of the main reasons we're going to lose this war, and I think a couple of things buried deep in the military's value system have created the problem.

First, the Pentagon's one-year-tour policy has left them scraping the bottom of the barrel for senior officers. The best leaders long ago served out their single tour, leaving thousands of Desktops to clean up this mess.

It isn't going to happen.

Second, these Desktops are the military's best scam artists. Everyone thought this war would be over by now, and they did, too. They've spent the past few years actively *avoiding* Southeast Asia. Some spent years in graduate schools where they turned back into civilians. Some wormed their way into "directed duty assignments" like space technology where they were "locked in."

Other Desktops back home had their general sponsors protecting them: "Don't you dare send my aide to Vietnam, Sergeant. I need him here with me." When their generals retired and those Desktops lost their cover, assignment sergeants gleefully swooped in like hungry buzzards and packed the now naked aides off to hellholes like NKP.

Finally, the military warned these Desktops, "Get out of the cockpit as soon as you can. Only spend a few years flying, making connections as you go. Get a sponsor. That's the only way you'll be promotable. You're an officer first and a pilot a distant second. If you pilot airplanes for a living, we'll brand you a loser."

They got the message and now resent this interruption to their careers. They feel they're being punished by actually having to fly again. Many haven't flown in as long as twelve years. Some have forgotten how. Some are afraid.

◆ ◆ ◆

Desktop controls our performance ratings and therefore our military futures. Other junior pilots across Southeast Asia are getting top ratings . . . we called and checked. The standard everywhere else is, if you're getting shot at every night, your rating is automatically "firewalled"—top scores.

Raters like Wiley firewall our ratings, but Desktop overrides them every time. He scrawls big, black *X*s over the original ratings and downgrades them to the halfway mark. It's like getting a 5.0 at the Olympics while other competitors are getting 9.9s.

We've raised the issue with him, but all we get back is "When I was a lieutenant, we were happy to get a five. This will give you something to grow into."

At promotion time, we'll be competing against jet jocks with firewalled ratings. Our bottom-of-the-barrel scores will also affect our assignments back to the States. No commander back home is going to want a bunch of losers the way we appear on paper, so we'll be shuffled off to even more aviation backwaters.

Jack explained that years from now I'll be passed over for promotion. It's over for us. Desktop is single-handedly killing any thought we might have had of military careers. So we're all going to get out and become airline pilots. At least I hope so.

Desktop and others like him also create our mandatory flight rules. They don't understand *what* we do, but make up rules that don't fit and enforce them with a vengeance . . . the same arcane rules Rich is so committed to, though Rich hasn't yet made the connection. Rich seems to think some mysterious, expert brain trust created our Candlestick procedures.

While actually he's working for the Mad Hatter.

The Desktop rock would poison the stream if I put it back, so I rear back like a baseball pitcher and hurl it against a big oak tree. *Thwack!* It ricochets off and lands in a patch of poison ivy. Good. That's where it belongs.

Now a gentle breeze picks up and brushes along my cheek. A monarch butterfly flits by. The sweet smell of honeysuckle fills the air. In my mind, I pluck one of the yellow flowers, pull out the stamen, place it on my tongue, close my eyes, and savor the sweetness.

Wonderful.

"I'm gonna grab a Coke. You guys want one?" I ask Charles and Rich.

"Sure. Thanks."

We keep Cokes cold in two Igloos of ice water. One Igloo up front and one in back. I unbuckle, hop down to the back porch, pry the Igloo lid open, and pull out three cans of Coke connected by Crazy Mark's plastic rings. I tell them, "Here you go," and pass them up carefully into the dark cockpit so the cans don't drip on the radio console, sending icy water into the electrical connections below.

That was the last of that six-pack and I am left holding the plastic rings. I look around to make sure no one is looking, secretly stuff them down beside my emergency water bottle in the zippered pocket along my right calf, then leap backward onto Charles's chair and strap in. I have a whole stash of Crazy Mark's rings back at my trailer.

Mark was right. They're great entertainment and make the hours of a hot afternoon whiz by. I'll sit on the concrete-block steps of my trailer, hold the plastic up to my eyeballs, and s-l-o-w-l-y stretch it out. The world gets all warped and stretched out like amusement-park crazy mirrors. Like those of us who fly, the plastic stretches and stretches and stretches and stretches and the *real* world looks all out of whack.

Then suddenly, without warning, the plastic breaks. It gets to the point it won't stretch any more when suddenly it . . . SNAPS! and I smile. It's a relief to see the real world still out there on the other side. I'd just lost perspective.

Then I'll reach down to the stack beside me, grab another set of rings, and do it again . . . for hours. I'm a little concerned how much time I'm spending with the rings, but I think I have it under control. I can stop anytime I want.

I just don't want to.

Reluctantly, I reach into the stream and pick out a fat rock labeled *Kaniver*. I want to get these ugly rocks out of the way first.

Desktop has good company in one of his fellow senior officers. Like Desktop, he'd only flown a handful of times, but was having a wild night over southern Laos, the Steel Tiger . . .

I radioed ahead, "Candle 24, this is Candle 26. We're ready to relieve you, sir. Please give me an update."

"Candle 26. Stand clear! Remain out of the area!" he ordered sternly.

I thought, Remain clear? That's odd.

Normally we fly in at a thousand feet above the departing plane, in a wider orbit, to see what's going on before taking over. Why would he want us to stay clear?

"Roger, sir, we'll remain clear," I answered. "What's going on?"

"I've got the biggest convoy ever!" he bellowed. "Must be two hundred trucks lined up! It's one for the record books! I've got the front and back trucks blocked off and been hitting this thing for three hours. Remain clear! Confirm."

"I confirm, sir. We'll remain clear. But how many and what kind of fighters do you have in the stack?"

With such a massive effort, I knew he likely had several flights of different kinds of fighters stacked in overhead holding patterns awaiting their turn. Things happen and change so fast in this job, you need a three-dimensional, constantly changing picture in your mind. Writing it down is way too slow. By the time you've written it down, the picture has changed . . . you're behind . . . and losing control.

So one of the things we develop is a good short-term memory; like a short-order waitress taking six breakfast orders. If I was going to "mop up," I needed to know what fighters were available, what ordnance they had, and how long each could stick around before getting down to "bingo" fuel.

The first thing you learn about fighters is that they are *always* running out of gas . . . weak designs at the factory level and decision compromises at the Pentagon by even more Desktops. Design compromises that put fighter pilots under fuel and time pressures right after takeoff.

After a long pause, Kaniver scolded me, "Candle 26, I don't have time to mess with you. I've got so many fighters stacked up, I've lost track. Have your nav call mine on the secondary radio for an update. I've got A-4s, F-4s, A-6s, A-1s. You name it, I got 'em. Stand clear while I finish the job!"

Then he called the next flight in the stack. "Gunfighter 64 Lead, Candle 24. I'm going Christmas tree. If you got me in sight, you're cleared in *hot*." I watched him flick his exterior lights on, then back off to avoid becoming a target.

"Roger, Candle 24. Gunfighter Lead. I got you in sight. I'm in *hot*."

I watched the jungle explode.

I thought, You've *lost track*? How can you be in control if you've *lost track*? You idiot! If you don't know what's going on, how do you know what to do *next*?

Then one angry fighter pilot complained, "Candle 24. A lot of us are approaching bingo. We're gonna RTB without dropping if you don't get your act together soon."

I orbited clear while we watched the trail segment turn into a firestorm as wave after wave of fighters torched the highway.

I was dumbfounded. What were the odds? By what stroke of luck did this bozo stumble onto the biggest convoy in Candlestick history?

Finally Kaniver boasted, "Okay, 26. This is Candle 24. She's all yours. We're headed home. I'm putting us in for a one-time DFC."

I radioed back, "Roger, sir. Congratulations . . . taking over now."

I flew us over to the firestorm area and set up our standard left-hand orbit so my scope and I could both see the target area. Miles of jungle were ablaze.

We had to wait awhile for the fires to die down so the glare didn't overload the starlight scope. Finally I asked, "Scope, Pilot. What do you see?"

"Nothing, JT. Nothing," he answered sadly.

"You mean the fire's still blanking out your scope?"

"No . . . I mean there's *nothing there*."

"What do you mean 'there's nothing there'?"

"I mean there's nothing there. There never was anything there. There never were any trucks. The whole thing was a charade. He made it up."

He made it up. He made it all up.

He put all those fighter pilots at risk of being shot down making the same repetitive bomb run. Years of torture awaited them at the Hanoi Hilton if they made one slight mistake or developed engine trouble and were forced to eject.

It was a total disregard for the value of human life.

Oh . . . and one top-secret tidbit they shared with us? We're running out of bombs. Some snafu in the supply chain or something . . . I don't know . . . but we're supposed to conserve bombs and choose only *good* targets.

Knowing this, Kaniver decided to bomb monkeys and bananas. For his own glory.

I lied to the remaining fighters that the convoy was destroyed and that they could all return to base. I had to lie. If word got out, no fighter pilot would ever again trust the Candlesticks. The words *aiding and abetting* come to mind.

Kaniver summoned Charles, our "awards and decs" officer, to his office the following day. Charles had no choice but to believe the fabrication and submit the paperwork for a Distinguished Flying Cross. Kaniver relayed the *unapproved draft* to his stateside sponsor, who promptly upgraded his return assignment.

The man's credo is Duty, Honor, Country, Self. Take your pick.

Paul Revere must be rolling in his grave.

The Kaniver rock is too heavy to throw against the big oak, so I grab it with both hands, swing it back and forth, and hurl it . . . way downstream. *Ka-splosh!* It sinks out of sight.

Good riddance.

No tadpoles here. I'll have to keep looking. But time is running out. That tsunami is out there . . . offshore . . . a monolithic death force gathering strength and momentum in the black waters. All I can do is stand here on the shore and wait . . . no place to run.

What's important now is not to fight it . . . learn to live with it. It's probably just all in my head, anyway.

We'll be all right.

"Drop flare . . . drop flare . . . drop flare!"

"Flares away!"

I check my Seiko . . . only 10:44?

Gawd, this is taking *forever*!

CHAPTER *SEVEN*

Maybe I was right to begin with. Maybe there's a problem with the engines or props, but the warning signs are so subtle I'm only feeling them in changed airframe vibrations. Some early clue out of the range of normal senses. Like the early stages of mental illness families ignore. Maybe if I lean out the engines, I'll be able to focus on the problem.

And maybe time will go by faster if I keep busy.

I call Tyrone at his scanner position along the left portholes. "Ty, do me a favor. Give me another lesson on leaning 'em out. Seems like a quiet night, so I think it'll be okay if you come up."

"Sure, JT. Be right up."

Rich shoots me a disapproving look.

JT. JT. So that's what's bothering him. Rich expects enlisted crewmembers to address him as "Captain Eastwoods." He insists the formality promotes discipline, and by allowing the guys to call me JT, I'm undermining the very foundation of the military unit.

Baloney. I think it builds teamwork.

The argument keeps Rich and me apart and neither of us is going to budge.

Feeling antsy anyway, I unbuckle my lap belt and shinny down onto the back porch. I see Tyrone huffing and puffing up the first step, and then he teeters backward. I throw out a hand, he grabs it, and I yank him up the second step. My friend nods and stops beside me to catch his breath. Any physical effort at this altitude is like mountain climbing without supplemental oxygen.

We're all carrying equal our weight in survival gear—parachutes, survival vests, guns, holsters, bullets, water bottles—the whole schmear. But the water is the worst part. The two flasks in our calf pockets act like dumbbells; their weight pulls our flightsuits down against our shoulders. The constant pressure slams you into a wall of fatigue. Every step becomes an effort. And with that water sloshing around, you constantly have the urge to go to the bathroom.

Anyways, Tyrone's been teaching me how to lean out the recips. The job is like working a Ouija board. Most flight engineers don't share their trade secrets with pilots, so our work together builds a silent bond between us.

The other enlisted guys notice, too.

Good ol' nonverbal communication. Stronger than the spoken word. Watch what people *do,* not what they *say.* Do something together. Start small and build from there.

"Okay, Tyrone, let me try it myself, but help me if I get in trouble."

Ty pats my shoulder. "No problem, JT."

I catch Rich shooting me another dirty look. An enlisted man *touching* an officer!

I half-kneel on the cockpit floor to reach the confusing array of controls: throttles, prop levers, mixture levers, carb heat and friction lever. I feel as if I were kneeling at the altar of aviation history. The only thing missing is organ music.

Anyways . . . the pistons, valves, pushrods, prop shaft, and everything else out there have delicate surfaces slamming together under tremendous pressures that require a velvet touch. Leaning out the engines is like brushing your horse before going for a ride. You can feel this old warhorse respond to the care. This brushing bond lasts throughout the ride, sustaining you in ways neither you nor the horse understands.

Rich yearns to be alone again . . . back in supersonic T-38s where you could just *jam* the throttles into afterburner. Try that trick on these old engines and they'll collapse.

Maybe that's it . . . maybe this whole scene looks revolutionary to Rich. Maybe I'm *his* renegade. After all, I've got our navigator flying while I'm out of my seat doing the flight engineer's job.

I must be destroying the values he holds most sacred.

"Okay, Ty, I take the friction lock, turn it *left* to loosen the controls, and then push it forward to keep some tension so the controls don't move on their own. So it's 'righty, tighty; lefty, loosey,' right? I mean, *correct*?" I laugh.

"Exactly," he chuckles.

I make the adjustments.

I was right. Caring for this old machine *is* like grooming your horse before you go for a ride. You first brush off all the old dirt, sweat, and leftover pieces of hay in your horse's coat. That way, they won't blister up under the saddle pad halfway through your ride.

Grooming causes you to focus your attention. The more you look, the more you see. You notice that new scab on your horse's shoulder and put salve on the spot so it doesn't become a festering wound insects will attack. She points her nose at a small stone stuck in one hoof you pick out that would have turned into a major blister. Caring for that scab and that stone creates a bond between you that lasts a lifetime. You glide your palm over her, looking for any signs of bruised muscles or bowed tendons. Then you lunge her to warm her muscles, searching for signs of lameness.

I ooze the mixture controls up to "rich" and slide the prop levers up to 2,400 rpm to clean off the spark plugs.

After all that grooming, you slowly ooooze your weight

over her and go for a ride—together. She'll now fight snarling dogs, stomp rattlers, or swim raging waters for you. It's no longer you riding your mare or her carrying you. *Together,* you metamorphose into an entity I have no name for.

But it starts with that caring and attention to detail. And patience. Take your time. Throw your watch away. Rushing just embeds long-term problems.

I am trying to share this lesson with Rich, but he's not paying attention.

He'd prefer to jump on this old warhorse cold. No warm-up. No grooming. No checking for stones. No caring. No relationship. No oooozing. Just jump on like an old movie cowboy, jam his spurs in, hit afterburner, and go like hell: "Yeehaw!"

If this old warhorse of ours should try warning Rich she's about to stumble and fall, he wouldn't hear her until she was on top of him and broke his neck.

I notice I've been holding my breath, so I release it.

"Rich, you want to try your luck?" I try again.

He answers, "No. I.have.to.roll.the.dice.for.Charles," looks down at me, making a *whirrr . . . click* sound that reminds me of the Disneyland animatronic Abe Lincoln that *whirr . . . clicked* out the Gettysburg Address: "Four.score.and . . ."

That's Rich. Moving and talking in chunks like Disney's Abe, reading outdated words off a TelePrompTer someone else scripted.

I ooze the props back to 1,600 rpm and wiggle the mixture levers back to "lean."

I depend on Charles for any critical advice. He's a master navigator, having spent most of his twenty-year career teaching Strategic Air Command student navigators at Castle AFB, California. He knows navigator tricks so old they aren't in the books anymore. He flunked out of pilot training back in the fifties and admitted to me he still mourns his failure.

I like Charles, though he makes a lot of pilots uncomfortable. With his Coke-bottle-bottom glasses and middle-aged spread, he looks more like an accountant. His flight-suit, designed for men twenty years younger, fits him like a sausage casing. People chuckle, but the sausage look is not his fault. They should make flightsuits available in a "gentleman's cut."

Charles is an enigma. Pilots joke about him because he's standoffish. Nobody really knows him. He prepares all his meals in his trailer and never appears at the club. It makes people suspicious about what he's doing in there. Everyone trapped in the NKP purgatory copes in different ways. I have my plastic rings and Wiley has his singing. Charles hides in his trailer. I've tried to get to know him better, but he always pushes me away. Maybe to him we're just kids. Still, after Jack Ward, he's my first choice to fly with because he still has an open mind.

When the tsunami comes, I'll turn to Charles.

Not Rich. Never Rich.

I think men like Rich get into their twenties and decide they know it all. That's *it* . . . they're forever locked in: their music, knowledge, relationships, philosophy, flying, science, hobbies, sex . . . you name it.

I watch Rich roll my red die, courting randomness. At least I got him to do that part.

He tells Charles, "It's a two."

"Roger, two," Charles answers seriously.

As Ty and I finish "leaning them out," I close my eyes to listen and feel for what I've just done. I'm trying to catch the odd vibration or grinding that might indicate an impending failure . . . some hiccup, an out-of-place rumble, some prop governor surging or hunting. But all I hear and feel is smooth humming. It's when you get those purring-cat sounds and smooth vibes you know the machine has responded to your care.

I'm finally forced to conclude my worry was misplaced.

The engines and props are fine.

◆ ◆ ◆

You have to understand my concern: these planes have been over here for years and the jungle has taken its toll. Imagine leaving your car in the La Guardia Airport parking lot against the seawall and allowing the elements to chew away at it . . . for years.

You'd come back to a rusted-out hulk with things *living* inside.

Now listen; this is important. They say there's a fuel-eating algae over here that lives inside our fuel tanks. Now stop and think about that. Picture something *alive* and *growing* in toxic fuel.

They call it green goo. *Inside* the airplane.

At first I didn't believe the stories. The first time I saw a fuel gauge fall from *four thousand* pounds to *zero,* I panicked. I thought we'd taken a hit and had lost half our gas. There wouldn't be enough left in the other good tank to get back home.

But the engine kept running and the gauge *slowly* crept back up to normal.

So now when a gauge falls to zero, I tell myself, "Patience, patience. It's just the green goo," because then that gauge the size of my grandfather's pocket watch always rises to normal.

Always.

Our mechanics assured me the green goo stories are true. "Damnedest stuff I ever seen . . . this long, green, slimy thing like some snake. It's disgusting. We yank it off the fuel probes with our bare hands, but then have trouble getting the crap off our arms. We can't never get the fuel probes clean. We get most off, but it just grows right back."

Leaning out the recips is also known as "hanging it on the props," a disappearing part of aviation that belongs in the Smithsonian hanging next to the *Spirit of St. Louis.*

You see, while leaned out, we're *barely* flying. The engines are *barely* running. The props are *barely* turning. The wing is *barely* flying. One false move, one rough flight-control input, and we'll stall and tumble out of the sky. The deck angle is so high, from outside we might look like an ornament on some Christmas tree in the sky: "Hanging it on the props."

It's also a good way to conserve fuel. They say the only time you have too much fuel is when you're on fire.

There aren't many left who know this skill, and it's a privilege to be part of the tribe. It's a dying art form, something that will disappear after this war is over.

But *I'll* remember.

Everything now is going to turbojets you just jam forward. No relationship with the horse. Something important is dying and nobody cares. Someone should write these things down before they are gone forever. Somebody should shout at America, "These people *mattered*! We were here! This is how we lived!"

Otherwise, what does all this matter?

I've gone back and studied the props when they're rotating this slow. They reminded me of the ceiling fans from the bar scene in *Casablanca*. I even hear "As Time Goes By" . . .

I can never remember all the words, but that's the feeling I get.

I reach behind Charles and massage his aching shoulders. He nods thanks.

Now I hop back up on his chair, strap in, and scratch my back against my chute.

"Drop flare . . . drop flare . . . drop flare."

"Flares away!"

I tell Ty, "Thanks. We'll do it again tomorrow night."

"No problem, JT."

I watch my friend disappear into the darkness like an apparition. I can barely make out his shadowy outline peering out a porthole, scanning for trouble.

Tyrone is the best of America. I didn't have to say one word. He just went back to his post. The same dedication of American fighting men dating back to Concord and Lexington's minutemen. Values implanted in grade school and the Boy Scouts: Duty, Honor, Country.

Dedication *despite* Desktop and Kaniver.

Ugh . . . that's enough depressing rocks for now.

I peer down into the stream of memories, searching for a good rock. I need one to cheer me up . . . I spot the Jack Ward stone, pick it up, and hear a meadowlark in the big oak begin a mournful song. The sun warms my face. A red-and-black-striped woolly-worm caterpillar suns itself on a rock. I hear Mr. Elder next door start his lawn mower. He notices me wading in the stream, smiles, and waves.

I roll the Jack Ward stone around my palm . . . the perfect "lucky rock." Jack deserves one of those *Reader's Digest* "My Most Unforgettable Character" articles.

The memories wash over me . . .

CHAPTER *EIGHT*

We'd just landed from my first mission in command, and I felt apprehensive as Jack escorted me to the threshold of the inner sanctum of the quiet bar. An invisible sign announced Junior Officers Not Allowed. Jack pointed out two stools away from everyone else, nudged my elbow, and said, "Let's grab those."

We sat down. I looked around. Red leather stools. Rainbow-colored Wurlitzer jukebox in one corner. Dave Brubeck Quartet playing "Take Five." Wall-to-wall, gold-marbled mirror behind the carved teakwood bar. Get-lost-in leather booths with new-car smell. Three balding, middle-aged guys in flightsuits peppered down the bar stared into their beers as if into fortune-tellers' crystal balls.

The place had a sanctuary feeling . . . a place for confessions.

The bartender approached and asked, "Would you gentlemen like a San Miguel or a San Miguel?"

I laughed and told him, "We'll take two San Miguels."

Then I told Jack, "They're on me tonight, Major Ward," and slapped down a dollar. "I've got a couple things I'd like your opinion on, anyways."

"Okay, John, but I'll get the next round. And, please, my friends call me Jack. By the way, congratulations on checking out as captain."

The barkeep brought us two frosty bottles and tossed down three quarters change. He explained, "Happy hour."

We tapped our bottles together in celebration. *Clink!*

I got my bearings as we drank. Row upon row of hard-liquor bottles padlocked behind wire-mesh cabinets. Chivas Regal. Johnnie Walker Red. Dewar's. Apricot brandy? Drambuie. Dusty bottles. A neon Coors mountain-stream sign advertised "Rocky Mountain Fresh." Budweiser Clydesdales pulled a beer wagon in a yellowed-plastic showcase.

I was full of myself. I'd *finally* checked out as captain. It was only a no-brainer flare mission, but to me it was an important milestone.

I went fishing for Jack's endorsement.

"So, Maj—Jack . . . sorry . . . I'm not comfortable calling a senior officer by name. What'd you think?" I asked eagerly, and slid forward on my barstool.

Jack didn't answer. He unzipped a sleeve pocket, pulled out a crumpled pack of unfiltered Lucky Strikes, took one out, tapped it on his watch to compress the tobacco, struck a match, lit the Lucky, inhaled his first cigarette since takeoff, and closed his eyes in ecstasy. After a long while he exhaled, blew smoke rings one inside another, and stared at them as they faded away.

Uh-oh. Thinking about his answer far too long, I thought.

"Care for one, John?" he offered.

"No, thanks. I don't smoke." I tried to change the subject. "My grandfather blew smoke rings. Don't stop on my account."

Jack stayed on target. "You want it sugarcoated, or can you handle the truth?" He stared at the concentric smoke rings.

I felt apprehensive. "What do you mean?"

"A lot of pilots *say* they want the truth, but turn angry when they hear it. I'd rather keep you as a friend if that's what's going to happen."

I lied, "I want the truth. It's the only way I'm going to learn." I braced myself by slugging down more San Miguel. He could see I was nervous.

Jack began, "Okay, we'll start with the good news."

I nodded.

"The good news is you complied with all the rules perfectly."

Relieved! "Thanks, I memorized every procedure." My confidence restored, I asked, "So what's the bad news?"

Jack sucked at his Lucky. The tip glowed red. "Worst case? The way you flew tonight is going to get us both killed."

I heard the sound of a hundred glasses crashing to the floor . . . my shattered ego. I felt stunned . . . speechless . . . rocked back . . . shot down.

What could I have possibly done so wrong?

Jack blew more smoke rings and poked his Lucky through the middle.

Bull's-eye.

"Would you like me to tell you about it?" Jack prompted.

Dumbfounded, I nodded and stared at his ghostly rings.

"The published rules are going to get you in big trouble. That rigidity in your thinking can be deadly. You're gonna have to start breaking some rules. And not just any old rules, but the *right* ones. But then you can't stop there. Then you have to create substitutes in their place."

I stammered, "I . . . I . . . don't get it, Jack. They've been cramming rules down my throat since pilot training. And, anyhow, how do you know which rules to break and which ones to follow?"

The bartender plopped down two overflowing baskets of hot popcorn.

I shoved a handful in my mouth so I had an excuse not to say any more.

A Cheshire-cat smile crawled across Jack's face. "That's the whole trick, isn't it? Knowing the difference." I shook my head. "All right, let's start with something simple. You flew the same right-hand racetrack pattern hour after hour tonight, right?"

Popcorn falling out of my mouth, I mumbled, "Sure, we're required to. That's the published procedure."

"But can you see that by being so predictable, you were like the redcoats marching down those colonial dirt roads while our ancestors hid in the bushes and picked them off? Those redcoats would tell you, 'Hey! We were just following procedure,' and look who won. These bad guys'll pick you off just as easy."

I tried to respond, but was cut off by a blast from the main dining room . . . our NKP theme song the band played several times each night. Two hundred men yelled the chorus . . .

> *WE GOTTA GET OUTTA THIS PLACE . . .*
> *IF IT'S THE LAST THING WE EVER DO . . .*

We couldn't talk over the din, so Jack blew more smoke rings.

> *WE GOTTA GET OUTTA THIS PLACE . . .*
> *GIRL, THERE'S A BETTER LIFE FOR ME AND*
>   *YOU . . .*

Jack motioned the bartender we needed another round.

Fishing for a tip, he brought out two chilled mugs and filled them slowly behind the bar. Then the barkeep opened a coffee-can-size tin of Planters peanuts and dumped a heaping mound in a red glass bowl. I grabbed a handful and started munching.

The singing stopped. The sanctuary resettled.

"I was just doing what they told me, Jack. I don't understand."

"Well, let's try this story. What were you doing fifteen years ago?"

I subtracted. "Well . . . I was ten; so I was in fourth grade."

"I thought so." He nodded. "Remember those air raid signals warning of Russian bombers coming in for a nuclear attack? You'd jump under your wooden desks until the all-clear siren sounded and your teacher would tell you, 'Boys and girls, by now our military would have shot the Russians down. You can come out now.' And you crawled out, *knowing* you were safe?"

"Sure, we practiced that all the time."

"Well, I was a bombardier in the supersonic B-58 Hustler out breaking rules, being creative, and I could have nuked your school or any target to smithereens." Jack blew more smoke rings and watched them fade away. Then he held the cigarette steady in his mouth as the smoke crawled up his face like an animal and into his eyes.

He did not blink.

He continued, "Our job was to be ready to drop the Bomb on Moscow. You can't exactly practice that, so we prepared by making bomb runs on U.S. cities, mimicking Russian bombers. The Pentagon directed us to fly what they *thought* were Russian procedures. And Air Defense Command—you know, ADC—fighters were *supposed* to swoop in and shoot us down. But they never could. We broke procedure and created new strategies, the same way the Russians would. We always delivered the Bomb. The ADC fighter pilots whined, 'You're cheating! Stop that!' and we'd break more rules and drop more might-be nukes on American cities. We never missed. And they never learned."

"They *never* stopped you?" I asked as my shock turned to anger.

"Never. We could have leveled Washington anytime we wanted."

I was reeling. "So the ADC protection was a myth?"

"Yep."

The Thai band next door obliterated our conversation . . .

Left a good job in the city,
Workin' for the man every night and day,
But I never lost one minute of sleepin',
Worryin' 'bout the way things might have been,

Big wheel keep on turnin',
Proud Mary keep on burnin',
Lollin', lollin', lollin on the liver . . .

After all these years, the Thais still can't pronounce *r*. Two hundred guys join the chorus several times each night and everybody laughs. Especially the Thais. I think they could sing the *r*s if they wanted, but know we depend on them *not to*.

The chorus died down.

Jack continued, "These bad guys have our playbook memorized. They know *exactly* what you'll do in any situation, and that predictability makes you vulnerable. Tonight you flew like those marching redcoats. Keep that up and you'll be an easy target. You've got to create something new they haven't seen before."

I stared at the rising bubbles in my beer.

Jack prompted, "Hello? Anybody in there?"

"I'll have to think about it," I answered dejectedly, and stared into my beer.

Finally I asked, "So how would I get started?"

Jack got that I-thought-you'd-never-ask look. Then he reached into a zippered chest pocket and pulled out a single red die.

Not two dice as you might expect. Just one. A nice, big one.

He said, "Hold out your hand," and dropped the die. The red cube seemingly tumbled end over end in slow motion before landing in my palm. I rolled it around . . . hefty . . . like the ones at Vegas craps tables. I saw straight through the red translucence to the far-side white dots. It had the feel of those "lucky marbles" we saved as kids.

"You can start with that," Jack said. "Keep it. It's on me."

"I don't get it. What does this mean?"

"What do you think it means?"

"I don't have a clue . . . but don't dice normally come in pairs?"

"One's all you need. Your racetrack pattern tonight was too predictable. Add some randomness next time. Break a rule. Be creative. Instead of a racetrack, imagine a four-leaf clover. Put a random number on each petal. Have someone roll the die just before the next pattern and fly whatever turns up. You'll start *thinking* and become a tougher target."

I felt unsure. "I guess I could give it a shot, Jack."

"I won't lie to you. Don't expect this to go smoothly. This will be hard work. Take a few shuffling steps. You'll have to shuffle before you can walk and then walk before you can run."

"But what about Desktop? He'll crucify me if he catches me freelancing. I feel like I've got enemies on both sides of the river."

"Someone once said, 'Our greatest glory is not in never falling, but in rising every time we fall.' If they knock you down, you get back up. If they knock you down again, get back up again. No matter how many times guys like Desktop knock you down, you get back up and keep going."

I was still confused. "What if I roll a five or six? What then?"

The Cheshire-cat smile crawled across his face again. "Now we're getting somewhere. They're the whole point. They're the reason you need only one die. They will remind you to keep your mind loose. John, you're still looking at the die in its *literal* form. The die's true power is as a *symbol*. Focus *beyond* its form. It will remind you to look beyond the surface of things and focus on *pos-si-bil-i-ties*. JT, you have a tendency to substitute other people's judgment to the loss of your own. You have a good mind. Use it. The five and six can be *anything*. They will remind you to 'Do as you please.' You know, make something up."

" 'Do as I please'? 'Make up something'? Jack! Everything so far in the military has been 'Do as you're told, or we'll hammer you.' I had to stumble onto you to learn this? Maybe we could fly together more . . ."

One of the other majors invaded our space. He staggered to the jukebox behind us, plunked in a dime for three plays, and punched in his selections. The 45s spun around, then stopped. The automatic arm placed his first selection on the spinning turntable, the arm swooped over, the needle kissed the plastic, and Stan Getz began playing "Desafinado."

Jack answered, "Sure, we'll fly more, but first talk to Ray Peters. Have him tell you the story about Wiley's limousine."

"Wiley has a car! Where is it?"

"You'll have to ask Ray. He was there and tells it better. I don't recommend what Wiley did, but the story might loosen your mind."

I nodded. "I'll do that. But why didn't you tell me about this stuff after that first night with Wiley?"

"I didn't know you then. Now I do. A lot of you pilots won't listen to a mere navigator. They think it challenges their authority."

I shook my head. "That's stupid. But you should be at the Pentagon planning nuclear-defense strategies. How'd you wind up in this hellhole after flying B-58s? That's a slap in the face, isn't it?"

"Something you need to learn, JT, is the Church punishes guys they think got a 'good deal,' or those who embarrass the leadership. A lot of powerful people resented our good fortune being in B-58s. On top of that, we made a lot of ADC generals look stupid when they couldn't stop us. So this assignment is their way of getting even. Paybacks are hell, John. The next outfit they'll hammer is the SR-71 Blackbird. Those guys don't see it coming yet. They think they're bulletproof. But the Church will screw them over, too."

I didn't understand his reference to this "Church," but let

it pass. Instead I asked, "Why the punishment? You guys were the best."

"We were *too* good. When the unit disbanded, guys like Desktop sent us to the worst places flying the oldest planes they could find. And that's why at the peak of my career I'm lying on a filthy old mattress . . . punishment for good behavior."

"Why do they do that?"

"They can't help themselves. It's their nature." He laughed. "Actually, the joke's on them. I'm having the time of my life. B-58s was all pretend. Here I bomb *real* trucks or provide lifesaving light."

I admitted, "Looks like I've got a lot to learn."

Jack stood to leave. "Do yourself a favor. I imagine it must be thrilling to be in command, but there are lots of guys here who've put in twenty years and will *never* be in charge. Word to the wise? Tuck in your ego."

My cheeks flushed red. "Sorry," I said, hoping the darkness hid my reaction.

"It's okay. You're allowed one night. Congratulations, again. Oh . . . one final word of warning: the Air Force eagle is a bird of prey that likes to eat its young. Get the hell out as soon as you can." Then he jackhammered his Lucky into the ashtray and dribbled beer over the embers.

I stared at the mess.

Jack patted my shoulder. "I'm tired. I need to rest now. We'll talk more later. Remember to ask Ray about Wiley's limo. Good night, JT."

I watched him slip out the back door into the 5 A.M. darkness and fade away like his smoke rings.

I look at the Jack Ward stone nostalgically. I think about putting it back into the stream with others I see: Wiley's Limo, My Helicopter, The Bangkok Dinner Party, Bandit, Thunder 58, and others still out of focus in the shimmering water. It's hard to know which memory to choose next. Events over the past five months have swirled together like cake ingredients I watched churn together in Sharon's Mixmaster.

My job now is to take that batter and separate out the flour, sugar, water, eggs, baking soda, salt, and vanilla while the beaters whirl at top speed. And not jam my fingers in the spinning blades.

That's why I jump around so much. I'm uncertain what comes next.

I take the Jack Ward lucky rock and tuck it away. It's a keeper.

In the days and weeks that followed, Jack taught me much more, but we always came back to the basics: *Break some rules. Make something up. Do as you please. Pos-si-bil-i-ties.*

Thanks, Jack.

I watch Rich roll Jack's red die against the flat space below the engine instruments. He asks, "John, it came up six. What do you want us to do?"

"Do as you please, Rich. Make something up," I try, nudging him along.

Charles nods and starts a random pattern.

He *understands*.

Rich shakes his head.

I check the windup clock on my instrument panel in front of Charles's right knee . . . it's going on eleven o'clock.

"Charles, it's almost the end of your half hour. How're you doing up there? I think I'm gonna stay back here and relax. You want Rich to take his turn now?"

Our navigator answers, "Are you kidding? I'm having the time of my life! I've waited *twenty years* for this and I'm not going to miss one minute! I'll fly the rest of the night . . . if it's okay with you, JT."

"Great, Charles," I tell him. "She's all yours."

"Drop flare . . . drop flare . . . drop flare."

"Flares away!"

I haven't checked on my Laotian friend Tonto in a while; things have been so quiet.

I radio, "Tonto, Candle 23."

No answer.

He *always* answers right away.

Trouble?

"Tonto . . . Candlestick 23 . . . *over,*" I say urgently.

My sleepy-voiced friend answers, "Candle 23 . . . Tonto . . . go ahead."

"Tonto . . . want to check light still okay."

"Light number one. Tonto sleep now."

"Sorry, Tonto . . . good night."

Sometimes I forget our light provides Tonto and his small band of men their only opportunity to sleep. If we were ever to let the light go out, the bad guys would swoop in and Tonto would be toast.

This is like leaving a night-light on for a frightened child so the monsters hiding in the closet don't spring out and eat him.

Except that, as I said before, the monsters here are *real*.

I hear, "*MAYDAY! MAYDAY! MAYDAY!* This is Thunder 58 on guard. *MAYDAY! MAYDAY! MAYDAY!*"

CHAPTER NINE

Against my better judgment, I've picked up the Thunder 58 rock. I saw it in the water earlier and hoped it would be carried downstream, out of sight. But it remained; so I might as well get it out of the way.

The rock is so hot, I won't be able to hold it long.

NKP vets tell the story to every FNG. I don't know if it's true or not. NKP is a black hole of misinformation. Incoming truth about the world is obliterated. No information escapes. We exist on rumor and fables.

The point is, *we believe* it.

The F-105 pilot was flying back to Thailand at "first light" after a raid up north. He'd taken heavy battle damage. He was over this same northern-Laos area when it happened.

The F-105 is the fastest thing "on the deck." It's an ICBM with stubby wings. It has a reputation for being able to take lots of hits and still limp home.

But this time it was different . . .

◆ ◆ ◆

"*MAYDAY! MAYDAY! MAYDAY* . . . I'm shot up bad . . . my engine fire-warning light's been on five minutes!" he pleaded.

A patrolling Jolly Green chopper made immediate contact. "Thunder 58, say your position . . . say your position! We'll be right there!"

The fighter pilot radioed the information and added, "I've got smoke in the cockpit now . . . smoke in the cockpit . . . I'm gonna have to bail out!"

"Roger, sir, we'll pick you up! Our ETA to your position . . . five minutes. Hang on!" the Jolly Green reassured him.

The fighter pilot's voice—normally composed—uncharacteristically screamed, "I've got flames in the cockpit . . . Holy shit! . . . Flames through the floorboards! . . . My God, the fire's at my feet! . . . I . . . can't stay! . . . I'm punching out!" And he was gone.

The Jolly Green *saw* him eject. They saw his parachute open and watched him land safely. They made radio contact and maneuvered in for the pickup. It was going to be a piece of cake. He'd spend only a couple of minutes on the ground.

The Jolly Green radioed, "We've got you in sight, sir . . . moving in to pick you up . . . hoist is coming down . . . we've almost got you, sir . . . you'll be home for breakfast . . . hang on!"

Then it fell apart.

Bad guys moved in from all sides and threw heavy automatic weapons fire at the hovering Jolly Green. Aircraft monitoring the frequency later reported they heard rounds hit the chopper. *Ping! Ping! Ping! Ping! Ping!*

The chopper radioed, "You're too hot, sir! . . . Too hot! . . . We're pulling out, or we'd join you down there!"

"You can't leave me! For God's sake, don't leave me! I hear them coming! For the love of God! Please!" he pleaded.

"Sorry, sir . . . you're too hot . . . find cover and we'll be back."

"BUT THEY'RE COMING!" he screamed to the departing chopper.

And that was it.

They found him later that day.

In pieces.

The bad guys tied him to their truck bumpers and pulled him apart.

Alive.

Now stop right there. Think about that image for a moment. Hold it in your mind. Don't push it away the way you want.

Now put the face of someone you love on the image: your husband, father, brother, favorite uncle, best friend, or sweetheart. Study the terror on his face.

We figure they pulled him trampoline-tight, revved their engines to add to his terror, and then slooooooowly pulled him apart. He had lots of time to think about it.

And *feel* it.

Like I said, the monsters here are *real.*

We got their damned message.

I have a message for them: paybacks are hell.

The Thunder 58 rock scalds my hands. I let it go. It falls into the water and turns the surface to steam. *Hsssst!*

Permanent burns, I'm afraid.

CHAPTER TEN

can't keep beating myself up that way.

I can see my seven-day clock ahead of Charles's right knee. It says 10:58. Only an hour till bingo fuel. The second hand stumbles across each second in slow motion . . . tick . . . tick . . . tick. Gawd, this is taking forever!

The second hand struggles its way up to twelve again.

C'mon! C'mon!

I check the time . . . 10:58 . . . 10:58? Wait a sec . . . it was 10:58 a minute ago! Bad sign. I'm losing track of time.

Feeling woozy now. Maybe if I rest my eyes a couple secs, I can recharge my batteries.

I lean back in Charles's director's chair, hang my chute's dead weight on the roll cushion in the crook of his chair, and relieve my aching shoulders. Wonderful. I prop my feet up on the bulkhead behind Rich and feel the blood flow rush . . . umm . . . better.

I can watch everything from here.

Jack Ward taught me, "The worst things happen at the end. Most of you new pilots' candles burn white-hot all the

way from takeoff, so there's only a stub left when the unex-
pected happens. When a strong wind comes up, it blows
your candle out."

I study Rich.

He's already down to a stub.

The crescent moon rises slowly up the front window, moving left as Charles turns right, then right when he goes left,
and chases us around the sky. I see the pale moon arisin'. I
see trouble on the way. I see earthquakes and lightnin'. I see
bad times today . . .

> Don't go around tonight
> Well, it's bound to take your life
> There's . . . a bad moon on the rise

The bad moon rises higher and higher up the windscreen
and mixes with the whirling standby whiskey compass in the
front window, and the moon jumps out of sight in a magic
trick and we are wrapped in darkness . . . no difference between the sky and earth and suddenly I'm standing on the
dark beach again that morphs into black ocean and into
black sky. A sliver moon catches cresting waves that lurch at
us. The pressure and temperature drop. I ask the vague
shadow on my right, "Did you feel that?"

He never answers.

The incoming tide we can't see laps at our toes, warning
us to move back before we become part of the ocean. No one
says a word. I hear surf sounds. A rush of cold air hits.
Something comes alive in the dark water. I turn to the left
shadow—can't see his face, either—and ask, "Did you feel
that?" He answers, "Feel what?" and I turn back to the first
shadow . . .

. . . but he's gone . . . again. Nowhere. Vanished.

I scan the beach. Nothing but darkness. I turn to ask the
left shadow where our friend went . . .

And I bolt upright in bed.

I keep my room cold enough to hang meat, but wake up

drenched in sweat. Clammy sheets. Heart racing. Hyperventilating . . . terrified by the recurring nightmare.

I can never get back to sleep. I stumble around the base in the middle of the night like a zombie . . . trying to erase the images. I watch young men in flightsuits cheerfully hop aboard hearses cleverly disguised as crew vans that whisk them off to their graves. Don't they know they're going to disappear, too?

Why don't they understand?

I want to grab their shoulders to warn them . . . but they'd think I'm crazy.

> *Hope you . . . got your things together*
> *Hope you . . . are quite prepared to die*
> *Looks like we're in for nasty weather*
> *One eye is taken for an eye*

I hear, "Candlestick 23, Moonbeam."

I sit up and tell Rich, "I'll answer them." I don't trust what he might say.

I answer, "Moonbeam, Candle 23. Go ahead."

"Candle 23, we just got word that your replacement, Candle 25, had maintenance problems back at NKP. He'll be about twenty minutes late. Can you hang in there till he shows up?"

I answer, "If we can keep the engines leaned out, fuel shouldn't be a problem. But stand by. I'll check with the rampers whether we'll have enough flares."

"Standing by, Candle."

"Ramp, Pilot."

"Yes, sir, JT. We were listening. We're okay on flares. No problem."

"Great. Good job, guys," and I relay the information up to Moonbeam.

I turn to ask Tyrone to come up and lean 'em out again to conserve more fuel, only to bump into him coming up the steps.

◆ ◆ ◆

Moonbeam, our C-130 mother ship, links us to the rest of the world. The mother ship pilots fly their own giant racetrack patterns on autopilot for twelve hours, but they don't have much to do with us. The Air Force sausaged a capsule and crew into the back of their plane. Those are the people I work with.

The capsule crew provides us weather information, relays targets of opportunity from Task Force Alpha, and gets us fighters . . . stuff like that. I talk to midrank NCO coordinators who do a fabulous job managing lots of moving pieces. There's a full colonel aboard managing the Barrel Roll air war, but we never talk to him.

I've decided the next rock will be Wiley's Limo. I meant to pick it up earlier, but got sidetracked. Sorry.

I should say again I don't know if the story is true. But there's no way anyone could prove it *isn't*.

"Who told you about Wiley's limo?" Ray asked suspiciously when he poked his head out his trailer door.

"I didn't mean to startle you," I explained. "Jack Ward told me to ask you. I hope it's okay."

Ray remained wary. "Well, if Major Ward sent you, that's different. I'm surprised he mentioned it. We agreed not to tell *anyone*. Anyway, come in and I'll tell you the story."

I stepped up into his trailer. I turned around and saw him look side to side. Apparently satisfied no one was around, he closed the door and bolted it shut. Then he faced me, raised a finger to his lips, *shush,* went through the shared bathroom and locked the door to the adjoining bedroom. He hollered, "Sam, I'm gonna take a shower, so I'm locking the door. Won't be long." Sam shouted back something muffled. Ray turned the shower on and then closed and locked his side of the bathroom. Then he turned on his radio real loud to WNKP, shoved two folding chairs together, and motioned for me to sit down. He opened his fridge, pulled out two San Miguels, and stuck one in my hand.

We sat facing each other. Our knees nearly touched. He whispered, "You can never—*never*—repeat this to anyone. A lot of people could get in hot water if this ever got out."

I assured Ray he could trust me.

I could see by his expression he was excited. I mostly lip-read as he began, "It started down in Saigon. Wiley and I flew our basketball team down to compete in the Southeast Asia tournament. Our team lost their first game and were eliminated from the competition. The game was rigged. The referee was stationed in Vietnam and there was no way Saigon would let anybody from a Thai 'country club' win. They think we got a good deal and they resent it. The ref was all over our guys with crooked foul calls.

"*But,*" Ray said emphatically, "they didn't count on Wi-ley. The problems started that night at the bar. Their team was shoving their victory down our guys' throats. Wiley got a little drunk and started bad-mouthing the refs, claiming the game was fixed. It was true, of course, but they didn't want to hear it. I tried to quiet him down, but he kept getting louder. That's when the trouble started."

"What happened? Did somebody deck him?"

Ray wiped beer foam from his mouth. "Oh, no, nothing that violent. But it just so happened the old fart on the stool beside Wiley was the commanding general of the whole fucking place! And, boy, was he *pissed*. I thought to myself, 'What are the odds? Of all people.'

"Anyway, this general started spittin' venom. He got right in Wiley's face and yelled, 'You *shut up,* get your ass out of *my* bar, get your fuckin' airplane off *my* base by sunup, or you'll live to regret it.' John, I about peed in my pants! Wiley leaned over like he was going to take on the old fart. So I grabbed Wiley and got him the hell out of there."

"Good for you," I said. "You saved his skin. So that was it?"

"Naw, I'm just coming to the good part. It was still pitch-black out when we got up the next morning. Wiley told me, 'Go get the plane ready. Have the team strapped in and the engines running. Leave the ramp down. Be ready to taxi as soon as I show up.' Then he disappeared."

"Where'd he go?" I asked, and inched forward on my chair.

"That's what I wondered, too. I had the engines turning like he said, but got nervous when it turned first light . . . the sun wasn't technically up . . . but there was no sign of Wiley *anywhere*. I was sweatin' bullets, man.

"Then I came unglued. Down the ramp raced the general's staff car . . . one of those huge, '69 black Lincolns . . . little American flags on the bumper along with that gold-star plaque. I looked down the ramp, but there was still no Wiley. I thought to myself, 'We're in real trouble and Wiley's deserted me.' There was no way out."

I told him, "I can't believe Wiley would leave you hanging like that."

Ray took another sip. "John, I was terrified. I thought they might confiscate the airplane and not let us fly back. Who knew what that old fart could do! Anyways, the limo zoomed under the right wing and disappeared. I whipped around to see what would happen next . . . and *here comes the general's car!* Right up *into the plane!*"

I became suspicious of Ray's tall tale. I leaned my chair back and crossed my arms. I told him, "I may be the FNG here, but I'm not stupid."

He said emphatically, "John, I *swear* it's true. I tried to see in the car, but couldn't see through those smoked security windows. Then, after a long time, the door *slowly* opened. One boot hit the floor . . . then another . . . then the driver slowly stood up."

Ray paused for a swig.

"It was Wiley!" he exclaimed. "With this big shit-eating grin! He stole the general's Lincoln! The basketball team gave him a standing ovation. Wiley bowed, ran up to the cockpit, jumped in the seat laughing, and told me, 'Call for taxi.' John, I was flabbergasted!"

"But isn't that a court-martial offense?"

"You bet your buns. I asked Wiley, 'How'd you . . . ?'

"He answered, 'Later . . . let's get the hell out of Dodge . . . call for taxi.' "

I wasn't sure where Ray's wild yarn was headed, but decided to humor him. What the heck? The beer was free, so I played along. "What happened next?"

"Well, when we got up to altitude, Wiley explained how he got it started. He said he grew up driving his grandfather's tractor . . ."

Aha! I thought to myself. I *knew* he grew up on a tractor.

". . . and he had to hot-wire the old machine to start it. Then I asked Wiley, 'What are you gonna do with it?' He answered, 'You'll see.' "

I said, "I *hate it* when he does that."

Ray nodded. "Me, too. Anyway, John, we had a blast! Everybody took turns driving the car back and forth a few feet inside the plane 'cause most of us hadn't driven in a year . . . it was great! Then as we approached NKP, Wiley radioed the command post to ask the Hawk to come meet us because we had a present for him."

"No! The wing commander! He must have been furious."

Ray grinned. "The Hawk? No way. He laughed his ass off. He said he appreciated the gesture, but told us, 'Get that thing out of here. I don't care what you do with it; just get it out of here.' Then he drove off."

"Sounds right. So what happened next?"

"We dropped off the basketball team and took off with Major Ward, the engineer, and one ramper. Wiley said we'd head for that base an hour west . . . Udorn? . . . Ubon? . . . One of those U-places . . . they all sound the same. So we flew over there."

"What did he hope to do?" I asked. Ray's details make me realize this tall tale might actually be true.

"Well, Wiley's plan was to land, taxi to a remote spot, back up against the grass, open the back, drive the limo off, shove it into the weeds, close up, and take off. Wiley figured it would be days before they discovered it. It would just be this mystery car."

"How does he dream up stuff like that? Did it work?"

"No. We were ambushed. Security police cars charged in with flashing lights; along with their commander . . . the whole schmear. Somebody from our command post must have tipped them off. I thought we were going to be arrested. I could see any future I had as an airline pilot going up in smoke."

"Did they arrest you?"

Ray smiled. "Nope. They couldn't stop laughing. But their commander said the same thing, 'Get that &*%#@ out of there.' So we took off *again* . . . stuck with that albatross . . . hoisted on our own petard, as they say."

Ray reached for the fridge and opened two more beers. I was on the edge of my seat. I couldn't see a solution.

"Ol' Wiley headed us east, back toward NKP. He stayed quiet. Thinking about how they were gonna hammer us, I guess. But after a while he started smiling. I asked him what we were gonna do and he answered, 'We'll see.' "

Again I interrupted, "I *hate* that!"

"Me, too. He had me fly east while he went back to talk with Major Ward at the nav table. They kept pointing at the map and nodding. Then Wiley went to the back and talked to the ramper, and there was a bunch of animated pointing at the car and the ramper looked excited about *something,* and then Wiley came back up to the cockpit with a grin the size of Nebraska. When I saw NKP sail by outside Wiley's window, I didn't know what to expect."

Ray wiggled closer. Our knees *touched.* I backed away. He leaned forward, lowered his voice, and motioned me closer. "Following Major Ward's headings, Wiley sneaked us into the Steel Tiger—"

I interrupted, "Southern Laos. Is he *nuts*? Even *I* know you can't fly into the combat zone without an official mission frag. You guys could've flown right through the middle of an airstrike."

Ray nodded and said emphatically, "Wiley flew us out over the Ho Chi Minh Trail. And then instead of 'Drop flare,' Wiley commanded, 'Drop limo!' "

"He chucked it! No way! Not even Wiley . . ."

Ray pledged, "He did. I swear. It was fantastic. I'll never forget it. Our loadmaster rolled that sucker down the ramp right out into the open sky. It just sat there suspended in midair . . . confused . . . like those old cartoon characters who'd run off a cliff and hang there and stare at the audience with that 'Good grief' look. That Lincoln flew formation with us for a while like it thought it was still attached, and then it slowly skydived out of sight."

I was stunned. "Wow!" was all I could manage.

"You know, John, I've always wondered what happened to it."

"What'd'ya mean?"

"I've thought maybe it skydived the whole way down, hit the thick jungle canopy, gently fell through the limbs, hit the ground in pretty good shape, and some bad guy is proudly driving it up and down the trail right now."

I started laughing.

"Or maybe it nose-dived into a swamp . . . that was the rainy season, you know . . . and it went five hundred feet straight down and some archaeological dig will come along a thousand years from now, find the damned thing, and conclude Laotians of 1970 drove Lincoln Continentals."

I laughed so hard my stomach hurt.

"Or maybe the bad guys started thinking we're almost out of bombs . . . and were so desperate we were hurling cars at them."

I laughed so that I couldn't talk. Finally I was able to ask, "How in the world does Wiley come up with stuff like that?"

Ray shook his head. "I don't know. I'd have never dreamed that up."

"Me, neither. Look what he did. He violated three major rules . . . stole a car, flew into the combat zone without authorization, and jettisoned an object without Pentagon permission."

"That's why the five of us agreed to keep it a secret." Ray asked, "How'd we get started on this, anyway?"

"Jack Ward told me to ask about breaking rules and making things up. But I could never do anything like that. *Never.*"

• • •

"Drop flare . . . drop flare . . . drop flare."

"Flares away!"

Rich tosses my die and tells Charles, "It's a four."

I watch Ty finish leaning out the engines and then return to his left-side portholes with a quiet dignity.

I know all this must sound bizarre, but the most bizarre parts are still ahead . . . so stay with me. I've got to hurry and get the rest of these memories picked up and studied before they're washed downstream. Months of mud and silt of other events cover others. Some memories are overgrown with fuzzy algae waving at me in the current, obscuring their labels. Some rocks have disappeared . . . lost forever.

Good.

I think some are best left untouched.

I wish I'd kept notes. At least I have those cassette tapes I sent Sharon.

I guess the next thing I should cover is Rich's (don't call him Dick) Great Zipper Attack from earlier this evening.

CHAPTER *ELEVEN*

My boots feel like barbells. I suddenly realize the metal edge of Charles's perch is cutting off circulation. I bend over, unzip each boot, and take them off.

Ahhh . . . better.

I feel blood rush below my knees . . . fighting fatigue now so I have something left in my personal gas tank for the end.

I hold my boots together, bend forward, aim for the back porch corner, and drop them from three feet up. Most times I try this stunt they simply flop all over. One tumbles left and the second bounces down to the cargo floor. I watch them hit . . . wobble . . . and . . . stand!

Ta-dah! Good shot, JT! Maybe this is going to be your lucky night.

I raise my leg zippers to let heat escape . . . better.

I remember Rich and I were sitting on a small wooden bench outside the chute shop while the technicians helped us suit up. Given our ongoing arguments, I was apprehensive about flying with him again. So I threw out an olive branch to start the night. "So how's Peggy doing down in Bangkok?"

No answer from him.

I tried again. "Any word from her doctor visit?"

Nothing back from him.

I should have known better, but asked, "Rich, what's bugging you?"

He pointed at my boots and blurted, "It's those zippers you *insist* on wearing."

I saw he *really* was upset. "What are you talking about, Rich?"

I didn't have a clue. Everybody modifies their boots with quick-don zippers. After the two hundredth time you bend over to tie and untie and retie and untie laces, you install zippers.

Rich continued his attack. "John, you know very well zippers are illegal. The regs clearly require *laces*. If we have to bail out, those zippers of yours'll pop wide open when you hit the ground. You'll wind up with two sprained ankles. Boot laces would reinforce your ankles and you'd be fine. And those zippers'll be so ripped up at impact, you couldn't get your boots to stay on. You'll be barefoot in the jungle."

I studied Rich's boots. Sure enough . . . tourniquet-tight laces.

As Rich droned on, I thought, We're going off to combat and he starts off with a stupid asshole statement about zippers. No *Howdy do*. No *How's Sharon doing?* Just *zippers*.

I try to get along with him; I really do.

I explained, "Zippers keep me comfortable. I'm not as tired at the end of a flight. Jack Ward said—"

Rich interrupted, "I don't give a shit. That was just his personal opinion. He didn't write the regs and he's not even in the unit anymore. Besides, he was just a navigator."

Trying to stay calm, I said, "Jack Ward knew more about flying than you or I'll ever know—"

Rich cut me off. "You *have* to follow the regs! That's the

trouble with guys like you and Wiley. You think you can just waltz around breaking any rule you want. The rules are there for your own good."

"I'm aware of the rule, Rich. I just choose to ignore it. If we're so far in the tank I've got to depend on *shoelaces* to save my life, I might as well bend over and kiss my ass good-bye. I'm going with the odds. The Candles have been doing this job for years and only one crew had to bail out."

Rich threatened, "Somebody's gonna catch you wearing those things and then you'll be in big trouble—"

Meaning he'll report me to Desktop . . . someday. In the meantime, he'd leave the issue hanging over my head.

I should have told him, "Don't you dare *threaten* me. I don't give a damn about zippers. I'm in command tonight. Not you. Now shut up and let's go fly." But I didn't.

Instead, I said quietly, "Thanks, but I'm keeping the zippers."

"But they're illegal!" he protested, droning on. I knew I had to stop him, or there would be no peace. He'd drive the whole crew batshit.

Then I realized his argument wasn't about zippers at all. It was about him not being in command.

He was using the zipper issue as a crowbar to begin to undermine my authority. After shoelaces, he'd move on to haircuts, allowing Charles (just a navigator) to fly, my bare hands, my unauthorized POW bracelet . . . the list was endless.

I sat there thinking, as always, while the situation got worse and Rich kept yammering about the evils of zippers.

Anger finally reached me. I had to stop him right then and there. I stood up, faced him, jabbed my finger in his face, and snarled, "Listen, *Dick* . . ."

His face exploded. Then he bellowed, "DON'T CALL ME DICK!"

Bull's-eye.

I turned, smiled, and walked away.

Gotcha, Dick.

♦ ♦ ♦

We haven't talked much since.

Now I study Rich and realize he's just one big fur ball of rules.

His mind is locked up in chains tighter than the laces that now chew into his ankles. The laces around his mind cut off any independent thought from reaching his brain.

I guess it's a subtle form of incapacitation. My earlier anger at him has evolved to pity.

Poor Rich. When he's faced with any new situation, he scans his memory for a rule. If his rule doesn't quite fit the situation, he breaks out the largest mallet he can find and pounds and beats and smashes and shoves his square-peg rule into the situation's round hole until there's nothing left but a floorful of wood chips. Then he stands back and proudly labels the obliteration "success."

There's no real Rich . . . just someone's ideas of what a pilot *should be*.

But here's the question: If Rich and I can't agree on *zippers,* what happens if all hell breaks loose? What if we stumble onto something his beloved rules don't cover?

If that happens, I'll turn to Charles.

Not Rich. Never Rich.

I know I'm making him out to be an unlikable, one-dimensional character, but I just don't feel up to fleshing out his good qualities. He must have some, or Peggy wouldn't have married him. She's so sweet and he's so . . .

"Stand by, everybody . . . drop flare, drop flare, drop flare."

"Flares away!"

There I go again . . . overanalyzing things . . . have to move on.

Besides, I want to finish inventorying this stream before we head home in less than an hour. I'm tired of carrying these memories around. I've decided to bury them, once and for all. But before I do, I want to go over them in as orderly a manner as possible.

After I'm done, I'm going to call in a fleet of mental cement trucks . . . five hundred or more . . . and bury these rocks under a hundred yards of cement. Then maybe I can get some sleep.

I want to talk more about Jack Ward next.

CHAPTER *TWELVE*

I check my watch. Twelve after eleven. Forty-eight minutes till we head back . . . if Candle 25 isn't too late. Let's see . . . a little over an hour to cross the Mekong into Thailand . . . thirty minutes south to NKP . . . twenty to shed this gear, debrief Intell . . . change clothes . . . mark an *X* through today . . .

I should be ordering Kobe steak by 2 A.M.

I'll party with Wiley and the guys, listen to the band till the sun comes up, set the alarm for 5 P.M., and come back up here tomorrow night and do this all over again. And the night after that and the night after that. And the night after *that*.

So there's no rush.

As Charles, Rich, and Ty talk, I back out of the conversation. I struggle to make small talk. I've studied people good at general chitchat. I mimic them, but it doesn't come naturally. People think I'm a good conversationalist, but I'm really just faking it.

Mental reflection is far more interesting. You can go

places with internal analysis no conversation could
venture . . .

I take the Jack Ward stone out of my pocket. Only bits of our
conversations remain. His lessons have become part of me. I
take them for granted . . . like walking or breathing.

I regret not keeping a journal. All that remains are these
stupid metaphorical rocks, a few bar napkins, and the
ledgers.

I'll try now to follow the sequence of events, as best I can.
But sometimes things jump out from memory under a power
of their own; so there are bound to be interruptions and mis-
connects ahead. So please bear with me.

If I plod through enough rocks, maybe I'll find what has
me spooked.

I remember Jack and I walked into the deserted, quiet bar after our second flight together. The Miller High Life clock
said it was 2:11 A.M. It was a Tuesday. We took stools
halfway down the bar.

Jack ordered a pitcher and put a dollar bill on the bar.
While the bartender left to fill the order, I excused myself
and walked over to the Wurlitzer. For a dime, I selected
"Sounds of Silence," "Mrs. Robinson," and "Bridge over
Troubled Water."

Then I sat back down beside Jack. The bartender tiptoed
toward us, trying to keep beer from sloshing out of a brim-
filled clear-plastic pitcher.

He took Jack's dollar, took the dime tip, and discreetly re-
treated to the end of the bar.

Jack trickled beer down the sides of our mugs; he looked
at me searchingly. He asked me, "Where do you think the
procedures we used tonight came from?"

"I don't have a clue," I replied. "Desktop shoved a bad
Xerox copy of a regulation in my hands titled 'Candlestick
Tactics' and told me, 'Memorize this.' "

Jack prodded, "But where do you think those tactics came
from?"

I shrugged. "I suppose they got some experts together at a conference and came up with the best ways to do the job."

He nodded. "That's what most guys think. Would you like to know where they really came from?"

Unsure where he was headed, I answered, "Sure."

He began, "Some of the tactics didn't make sense to me. So I dug into the records and found the guys who were here at the very beginning. I got Desktop to let me use his phone on the pretext of researching unit history, and I called those guys back in the States. I asked them the same question. They told me that when they started, nobody knew what to do. So they made it up."

I sipped my San Miguel and nodded.

"They experimented. Every night was trial and error. Some things worked. Some didn't. Nobody up the chain of command paid them any attention. After all, what could a dilapidated old cargo plane do against trucks two miles below? With no one watching, they were free to do as they pleased."

The bartender brought a silver platter packed with spring rolls. He explained, "Leftovers from dinner. They're on the house."

We said thanks and dove in.

"After they landed, they compared notes. They scribbled their experiments on napkins like this." Jack dangled one of the white squares. "To their wonder, sometimes when they combined two failed experiments, the results were pure magic. And their experiments started paying dividends. They started killing trucks. They destroyed so many that Saigon didn't believe their reports and gave them credit for only a quarter of what they reported."

"Saigon assumed our guys were *lying*?"

"Yep. But our guys didn't care they didn't get credit. They went right on taking out more trucks." Jack looked excited. "They were having the time of their lives. No one was around to hold them back. No one was around to stamp 'DISAPPROVED' on their napkins. There was an electricity about their efforts. It was fresh, alive, and changing every night. It was wild!"

I stared at him, thinking about what he said. Then I said, "It sure doesn't feel that way now."

"No, it doesn't," he said sadly. "Those guys were artists working on a group sculpture. Along the way, they learned their mistakes were the *real* treasures. Their failures taught them what *didn't* work. Nobody was watching them . . . yet. Those early guys were a marvel in a sea of average performances."

I jumped in, "I wish I'd been there. It must have been great."

"I'm sure it was. They were free men for the first time in their military lives. I could still hear the excitement in their voices. They'd broken out of the master-slave mentality of the Church of the Air Force."

I interrupted, "Whoa. You're losing me. The *what*?"

"Later. You're not ready for that yet. We have other things to cover first. But they made one fatal mistake. Hold on a sec."

Jack brought out a Lucky, lit it, and began blowing smoke rings. I glanced in the bar mirror and saw him studying my reflection.

I looked away, self-conscious.

The music stopped. I started to get up, but the bartender waved at me. He hollered, "Your money's no good in here tonight." I thanked him, then he pointed a remote control at the jukebox and my songs started over.

Jack asked, "Where was I?"

"You said they made a fatal mistake."

"Oh, yeah. During one of their no-holds-barred discussions, someone said, 'You know, we're about to rotate back home. But there's no record of what we've learned. We should *write it down* so new guys won't have to start from scratch. We'll create a series of ledgers where we'll log everything we know.'" Jack took a drag and blew smoke rings.

He continued, "They got together over beers and wrote down their discoveries on legal ledger pads complete with cross-outs and beer stains . . . with no organization. It was the same creativity you find in a Beethoven piece. It was glorious!"

I waved to the bartender for a refill and asked Jack, "So what happened?"

"Well, they went home. Then somebody like Desktop showed up, found FNGs using the dog-eared, beer-stained ledgers, and concluded, 'I can't allow this mess. We can't have people flying around doing just about whatever they damn well please. This is a military unit, not some goddamn barnstorming flying circus. Besides, there must be *twelve* ledgers here . . . way too much stuff. I'll cut out the things that I don't understand and keep the useless ten percent I do. Then I'll dice it, slice it, and chop it into a formal regulation of chapters, paragraphs, headings, subheadings, footnotes, exceptions, wherefores, warnings, a glossary, and a bunch of other clerical mumbo jumbo no one but an attorney could love, and in the process of writing about something I don't understand, I'll choke the life and vitality out of this bubbling cauldron of ideas. What this place needs is *order*.' "

Jack took a break and gulped some of the new pitcher.

He continued, "Then I'll send *my* document up through channels for the general's signature. He'll see how smart and organized I am, how I've brought order to this renegade outfit they warned me about, and I'll take credit for those other people's work. In claiming their ideas as my own, I'll land a better job back in the States. The original drafters have all gone home; so nobody's left to raise a stink. When the copy of *my* regulations comes back from headquarters, I'll shove it down my slaves' throats.' "

Jack looked at me seriously. "Then he destroyed the old ledgers. When those printing presses stopped, the full flower of their ideas were wiped out. There must be hundreds of ways of doing our job, but few people try to find new ones anymore."

The bartender began washing glasses in the sink, rinsing and then hanging them overhead upside down to drip-dry.

"So you wind up with a system of blind obedience. Today's regulations are a mental straitjacket for Rich and all the others like him. But the problem is much bigger than that. It gets worse."

I grabbed a stack of napkins and started taking notes.

"Now they have quarterly tactics conferences in Bangkok ostensibly to see if they should make any changes. This crop of Desktops assigns their suck-up protégés who know no more of what's going on than their bosses to attend what amounts to a bonus combination CTO and stateside job fair. The protégés make speeches proclaiming how wonderful their programs are and then head for the bar. Those attendees who can't see through the charade and came to actually discuss improvements commit political suicide and are never invited again."

I caught the eavesdropping bartender nodding agreement.

"So nothing changes. Over time, the rules take on a life of their own. Instead of being a means to an end, they become an end unto themselves. They become the religion of the Church of the Air Force . . . the way it's *always* been done. A few years from now, our current tactics will mature into DOCTRINE . . . carved in stone like the Ten Commandments. At that point, this unit and its mission will be dead. And consider this: there are *thousands* of Desktops across Southeast Asia choking the life out of something that once was alive, vital, exciting, energetic, and which once stood some slim chance of success. No more."

Jack took out another Lucky, but this time the bartender rushed over, produced a silver Zippo lighter, and offered a light.

"As I said, there are hundreds of ways to do this job, JT, but when you publish only a few, people begin to comply without understanding the overall problem. They lose all feel for the work. The hard-to-follow instructions force them into making mistakes. Those mistakes drive them into greater mistakes, and the increasing errors snowball until there's no way out."

"Wow, Jack, how do you know all this stuff?"

He avoided the question. "That leaves one big problem.

The published tactics don't work anymore. The situation has changed."

I was scribbling, but couldn't keep up. I filled one napkin and reached for another. I said, "You're going too fast. I'm missing some."

He went slower. "Compare our dogmatic rules to what the bad guys are doing. They don't have printing presses in the jungle, so they *have to* make it up. They do what works. It's messy, dynamic, and different every night. They're making decisions as they go. They constantly outflank us because they know our next move. They're like an NFL defense who knows the offense is going to run up the middle every play."

I filled a napkin, reached for another, started writing, but my pen broke through the thin paper. I gave up and just listened.

Jack wrapped it up. *"And what that means is* . . . we're gonna lose this war on the printing-press issue alone. It's over. The people in charge haven't realized their penchant for control is a growing cancer they've implanted in the patient. The creativity that *might* have won this war requires *a loss of control,* but that's something the Church will never tolerate."

I stared at Jack in silence.

"And the higher you go, the sillier it gets. The worst are the Pentagon's rules of engagement."

I got a word in. "I tried reading those, but couldn't get through them. They read like an IRS tax form."

Jack nodded. "Did you see the one that says we can't take the first shot at an enemy gun? That we have to *wait* until the gun is a *direct, continuing* threat to us *personally*?"

"I did. This is a war, for cryin' out loud. What idiot came up with *that*?"

"I called my Pentagon contacts. They swear it came from Defense Secretary McNamara's snot-nosed, draft-deferred, politically connected Whiz Kids, who sip dark Becks in Georgetown every night. They overlay their stuck-up, East Coast, Ivy League value system on a war half a world away they've never even seen. I'd like to take one of them up with us for a night of flak and see if they still feel the same."

I thought about what he said. Then I asked, "Jack, are you saying I'm supposed to feel sorry for guys like Rich? That he's somehow a victim of a corrupt system?"

"No; I'm not saying that at all. We all bear personal responsibility for our behavior. My point is, there are thousands of Riches over here who are like Pinocchio to the Air Force's Geppetto. Geppetto is hovering over Rich, pulling his strings. Meanwhile, Rich thinks he's making his own decisions. The hope is that someday Rich will look up, see Geppetto, and cut the strings. But before that can happen, he'll have to do some direct seeing of his own. If you tried cutting his strings for him, he'd wind up as a pile of sticks scattered across the floor. Rich will have to cut his strings for himself. Only then will he become a real boy."

"Cut to the chase, Jack. I have eleven and a half months left. What the heck am I supposed to do?"

He spoke slowly. "Throw the rules out the window. Go back and capture the spirit of those beer-stained napkins. Architect Frank Lloyd Wright once said he made 'order from chaos.' And that's what you have to do: make order from chaos."

"Where do I start?"

Jack smiled. "With those old dog-eared ledgers."

"What are you talking about? You said they were destroyed."

"I lied. I wanted to see your reaction. I've mentioned them to some guys who said, 'That's interesting,' and ordered another beer. I didn't want to be disappointed again. Anyway, I knew the Air Force never throws anything out. So I poked through the bottoms of desk drawers behind Admin, and sure enough, there they were . . . shoved under a stack of old Teletype messages. I thought, 'What a gold mine!' So I sort of liberated them . . ."

"You stole official records?"

"Absolutely not. I *liberated* them. Wiley and a few other

guys have studied them. They're at my trailer if you'd like to borrow them."

I jumped at the chance. "I'd love to."

The bartender brought a third pitcher. We said, "Oh, no!" and gleefully began to make it disappear.

I said, "Jack, you should write all this down."

He looked at my notes and started laughing.

I said, "Oh," and started laughing, too.

We sat in silence, drank beer, and listened to Art Garfunkel until the sun came up.

The rampers drop another set of flares, Rich rolls my red die, and Charles flies us around another racetrack.

So round and round she goes and where she stops, nobody knows . . . with a little conversation, a few rocks from the stream of memories, a couple bars of music to make the medicine go down, a metaphor here and there, a dash of technical information, and a touch of mental reflection to round out the evening entertainment and make the lingering minutes pass . . .

. . . and keep my nightmare back in its cave.

My mental gymnastics amount to whistling in the dark.

Sure hope it works.

Eddie? I haven't heard from our right scanner in a long time.

CHAPTER *THIRTEEN*

I spin Charles's chair around to look down the right side of the dark cargo compartment to look for Eddie. I see his black-shadowed outline perched like a small bird on the narrow wooden catwalk that rings the cargo area about two feet above the metal floor. That's right, I said *wood*. This old warhorse is probably the last airplane with some components made of wood.

Eddie has managed to wedge himself into the tight space between the forward flare pallet and the aircraft wall. He's supposed to be scanning out the right-side portholes for artillery fire, but he's fast asleep. Worn-out.

If Rich were in command, he'd blow a fuse. I can hear him now: "Airman, wake up! You can't sleep here! This is a combat mission! That's dereliction of duty! You're in a lot of trouble, mister! Now stay awake, or I'll put you on report!"

I decide to break another rule and let Eddie sleep. If he can sleep through all this noise, he must really be exhausted. I may need him later with his batteries fully charged.

Eddie and all the right scanners we fly with are "volunteers." His real job is as one of our squadron administrative clerks. He works a full shift during the day, gets an hour off, then suits up to fly with us until about 2 A.M., gets a few hours' sleep, and starts his day shift again at 7 A.M. Night after night after night. No wonder he's asleep.

I was surprised to learn the Air Force never staffed these missions with a right-scanner position to make it a full crew. They rely totally on *volunteers*.

Volunteers, my ass.

A long time ago, I asked Eddie, "Why do you choose to come up here and get shot at with us every night? You certainly don't *have* to. You have a wife and twin infant daughters back home, don't you? You could go home to them in a box if somebody gets off a lucky shot."

"My wife and kids need the money," he explained. "You see, I had a real good apprentice position on the assembly line back in Detroit. We were poor, but we were doing okay; the future looked real good. Then I got my draft notice. My wife was terrified I'd wind up in one of those black body bags they show on TV, so I hurried up to join the Air Force to avoid being in those rice paddies carrying an M16. I told the Air Force I was a mechanic by trade and that I wanted to work on airplanes, but they made me a clerk."

"But, Eddie, you wound up in the same place you were trying to avoid. We could get shot down any night. Why do you do this?"

He laughed. "For the Pampers. We have two baby girls and my wife says the only way she can keep up with taking care of them herself is with disposable diapers; flying combat is the only way I can afford them. With the combat pay and the full income-tax exemption, she can just squeeze by."

"I'm sorry, Eddie. It's terrible that they don't pay you enough to take care of your family, knowing you'll need to 'volunteer' for work the Pentagon should man and fund as a full-time job. They're using you, can't you see that?"

"Thanks for your concern, sir. But I'm using them back.

When I get out, I'll go back to college on the GI Bill to be an accountant and get off that assembly line."

But Eddie works for Desktop, and if Desktop thinks Eddie isn't volunteering enough or if his office performance falls off, he'd cut him off flight orders immediately. Permanently. No combat pay. No tax break. No Pampers. No saving for college.

The Air Force bird of prey at work again, I thought to myself.

So I let Eddie sleep when things are quiet, like tonight.

Earlier this evening I tried one last time to remind Eddie of the consequences of his decision. "Eddie, you could get killed doing this. Then your daughters wouldn't have a father."

"That's why I like to fly with you, sir," he explained. "I know you'll get me back safely."

No pressure there, of course.

I watch Eddie readjust himself so as not to fall off the catwalk, and now I turn back around to check on Charles and Rich in the cockpit.

Even without the weight of my combat boots, the metal ridge at the front of Charles's chair cuts into my thighs and cuts off the circulation. If someone had just designed the replacement seat cushion to lap *over* the ridge like the original instead of resting just *inside* the frame, hundreds of crewmembers wouldn't have been so uncomfortable all these years.

Oh, well. Maybe someday in the future the manufacturers will actually talk with us before they design these things.

I shinny down off Charles's chair onto the back porch to get the blood flow going again. Ahhhh . . . that's better.

I stand up on the one remaining short step just below the cockpit floor. From here, my head grazes the ceiling and I look straight down on Rich's bald spot.

I peer out the cockpit windows, surprised I can see all the way to the surface. We just moved into the rainy season. So most nights, rain clouds fill all the valleys below us and cover all but the ridgelines of the mountains. Our candlelight can't burn through the thick undercast and rain, nor can we look for truck convoys to kill. On most nights these days, we just drone up and down the trail above the clouds, following the navigator's best-guess headings. Boring holes in the sky. Burning fuel. Accomplishing nothing.

It's a complete waste of time.

While the rain must make the dirt trail difficult to pass, I'm sure most nights the drivers are down there laughing at our futile efforts.

We often ask Saigon to release us to go home after we fly all the way up here and relay a cloud-cover report through Moonbeam. After all, there's nothing we can do. But the answer is always the same: "Disapproved. Complete your mission as tasked. You may not be able to see anything, but the enemy can hear you. They know you're there. You are demonstrating the continued U.S. presence."

U.S. presence. What a crock. We're fighting a great war machine with *noise*. Yep, that'll work. That'll make them think twice about messing with us. They must be shaking in their boots down there on nights like that. Never mind that some enemy gunner might get off a lucky shot.

So night after night, we come up here above the clouds and waste our time. The rain even tries to spoil the movies back at NKP.

They show us old movies on a dilapidated, 1950s, surplus grade-school projector some organization back home like the VFW donated. Guys before us built a makeshift outdoor theater in a stand of trees on a small hill up the street from the club. They felled just enough trees for seating and left the rest. Nice. The movie screen is a sheet tied with clothesline between two trees. Simple, but effective.

Early arrivals rush to get a good seat—one of the flat tree stumps. Nice and flat for your rear end. Late arrivals have to sit on logs that used to be the trees. There's no flat surface, so your butt gets real sore where it meets the curve of the log. Log-sitters spend most of the night rolling their log back and forth from thighs to butt to stay comfortable.

They show us mostly old Westerns where the good guys always win. All of us see through their ham-fisted brain-washing, but we watch because there's nothing better to do.

A few nights ago they started the movie under clear skies . . . Gregory Peck in some Western nobody cared about, but the hillside was packed with people. Halfway through the movie the gust front of a rainstorm started blow-ing the sheet around, so it looked as if the movie were being shown on ocean swells. The first raindrops hit the ground like little dust bombs, each sending up small dust explosions.

No one moved.

The rain came down harder and turned the ground a darker shade. The drops started mixing with the picture so it looked as if Gregory Peck had some disease. The man oper-ating the projector covered it with a green, waterproof mili-tary poncho and kept on rolling.

No one moved.

The rain dotted the ground, then soaked it completely. Rivulets of rain worked their way down the hillside we were perched on, running along both sides of my tennis shoes. The movie-screen ocean swells became one of those old amusement park "crazy mirrors," and we couldn't tell one actor from another in the blur.

The hair of the man seated ahead of me grew soaked. The cloth tops of my tennies became saturated. The projectionist turned the volume up to max so we could still hear the dia-logue above the roar of the rain. The actors' voices rumbled like thunder. Gregory Peck shouted his lines above the roar, but we knew most of the lines by heart anyway. So it didn't matter.

We all just sat there.

The rivulets of water swelled into small streams and then larger rivers. The movie screen sheet slipped from the weight of the water and became half its height. The hillside became a spillway. The roar drowned out the sound, but we could still read Gregory's lips on the crazy mirror.

No one moved. We all just sat there.

Pretty soon, the clothesline couldn't support the water and the sheet rolled down between the trees until about only a foot remained. But it didn't matter. We didn't need the picture. We'd all seen the same movie so many times, we could play the scenes in our mind. All we needed was the dialogue. The projectionist dangled the extension cord over a tree limb to keep it out of the spillway and kept on rolling.

The movie sheet finally became so heavy with water it became the width of a clothesline. The whole thing sort of slid together. But that was okay, because the rain was so hard we could still see parts of the movie on the wall of water; I swear. The spillway of water turned into raging white-water rapids. The rapids rushed into my tennies and soaked my feet. The roar of the rain completely drowned out the actors' voices. I looked at the man on my right and saw him silently mouthing the script . . . for all the characters. He saw my predicament and raised his voice so I could hear.

And then it *really* came down. It wasn't just raining anymore. This was a mugging. The rain beat us up, slamming down on our heads and shoulders. It roared like a freight train. I looked at the man on my right and saw him holding—no hiding—his face in his hands. And we all just sat there.

No one moved.

The interphone is quiet now. No one has anything to say. I guess everyone's stuck in the cotton-candy silences of their own thoughts. Me, too. Everyone's entitled to some quiet mental space, so I don't say anything.

I am just looking around.

The clock by Charles's right knee says 11:19.

I take the short step backward down onto the back porch, turn around to my left, and scan the cargo compartment. No signs of trouble there.

The weight of my parachute pulls against my shoulder blades and I feel like a mule in front of an old plow, straining against the earth. So I lean backward against the bulkhead and rest the chute's dead weight against it for a while. My legs still ache, so I draw my right thigh up to my chest and hold it there, stretching the violin-tight ligaments and tendons. I repeat the process with my left leg.

Manage the fatigue. Have something left for the end, I tell myself.

Whew! . . . Much better.

I get the feeling now I'd get on those summer family car vacations out West back in the 1950s. We had to cross the desert at night or the old '51 Ford sedan would overheat. You'd go for miles and miles and not see any other cars. That was all pre-interstate highways, so we'd barrel down two-lane blacktop roads in the middle of the night with nothing to do but gaze out at the blackness.

Just like now.

A couple hours before the sun would come up, Dad would start looking for a mom-and-pop motel. The chain of reliable, clean Holiday Inns was still years away. Dad would get out of the car while we stayed inside, wake the owner with the night call bell, and wander down the outside walkway with him to inspect the sample room. Soon Dad would walk back to the car shaking his head. We'd all groan while he pulled back out onto the road and explained, "The place was filthy. There'll be a better place ahead."

He'd try to distract us by making us sing along with some of those dumb old Western songs like "Something, something, something . . . on the lone prairie . . ."

What cornball.

God, it was wonderful!

That's the feeling I get with these guys, anyway.

Family.

Except now, *I'm* the dad, driving us down this black, two-lane road toward an uncertain future.

I wave at Tyrone and he waves back.

◆ ◆ ◆

"BANDIT! BANDIT! BANDIT! This is Arizona Pete on guard with a warning! Do not answer! Do not answer! BREAK . . . BREAK . . . Bandit one-eight, channel forty-seven, three three five degrees, one hundred twenty nautical miles . . . Arizona Pete on guard . . . out," the voice bellowed.

CHAPTER *FOURTEEN*

I've been avoiding the stream of memories. I didn't know which rock to pick next. So I might as well jump in with both feet, pick the next one I see, and hope for the best. I could spend all night worrying about which memory comes next . . . until nothing gets done. Besides, I want to finish before we head home and those cement trucks roll in; so I'd better get a move on.

This Bandit rock is covered with so much moss and slime, I know much of what follows is wrong. Major parts of the episode have washed downstream. For instance, I can't remember my FNG copilot's name. So I'll call him Fred. I'll fill in the rest of the gaps as best I can, knowing some will be wrong. It's the best I can hope for.

I may bounce off this story a couple times before the end. Whenever I think about the episode, I feel a momentary fright. My stomach cramps and I rear back before I'm able to continue.

I hope you'll understand.

◆ ◆ ◆

The first broadcast didn't make sense, so I ignored it.

But the barely audible warning came again a few minutes later:

"BANDIT! BAN . . . ! This is Arizona Pete on guar . . . Warn . . . ! Do not ans . . . not answer Break! . . . dit one eight, channel four sev . . . three two . . . degrees, one hund . . . sevent . . . naut . . . mi . . . zona Pete on guard . . . out."

Fred bolted upright. "What's *that*? That's the second one of those."

I explained, "A MiG warning from Arizona Pete."

My copilot looked confused. "Who?"

"That radar facility on Monkey Mountain over in Vietnam. If they spot an enemy fighter going after one of our guys, they announce an alert on guard like that."

"What's all that gibberish? I couldn't make out most of it."

Jack announced, "I got it back here."

I continued, "The site is so far away we're only receiving pieces of the transmission." I turned up the radio volume so we could hear it better next time. "If it comes again, we'll write it down for practice."

"Okay." Fred pulled out a pencil to be ready. "What's it mean?"

"They're giving the location of a MiG referencing the azimuth and DME off a TACAN channel somewhere."

Fred asked nervously, "There's no history of them going after a Candlestick, is there?"

I told him not to be concerned. Then I told him the story about Wiley circling near Vinh my first night. I added what Wiley said about the C-123 not being a worthy target.

"Okay," Fred replied, and relaxed back in his seat.

I turned around and asked Jack what he thought. He agreed an attack on a Candlestick would be unprecedented. The only warnings he'd heard were way over by the DMZ . . . hundreds of miles away.

So I turned back to my instruments and followed the

scope's headings, all relaxed and easygoin'. Just like Wiley.

No problem.

Come to think of it, we were at about this same spot. Strange.

We followed the trail south several minutes.

Finally I asked Jack casually, "Out of curiosity, do me a favor. Plot those positions and let me know where they are."

"Way ahead of you, JT," Jack answered seriously. "I plotted the first warning and am working the second now. The answer'll give us his trajectory. Stand by one."

I remember thinking his anxious tone seemed melodramatic for what amounted to a nonevent. Fred looked at me apprehensively.

I shrugged. "Beats me."

The situation did not make sense. Even *if* the warning was real, it couldn't possibly involve us. With hundreds of planes airborne over North and South Vietnam, northern and southern Laos, the odds were astronomical of *us* being the target.

So I took a deep breath, leaned back, and dropped the issue. I was confident Jack's plots would prove that MiG was an entire country away.

Big mistake.

I got stomach butterflies. What if I was wrong?

I nervously prompted Jack, "How're those plots coming?"

He answered ominously, "Bad news. There's a MiG-17 headed up our tail at point nine Mach. He's after *us*."

CHAPTER FIFTEEN

I got the cold sweats. I whirled around and saw Jack bent over his maps. In the light of his desk lamp, his calipers, compass, plotter, pencils, and slide rule were a blur. I exclaimed, "You gotta be shittin' me!"

"I'm dead serious," Jack insisted. "He's overtaking us at nine miles a minute. He *knows* we're here. He'll be in missile range in under three minutes. Looking up his armament . . . stand by."

I looked over at Fred. His expression changed from bewilderment to surprise to uncontrolled fear in less than a second.

I froze. I told myself, This can't be happening! Not to *me*! I'm not *ready*! I need more of that "seasoning" they talk about. If Wiley were here, he'd know what to do. I machine-gunned his old commands: "Ramp, Pilot. Close the back. Hurry! Tell me when it's closed . . . Engineer, start both jets. Bring them up to max ASAP . . . Jack, how long? What's he got?"

Jack replied calmly, "Stand by . . . in progress."

I called Moonbeam, declared an emergency, and asked them for fighter rescue.

Moonbeam answered, "Stand by."

I reassured myself, we're gonna be okay. Our interceptors will zip in and scare this guy off.

I suddenly realized my orders were like spitting in the surf to raise the ocean. There was no way we could outrun the Russian-built fighter. By the time we got the back end closed and the jets up to max, he'd be on top of us. It dawned on me how different this situation was from my fifty-seven-millimeter initiation: Wiley's radar-controlled gun was stationary.

This one was racing up our tail at 90 percent of the speed of sound.

Realizing the futility of my knee-jerk commands, I canceled them.

The loadmasters replied, "The ramp's already closed, sir. You want it reopened?"

I answered dejectedly, "No." Then I told the engineer, "Leave the jets at idle," although I couldn't imagine what good they'd do.

Moonbeam called back and advised us that our fighters were coming to help, but were at least twenty minutes away.

We were on our own.

I smacked my forehead. You idiot! If you'd called for help at the first warning. Stupid, stupid, stupid!

I watched Jack feathering through the thick enemy-aircraft reference manual. "Got it!" he announced. "He's *loaded*. Hard to know exactly what he's got, but this says he can carry radar-guided missiles, heat-seeking rockets, hard bombs. He's even got a Gatling gun, airborne radar . . . wait a sec . . . *Oh, shit* . . . this says *some* MiG-17s have IR capability."

"What if he's got IR?"

"He'll pick up the heat signatures off our exhaust stacks no matter what we do. It'll be shooting fish in a barrel."

The contest was a complete mismatch: his Soviet-made fighter stuffed with computer-generated fire-control systems against our museum relic.

We were outgunned and outperformed.
Not to mention defenseless . . .

There's something you need to know before I go on. We might have stood a fighting chance if the Pentagon had equipped us with any of the readily available radar-jamming equipment. Instead, they give us a "nuclear protection kit" . . . I swear to God. Like the bad guys are *really* going to launch a nuclear attack.

"Nevah happen, GI," the Thais say. "You *clazy* man."

And the silliest thing in the kit is the nuclear blast monocle. We're supposed to wear it like Long John Silver's eye patch. They won't give us two. We're "authorized" one. They briefed us, "One eye will instantly turn to dust from the blast, but your golden monocle with that tiny center hole will leave you one good eye . . . enough to get the aircraft back home. So choose ahead of time which eye you want to lose. And remember, that coating's real gold. Lose the patch and they'll dock your pay."

They couldn't spring for the dough for a second monocle? Give me a break. But, outside the eye patch and starlight scope, the most sophisticated equipment we have onboard is a broom.

Sorry; I bounced off there. Back to the story . . .

We barely heard the third warning. "BANDIT! Ariz . . . ete on guar . . . Warn . . . ! Do not ans . . . not answer! Break . . . bandit . . . chan . . . forty-seven . . . two eight fi . . . degrees, one und . . . three . . . naut . . . mi . . . zona Pete . . . out."

Jack said solemnly, "Two minutes to missile range. You've got to *do something,* JT. He's prob'ly got a skin paint on us. When he gets inside ten miles, he'll spot us visually."

I imagined the MiG pilot focusing computer-driven crosshairs on the neck of our albatross.

In my mind I was six years old in front of class after the teacher asked me a question whose answer I didn't know. The kids snickered . . . knowing I'd fail. The angry school-marm with that harsh hair bun crossed her arms and tapped her foot. Chalk in hand, I stared at the empty blackboard in complete internal panic . . . exposed as a phony.

Then my pants fell down.

I remember not wanting to do anything about that MiG because anything I might do could be wrong. I was that deer trapped in the headlights.

My crew waited for my decision. They couldn't know they'd wait forever. I was mentally paralyzed. My heart felt as if the devil himself had punched his hand through my chest wall and was squeezing as hard as he could.

The loadmasters sensed my panic. They prodded, "Pilot, Ramp. You want us to deploy the chaff, sir?"

"No! Absolutely *not* . . . his radar'd hit on the foil and tell him exactly where we are."

"Sorry, sir."

Jack appeared in the doorway with a running stopwatch in his right hand. He shook my shoulder and pointed out my left window. "JT, you see that next valley over?"

I looked out the window. In the full moonlight, I spotted it . . . a long, dark valley maybe three miles wide between two jagged ridgelines. I asked him, "You mean the crooked one that goes south a few miles, makes a left forty-five, and finally makes a hard ninety-degree right?"

"That's it. We stand out like a sore thumb up here. If you get us down just below those ridgelines, his radar might lose us in ground returns."

"What!"

"We might blend into the background."

"Oh . . . right. But what if he's got that IR?"

"We're history. He'll spot us no matter what."

"On my way." I turned left, yanked the throttles to idle, and nose-dived for cover.

Jack pointed out the front window. "Aim for the middle. Hurry! One minute! All he needs is one shot."

I swooped down into the valley. I nestled us down between the relative safety of the craggy, parallel ridgelines. Their saw-toothed walls rose above us.

I stared in horror out my front window. The view was terrifying.

The safe harbor we thought we saw from above was filled to the brim with a carpet of white clouds. I instinctively leveled off and skimmed along the creamy tops.

A giant white moon rested atop the far-end ridge before the valley turned left. Moonlight splashed in through the windows, filling the cockpit with a gossamer light. I watched Fred's head cast a shadow against the aft circuit-breaker panel and imagined our aircraft shadow against the clouds.

Our blend-into-the-background plan had blown up in our faces.

From the MiG's view, we looked like a black horsefly on the back of a white horse. Our black fuselage against the carpet of white screamed, "Here we are! Come shoot us down!" I'd succeeded in making us an even better target.

If I ducked inside the clouds, we might stay between the ridgelines for a while. With a lot of luck, we might even make that first blind half-left. It was that second hard right that worried me most. That would be the knockout punch . . . if the MiG didn't get us first. If I stayed on top of the clouds, he'd smash us with one easy *swat*.

It was Russian roulette with five of the six chambers *loaded*.

There was no way out.

Staring out at the whipped-cream clouds, I asked myself, *Okay, JT, what's next?*

I answered, hide in the clouds.

I told myself without hesitation, *Okay, dive in*. I nudged us in and out of the tops; getting my feet wet.

Another voice inside said, *You can't do that. Who the hell do you think you are? You're no Wiley. Give it up.*

Arizona Pete warned again, "BANDIT! BANDIT! BANDIT!"

Fred asked nervously, "You're not thinking of hiding in the clouds, are you?"

Jack yelled, "*Just do it!* Thirty seconds."

I asked Jack, "Are you *sure*? Your maps're so unreli—"

"Yes, dammit! Get in the fuckin' clouds!"

Fred yanked my sleeve. "We're not in radar contact. You can't—"

I yelled back, "I'm breaking that rule. You want to stay up here and get your ass blown off?"—trapping him.

"BANDIT! BANDIT! . . ."

My mind screamed, SONOFABITCH! SONOFABITCH!

I felt my cranium would crack from internal pressure. I let go of the controls, flew with my knees, grabbed my skull between both hands, and *squeezed* to keep the bones from splitting.

The hunter's moon disappeared and reappeared as I dipped in and out of the cloud tops.

Jack yelled, "Fifteen seconds!"

Fred's expression turned furious. He leaned across the radio console and shouted in my face, "You can't go in the clouds! It's suicide! You don't have the authority!"

Rage consumed me. Lightning raced through my veins. Thunder rumbled inside my skull. My mind burst into flame. A beast blasted through the doors of the wood cellar of my mind. "You don't think so?" the beast growled out. "You just *watch me*."

Fred look stunned and jerked back.

I was startled. I thought, My Lord, did *that* come out of me?

Jack patted my shoulder and chuckled, "Now we're getting somewhere." Then he disappeared back to his maps.

Fred gasped, "You go in there, we're dead meat. You can't—"

I dove into the foggy valley. Clouds enveloped us and . . . *Pouf!*

We were transformed into a submarine careening through underwater canyons. I wondered if I'd made a terrible mistake. The *idea* of flying blind had been easy to contemplate. *Actually* flying blind between the two killer ridges was terrifying.

My imagination played the scene from *20,000 Leagues Under the Sea* with Captain Nemo trying to save the *Nau-*

tilus from surface-ship depth charges. Nemo raced through underwater caverns to evade his attackers as the *Nautilus* careened down sides of plaster-of-paris mountains. Their peaks raked down the sides of the sub, ripped it apart, and sent the toy sub to the bottom of the soundstage water tank.

But that was Hollywood. This was *real*.

I said, "Jack, please tell me you've done this before."

"Not blind like this. I'm just makin' this up as we go."

I looked over at Fred. His face had a look of fear and contempt that screamed, "You crazy bastard! You're gonna kill us!"

I felt Jack move in beside me. He cupped his hands over my right ear. I felt his mouth moving. He whispered, "You're doing fine. Keep going. You can do it. Don't be scared. I believe in you."

I nodded, turned to answer, but saw him strapped into his director's chair, concentrating on his maps. I thought, How'd he get back there that fast? I turned back to my instruments.

Long-ago-rusted-shut windows across my mind slammed open. Wham! Wham! Wham! Ideas started flowing unself-consciously.

I asked myself, *What's next?*

And I answered, I need to change the game to keep that MiG off-balance.

How could you do that?

I could slow down and hope he'll rip by before he's realized he missed us.

Okay, what's next after that?

I don't know.

That's okay. We'll figure it out one step at a time. Get slowed down for now.

I asked Jack, "If I slow her down, can you still make the turns?"

"Yeah . . . good idea. Remember, I've got remote heading, altitude, and airspeed indicators back here . . . I'll adjust to you."

I looked around, expecting to see Jack concentrating on our unreliable maps.

I was stunned. He had shoved his charts off to one side like a pile of old newspapers. We were navigating solely by his stopwatch.

I thought, Oh my God. What if he's just an old sot who told good bar stories and I've fallen for the performance?

Arizona Pete updated their ominous warning: "BANDIT! BANDIT! BANDIT! . . ."

"JT, that position puts him in rocket range. His fire-control systems'll lock on any second. Even if he misses, he'll have hard bombs left when he gets overhead."

I throttled back and watched the speed slow . . . 130 . . . 120 . . . 100 knots . . . trim, trim, trim . . . the nose rose higher and higher.

Fred blew up. "What the hell're you doing! If you get any slower, she'll stall! Stalls are prohibited," he warned.

"She won't stall." I didn't have time to explain my tortoise-versus-hare defense . . . using the MiG's speed advantage against him . . . hoping his rabbit might zip by our tortoise as if we were standing still, cutting his time on target to almost nothing. He'd have to make that perfect shot Wiley talked about.

At one hundred knots and slowing, Fred said, "I'll look up the stall speed," and turned to dig into his kit bag for the performance manual.

I ordered, "Stop! No time."

"But you don't know when she'll stall!"

"Yes, I do. We'll *feel* it. Put your hands on the controls with me. It'll shake in your hand before we stall."

The airspeed fell to ninety . . . still flying. I waited to feel that shake you get from the end of the line when a fish nibbles at your bait.

We got a single nibble at eighty-five knots.

Fred got excited. "I *feel* it! I do!"

But I needed to get even slower so our rabbit would rip by before he figured out the game and compensated. A slower speed would also give Jack an easier time making those blind turns racing toward us.

Still terrifying, but easier.

Now what's next?

I answered, I have to find that first left turn.

There's nothing you can do about that. Let Jack worry about the turns. Just fly the damned plane.

I figured Jack could find the first turn, but started worrying about the second one. By the time we got that far down the valley, guess upon guess would create error upon error, and that growing cat-fur ball of errors would turn Jack's good guesses into a crapshoot. And where the hell were our fighters? How long could we stay submerged and not hit? What if he had IR? What if . . .

Stop that! Just fly the damned plane.

The control column nibbled a second time.

Fred panicked. "Look out! If we stall, these old instruments'll tumble. We won't know which way's up. We'll spin in!"

I ignored him.

So what's next?

I have to get even slower, but we're almost stalling.

So how can you do that?

The ledgers talked about prop wash! I could try prop wash!

Okay, try that.

"Engineer, set twenty-eight hundred rpm, then max manifold pressure. Now!"

"Yes, sir!" I watched his hand fly forward, set max prop rpms, and then wiggle both throttles up to the firewall.

I slowed . . . eighty knots . . .

No nibbles.

Fred saw the speed coming back and yelled, "What the hell're you doing!"

"Hangin' it on the props. Now shut the fuck up!"

He hollered, "Twenty-eight hundred! The flatter blade angle'll add even more drag. Are you *crazy*! We'll stall for sure!"

I ignored him.

The speed indicated seventy-five knots . . . no nibbles.

I trimmed more and more and the nose rose higher and higher. The nose was so high I felt like an Apollo astronaut on the launchpad.

Seventy knots . . . still flying! Glory hallelujah! Even the old Fairlane would have passed us! The ledgers were right!

Jack announced, "He's too close now for missiles or rockets. He'll switch to hard bombs from here on in."

My stomach's in knots . . . my dad's ulcers again. I unzip a pocket, pop out two Gelusil tablets from their foil pouch, toss them in my mouth, and swallow.

I need a break for the pills to work before I continue. Besides, there's something I need to tell you so the rest of this story makes sense. Otherwise, you might not believe me.

The ledgers theorized about prop wash. The original Candlestick pilots were convinced the glider-shaped, high-lift wing on the old bird might fly as slow as fifty knots in prop wash, but they'd never had the opportunity to flight-test their theory.

We were the test bird.

I knew the basics: Airflow at the wing's leading edge separates into top and bottom airflows that rush to meet each other at the back of the wing—the trailing edge. Because of the shape of our wing—the fat camber of a glider, designed to land gently in European fields and allow troops to survive crash-landing—the air on top of the wing has to race like hell to meet its partner at the trailing edge.

All that top racing creates a low-pressure area people call lift. Lift is a misnomer. Instead, the wing is sucked up into the air like Coke through a straw.

That top sucking occurs at the boundary layer where metal meets airflow. The boundary layer can be a fraction of an inch thick, like on a jet fighter, or a couple *feet* deep, like on our glider.

As I raised the nose to increase the angle of attack against the relative wind, more and more airflow hit the *bottom* of the wing, making it increasingly difficult for it to reach the *top* . . . where all that crucial sucking happens . . . causing the boundary layer to shrink.

When that happened, an eddy of turbulence appeared at the top trailing edge . . . like an undertow at the beach when the water rushes back out to sea. That eddy of air began to destroy our boundary layer, causing the wing to shake . . . not enough sucking going on.

Fred was half right. At 2,800 rpm, the prop face was so flat against the wind, it *did* add drag and destroyed some of that critical sucking.

But, boy, oh, boy . . . what prop wash *also* did was magic. The ledgers theorized that at 2,800 rpm, with the prop tips nearly supersonic, the props would *create their own lift!*

Their theory was that when the wing was about to stall— when that eddy of turbulent water ripping out to ocean destroyed the last of that top sucking— you could use high prop rpms to *slap!* that boundary layer back down where it belonged and fly slower than the designers ever imagined.

Hot damn! Now that's power! Instant lift out of nowhere!

Feeling better now. Thanks for the break. Back to the story . . .

I watched my airspeed pointer slow to fifty knots. No nibbles!

Pure magic.

Jack announced gravely, "He'll be on top of us in ten seconds."

Fred looked aghast.

Jack warned, "In five . . . three . . . bombs away."

Fred stared at the ceiling like Nemo's men. No one said a word while we waited for the bombs to find their mark.

My imagination and fears jerked me outside, looking straight down on us from above. I watched bombs hit both wings. They exploded in flames. Twin fireballs consumed both airfoils. I saw the wing structure poke through like an Erector set. The wings melted; then separated. Then our fuselage settled to the bottom of the ocean of clouds . . . like the *Nautilus*.

"He missed, guys," Jack advised. "He's gone by."

Fred looked relieved.

I asked Jack, "Help me remember. He's probably only got enough gas for one pass, right? He'll have to head home now, don't you think?"

"Unless he's got tip tanks. We won't know he's gone until we hear the all-clear broadcast. If he's got tip tanks, he could circle back and loiter overhead till our guys show up. Remember, if he's got IR, he'll see the heat signature off our exhaust stacks. Either way, it'll be a turkey shoot."

Fred was speechless. He opened his mouth to say something, but nothing came out.

Jack continued, "I can't keep us clear of these walls forever. We'll eventually have to pop back up to get our bearings. So even if he doesn't have IR, if he has tip tanks, all he has to do is outwait us. We wouldn't last ten seconds up there."

Arizona Pete warned again, "Bandit! Bandit! Bandit . . ."

"Jack, where's that one?"

"Stand by . . . have it in a sec. Got it! That puts him twenty miles south. Valley wall dead ahead in twenty seconds . . . stand by to turn left fifty degrees . . . new heading one two five."

Fear rippled across Fred's face. He hollered, "We can't turn! She'll stall! And the rudder's no good below sixty knots. You've boxed us into a goddamned corner."

Jack announced, "Fifteen seconds to the turn, JT."

What's next?

I have to turn.

"Ten seconds, JT."

How could you do that?

Fishtail like Wiley that first night.

And how could you do that?

I forgot . . . the jets are running! I could use asymmetrical thrust!

"Five . . . four . . . three . . ."

Go for it.

Jack bellowed, "Turn! *Now!* New heading one two five."

I reached below the main throttles, felt for the right-jet

electric switch, toggled it to max, we fishtailed left, and then I idled the jet.

I checked our new heading: smack-dab, dead-on 125 degrees.

It worked! My confidence soared. We were gonna make it, after all!

Fred looked amazed. "Where'd you learn *that*?"

"Later." I waved a hand in the air to shut him up.

Arizona Pete warned us again, "Bandit! . . . dit! . . . Bandit!"

Jack barked, "I'm on it!"

I wondered aloud, "That doesn't make sense, Jack . . . it sounds like he's hovering at the same position as their last warning."

"It *is* the same, JT."

"But he'd have to be a helicopter, not a MiG."

"JT, it makes all the sense in the world. He made a one-eighty. He must have tip tanks, after all. He's headed right back at us."

CHAPTER *SIXTEEN*

Jack warned, "He'll be back on top of us in forty seconds."
I thought, Trap!

He'd changed the game.

My stomach turned to concrete.

I realized the MiG had been herding us as if he were a cattle dog, scaring us down that valley cattle chute toward an awaiting guillotine.

I'd flown us right into his trap.

We were stuck in an energy-deficit corner, having wrenched every ounce of performance out of the aircraft.

What was left?

Then I recalled reading somewhere, "When your opponent has you backed into a corner, when he's pummeling you to death, when things seem hopeless and your back is to the wall, when you're about to take your dying breath . . . there's only one thing left to do . . .

". . . CHARGE!"

So I charged right at him.

I slammed the nose down to level. The speed crept up . . .

80 . . . 100. I yelled, "Engineer, gimme max power on both jets . . . now!"

I watched the speed creep up . . . 120 . . . 140 . . . 150 . . . and stop at 180 . . . the max.

Fred screamed, "Have you lost your mind! What the hell're you doing?"

I answered solemnly, "Changing the game. Jack . . . new speed . . . no other choice . . . how long?"

"Gotcha covered . . . compensating . . . stand by."

Fred yelled, "But that solid granite wall's less than two miles ahead. You saw it yourself. That's—"

Jack filled in, "Thirty seconds. Stand by for that hard right turn in twenty."

I flew on.

My mind leapfrogged ahead. Surviving the turn in this soup was a crapshoot. But if I popped up to see it, he'd pick us off. Even if we survived the blind turn and his bombs missed, what then? Our wingtips might be ready to scrape granite. But which one? Turn left? Right? How much longer could we stay submerged before . . . ?

Stop that! Just fly the damned plane.

Jack announced, "Ten seconds. We'll meet him right at the corner."

Fred exclaimed, "I get it! It's the old squeeze play!"

I flashed him the thumbs-up signal.

"Bandit! Bandit! Bandit! . . ."

Jack squeezed into the cockpit past the engineer, staring at his stopwatch. "He's directly overhead! Hard right *now!* New heading two two zero."

I slammed in full right rudder, toggled the right jet to idle, kept the left at max, jerked us over the right wing, and yanked back with both hands.

My spinning heading indicator was unreadable.

Jack yelled, "Roll out, or we'll overshoot!"

I rolled out, idled the left jet, and checked the new heading.

Dead-on: 220 degrees.

Hoohah!

Then we heard, "This is Moonbeam on guard with a relay

from Arizona Pete . . . All clear . . . all clear   terminate Bandit alert . . . I say again . . . all clear."

I yanked back and ordered, "Engineer, max power . . . both jets!"

Like a Polynesian pearl diver who'd stayed under too long, I madly kicked for the surface. Lungs bursting for a blessed gulp of air, I paddled upward, praying for the sky to reappear. I needed air, air, air!

We kept going up . . . up . . . the altimeter spinning . . . up . . . up . . . where the hell was that moon?

Then we popped out . . . smack-dab in the middle of the moonlit valley.

Fred looked astonished and collapsed back into his seat.

It was a miracle. I still don't understand it these many months later. Jack was perfect. It was as if he'd been able to see through the clouds.

I turned and asked him in wonder, "How'd you do that?"

He laughed. "Made it up, JT. Trade secret . . . tell you later."

The rest of the crew celebrated. Cries of "Yahoo! *All right, JT!*" and "Major Ward! Shit-hot!" and "Candlesticks rule! That'll teach 'em not to mess with us!" filled the interphone.

I remained quiet.

They didn't know how close they'd come to meeting the grim reaper.

We had only a half hour left in the mission, but I decided we'd had enough for one night. No sense tugging on Superman's cape. Anyways, I was anxious to find out how Jack had pulled off that navigation miracle.

So rather than *asking* Moonbeam's permission to return to base, I *told* them.

They answered, "Approved," but I'd have left whatever their answer.

I told the engineer to shut down the jets and I headed us back to NKP.

My eyes watered until I couldn't read my instruments. I told Fred to fly and felt him wiggle the wings to acknowledge. I turned away and stared out my window at the passing moonlit ridgelines.

Fred asked, "You okay?"

"Something in my eye," I reassured him.

I suppose at this point someone could rightfully ask why it ended so quickly.

And I suppose my answer is this: I don't think I'll ever understand why that MiG went home when he did. Not trusting Jack, I'd soon have popped up to get our bearings. Picking us off at that point would have been easy money. Maybe he was short on fuel. Maybe he'd dropped all his bombs, missed both times, and they exploded harmlessly in the valley. Maybe our hide-in-the-clouds strategy worked and he lost us in the clouds.

Maybe it was a terrifying game of cat and mouse and he just wanted to sink his claws into our minds. Maybe he only meant to scare the bejeebers out of us in payback for Wiley taunting them the month before. Maybe he knew if he took out a defenseless aircraft, the injustice would urge our B-52 friends to turn Vinh into dust. Maybe it simply wasn't our turn. Jack thinks we might have been saved because I have other things left to do.

Maybe, maybe, maybe. I just don't know.

Oh . . . and those fighters we asked for?

They never showed.

Crossing the Mekong, we spotted Candle 25 cruising out to replace us. I warned the pilot, urged him to verify the attack with Moonbeam, call the command post for permission to cancel his mission and turn around before the same thing happened to him.

The pilot answered sarcastically, "Yeah, *right,* JT. A MiG. Like that could happen."

I assured the disembodied voice that our encounter was real, but it answered, "We'll go check it out ourselves."

Come to think of it now, the voice sounded like Rich.

Anyways, I couldn't wait to get to the quiet bar and celebrate with Jack.

I'd done it all . . . everything. I was going to buy nonstop San Miguel pitchers and smoke one of Jack's Luckies to mark the occasion. After all, I'd finally turned into Wiley. We were going to have a great time.

"Flares away!"

I check my watch: 11:24. Thirty-six minutes to go.

CHAPTER *SEVENTEEN*

I'm tired of holding my chute up against the bulkhead. I lean forward, but the straps cut into my shoulders again. I roll my shoulders to relieve the burning sensation, but the pain persists.

Feeling jumpy. I try staying quiet, but can't sit still . . . not like me . . . can't put my finger on what's wrong.

Odd.

I get that creepy feeling again now of being *watched*. Measured. Sized up. Studied like a lab mouse. Lately I get the feeling walking down the street when you *know* someone is following. Women listen to this feeling more acutely. Walk behind a pretty woman down a busy city street to admire her beauty, she'll turn and glare: "Back off!" Somehow, she *knew*.

Try it sometime. It's real.

I've an urge to whip around and glare, but know again no one will be there.

Stupid feeling. Still, it's *there*.

Now the watched feeling blends with the dark cargo compartment and the dark sky and the darkness in our hearts and feels as if it belongs. I hold the back of my hand up to my face and spread the fingers . . .

Rock steady. Good. I'm fine . . . must all be in my head.

I turn around and peer into the cockpit to check on Charles and Rich. No problem there, either.

I pry the top off our spigotted water jug and let the top dangle from its chain. I pick off two of the last three Dixie cups from the stack, dip each cup into the icy water, and fill them to the brim. Then I step up in the cockpit doorway and offer them to Charles and Rich. I pass the cups behind their backs so we don't spill water on the radios.

I tell them, "Save those cups. We're out."

They drain them and pass them back. Nothing else is said. I didn't have to ask if they were thirsty; we're *always* thirsty. I refill each cup and pass them back up. Then I take the last cup for myself and shove the lid back onto the jug.

Now I lean forward across the throttle quadrant and lightly rest two fingertips on the prop levers; then the throttles. I close my eyes, trying to pick up hidden vibrations. I listen for a surging prop that indicates a failing prop governor, or a coughing cylinder . . .

Nothing. Everything's fine. Except my unease.

Puzzling.

I step back down onto the back porch, set my *J* cup on Charles's table, hop backward onto his chair, and buckle in. I hit the recline lever and rest my chute's dead weight against the chair back to relieve my burning shoulders.

Still uncomfortable. We're *supposed* to wear the chute tight at all times, but I loosen the vise-grip chest strap and take my first unconstrained deep breath in hours.

Whew!

Now I want to get you back to that quiet-bar celebration with Jack after we avoided that MiG . . .

I got there first. The place was packed. I found two open stools halfway down the bar, sat down, and put my flight cap on the only other to save it for Jack. I ordered a pitcher of

San Miguel and put three dollars on the bar. The bartender brought back an overflowing plastic pitcher with two frosty mugs and took one dollar. I told him, "Keep 'em coming."

Jack appeared in the doorway, waiting for his eyes to adjust to the dark. I waved. He walked over, sat down, and drained half his mug. He looked disappointed.

I hesitantly asked, "So what'd you think?"

"You're still *thinking*."

I defended myself. "Of course I was thinking. What'd you expect?"

He frowned. "You still don't get it. You've got to stop thinking and start *feeling*."

I snapped, "I don't have a clue what you're talking about."

Jack sighed. "No one talks about the delay between recognizing what you *see*, *thinking* what to do, and finally *doing something*. But that delay is deadly, and tonight you and that delay put the whole crew at risk."

I hung my head. My best work and *still* he wasn't satisfied?

Jack nudged the conversation along. "Would you like me to tell you about it?"

Reluctantly, I nodded yes. I took out a pen and grabbed a handful of napkins.

Jack asked, "What're you doing?"

"Making notes for the ledgers."

He smiled. "JT, you made mistakes that could have gotten us killed. First, you ignored the first two bandit advisories. I went right to work plotting after the first call. If you'd started to find a solution right then and there or called for fighter assistance, maybe we wouldn't have gotten in such a jam. But you squandered that time. Then when you finally realized the warning *was* for us, you froze."

"I didn't—"

"Don't bullshit me. You froze," he said sharply.

I admitted, "Yeah."

"It's okay to be frightened. I was scared, too. But you need to learn to put your fears on a shelf and still function."

I said nothing.

"And if I hadn't pointed out that valley, we wouldn't be sitting here."

I admitted, "Yeah."

"Then when we discovered that undercast, you *thought* about the situation. You wasted precious seconds *talking* about it. Then when I gave you the only answer, you *hesitated*. Then you squandered more time arguing with Fred to get his concurrence you never needed in the first place."

I scribbled and grabbed another napkin.

"Then you wasted more time scanning your memory for an applicable rule, more time convincing yourself to break it, then went through the mental anguish of deciding to break it. You *knew* what the answer was, but wanted someone else to shoulder the responsibility . . . me."

I kept writing, hoping Jack wouldn't notice my embarrassment.

He slugged down half a mug. "You waited for me to shove you from behind, but I may not be there for you next time. You'll have some FNG nav. Nobody talks about time as a scarce resource, but you squandered it tonight."

I started another napkin and saw him smile.

"You're *reacting*. You're not *feeling*. You've got to move seamlessly from the problem to doing the right thing intuitively without all that talking and thinking. You're not moving with the horse. You're worrying about what the horse *did* or is *going* to do. That leaves you going *down* while the horse of reality is moving *up,* so you're always out of sync. The military molds you pilots into rigid thinkers, but you've got to break out of that mold."

I felt depressed, but kept writing.

"And on top of that, you didn't trust me—"

"No. I trusted—"

"Don't bullshit me and don't BS yourself, either. I *saw* the look you gave me. If you're going to make it through this year, JT, you'll have to trust other people . . . you okay? You look shell-shocked."

I answered wearily, "I'm disappointed in myself. I thought I got it right this time, but you're right. It wasn't until you came up and whispered that stuff to me that I got the confidence to hide in the clouds."

Jack looked confused. "What are you talking about?"

"Oh, you know . . . that stuff about 'Don't be scared. You can do it. I believe in you' . . . you remember. I thought if you thought I could do it, maybe I could."

"I don't know what you're talking about. I may have been *thinking* those things at my desk, but I didn't have time to come up to the cockpit."

I insisted, "Don't kid me, Jack. I heard you. I recognized your voice."

"I don't know what to tell you. It wasn't me."

I was dumbfounded. I'd *heard* him. But knowing we'd go round and round the same loop, I consulted my notes and let it go. "You were saying I was scared, reacting rather than feeling, and didn't trust you."

Jack patted me on the back. "I was scared, too, but you can't let fear affect your performance. Put your fears on a shelf. Cultivate mental quietness while chaos surrounds you, or you won't be able to function and you'll be no good to me. It's mental quietness that lets you do each thing right in its natural sequence, rather than *forcing* things."

I took a deep breath and didn't say anything. I'd never heard anyone talk about flying in those terms. All the things they'd taught at flight school were technical issues like hydraulic pumps, electrical fires, and prop limitations. I was back in flying first grade. But I had to fly again the next night . . . unprepared.

I heard air escaping from the balloon of my newfound self-confidence. *Whoooooooooosh!*

Jack pumped some air back in "It wasn't all bad. That thing about 'hanging it on the props' and those fishtail turns were a good start, but you can be even better. Instead of forcing things, let them come to you. You must be an artist moving instinctively with the clay of reality. These flight rules have you looking at reality through those thick, glass-brick walls of 'future homes' from the 1950s that were the rage; remember those?"

"Sure. There was one in my neighborhood. I think people didn't buy them because you could see inside. Wavy images, but anybody on the street could see you in the bathroom." I laughed.

"Right. Well, the rules the Church has stuffed in your head distort your view of reality like those glass bricks do. But the worst part is, after a while, you forget what reality looks like and assume the wavy images *are* reality. After a while, your thinking becomes as rigid, brittle, and opaque as the glass. You have to smash through your own glass bricks and do some direct seeing."

I took a deep breath and let it out. "Whooh, that's a lot to swallow, Jack. You lost me back there a ways."

"Okay, take Wiley, for example. He *understands*. Maybe he comes by it naturally . . . it doesn't matter. Wiley doesn't see rules. He's not trapped behind someone's glass-brick ideas about reality."

The two men on my left asked the bartender for a dice cup and began playing liars' dice. They took turns shaking the red leather cup, CRASHing it and the dice onto the bar, then the shaker peered under the cup to announce his total, challenging his competitor to reckon if he was lying. The loser would buy the next round.

I leaned toward Jack to hear him over their smashing. "Wiley's making it up in the present—moment by moment, based on direct seeing—and you need to develop that skill. You have to cultivate a craftsmanlike feeling for the work."

CRASH!

I shot the crasher a dirty look and hollered at Jack, *"Please go on."*

"Wiley's a potter working in wet clay on a spinning wheel. He *feels* the work. Nothing is forced. He *guides* the clay, moving with its ever-changing shape, but has no pre-conceived idea what final form the bowl or cup might take . . . no biases that would make the work clumsy. He's making decisions as the clay changes shape through his fingers. Sometimes he closes his eyes so *seeing* the clay doesn't get in his way of *feeling* it. He's comfortable with that sort of 'letting go' . . . a loss, or at least a sharing, of control most pilots can't tolerate."

CRASH!

"I won't kid you, this 'letting go' can be like walking a tightrope over the Grand Canyon blindfolded in a howling thunderstorm without a safety net. But if you can move beyond your fears to that level, unseen beings will rise up to assist you."

CRASH!

I turned to the crasher. "Do you mind! We're trying to have a conversation."

The crasher answered, "Sure. No problem."

I turned back to Jack and asked him to continue.

"You see, by contrast, a guy like Fred tonight would slam the brakes on the spinning clay, rip it off the wheel, grab one of a hundred commercially made molds hanging on the wall, smash the wet blob into the mold with the butt of his hand, crudely knife off any clay that dared squeeze over the edge, toss it overeagerly into a hot kiln, and produce the billionth crazed, ugly ashtray for a mother who doesn't smoke. See the difference?"

I laughed at the image of Fred and the ham-fisted ashtray. "Yes, I see."

Jack smiled and kept going. "If you were to ask Wiley what principles he's following, he couldn't tell you. But before you can come over to where Wiley is, you have to let go of the values they've poisoned your mind with, or you'll never see the right answer even if it's staring you in the face."

CRASH!

That's it! I thought. I turned, grabbed the dice cup, and stuck it between my legs. I told the crasher, "Thanks for your support."

The man looked startled, opened his mouth, but said nothing.

I turned back to Jack, consulted my notes, and reminded him, "You were saying, '. . . even if it's staring me in the face.'"

Jack laughed at something I didn't understand. "The best facts don't stand up and shout, 'Here I am!' It doesn't work that way. You have to develop a capacity for mental quietness, to focus on just one or two key facts and, well . . . just *stare* at them while a thousand others scream, 'Pay attention to us!' That's what Wiley's doing when he doesn't answer you."

The Thai band's guitarist in the main dining room strummed the opening bars of "Yellow River." Jack raised his index finger. "Hold on, I want to hear this."

> *So long, boy, you can take my place*
> *Got my papers, I got my pay*
> *So pack my bags and I'll be on my way*
> *. . . To Yellow Liver*

I motioned the bartender we needed another pitcher while we listened to the chorus. Jack blew smoke rings that blended with the music.

> *Yellow Liver, Yellow Liver*
> *Is in my blood, it's the place I love*
> *Got no time for explanations, got no time to lose*
> *Tomorrow night you'll find me sleeping underneath*
> *   the moon*
> *. . . At Yellow Liver*

As the band played, I sat and thought. After a while, I admitted, "I have a long way to go, Jack. I thought I did a good job tonight, but now I realize I just made another ugly ashtray."

Jack put an arm around my shoulders. "It wasn't that bad. Don't worry; we'll get you there. You're just a product of the system. The Church has taught you everything except how to handle a new situation, but we're working on that. We'll call you a work in progress."

I was having such a rockin' good time, I didn't want it to end. I felt we'd never again reach the same depth of honesty, so to keep him talking, I said, "Jack, this stuff's terrific . . . you got anything else?"

He blew concentric smoke rings, studied them, and finally answered, "Here's one that's helped me. Imagine walking in your bedroom to make love with Sharon wearing a medieval suit of armor. Imagine how clunky, hot, cumbersome, and uncomfortable the act of love would become. You'd lose all feel for the activity, plus it'd scare the hell out of her."

I got an image of the armor's visor falling down with a huge CLANK! as I staggered into the bedroom, seeing Sharon's reaction through the narrow slits as she backed away. "I see what you mean."

"Right! The Church of the Air Force has your mind shackled inside a mental suit of armor, preventing you from touching reality directly."

There it was again. I finally asked, "What's this 'Church of the Air Force'?"

Jack's image looked troubled. "It's dark stuff. We've had a good talk and I don't want to spoil it. Maybe another time."

I shifted tactics. "Just one more thing. I've been wondering . . . how'd you get us through that valley? You weren't looking at your maps. How'd . . ."

He smiled. "An old navigator trick. Our maps aren't reliable enough for the type of detailed navigation I needed, so I got rid of them. They were just glass bricks."

"But how'd you wind us through the valley? It was like you could see through the clouds."

"Memory, JT . . . memory. Other nights I'd flown down that same route segment and didn't spot any trucks, I spent time looking into the adjacent valleys in case we ever needed the information. You always need a plan B . . . an escape plan. I've spent months memorizing those nearby valleys. It's an old navigator trick they don't teach anymore. The map was in my head."

I was mesmerized. "Well, thank God for old navigators. It sounds like you've been working on these ideas a long time."

"About twenty years," he answered seriously.

I felt we'd crossed some boundary in our relationship, so I pushed the envelope. "What's this stuff about the Church of the Air Force?"

Men on both sides stopped drinking. Jack saw them eavesdropping. I thought their invasion of our privacy might stop him. But with an "Oh, well, what the hell" look, he started. "I'll tell you about the Church if you'll promise to do me one favor."

"What?"

"Where was that red die? I didn't see you using it."

I answered sheepishly, "In my pocket."

"It won't do you any good in there," he said sternly. "You won't remember it. You've got to promise me to put it where you can *see* it. Put it on the console below the engine instruments to catch their light as a constant reminder of what we've talked about."

"I promise . . . but I have to go back out there tomorrow night . . . I'll never remember all this stuff . . . what the hell am I supposed to do in the meantime?"

He thought seriously. "Fake it . . . just fake it. Pretend you already have the skills . . . let them come to you. Don't force anything."

His answer left me more confused. "I don't get it. What's the bottom line?"

"The bottom line . . . you can look a thousand years and not find one rule that stands the test of time. Today's commandments are tomorrow's folly. Look everywhere, but you won't find one single lasting rule. And every time 'they' make up a rule, part of reality quietly dies in the process, but no one notices. Who's to say what reality is? Maybe our images in the mirror are reality staring at us thinking we're *their* reflection. How would you prove otherwise?"

I scrunched my face. "Cut to the chase, Jack. What the hell am I supposed to do *tomorrow night*?"

He took a long drag on his Lucky, held the smoke in his lungs, then slowly exhaled these smoky words: "Be the

rocks in the stream to the bubbling clear water of reality . . .
let it wash over you."

Ty's voice booms in my headset. "Pilot, Engineer!"
   Damn! Just when I was getting to the good part.

CHAPTER *EIGHTEEN*

What!" I snap back at Ty for interrupting.

My friend sounds concerned. "Moonbeam's called you *three times,* sir. They sound pissed. You okay, JT?"

I reassure him, "I'm fine, Ty. Sorry about snapping your head off . . . thanks . . . I'll call them back."

I sit up in Charles's chair and switch his comm box over to UHF 2. "Moonbeam, Candle 23. Go ahead . . . sorry . . . I was busy."

"Candle 23, Moonbeam. We just got word your replacement, Candle 25, finally got airborne after that maintenance delay. It's worse than we thought. He says he's going 'straight out' . . . got his jets going full bore . . . but won't be on scene until two zero . . . maybe two five minutes after midnight. We know you're scheduled to RTB on the hour, but could you hang in there fuel-wise until he gets on station? We checked the NKP weather . . . they're forecasting 'severe clear' all night and the runway is not . . . I repeat . . . *not* fouled. Can you remain on station and flare Tonto until 25 shows up?"

I key the radio. "Stand by."

I switch to interphone. "Okay, guys, here's the way I see it. The airplane's running well. Bingo fuel's six thousand pounds . . . if we can keep 'em leaned out, we should squeeze out an extra fifteen minutes. We could drop a last set of flares about midnight fifteen, head south, and they'll burn till midnight twenty. Tonto might be in the dark for five minutes tops . . . maybe not at all. Anybody see it differently?"

Silence. Not even Rich objects.

"Ramp, Pilot. You guys got enough flares left?"

"We're running short, sir, but we should have enough."

I call Moonbeam back. "Don't worry . . . we won't let the light go out."

"Thanks, guys . . . good job . . . Moonbeam out."

Fatigue runs over me. Hard to know what the problem is . . . not like me to miss radio calls. Still uncomfortable and we still have a long time left. I figure I'd better do something about it, so I reach down and loosen my chute crotch straps.

Only one adjustment left. I take my chest zipper and yank it down below my waist.

Ooooooooh! That's it! Blessed relief from this oven.

I take an ice cube from my *J* cup and rub it over my face, inside my ears, around my neck, along the insides of my forearms, and finally down my bare chest. "Pacing, JT," Jack taught. "Save something for the end. The worst things always happen at the end of a mission."

Sometimes I drop the ice cube down my shorts. Yikes! That'll *really* wake you up!

I look down and see a view that would drive Rich into orbit . . . no boots . . . comfy white cotton socks instead of the military's hot black nylon . . . unzipped leg zippers . . . loose crotch straps . . . regulation gun belt, holster, revolver . . . floppy chest strap . . . bare chest down to my shorts . . . no gloves . . . nearly undressed . . . and the unauthorized *Jim Sehorn* POW bracelet on my right wrist I hide when they "sanitize" us . . . illegal from head to toe.

I love it.

But I want to get back to that Church of the Air Force discussion before another interruption. This is important, so pay attention.

Jack had continued my lesson in the Quiet Bar. "JT, how do you suppose Desktop and the new commander view their jobs?"

I answered, "I guess it's to make sure the mission gets accomplished so we do our part to stop war materials coming down the trail so the rest of the 'tiger nations' don't fall like dominoes."

"No, no, no. Winning this war has *nothing* to do with it," he corrected me. "Everybody knows this war is lost. It's *over*. Maybe there was a time years ago when winning was a possibility, but that time is gone. So you see, Desktop and the commander serve as high priests in the Church of the Air Force. Their primary job is to preserve the sanctity of the Church for the future so there's something left after this war's over. Everything else is subordinate to that goal. They don't give a damn about you, me, trucks, or guys like Tonto."

"Go on."

"Like that of the Catholic Church, Desktop and the other high priests work within a rigorously structured hierarchy with a firm set of traditions, complete with ceremonial robes. Their power comes from—and is vested in—the Church itself. They constitute a religious bureaucracy whose primary goal is self-preservation."

I stared at Jack to see if he was serious and then went back to writing.

"They see Wiley and others like him as barbarians hellbent on attacking their beloved Church to burn it to the ground. They see Wiley as one of those 'long-haired hippie-freak bastards' on the Kent State lawn last May, who those National Guardsmen had 'every right to shoot.' They *know* the only reason Wiley's here is because the draft yanked him off a campus like Kent State, shaved his head, shoved him into a cockpit, and sent him here to make their lives hell and destroy their beloved Church."

"Jack, that's crazy. Wiley's my best friend. He's not like that."

"*I* know that and *you* know that, but the Church priests don't see it that way. And the sad part is that the few guys around like Wiley are the Church's only hope it will survive and prosper into the future. Wiley represents the future; at least I hope so, while the priests represent the past. They're *terrified* of him. Our whole society is changing in fundamental ways, and somebody like Wiley has to be the first to change. But whoever's out front is always going to be in conflict with the status quo—the Church."

I picked up another napkin and scribbled more notes.

"Even their power bases are different. Desktop's power comes from those *above* in the organization. Wiley's power comes from those *around* and *below* him. That's *real* political power, and it's what Desktop and the new commander fear most. People are naturally drawn to Wiley and are gradually shifting over to his approach. The high priests *know* he's out to destroy their Church and are convinced it's their job to destroy him first. But he's beyond their control and it drives them crazy."

Jack went on, "They think Wiley's building up his own power base at the cost of their own. They feel Wiley has some master plan to undermine their authority. But there's no plan. He's just following reality as it changes moment by moment; making it up as he goes. Wiley's just being himself, but the priests see him as evil incarnate. And they're sending him a strong message: 'Comply, or we will destroy you.'"

"Does he know all this?"

"Yes."

"Then why continue?"

"He's decided to do the right thing *in spite* of the punishment he knows is coming. Desktop and the new commander are just more glass bricks he's decided to ignore." Jack paused. "So, JT, you have a choice to make. You can be like Rich and remain in the Church, or join Wiley outside and be attacked for heresy. A lot of guys like Rich decide to remain within the Church. It's easier to get along. But that approach puts Rich at risk in-flight. On the other hand, Wiley is in *direct* contact with reality. He'll probably survive combat, but the priests will destroy him back on the ground. Being Wiley puts your neck on the chopping block down here."

I couldn't think what to say.

After a while I offered, "You make me feel I have enemies on both sides of the river, Jack. Either way I choose, I lose."

Jack drew on his Lucky. "That's about the size of it. But the sad truth is that Wiley is the only Candlestick pilot left who understands. When he leaves, this unit will enter its death throes."

I stared at Jack's ashen face in the mirror. I couldn't think of anything to say.

Finally, I played devil's advocate. "But that means *everybody* else is wrong and Wiley's right? How do you account for that?"

"Organizational brainwashing," Jack explained. "If you repeat a lie enough times, it becomes the truth and thousands of people believe it. Take Hitler. He convinced an entire society that killing thousands of Jews was good. Or McCarthyism . . . the frenzied hunt for Communists hidden in our government. Or the Salem witch trials, where citizens burned their neighbors at the stake. It happens more often than you think."

I was getting a headache. I poured us two more beers to hold the pain at bay. We sipped and said nothing.

Then Jack dropped a bombshell. "I know you and Wiley are friends, but you should know you're being *watched*."

I said, too loud for the quiet, crowded bar, "What do you mean 'watched'? Wiley's my best friend."

"Keep your voice down," Jack whispered. "I thought you knew. You're being *monitored*. Desktop and the others are watching to see which side you'll choose . . . Wiley's, or the Church. You've been seen going into Wiley's trailer on several occasions to listen to 'that music.' They've noted you allow enlisted guys to call you JT instead of Captain Halliday, and they don't like it much. You're getting quite a reputation, and this thing tonight with the MiG won't help. If you know what's good for you, you'll keep quiet about our little adventure."

I blurted, "But Wiley's my best friend. I have a right to choose my own friends."

Jack shook his head. "The Church doesn't see it that way. And being watched isn't unusual. You know they assign ghost riders to monitor the time Ginger Berano and Peggy Eastwoods spend visiting Rod and Rich up here, don't you?"

"What? That's *nuts*. They're spying on Ginger and Peggy! Who?"

"Pilots like you," Jack explained matter-of-factly. "If the women stay *one hour* past their authorized four-day visit, the priests would keep their husbands here an extra six months, because that hour delay would make this a 'spouse-accompanied' assignment. To avoid that, the women leave a whole day early, in case the shuttle breaks."

"Jack, you're scaring me. What the hell's going on?"

"It's simple. The high priests are hell-bent on preserving their *Ozzie and Harriet* and *Father Knows Best* 1950s world. That world is gone forever, but they're fighting to hold on to its remnants. I think they know it's nearly dead, and that's why they're so fanatical about preserving it. It's their *lack* of faith that makes them so vicious. If they had confidence in their own institution, they could afford to ignore Wiley."

I asked, "How do you know who's right?"

"You can't. We'll know ten years from now when we look back. And look at it this way: to the outside observer back home, the Church *must* be right. It has all the money, power, buildings, reports, reward-and-punishment systems, uniforms, the pomp and circumstance . . . the whole organizational shebang. And then there's Wiley alone over in one corner 'doing his thing.'"

"If Wiley's such a big problem, why don't they do something?"

Jack chuckled. "They're afraid to make a move because

he's so popular . . . especially with the enlisted. When the priests do go after him, it'll be a coward's attack . . . in the dead of night when no one's looking."

He went on, "The saddest part is that Wiley represents the future. For a society to change, it must start with one individual. Somebody like Wiley has to be the sacrificial lamb. Any organization is an established pattern of fixed, concrete values, and unless they're changed, they remain the same year after year, decade after decade, until the system becomes decadent and implodes."

"Does Wiley know he's this sacrificial lamb?"

"Sure, but he's decided to take the punishment he knows is coming. And that puts him beyond their control."

I said, "Makes you wonder how Desktop and the new commander became such vile characters."

"They're trapped, too. They're victims as much as Wiley. They *can't* let the squadron degenerate to everyone doing as they please. The results would be chaos. Nothing would get done. And they have no management tools to fix the problem. The Church's primary means of control is the old master-slave model Lincoln obliterated with the Emancipation Proclamation. The final place you'll find that model is here in the military. The priests' message is clear: Comply and we'll ignore you. Think for yourself and we'll destroy you."

My headache came on hard.

Jack surged ahead. "There's one thing wrong with the military master-slave model: it conflicts with the basic American value of *freedom*. Our country is best served by free men and women who think for themselves, but the priests can't allow that. The result would be anarchy."

"What are Wiley's odds of survival?"

"Probably good, short-term. But even Wiley can't hold out forever. It's *wearing* knowing you're the only sane person trapped inside a mental ward."

I suddenly realized Jack wasn't talking about Wiley. He was talking about himself. In my naïveté, I had pushed my friend into a painful conversation. I held up my hand to stop him. I said gently, "Jack . . . you don't have to . . ."

He held a finger to his lips. "Shhhhhh. Yes, I *do*. I've got to get this venom out of my system. Let me finish."

I said nothing.

I looked into his eyes. They were wet.

"After years of beating his head on the Church door, a certain numbness will set in. Wiley'll become increasingly isolated and pretend that he just doesn't see. He'll forget how to move with the wet clay. To protect himself, he'll don a mental suit of armor and be dead inside."

I wanted to put an arm around Jack to offer comfort, but too many people were around. I should have done it anyway. "So what's the bottom line, Jack?" I asked to close the evening.

"The scariest part about being here is we're trapped in a situation where organizational goals and support have collapsed, and all you have to keep going every night is your own spirit . . . that personal connection you have with the guy on the ground your flares keep alive . . . or the knowledge that the truck you blew up is one fewer load of shells that might otherwise blow some faceless eighteen-year-old draftee to smithereens. The push must come from *inside*, JT. The only place you'll find the right answers is within yourself."

I knew we'd never talk this way again, so I asked, "Anything else?"

"Yes," he said ominously. "You'd better learn to be a killer, or you're not gonna last long."

Suddenly I'm slammed around in Charles's chair.

What the hell was *that*?

I bolt upright and look around . . . the engine instruments are fine. Did we take a hit? I see Rich and Charles exchange glances of understanding.

They laugh.

Oh . . . I get it . . . nature's wake-up call . . . prop wash.

We flew through our own prop wash that's been rolling around the drop point from four minutes ago. There's no wind tonight, so the ever-growing ball of clear-air turbulence sat in space, silently awaiting our return.

I relax back in the chair and rub my eyes. I shouldn't have been surprised. Our flares have been falling straight down all night . . . no wind drift. Most nights the scope nav has to apply "Kentucky windage," but not tonight. The valley below has filled with flare smoke and the scene has taken on the eerie look of an Edgar Allan Poe tale . . . maybe "The Telltale Heart."

Creepy feeling.

Feels now like ants crawling underneath my forearms. I scratch at them.

Flash! Crack! Boooom!

That William Shatner feeling hits me again.

CHAPTER NINETEEN

Sometimes lately I get the feeling I'm the William Shatner character in that black-and-white-TV *Twilight Zone* episode. Shatner had a window seat over the left wing of a Boeing 707 on an all-nighter transcon from Idlewild to SFO. The big plane was dodging a line of thunderstorms, rolling through heavy rain and bone-jarring turbulence.

Shatner cinched down his seat belt, punched on his overhead reading light, and picked up his book to move his mind off fears of crashing.

Lightning *flashed!* outside his oval window. Then a *crack!* of thunder. Close! Out of the corner of his eye, Shatner thought he glimpsed something *moving* on the silver, rain-soaked wingtip.

He shook his head and went back to reading . . . just nerves.

He slowly turned and peered out the window to see . . .

Flash! Crack! Booom!

In the lightning strobe, he saw a gremlin . . . *devouring* the wingtip . . . eating the metal! It *stared right back at him*.

Shatner turned to the sleeping little old lady beside him. He shook her awake.

"Ma'am, ma'am! Wake up! There's a green-eyed gremlin *eating* the wing!"

She leaned across his lap. They pressed their faces to the porthole just as . . .

Flash! Crack! Booom!

The drenched wing looked normal. No gremlin. The grandmother shot Shatner an "Asshole!" look and went back to sleep.

He peered outside.

Flash! Flash! Craaack! Booooom!

The gremlin was back! Glowing eyes staring him down! Holy Christ! A quarter of the wing was gone! He had to warn the pilot!

Shatner punched the red flight-attendant call button.

Ding . . . ding . . . ding . . . ding . . . ding . . . ding . . . ding.

An irritated stewardess snarled, "One ring will suffice, *sir*. Others are trying to sleep. Can I help you?"

Sweat poured down his face. "There's a green-eyed gremlin eating the wing! You've got to tell the captain to land. Hurry!"

The flight attendant glared at Shatner, then marched away.

Flash! Crack! Flash!

He yelled, "Miss! We're all gonna die! Please! Tell the captain."

I look outside.

Green, glowing eyes fill the porthole . . . staring back.

The scene then cuts to a woman in a cornfield speaking into a microphone. "Ladies and gentlemen, I'm reporting live from the scene of a 707 crash near Madison, Wisconsin. Investigators are puzzled because there was no emergency call from the pilot. And in a bizarre twist, they are unable to find any trace of the giant plane's left wing."

That's the feeling I've been having . . . the William Shatner feeling. No one sees the monster but me . . . and Wiley. Wiley believes it's there, too, so there's comfort in that. But the whole thing leaves me jumpy. Can't shake it.

Crazy feeling, I know. But still; it's *there*.

Something is going to happen. Something bad is *definitely* going to happen.

It's a matter of time.

That's funny . . . Charles and Rich look as if they were at the end of a sewer pipe and their bodies have fuzzy edges. Neat-looking . . . never seen *that* before.

Now their voices sound tinny . . . as if they were talking through a tin can.

The maps on Charles's desk have turned black-and-white. Odd . . . I thought our maps were color . . . must be some new cheap issue.

Some guys have been kidding me that I'm the last survivor of what they're calling the Bangkok Curse. They laugh, but I can tell they're serious.

I can't ignore the signs. I've been getting strange looks from way across the dining room. Pilots I don't even know point at me warily. I read their lips. "Yep, *he's* the one," they say, nodding seriously. They notice me staring back and jerk away.

I get the impression people are beginning to shy away from me. For the past week, I keep getting assigned doofus copilots like Rich . . . don't get the good ones anymore . . . just the bottom of the barrel . . . maybe I'm misreading the signs . . . I don't know . . . it's subtle.

So, on Wiley's advice, I've stopped telling the Bangkok dinner-party story. Only one problem . . . that leaves it bottled up inside.

Feeling nauseous now. I concentrate on holding it down.

Odd . . . never been airsick before.

CHAPTER *TWENTY*

Charles turns and stares at me bug-eyed. He's saying tin-canny words I can't understand . . . must be my inter-phone connection. I wiggle it around. It's okay.

Feeling woozier.

Now I see those shooting white stars in my eyes . . . not enough oxygen. Let's see . . . at 12,000 feet the partial pressure of oxygen in the lungs is two-thirds of the half-atmosphere at 18,000 feet . . . so that makes . . . what? . . . two-thirds of half is? . . . so that's? . . . oh, for cryin' out loud . . . Halliday, you idiot . . . you're hypoxic.

I realize I can't figure out the simple math problem, so I reach over, grab Charles's oxygen mask lying on his desk, hold it to my face, and take a few deep hits.

Charles still looks concerned, but I flash him a thumbs-up. As I suck on the mask, I try to figure out what happened.

We're like high-altitude mountain climbers who generate extra red blood cells to deliver the rare 12,000-foot oxygen molecules to the bloodstream. When we take a four-day CTO in Bangkok, those extra cells pass out of the body. So the first couple nights back, we're woozy until the body makes more.

But I haven't been to Bangkok in . . . what? . . . two weeks? . . . since Jack Ward's going-away dinner party last month. So red blood cells shouldn't be the problem.

The oxygen takes effect . . . ahhhh . . . better. The shooting white stars disappear. The colors return to Charles's maps, and Charles and Rich aren't fuzzy at the end of that shotgun barrel. The rest of the cockpit slowly rematerializes. The ants on my arms vanish and the wooziness recedes.

I wipe anxious sweat off my forehead.

Charles's non-tin-can voice asks, "You all right? We lost you there awhile."

I take the mask off and press my interphone button. "Thanks. I'm okay . . . just hypoxic."

I take an alcohol swab out of a Handi Wipes pack, swab out his mask, and lay it down on his desk within easy reach.

I watch Charles and Rich return to a heated argument. Good . . . at least they're talking. I have nothing to add, so lean back into the cottony silences of my own thoughts again . . . quiet and meditative . . . whatever comes to mind . . .

I suppose at this point someone could ask, "Why don't you get some counseling? You should see the base shrink."

The answer is, I know what happens, from other guys who sought help. First, the shrink assumes you're faking it to avoid combat. They say he gets this smirk as he makes notes. If the slimy little bastard ever came with us on a hardball mission, that smirk would disappear.

Don't get me wrong. The docs are good guys, but they just watch from the sidelines.

And there's this undercurrent of resentment between us. You see, the docs are required by regulation to fly with us once a month to get insight into our problems.

That's where the resentment starts. The docs can pick any flight. After all, they have no specific crew duties. They simply observe, yet collect the same combat pay and $100 tax exemption. Lots of times they'll sleep the whole flight. On top of that, they choose only slow-pitch softball missions, like tonight's. You'll *never* see them volunteering for a mission that expects hundred-mile-an-hour fastballs.

So there's a hole in their knowledge. They can't help us scratch an itch they've never felt.

Second, the shrink writes you a prescription for an extra Bangkok CTO to rest up from battle fatigue. No advice on dealing with your nightmares; just a slip of paper any commander *must* comply with. The doc wins hands down. Sounds good at first, but our new commander was born angry. And that extra CTO you just shoved down his throat from an external authority *really* pisses him off.

Third, they say the shrink documents the counseling in your permanent medical record in psychobabble mumbo jumbo that makes anyone who reads it suspicious. I can imagine the airline hiring administrator years from now asking politely, "Ooh, this is interesting. Tell me about the time you sought counseling at . . . what? . . . Nak . . . Phan . . . am?" And I'll explain, "Well, it was like battle fatigue, but we were all a little nuts. But I'm okay now."

"Thank you for your interest in our airline . . . *Next!*"

And fourth, while you're off partying in Bangkok, your buddies have to fly *your* missions. We don't have extra pilots, so your friends have to pick up the slack and work on their day off. They dodge shells with *your* name on them. They're just as frightened as you, but they didn't pull the emergency stop cord on the subway train of their own nightmares.

So when you get back from that extra CTO, the big freeze-out begins. They maneuver chairs at the dinner table so there's no room for you. Try sharing a log at the movie and everyone moves away. That leaves you no one to share your fears with. And your commander's still pissed for shoving "that psychobabble bullshit" up his ass, so he makes sure you fly only the worst hardball missions when you get back. Night after night.

And last, that extra CTO telegraphs your shrink visit.

Enlisted crewmembers begin questioning your abilities.

Just when you need them to comply unhesitatingly, they might give you a no-confidence vote.

So nobody visits the shrink.

Nobody.

Only another crewmember can scratch your itch. Wiley is my shrink. And the music. That wonderful, mind-numbing music! And those *lyrics*!

Karen Carpenter understands . . . somehow . . .

> *Talkin' to myself and feelin'. . . old*
> *Sometimes I'd like to quit*
> *Nothin' ever seems to fit*
> *Hangin' around, nothin' to do but frown*
> *Rainy days and Mondays always get me down*

Wiley is my best friend. To hell with who's watching.

I can't afford a stereo system, so Wiley lets me hang out in his trailer. We'll listen to his tapes for hours. Before I moved into my own trailer half, the visits let me escape Crazy Mark and the Dungeon. Now the visits are a way of life. We talk about what's going to happen when we get home, if we have a prayer of becoming airline pilots . . . stuff like that.

And sip beer. Never drunk . . . just enough to keep a buzz on.

Our shrink is Dr. San Miguel.

But music is the centerpiece. We'll spend hours, headphones blasting at full volume, singing along with his pirated tapes. Karen has it right . . .

> *What I've got they used to call the blues*
> *Nothin' is really wrong*
> *Feelin' like I don't belong*
> *Walkin' around*
> *Some kind of lonely clown*
> *Rainy days and Mondays . . .*

Choosing Wiley's path over the Church's wasn't that difficult. I never got along with military people growing up in

Arlington, so remaining outside the Church seemed natural.

I figure, what else can they do to me? They've already taken me away from Sharon, housed me in that hot-box dungeon, screwed up my pay so we're about to lose the house, and sent me out dodging flak most nights.

I've decided to get out of the military at the first opportunity, so I figure I'm bulletproof. The priests can't touch me as long as I fly my missions.

Remember when I got off the shuttle that first day and I thought Wiley looked older? Remember that?

Shaving this evening, I saw Wiley's face staring back.

Yesterday a baby-faced FNG called me "Sir."

I asked him how old he thought I am.

He guessed thirty-five.

I'm only twenty-five.

When I told the kid, "Please call me JT," his voice snapped to attention: "Yes, *sir,* JT."

I'm not sure Sharon will recognize me at R & R in Hawaii next spring . . . or if she'll even like this new person . . . no . . . *killer* . . . I've become.

Remember when Wiley offered to escort me to the base exchange trailer my first time? And his Vincent Price smile that said, "You'll be next . . . you can't stop it."

And I thought, "Stop *what?* I won't be *next. I* won't read can labels for entertainment." And I thought *he* was nuts? Remember that?

Now I'm a food-label fanatic. Campbell's vegetarian vegetable soup is my favorite. But I like beanie-weenies and Vienna-sausages cans, too.

Can labels are an undiscovered art form. You can lose yourself in the colors.

Wiley escorted me for my first BX visit. He made me close my eyes before we went in. He cautioned me, "No peeking, or you'll regret it."

I felt silly walking in with Wiley steering me from behind, but I thought I would humor him. Other patrons must have been gawking and giggling.

Wiley guided me to one corner and said, "Okay, open." He restricted my viewing to a single shelf. "Pick one section and *spend time looking*. Don't glance. *Look*. The more you look, the more you see."

When my eyes drifted down to the toiletries shelf, he grabbed my shoulders, made me close my eyes, and shoved me out the door. "That's enough for your first time. Save something for tomorrow and the day after that and the day after that . . . trust me."

Now I can go unchaperoned. I don't shut my eyes, but charge past items I haven't yet seen.

It's been six months.

Jack was wrong on one thing about Wiley. My friend *does* have a hidden agenda.

Wiley chuckles, "Remember those wood, black-and-white doggy pull-toys we had as kids? You pulled one around and it would go, 'Arf! Arf! Arf! Arf!'" He laughed. "The priests are my personal pull-toys. I pull their chains and watch them: 'Arf! Arf! Arf!'"

When we have to attend one of Desktop's stupid mandatory briefings about how we're not killing enough trucks, we'll explain, "Sir, if you look at the historical record, the kill rate normally falls off in the monsoon season. We can't see the trail because of the carpet of rain clouds and the trucks bog down in the washed-out dirt roads."

When he berates us with yet another "You've got to do better. You're making me look bad at higher headquarters," all I hear is "Arf! Arf! Arf! Arf!"

To an outside observer, Wiley might seem an arrogant jerk. But there's something serious going on below the surface of his shenanigans.

He explained it this way: "Desktop and the other priests have forgotten their proper role in American society. They've become a law unto themselves. They have a complete disdain for the people. They've forgotten they serve the people and that includes you and me. But it's worse than that. They think the American people *are* the enemy. They've forgotten the framers of the Constitution put civilian authority over the military because they were afraid of the very arrogance the priests exhibit daily. You following me, JT?"

I told him yes.

My friend continued, "They've forgotten that civil disobedience, free speech, and the right of assembly to demonstrate against government policies are constitutional basics they swore an oath to uphold. They feel those kids gunned down at Kent State 'got what they deserved.' It's disgusting.

"Our country was founded on the citizen-soldier concept in which farmers laid down their plows and picked up their guns . . . normal people serving their country in time of war, but then returning to the land. As civilians, you and I will always outrank the priests, but they've forgotten those grade-school lessons. Desktop works for *us,* not the other way around. Don't get me wrong. I'm no protester. I'll serve out my minimum time honorably, but then I want to go back to my plow. But while I'm here, I'm gonna give these clowns a basic civics lesson."

I told Wiley I agreed with him.

I added, "My grandfather came over on the boat from Ireland's County Cork in 1903 to escape the great potato famine. Thousands were dying from starvation. The trip lasted eight weeks with hordes crammed together in unsanitary conditions. My grandfather told me when they steamed into New York harbor, the first thing he saw was the Statue of Liberty—'the Lady,' he called her out of respect.

"He talked about seeing her torch of freedom held high as she beckoned the world to give her 'your tired, your poor, your huddled masses,' and how he broke down in tears. He walked down that gangplank onto Ellis Island with nothing but the clothes on his back and the hopes for a better life. He took a job carrying a brick hod.

"My grandfather later worked two jobs: theater doorman

and Long Island Rail Road conductor," I continued. "They lived in a three-room walk-up in Astoria near La Guardia Airport. The apartment 'doors' were see-through sheets . . . one living room and two bedrooms for seven people . . . a single bath by the front door. He raised five sons, all of whom went to college and are successful family men. When I was six, I asked him, 'Grandfather, aren't you bitter? Your life has been so hard. Things are so much better now.'

"Wiley," I explained, "my grandfather kneeled down, smiled, cradled my small shoulders, looked me straight in the eye, and said proudly in his beautiful Irish brogue, 'Aye and begorra . . . Johnny, me boy . . . I *bless* the day I came to this country. When I got off that boat, I got down on my hands and knees and *kissed* the ground. I *bless* the day.'"

His words still water my eyes.

Unlike my grandfather, Desktop and the other priests have forgotten what it is to be American. They consider their exalted status to be their *birthright*. They've forgotten it's a *privilege* earned for them by thousands of immigrants like my grandfather.

Except for the Hawk . . . he hasn't forgotten.

And I think that's why he pees on the curtains.

That's something I never understood before now. Those immigrants were the *true* Americans. Those ragtag people stumbling down those gangplanks were more American their first day here than the priests will ever be.

There. I'm glad I got that off my chest. I've been debating this whole flight whether to include these hokey issues, but there they are . . . out in the open for anybody to laugh at if they want. And now that I've said it, I think it was absolutely necessary.

Sorry, I got off on another tangent there.

Now I want to get back to telling you about Wiley . . .

There's this second small trailer beside the BX devoted to Japanese stereo equipment. I'll hang out there with Wiley to

avoid being left out. I'll lie to the salesman, "Just shop-
ping . . . waiting till that new system comes out."

I'm too embarrassed to let guys know I can't afford a
sound system. I'll even stand in line outside the stereo trailer
for hours for first chance to buy the latest tapes, then
"change my mind" . . . another charade. I'm broke.

Wiley and I flew the dawn patrol last week—the mission
that comes back at sunrise. After landing we made a beeline
for the stereo trailer.

Rumor was the brand-new Sony reverb unit would be
available. Wiley desperately wanted one. Although the store
didn't open for two more hours, the line circled the block.
People had spent all night in line.

Wiley and I took a place at the end.

Lots of guys didn't intend to buy one. They just wanted to
see the reverb, touch it, read about it, hear it, talk with the
salesman, and leave it right there on the shelf. On their way
out empty-handed, people in line yelled, "Did you see it?"

They proudly hollered back, "Yep, I saw it. It's *awesome*!"

Wiley and I finally made our way inside about noon. Wiley grabbed one. Then we stood in line to pay for it. When
no one was looking, Wiley slipped me the cash so it would
appear *I* was buying the unit. Then he let me carry that fabulous reverb out into the sunlight.

Guys still in line pointed at me and shouted, "Look! *He*
got one! Lucky dog!"

Wiley and I walked off to his trailer, me proudly showing
off that reverb as if it were mine. My feet never touched the
pavement. It was an act of kindness I will never forget.

How such compassion and that nitroglycerin violence I
saw that first night can coexist in one person is something I
will never comprehend.

Whenever someone gets shot down, word spreads like wild-
fire about the upcoming rescue attempt. Along with the
whole base, Wiley and I race to the flightline auditorium. We
eavesdrop live on overhead speakers as the A-1 Sandys and
Jolly Green Giants attempt a pickup.

The Sandys swoop in at treetop level and hose down the area so the Jolly Greens don't need to be rescued themselves. One chopper is the "low bird" to attempt the pickup, while the second Super-Jolly "high bird" hovers overhead, ready to dive in and rescue the low bird if it's shot down. It's serious business.

The packed auditorium is expectantly silent. The chaplain quietly slips in by a side door and hides behind a screen.

Sometimes it all works. Sometimes the Jollys report, "We got him!" Then the auditorium explodes in celebration. People jump up and down and hug each other.

Sometimes it doesn't work. *Lots of times* it doesn't work.

Wiley and I have listened to that solemn radio call too many times.

"Jolly 32, Sandy 08. Might as well pull off . . . a bunch of bad guys grabbed him and hauled him off into the jungle. He's a goner."

If the bad guys capture them in the Steel Tiger, there's hope they might survive. Months go by with no contact while family members back home wonder whether their husband or father is dead or alive. If they're lucky, a year later, a single-page, chicken-scratched letter arrives from the "Hanoi Hilton."

Then someone makes a POW bracelet bearing the name so we don't forget.

I look at my wrist and jiggle my *Jim Sehorn* bracelet so *I* don't forget.

If a plane gets shot down during the day up here over the Barrel Roll and they're not picked up immediately? They never make it to the Hilton. They never last the day.

And at *night*? Forget it. The Air Force has no night-rescue capability.

Guys downed at night in the Steel Tiger sometimes evade till morning and get picked up.

Guys shot down after dark up here in the Barrel Roll? They never see first light.

Never.

When we lose one, our auditorium vigil turns into a memorial service. Remember back to my first day, how I was shocked the veterans grieved so quickly? That's how it happens.

The chaplain emerges from behind his screen to begin the memorial. He moves about the congregation, consoling crewmembers, who bawl like babies. The few women stationed here sprinkle themselves through the crowd, cradle their arms around those most shaken, and rock them back and forth.

Wiley and I stay just long enough to pay our respects and hear the chaplain recite the Twenty-third Psalm. But after a while, we slip out to conduct our own memorial at Wiley's sanctuary.

Our hymn of choice should be obvious.

Wiley cranks his speakers up to a thousand dBs. His trailer floor, door, walls, and window shake. My chest reverbs. My eardrums ache from the MIND-NUMBING BLAST. Wiley hands me my microphone. We shut our eyes, rock back on our heels, and howl along with Marmalade:

> *All my cryings; all my cryings*
> *Feel I'm dying, dying*
> *Take me back . . . to my own home . . .*

Over and over . . . hours and hours . . . until our voices give out and we fall asleep propped up against the wall.

On my six-month physical last week, the doc noticed a dramatic hearing loss. He cautioned me, "I know they're uncomfortable, but wear earplugs under your headset . . . that prop noise is making you deaf."

I lied that I would. But the doc was wrong. The props aren't the problem.

It's Wiley's body-shaking, mind-numbing, jackhammering, eardrum-blasting, kick-ass music.

I don't care about my hearing loss. Let 'er come. I have no intention of stopping . . . until Wiley leaves in three days.

◆ ◆ ◆

I don't know how I'll cope after he's gone. His trailer is my only sanctuary. Jack already went home, so I'll be alone.

> *Lean on me, when you're not strong*
> *And I'll be your friend*
> *I'll help you . . . carry . . . on*
> *For . . . it won't be long*
> *Till I'm gonna need*
> *Somebody to lean on . . .*

When Wiley leaves, I'll be alone. No one to lean on.

No Karen Carpenter . . . no "American Pie" . . . just Church-approved hymns over WNKP on my GE clock radio.

The prospect scares the hell out of me. I know I'm not doing well, but with Jack and Wiley gone, I fear I'll degenerate into Crazy Mark. That's what you get from the Church's nonsupport system . . . human trash no one bothers to bend down and pick up.

When Crazy Mark rotates back home, for the new FNGs, I'll be "Crazy JT." They'll say, "There goes Crazy JT with his plastic rings." Guess I'll have to play with them in private from now on.

Oh, my God! I never realized that before this moment! Wiley must have felt as alone that first day. He'd had his own "Jack" and "Wiley" who had left him solo, too.

That was no chance meeting . . . he *molded me* into his best friend!

That's enough now about Sharon and Jack and Wiley. I've already stepped over the bounds of their privacy, so I'll be quiet about the rest of their lives. They're my wife and friends, not one-dimensional characters in some cheap dime-store novel. They deserve respect. So you'll have to fill in the rest yourself . . . if you want.

But now that I've come to the end of Wiley's story, all I see before me is an empty stream. I find myself thinking about nothing at all . . . daydreaming . . . freewheeling . . . a car coasting down a hill with the transmission in neutral. Maybe all the memories are gone and I have reached the end.

Nice feeling.

As I stare down into the stream, the rocks reappear.

They were there the whole time. I just didn't see them.

I reach into the water and pick up the *Jim Sehorn* Bracelet and Sanitized stones. I keep getting sidetracked, forgetting to cover these smaller issues, yet they're important in their own right. So I'll cover them next.

Charles's voice yells, "What do you think about *that,* JT?"

Dammit! I'll never get this story finished!

CHAPTER *TWENTY-ONE*

I snap, "What do I think about *what,* Charles? I was refiguring our fuel reserves . . . wasn't listening." A lie to cover my mental excursions.

"Rich and I were arguing about Major Peterson and Jeff Hamilton. We wanted your opinion."

"Sure. Go ahead."

"You heard the news about Peterson?"

"No. What?"

"You know him . . . the pudgy navigator who looks like Tim Conway, the comedian . . . keeps to himself . . . not the spitting image of a killer, if you know what I mean."

I shake my head. Neither are you, Charles.

I answer, "Sure, I've flown with him . . . looks like a shoe salesman."

Charles laughs. "Yeah, but he's our best scope. You didn't *hear*?"

"Hear what?"

"Well, you know he's been over here two years—"

I blurt out, "Two years! Can they make us stay that long?"

"No, no, no. They can only *make* you stay three hundred and sixty-five days. But Peterson loves this job; so back a year ago, he volunteered to extend six months. The squadron jumped at the chance to keep their best nav. Well, his wife back home threw a fit. She threatened to leave him, but he convinced her our work was of national importance and that the time would go by quick. So he stayed on. Then at the eighteen-month point, without even telling his wife, he extended a *second* six months," Charles says sadly. "Nobody could believe it. His wife left him, but he stayed here anyway. And the new commander? Didn't give a damn."

"Growler?" I asked. "Why didn't he send him home if there were family problems?"

"And lose his best scope? Have his truck kill rate drop off? No way, José. But here's the kicker . . . Peterson just tried extending for a *third* six months!"

"What do you mean 'tried'?"

"The Pentagon intervened and yanked him home."

"Why would a middle-aged, overweight major who's not promotable ruin his life like that?" I wondered.

"I don't know . . . maybe hooked on the adrenaline rush."

"How did he come up?"

"I'm surprised you didn't hear," Charles says mournfully. "He finally left a couple days ago and was arrested down in Bangkok by U.S. Military Customs. He was trying to board the 707 Freedom Bird smuggling a *live* North Vietnamese AK-47 machine gun."

"*What!*" I exclaim. "What'd they do to him?"

"He even had live ammo, JT. The cops might have given him a break if the damned thing had been 'rodded out'; you know . . . barrel filled with lead. But it was the real McCoy . . . ready for action."

"Charles, that doesn't make sense. He had to know the MPs and search dogs go through everything with a fine-tooth comb."

"I know, I know. Normal procedure would be to send him back up here for Growler to deal with . . . but he's disappeared without a trace."

I ask, "What'll they do to him?"

"Because he's a senior officer, prob'ly make an example out of him. Prob'ly prosecute him to the full extent under the Uniform Code of Military Justice. He could do hard time at Leavenworth . . . forfeit his rank, pay, retirement . . . everything."

Rich spits, "Serves him right. He knew the rules."

Charles looks shocked at Rich's coldheartedness.

I feel my face flush red . . . my grandfather's Irish temper. I count to ten to cool off the way Dad taught . . . one thousand one, one thousand two . . .

Charles stammers, "Rich, don't . . . don't you . . . isn't there room for seeing Peterson as a *victim*? Don't you think after getting shot at for two years, maybe he'd lost his way and made one simple, human mistake that deserves a little kindness and understanding? Couldn't they have confiscated the weapon, turned their heads, walked away, and said it never—"

Rich cuts off our senior officer, "Nope! He knew the rules. He'll have to pay the consequences like anybody."

. . . one thousand six . . .

Charles shakes his head sadly and is quiet.

At least I *knew* I was wrong to interrupt my senior officer. Rich didn't give it a second thought. That's one of the differences between us. He treats conversations like a switchblade street fight.

No one says anything.

Pissed.

. . . one thousand ten . . . deep breath . . . better now.

I try to smooth things over. "How'd he get nicknamed Growler? 'Moray' fits better. He has that angry scowl of those green eels on those nature shows, hiding in his office—appearing only to rip a bite out of an unsuspecting diver, then slithering back into his hole."

They both laugh.

The tension cleared, Charles continues, "JT, did you see what happened last night at the Candlestick hooch?"

"No. I was over at Wiley's."

"You know Jeff, the pilot your age with that poker habit? I mean, he plays every night all night long."

I answer yes.

"Last night the stakes got out of control. By sunup, Jeff'd lost his entire month's paycheck."

"The whole thing! How's he gonna live? He's got a wife and kids back home. What's he think they're gonna eat? Dirt? How's he expect to pay the mortgage!"

"I saw him still sitting at the poker table this afternoon, shuffling those cards over and over; looking for someone . . . anyone . . . to start a game . . . must have sat there on that hard, metal folding chair since sunup, shuffling those cards. Looking to win it back, I guess."

Silence.

After a while Rich says, "Serves him right. He knew the rules. Nobody stuck a gun to his head."

I scowl at Rich. Charles looks disgusted, turns away, and stares out my left window.

After a while he turns back and pleads, "Rich, you don't think the organization bears *any responsibility*? They rip these guys from their families and send them half a world away. They get shot at most nights, listen to their friends dying over those auditorium speakers, exist on nothing but worn-out movies, beer, and poker . . . they bear *no responsibility* for people they're *supposed* to be leading? What the hell's wrong with you?"

"Nope," Rich says emphatically. "Jeff knew the rules when he sat down to play."

Charles tries again. "You don't think Growler had a responsibility to send Peterson home after his first extension, or see that Hamilton got to the shrink? For crying out loud, Eastwood, the man obviously has a gambling addiction. I see them as *victims*. Isn't there room for that point of view?"

"Nope," Rich answers sternly. "They made their own beds. They'll have to lie in them. And it's Eastwood*s* with an *s*, not Eastwood."

I glare at Rich. I think to myself, I hope you meet *your* limits someday and have them shoved down your self-righteous throat. I just hope I'm there to watch.

Charles asks, "JT, what's your opinion?"

"I can't give you an unbiased answer."

"Why not?"

"Sharon's mom has been in the hospital back in Rockford, Illinois, the past three months. I asked Growler for emergency leave so I could accompany Sharon to Rockford for a final good-bye. Without that emergency-leave statement, Sharon isn't eligible for a military discount fare to fly there alone. But we don't have money for a full fare because my pay's so screwed up. My paperwork came back with a big black *X* scrawled in the 'Disapproved' box, because I'm not a blood relative."

Charles sounds furious. "That's inhuman! You should be back in Rockford right now. Growler could put your November and December CTOs together . . . you'd be back before anybody blinked. You should make an appointment with Growler to appeal . . . I'll go in with you if you want."

I explain, "Thanks, but I already tried that. When I went in, Growler was sitting at ramrod attention with the leave regulation spread open on his desk. He quoted page and paragraph: 'The rules allow emergency leave only for blood relatives—father, mother, brother. Not in-laws. Request denied.' Then he slammed the reg shut. I pleaded I was as close to Sharon's mom as to my own, but he said his hands were tied and that I was dismissed."

Charles explodes. "Bullshit! He can do anything he goddamned well pleases! Commanders make exceptions . . . that's his fucking job. You should ask the Red Cross to help."

"Sharon and I both did. But it's a catch-22: they said they can't help unless Growler approves an emergency leave, or we have a death certificate. The Red Cross said that when her mom dies, they'll get me the leave and I can fly home, get Sharon the discount, and we'll attend the memorial."

Silence.

Sharon will never forgive me.

I should be there.

Rich doesn't say a word. He'd better not, or I'll dive for his throat.

Off in the distance I hear the bird of prey *screeech* a victory cry.

No matter how many times they knock you down, what do you do?

I whisper to myself, "Get back up."

Now I try to find some intellectual middle ground to keep the crew from falling apart.

"Charles, I didn't answer your question. It seems to me we all have small, preexisting personality fissures. Back home, they're held together by wives, kids, PTA, softball leagues, Scouts, Lions clubs, weekends, friends, family, doctors, in-laws, mowing the lawn, paying the bills, bathing the dog, football games, making dinner, taking out the trash, getting the car down to the shop . . . the day-to-day glue of normal living you take for granted. These fissures, these weaknesses in all of us, lie dormant for years and never become a problem because the support system keeps them glued together. There isn't *time* to weird out."

I see Charles nod, so I go on. "That's why Rich and Rod are still stateside normal . . . Ginger and Peggy are the glue keeping their fissures from cracking wide open. And you, Charles? Staying in your trailer insulates you. People may think you're aloof, but it's a great way to cope. On top of that, you *know* what the future holds. You *know* you're going back to Castle AFB and your house in Merced. For most of us, life after NKP is a crapshoot. And Peterson? He lost his way; and no one offered him a helping hand to find his way back. Growler should have sent him home after his first extension; but when he approved the second . . . well . . . the die was cast."

Charles nods.

Rich says nothing.

Thinking, maybe . . . I hope.

"Drop flare, drop flare, drop flare."

"Flares away!"

Rich rolls a snake eyes, Charles turns left, grabs a couple handfuls of nose-up trim, adds two inches manifold pressure, and the Big Dipper slides across his window over to Rich's, then disappears.

There's still one hanging issue, so I bring it up now. "Did you guys hear what they did to Wiley's stateside assignment?"

Charles answers, "He's only got a couple days left, doesn't he? Too bad, this place won't be the same without him. He's the best. I mean, you're a close second, JT, but Wiley's the best. Wasn't he forecast to go to one of those new C-5 units at Travis?"

Rich looks shocked at Charles's high regard for Wiley.

"Yep. That C-5 assignment was critical. With heavy-jet time on his résumé, he'd be snapped up by any airline. But somehow it got changed at the last minute," I tell them. "Wiley got hammered. I didn't think there was a place worse than NKP, but they found one . . . Reese Air Force Base out at Lubbock, Texas."

When the priests go after him, it'll be a coward's attack . . . in the dead of night when no one's looking.

Charles looks startled. "The West Texas desert? What a screw job! Somebody had it in for him."

"Charles, it's worse than that. They added insult to injury by assigning him in the slow T-37 teaching brand-new students, even though Reese has openings in the supersonic T-38. When it's time to apply to the airlines, Wiley won't be competitive, so this assignment cost him an airline career. If they'll nail *Wiley,* what chance do the rest of us have?"

The last-minute switch has Growler's grubby fingers all over it.

I catch Rich smirking.

Now that I've dropped that conversation killer, I grab Charles's notepad and scribble shorthand notes for the ledgers . . .

♦ ♦ ♦

Next I want to get back to those Sanitized and *Jim Sehorn* rocks. Time's running out . . . still have to tell you about the My Helicopter, Bangkok Curse, and Four Little Indians boulders before we head home . . . but it seems the more I remember, the less I understand.

> *But I knew I was out of luck*
> *The day . . . the muuusic . . . died*
> *Singin' this'll be the day that I die . . .*

CHAPTER *TWENTY-TWO*

Remember that first night with Wiley, Jack Ward, and Charles and the Intell officer with the belligerent attitude? On his way out he told us, "Stay put because someone will be along to sanitize you." Remember that?

I didn't know what to expect. I couldn't imagine how they were going to sanitize an entire *human being*. I felt apprehensive. I didn't know if they were going to spray us for those finger-chomping Laotian insects, or some hideous fungus no one had mentioned.

It was the same that first night as every night since . . .

A bulldog-type Intelligence sergeant stormed into the briefing room and barked, "Okay, listen up! I'm only gonna say this once. I'm here to sanitize you guys. Now, I know you've heard it all before, but these are mandatory briefing items before every flight, so listen up. Okay, here's your standard, one-each, green drawstring bag for your personal items. Take off all identifying items you may have on your person."

Falsetto aggressiveness, I thought, as Bulldog snapped

away. The man seemed driven to fulfill some false image of bravado that exists only in old John Wayne movies.

Courage isn't like that. Real courage doesn't bark. Real courage is quiet, like Wiley that first night dodging all that flak. Remember that? Remember he didn't say much?

That's courage.

Bulldog snarled away, "To remind you, that means your name tags, wings, rank, squadron patch, American flag patch, and your hats. The bad guys could tell you zeros"—he laughed alone for the hundredth time at his organizationally sanctioned slander—"sorry . . . could tell you *officers* from the enlisted by your flight caps' silver braid and you'd be singled out for extra torture because the bad guys'll think they can rip more valuable information out of you. Take off any wedding rings, leave behind your wallet, any family photos; anything identifying you with the United States Air Force or NKP, stuff it in the little green bag and give it to me. I'll give you the standard wooden chit to reclaim your personal items. And Captain Halliday"—he glared at me—"I'm warning you the last time: lose that POW bracelet you insist on wearing. It's illegal, so get rid of it . . . now. I'll be watching."

His insults and lies continued, "To remind you why you're going out sanitized is, we don't want the enemy to be able to identify who you are when you're captured, track down your families, and make threatening phone calls during your years of beatings and solitary confinement. So for your own protection, put all your stuff in the green bag and I'll lock it up in this cabinet. And, *remember*—I'll be *watching,* so don't hold anything back."

Horsepocky.

When I first got sanitized, I thought: boy, this is the *real thing* . . . like the beginning of that TV show *Mission: Impossible*. I thought I'd graduated to the Big Time, involved in top-secret government spy missions. Gawd, was I naïve.

That makes for good television, but it's different when it's *real* and happening to *you*. Now I find the process humiliating.

I didn't understand what was happening until my best friend, Norm Komich, came here on temporary duty from Vietnam with a Jolly Green helicopter detachment to sit "alert." Until then, I thought *everyone* across Southeast Asia got sanitized. But when Norm volunteered to come out and fly a Candlestick mission with me, the process surprised him. He told me in his beautiful Boston accent, "John, we fly dangerous pickups all over Nam and *never* get sanitized. The requirement's in the regs, but nobody does it in-country, and we could get shot down any day. I'm impressed you guys are so professional."

We aren't "professional." We're suckers.

For a long time, I believed they sanitized us for our own protection. Now I've come to understand it's to give the Nixon administration political cover. Sanitization is about *de-ni-a-bil-i-ty*.

Because we have no identifying marks, the Pentagon could tell reporters, "Gee, we don't know what you're talking about. The Air Force strongly denies having flightcrews in Laos or Cambodia. If anyone *is* there like you *claim*, they must be independent soldiers of fortune. I refer you to President Nixon's official statement from this spring . . ."

When we peel off our Velcro patches, the room fills with ripping sounds of something happening at a much deeper level . . .

Riiiiiiiip . . . goes the 606th Special Operations Squadron patch.

Riiiiiiiip . . . goes my name tag and pilot wings.

Riiiiiiiip . . . goes the American flag . . . into the green bag.

Riiiiiiiip . . . *Riiiiiiiip* . . . go my captain's bars off my shoulders, leaving telltale Velcro squares telegraphing my rank is captain or higher: "Torture this one first."

Riiiiiiiip . . . goes my *Jim Sehorn* POW bracelet.

Riiiiiiiip . . . goes your dignity, self-worth, identity, and existence.

Riiiiiiiip . . . goes any Nixon administration accountability.

Riiiiiiiiip . . . goes any hope of rescue should we be shot down.

Riiiiiiiiip . . . go our lives, all into the little green trash bag.

It's an organizational sleight-of-hand trick . . . we become the amazing, magical disappearing human beings. Now you see them, now you don't! Poof and they're gone! Right before your eyes! PFM—pure fucking magic.

The pieces fell into place with the rest of Bulldog's briefing. "The only thing you're allowed on your person, gentlemen, is your blood chit," as he held up a sample of the foot-square silk displaying the American flag printed with a request for assistance in Laotian, Burmese, Cambodian, Vietnamese, and Chinese. "Use this as a last resort to obtain assistance from the indigenous populace. The blood chit is old as World War Two and has assisted many to be repatriated. You are *not*—I repeat *not*—a military crewmember. You are a downed airman seeking assistance under the accords of the Geneva Convention."

I think the bad guys never even heard of Geneva, Switzerland, much less give a damn about any "accords." The downed-airman strategy is about more *de-ni-a-bil-i-ty*.

Bulldog's voice hardened into a monotone. "Your blood chit tells anyone, 'This is a downed airman. If you help him to return home, you will be richly rewarded.' Give it to anyone who appears friendly and may help return you to U.S. control."

I wonder, how are we supposed to tell the good guys from the bad guys?

"Now remember, the silk's expensive and therefore an accountable item . . . you'll have to sign for it on this here hand receipt and return it directly to me *if*"—he chuckled and corrected himself—"I mean, *when* you come back. Being pure silk, that crap cost the government a ton of dough. These chits are *not* your personal souvenirs. That loss is not going to happen on my watch, so don't get caught stealing . . . it's a court-martial offense. Do I make myself clear?"

We just wanted out of there.

"Oh, I forgot to brief one new required item," Bulldog snarled. "Remind your wives *not* to believe rumors of your death or capture unless a flag-bearing, uniformed officer presents himself at her door. That's it. Any questions?"

Now I look down and finger the silver links of my *Jim Sehorn* POW bracelet.

I smile; there goes another rule.

I palmed it again. The purchase is the second luxury I've afforded myself. They say the money goes directly to POW families.

Jim has survived the past four years in solitary confinement at the Hanoi Hilton suffering daily beatings, eating bug-infested rice. His six-by-six-foot, windowless cell features a concrete bed complete with iron brackets to strap him down. No toilet. No chair. He squats in his own urine, listening to the screams of other prisoners being tortured while he awaits his turn. Like most, he's skin and bones . . . eating *anything* to stay alive . . . maggots and all.

Jim's bracelet reminds me to consider the risks when I'm about to make a critical decision. When I jiggle the silver links against my wrist, they remind me what's at stake. We'd all be dead before my buddy Norm got his chopper up here at first light tomorrow morning . . . staked out on display like Thunder 58.

I won't fly without Jim's bracelet or Jack's red die.

I know it may seem as if I'm jumping all over the place, but later I'll show you how the pieces slide together . . . they do, I promise. This process is like . . . well . . . throwing a brick through a plate-glass window, filming the mess, and then playing the film in reverse. The shattered glass will reconfigure into a coherent whole as we go along; I swear. So please, stay with me.

I suppose what I should cover next is the My Helicopter boulder. Hold on; this is a big one, but I think I like it best. This memory is so fresh.

Jack Ward and I spent months going over the ledgers, but that night was the first opportunity I had to put it all together. We were a hundred miles north of here, searching for convoys . . .

CHAPTER *TWENTY-THREE*

"Pilot, Scope! There he is again! I've got him in sight! He's in the *same spot* as last night and the night before. He's got those two powerful searchlights blazing out front again. For cryin' out loud! The *nerve* of this guy! He's thumbing his nose at us, knowing we can't do a damned thing. You got to come down and see this, JT."

I answered eagerly, "Be right down."

I told my copilot and nav to fly a racetrack pattern and bring us around for another pass. I unhooked my lap belt, unplugged my interphone cord, scrambled down the back-porch steps, hit the metal cargo floor, and knelt down on the mattress beside the scope's prone body. Without a cue, the engineer and the right scanner appeared on both sides and hooked my chute harness onto the overhead cable system so I wouldn't fall outside two miles straight down.

The scope's shadowy image waved me forward. "Come on! Come on! Hurry up, or you'll miss him!"

I knelt down on all fours, crawled forward until I was over the gaping hole, then belly flopped down. Oooof! The extra bullets I've "liberated" one by one and keep in my chest pockets hit my ribs like metal fists, knocking the wind out of me.

The pain was worth it. I figure our six-bullet ration for which they make us sign yet another hand receipt won't do the job in a ground firefight, so I've stashed personal handfuls of extras over the months.

I crawled forward until my head was over the middle of the open hole, but couldn't see anything out the three-foot-square opening.

The *noise*! Holy moly! The howl from level-five hurricane winds two feet below our faces was deafening!

I reached down to key my interphone to talk, but realized in my rush I'd forgotten to plug in . . . dumb . . . no time left . . . we'd have to yell at each other.

The scope noticed my predicament and hollered against my right earcup, "HE'S JUST EAST OF THE CROOK IN THE ROAD. YOU'RE GONNA SEE HIS RED ANTI-COLLISION LIGHTS BLINKING THROUGH HIS ROTOR BLADES. HE'S STILL GOT HIS SEARCH BEAMS ON, TOO. THEY LOOK LIKE GIANT ICE-CREAM CONES. YOU'RE GONNA SEE THE OUTLINE OF HIS INSECT-LIKE FUSELAGE . . . NOTHING LIKE IT IN U.S. INVENTORY. REMEMBER . . . KEEP BOTH EYES *OPEN*. FOCUS ONLY WITH YOUR RIGHT EYE . . . IGNORE THE LEFT."

I nodded and lined the scope up with my right eye.

I yelled, "WHERE IS HE?"

"USE IT LIKE A TELESCOPE . . . HE'S RIGHT AFTER THE S-TURN . . . LOOK FOR THE RED FLASH . . . HE'S NOT IN VIEW LONG, SO LOOK QUICK BEFORE HE PASSES BY THE BACK OF THE HOLE!"

I hollered, "UNDERSTAND!"

My eyeballs turned to sand from the gale-force wind blasting up through the gaping hole.

Focusing the starlight scope is not as easy as it might sound. It's like trying to focus a telescope at Mars out the window of a car that's screaming down a bumpy country road at night at 130 miles per hour.

Then I saw him. I first saw his flashing red beacon with my dried-out, naked left eye. I yelled, "GOT HIM!"

The nerve! *Taunting* us! He knew we knew he was there, and he knew we knew he knew we couldn't do a damned thing about it. He knew we didn't have offensive weapons. And he was too small a fleeting target to call in fighters armed with hard bombs. He'd flit away from any such attack like an escapist mosquito on a summer's evening.

It was infuriating and an insult to boot. He could do whatever he damn well pleased. All we could do was watch. What was he up to night after night?

As my right eye focused through the scope, I saw his praying-mantis shape. His powerful search beams did look like giant ice-cream cones fanning out from his mantis head. Farther back was the thick upper thorax of the cockpit that narrowed to almost nothing in the middle, but then his fuselage broadened into a thick thorax at the tail . . . *two* huge rotating blades—one out front and one in back.

He was *huge*!

Then the mantis-chopper passed by the back of the hole and slipped out of sight.

I shifted the instrument back over to the scope and then made the mistake of looking *two miles* straight down through the gaping hole. My pupils had opened wide to capture what little moonlight existed, and that's when it happened . . . again.

YIKES!

A Jimmy Stewart–Alfred Hitchcock–*Vertigo*, an elevator-falling-out-of-control, queasy, telescoping-away, clammy-skin, sick-to-your-stomach, tumbling-to-the-center-of-the-earth feeling consumed me. The ground two miles below rocketed away as if I were strapped to the side of a Saturn rocket blasting off the launchpad. The scene tumbled and defocused simultaneously. In my imagination, I saw myself sucked outside; smashing against the bottom of the fuselage, buffeted by 130-knot winds. Would my restraint

harness hold? Could the guys pull me back in fast enough?
How long before the cable snapped? What if my chute didn't
open? How long before SPLAT!?

A minute? Thirty seconds?

Less.

I bolted to my hands and knees and scrambled backward.

The scope turned around, looking concerned. He cupped
his hands and megaphoned, "YOU OKAY, JT?"

I made up a lame excuse he didn't believe and flashed
him a thumbs-up. I couldn't let the truth out. You have to understand . . . I'm afraid of heights. I have acrophobia.

I know, I know, I know. You're probably saying, "You're a
pilot with a fear of heights? How can you fly a plane and
how'd you ever graduate from pilot training in the first
place?"

You have to understand, as long as I'm in my seat in control, I can look outside . . . no problem. It's when I look
straight down from high altitude . . . *WHOOOSH!*

I didn't even know I had acrophobia until *after* I'd graduated from pilot training. I did barrel rolls, loops, and high-
speed dives all day long as a student and never got a hint I
was carrying this internal time bomb. I didn't lie . . . the issue simply never came up.

I learned of my affliction when Sharon and I were honey-
mooning after pilot training. We were visiting Yellowstone
National Park's grand canyon. We marched up to the canyon
edge, to its knee-high guardrail good only for tripping over,
and I looked *straight down*.

I didn't see it coming . . . the sensation hit me like a
freight train . . . telescoping, dizzy, queasy, tumbling vertigo
accompanied by cold sweats and hyperventilating.

I sank to my knees and crawled backward from the edge.
Sharon smiled and teased, "And you just graduated from pilot training? Good thing they didn't see *that*."

I'd been hoping I'd outgrown my fear. One of my pilot-
training classmates threw up in his oxygen mask every flight
every day. He and his instructor pilot got used to it. He'd get
sick, his instructor would take the controls, and this guy

would detach his mask, barf into a plastic bag, zip it up, put his mask back on, and tell his IP, "Let's go."

He barfed every day he flew for fifty-one weeks. The supervisors warned him he'd have to quit throwing up to graduate.

Then one week before graduation, it stopped. He'd outlasted his fear.

I had hoped the same thing would happen for me. When I crawled forward to that scope hole, acrophobia was the furthest thing from my mind. It hadn't happened in what . . . three years? Since Yellowstone with Sharon. I thought it was in my past, or a onetime deal.

I was wrong. It was still *here*.

Two guys helped me up to my feet on wobbly legs. I stumbled up the back porch and plopped down into the left seat . . . badly shaken. The twin chest bruises from belly-landing on my liberated bullets didn't help.

We completed the mission, but my bewildered copilot did the rest of the flying and made the landing back at NKP.

"We saw the mantis again, Harvard," I told my Intell debriefing friend at NKP after I'd recovered. "Did you do that research I asked for?"

"Sure did," he answered proudly. "I went into our archives of photos and silhouettes of enemy choppers. Let's see if you recognize any."

I've developed a deep respect for Harvard. He even likes the nickname I gave him. He graduated with honors from the Cambridge institution and, like me, was about to be drafted and wind up toting an M16 through a rice paddy. So, also like me, he joined the Air Force, but as an enlisted man. When I asked him why he didn't become an officer and go to pilot training since he was qualified, he explained he just wanted to do his duty, get out of the military, and get on with his life. Somewhere along the line, someone actually recognized his intelligence and assigned him to . . . guess what? . . . Intelligence! *Quelle* surprise!

It's just so rare the Church puts a round person in a round hole.

Harvard began flipping through stacks of black-and-white overhead snaps of enemy choppers . . . it was like looking at mug shots. I kept saying, "No . . . No . . . Nope. Not him. *Yes!* That's *him*! That's the mantis!" My scope nav seated beside me agreed. "That's the one! What is it?"

Harvard flipped the photo over and read the narrative. "This says it's a Russian-built helicopter designed to haul large equipment into major construction sites. Apparently, this is their version of our huge Sikorsky 'sky crane.' Where is that?" He shuffled through more pictures. "There should be one of those . . . oh, here it is." He held up the two images for comparison.

The two helicopters looked similar, except the Russian version looked as if it had come out of that much-used clay mold someone yanked off the wall . . . a butchered copy of the original.

"If you're correct, JT, you've stumbled onto something *really* big. There's no record of the bad guys using large choppers, so this could indicate a major shift in their strategy and capabilities, or maybe some large new construction project. Great job. I'll pass it along up the Intell chain of command to Saigon."

Harvard got up, turned to walk toward the Intell inner sanctum where even *we* weren't allowed. But before he disappeared, I asked, "Are you *sure* it can't be one of ours on some deep-cover mission? Are you *absolutely sure* it's the bad guys? I've heard of black operations that go way beyond what we're doing here."

Harvard looked confused. "Well, I'm *pretty* sure, but I could check it out if you'd like. Why do you ask?"

I asked my scope to let us have a private discussion. After he left, I said seriously, "Because I'm gonna take him down tomorrow night."

Harvard looked stunned.

• • •

If Desktop or Growler got wind of my plan, they'd immediately put the kibosh on it. But I had to trust Harvard with part of my plan to make sure I wasn't going to knock down a friendly helicopter.

We're the same age, from similar East Coast backgrounds, so it's been natural for Harvard and me to analyze the war and the deceit that surrounds us. On top of that, the poor guy works directly under Bulldog, so our talks give him a few moments' relief.

One thing neither of us understands is what happens to our "truck kill" counts. If I report through Harvard to Saigon we *really, honestly* destroyed fifty trucks, the next day's official report credits only *twenty-five*. I mean, we can *see* the burning hulks lined up. There's no mistake. Each truck looks like a house afire. You can see each one with the naked eye. We might be off by two trucks out of a claim of fifty, but we're not off by double.

Saigon's cuts are an insult. They're telling us, "You're lying."

Their belligerent attitude has created a complete breach of trust. To get credit for an honest fifty trucks, we have to claim one hundred. When they cut *that* in half, at least we get credit and Saigon has a better understanding of how many supplies are reaching the South. But there's a problem brewing.

Saigon has started cutting our claims by 75 percent! They evidently caught on to our doubling strategy. They figure we're lying more now than when we were reporting the *truth*.

Do you know what that means? Can you see it?

To compensate, we lie more, then they cut more in a never-ending cycle of mistrust and misinformation so nobody knows *what the hell's going on!*

Soon we'll have to claim destroying every truck on the trail every night in a growing "pyramid scheme." Ask any mathematician . . . the numbers quickly get out of control.

• • •

Maybe now you can understand why Wiley liberated that general's Lincoln. He told me, "I don't know what came over me. That's not like me . . . I snapped. The crooked officiating at that basketball tournament was the last straw atop a haystack of lies. I mean, we're out here every night getting our asses shot off and they're calling us liars? So when I saw that pompous, cheating asshole laughing at me from his barstool . . . I lost it."

Bottom line here?

A gaping hole in the fabric of trust with the Church leadership.

Then again, sometimes Harvard and I think Saigon may be right in deflating our claims.

Just the other night, for example, we directed a stack of fighters in on a 150-truck convoy. Following my instructions, the first jets dropped their bombs in *front* of the lead truck to cut off forward progress. Then we dropped the second bombs behind the *rear* truck to block any retreat. That done, we took a break. We waited . . . even the aggressive fighter pilots.

At first I didn't understand this "pause." But now I do . . . it gives the drivers a chance to run for their lives before we incinerate their trucks.

No one will admit to the "pause." You won't find it in any rulebook . . . except the big one about American values and the sanctity of human life.

We figure our job is to restrict *supplies* coming down the trail. Period. End of report.

We're not here to kill *people*. Those drivers have families, too. And there's sketchy information that some "volunteer" drivers are forced labor. If they don't agree to drive? A gun barrel goes off down their throat.

Saigon would raise holy hell if they found we were giving the drivers time to run for cover; so we don't tell them.

Lies upon lies.

• • •

Anyways, that night we set that 150-truck convoy ablaze; we circled back overhead to conduct bomb damage assessment—BDA. My scope reported, "JT, you're not gonna believe this! We've dropped a couple hundred bombs the past two hours and the lead truck's *still going*. It's incredible! This guy's a Timex watch . . . takes a lickin' and keeps on tickin'. I can see his headlight beams shine *way up* in the sky as he grinds his way up out of one crater and then shorten as he rumbles down into the next."

Can you see what that lone driver represents?

We're gonna lose this war. You can't bomb that level of determination into submission. In fact, the United States has already lost this war; it's just nobody wants to hear the truth. Yet when we try sharing this with the Church, they tell us we don't know what we're talking about

Anyways, that's the kind of stuff Harvard and I mull over, but have no answers for.

Sorry . . . I got off track again . . . . back to my mantis chopper . . .

I'd just told Harvard seriously, "I'm gonna take him down tomorrow night."

My words stopped him in his tracks, his hand on the inner-sanctum doorknob. As he turned, his expression went from stunned to baffled to skeptical in a heartbeat. He walked back to the debriefing table, sat down, and stared at me.

I smiled . . . he was hooked.

My friend folded his arms and looked at me suspiciously. "How could you possibly do that? No offense, JT, but you're just a forward air controller. You don't have offensive weapons. It would take a fighter catching him out in broad daylight to nail his butt, and your mantis would never show himself under those conditions. From what you've told me, he's too cagey. How could you possibly take him down?"

I answered Harvard, "I'm not saying. I haven't told a soul and I don't want to put you on the spot. If anyone asks, you can honestly answer you didn't have a clue. Just do me one favor . . . when I show tonight for the Intell brief, tell me you've checked all the way up the chain of command . . . go all the way to the Pentagon if you have to . . . just make *damned* sure that mantis isn't a CIA operation using captured enemy choppers to mask some deep-cover operation. I don't want to kill any friendlies by mistake."

Harvard stared at me in confusion. He still didn't believe a benign, old C-123 could take out that mantis ten thousand feet below.

CHAPTER *TWENTY-FOUR*

I showed up that night and asked Harvard, "Did you check it out?"

He was excited. "Yes, I verified it with the Pentagon on our scrambler batphone in the back. They swear they don't have friendly helicopters in that location. They confirmed it's a hostile target . . . fair game."

"What'd they say when you warned them I was going to take him out?"

"They thought it was a joke. They think you're nuts. But they said, 'If he can do it, tell him to go ahead.' Then I heard their office staff erupt in laughter in the background. So how *are* you going to do it? I have to tell you, it does seem far-fetched."

"I'll tell you later if it works. But if I knock him down, I want credit for the Candlesticks annotated in the official record. That's all I care about . . . documentation."

As I climbed into the cargo compartment that evening, I saw our rampers securing the two flare pallets. I waved both arms to get their attention over the howling APU and forklift sounds. When the lead ramper finally looked my way, I jerked both palms up. "Did you get 'em?"

He circled his right thumb and forefinger and winked. "Got 'em!"

My weapons aboard, I knew we stood a slim chance of success.

I compartmentalized the information so nothing leaked. I told only my scope nav the entire plan. I only told the rampers about the materials I needed. I left them, the copilot, table nav, engineer, and scanner in the dark.

Even with those precautions, I was apprehensive word might leak.

During preflight, engine start, and taxi-out, I glanced nervously out the cockpit windows, half-expecting security police vehicles to surround us. I imagined Growler jumping out to demand, "What the hell's going on!" And ordering me, "Cease and desist. Gentlemen, arrest this man!"

I must have been roaring down the taxiway, because the control tower joked, "Hey, Candle . . . where's the fire?"

Once airborne, as soon as we got the gear and flaps up and turned north toward the Barrel Roll, I reached across the radio console, detuned our UHF number-two radio from command-post channel 11 preset frequency, and shifted it over to Moonbeam "tactical."

My pip-squeak FNG copilot dutifully reminded me in a high-pitched, Mickey Mouse voice, "Sir . . . sir . . . don't the rules say to monitor the command post in case they recall us?"

"We're not doing that tonight," I told him. "Leave it where it is. I want to listen to Moonbeam's frequency early to see what's going on."

Squeaky nodded apprehensively. A few moments later, I caught his left fingers tiptoeing across the radio console to sneak the radio back to channel 11.

"Didn't you *hear* me? I *said,* 'Leave . . . it . . . alone.' "

When Squeaky jerked his hand back, I knew we'd made a clean getaway.

◆ ◆ ◆

Not long after we arrived over the mantis area, my scope yelled, "Got him! The same goddamned place as last night. The arrogant bastard still has his floodlights on . . . thumbing his nose at us, JT."

"Let's get on with it," I told him.

"You want to come down and see him, JT, before we do it?"

The last thing I needed was another Jimmy Stewart–*Vertigo* episode. I didn't need to stick my head in that buzz saw again. So I answered, "No, thanks. Let's just get to work."

"Right. Damn! He just slipped by the back of the hole. Bring us back around, JT."

I told the table nav to give me directions to circle around for our first bomb run.

"Pilot, Ramp. You guys ready back there? Did you practice like I asked?"

Elated voices answered, "Yes, sir! All set back here!"

I rolled out wings-level on the bomb-run heading.

"Here he comes! Steady . . . maintain heading . . . perfect . . . stand by . . . NOW! Drop chains . . . drop chains . . . drop chains."

"Chains away! All three of 'em!"

I got excited. "Did we get him, Scope?"

"Couldn't tell. He disappeared out the back of the hole before I could see. Remember, it's a small field of view . . . can't keep him in sight long. Bring us back around for BDA and I'll verify. But I don't see how we could've missed . . . we were *right on top* of him."

As I rolled into a left turn to swing back around for a damage assessment flyby, I glanced over at Squeaky. The kid looked flabbergasted. I thought his eyebrows might fly off his face.

I chuckled, seeing in him my own image from months earlier.

"Sir . . . sir . . . what're you doing?" Squeaky stuttered. "We don't have a mission frag for any of this, do we? And

correct me if I'm wrong, but isn't throwing things overboard prohibited without prior Pentagon approval *in writing*? This appears to be a clear violation of Air Force
regulation 60-16."

I answered calmly, "We throw things off the airplane
every night."

Squeaky exclaimed, "But you don't have the authority!"

That was the moment of crystallization . . . the break-
over point . . . the moment I stopped waiting for someone
offstage to give me the signal to go ahead. I should find
Squeaky when we get back tonight and thank him.

"You don't think so?" I growled. "Well, you just *watch*.
You just *watch me*."

"But those chains are accountable items!" Squeaky
protested. "I mean, somebody's going to have a lot of explaining to do. Tie-down chains aren't cheap."

Meaning you'll turn me in to Growler, but don't have the
guts to tell me to my face. Typical stab-your-buddy-in-the-
back Church protocol.

I stared Squeaky down while my Irish temper did a slow
burn. Then I stiff-armed his argument. "Don't you dare
threaten me . . . don't even *think* about going there. You have
no idea what you're talking about. You don't deserve an explanation, but I'm gonna give you one, so you stop squeak-
ing. First off, I have all the authority I need. Second, these
tie-down chains are off the NKP scrap heap. They didn't
cost a goddamned dime. Isn't that right, Ramp?"

"Yes, sir. They've got a huge pile of surplus chains at
the junkyard. They keep sendin' new ones we don't need,
so we keep throwin' the good old ones away . . . no place to
store 'em."

I finished lecturing Squeaky. "Look, kid . . . you're off
the hook. I accept full responsibility for this. If anybody
asks, I'll tell them I continued over your protests. No one's
going to blame you. But now you have to be quiet. We need
to concentrate."

Squeaky looked stunned. I saw him swallow hard and nod.
He'd *better* have.

"Pilot, Scope. We missed! The mantis is still there! I don't see how we could've . . . but . . . there he goes . . . slipped out of view again."

Fake it . . . just fake it. Don't force anything.

I reassured the scope, "Don't worry, I'll bring us around again for another pass. We've got tons of gas and I told the rampers to bring at least twenty-one chains. So we've got six more shots. Take your time. Relax."

"Roger, JT. I'll try to be more accurate . . . somehow. Maybe the wind blew the chains off, but I wouldn't think these heavy chains would blow around much."

As we circled around, I remembered Wiley's limo flying along with the aircraft . . . confused . . . before dropping away . . . maybe.

"Scope, where'd you call that first drop? When we were right on top of him and the second and third chains after that?"

"Yeah . . . directly below."

"Okay, let's try this . . . on this next pass, can you find a spot on the road just *before* he comes into view?"

"Sure."

"This time," I instructed, "throw the first chain out *before* you see him, the second when he first comes in view, and the last overhead. Remember now, these chains are gonna fly along with us at one hundred and thirty knots before falling, so you have to apply some 'Kentucky windage' . . . lead the drop."

He shot back defensively, "Look, nobody's ever done ballistics tests on chain aerodynamics. Nobody's ever tried this before. But maybe you're right . . . I'll lead the next drop. I'm making this up as I go, you know."

I agreed, "Me, too. Just relax and do your best."

The scope announced, "Listen up, guys! Almost there . . ."

"Drop chain . . . drop chain . . . drop chain."

"Chains away!"

"That *must* have done it. We *couldn't* have missed. Bring us around again."

As I circled us around the tight racetrack pattern and waited for the good news, I looked over and saw Squeaky relax back in his seat.

"*Sonofabitch!* He's still there," the scope reported, "lights blazing away! Missed him *again*! Damn! I *knew* we had him that time. I don't get it. There he goes out the back again. Circle around, JT. We'll have to try again."

Don't expect it to go smoothly.

I responded, "Sure. No problem."

"Sirs, I hate to tell you this," the lead ramper interrupted sheepishly, "but we've only got enough chains for one more pass. JT, I know you told me to get twenty-one chains, but I couldn't imagine why you'd need so many. Sorry . . . we've only got . . . let's see here . . . three . . . enough for one more pass. I need the rest to keep our flare pallets tied down."

Damn, I swore under my breath. My Irish temper took over. I thought about saying, "If you people would *just do what I tell you* rather than second-guessing me," but kept my mouth shut.

I knew our antics were too juicy not to leak out once we landed . . . Growler would intervene . . . there would be no second chances. This one last pass was it.

You'd better learn to be a killer, or you're not gonna last long.

I looked over at Squeaky for advice. He scratched his head and shrugged . . . no help.

I let the loadmaster off the hook. "It's okay, Ramp," I said easily. "We'll have to get him on this last pass." As I circled back, I picked up Jack's red die and closed my fist around it.

Don't think. Let it wash over you.

Then it hit me. We'd been doing it wrong!

I asked, "Ramp, how are you tossing the chains overboard? *Horizontally,* or *vertically*?"

"What'd'ya mean?"

"I mean, are you dropping them length-wise, or nose-to-tail?"

"Nose-to-tail. Sir, there's just the two of us back here

wrestling with these tugboat-size babies. They're monsters, so we've been dumping them out *vertically*. They're too long and heavy to drop the other way with only two people. If we could get some help . . ."

"No problem. Nav . . . left and right scanners . . . get back there and help."

"Roger, JT! On our way."

"Pilot, Nav. How're you gonna find him without me?"

"The scope and I'll manage. Right, Scope?"

"Can do!"

I turned to the table nav. "Get your butt back there. Hurry!"

I watched him unbuckle, slide off the director's chair, land on the back porch, turn, and disappear into the darkness.

"Ramp, Pilot. This time, I want the five of you to place the chains in sequence on the ramp edge, pick each up like a giant snake, and give the old heave-ho *horizontally*. Now I don't want anybody falling overboard . . . so make damned sure everyone's safety-strapped onto the floor. Be ready to throw them out in quick succession to blanket a large area. See what we're doing?"

"No, sir."

"We're trying to smack him with a huge flyswatter, but so far we've been trying to hit him with the *edge*. You had to be a perfect shot. This new way, we'll make our flyswatter into a huge, open-faced tennis racket. See what I mean?"

"Yes, sir!"

"Now remember, Scope, lead it . . . last chance."

"Roger."

"Ramp, Pilot. Ready back here."

"Crew from Scope . . . stand by . . . here comes the lead point! Steady . . . steady."

"Drop chain . . . drop chain . . . drop chain," he announced ominously.

"Chains away!"

I held my breath.

"We got him, JT! I don't believe it! It worked!"

Gotcha.

I asked gleefully, "What'd you see? Can you be sure?"

"There's no question. I saw his red beacon go out about the time the chains would've arrived. Then his snow-cone searchlights tilted sideways and lit up the mountainside at a cockeyed angle. Then they flickered off and on; then went out for good. You got him, JT! Way to go! I don't believe it!" The interphone exploded in cheers.

Even Squeaky laughed.

"You *did it*!" Harvard exclaimed. "You took down the mantis?"

"Well, we think so, but we're not sure," I replied.

I told my friend the whole story. He started laughing, then laughed harder as I went along.

"It's unprecedented," he said in amazement when I finished. "Nobody's going to believe this. As far as I know, a cargo plane has never taken down an enemy aircraft. But let me get one thing straight . . . you did this on your own? You didn't get approval or tell anyone before trying out this harebrained scheme?"

"I didn't need permission," I answered firmly. "The Candlestick mission is to pursue 'targets of opportunity.' This is a war; remember? We're *supposed* to kill the other guy. Besides, asking approval would have given the Church an opportunity to say no. Only my scope knew everything. I kept everybody else in the dark."

"Even the loadmasters? They had to get those extra chains. They had to figure something was up."

"I told them only after we got airborne. I didn't want any leaks. I thought if we could show Saigon hard evidence the Candlesticks could take on a new mission, they'd have to pay attention and expand our role. Think of it . . . for the first time, we have a cheap, safe way to take down more choppers . . . which is why I want you to do me a favor. Could you order a reconnaissance flight by one of our RF-4s to document whatever happened? Like I told you, all I care about is documentation."

"JT, if your claim is true, you know what you did? You took out a major enemy weapons system for next to nothing! Talk about bang for the buck. It's incredible! I'll get on this right away."

"Actually, from a cost standpoint, it was free. The chains were surplus scrap."

He laughed harder and shook his head. "JT, they are not going to believe this. I'll order an RF-4 for later this morning so we'll know for sure, one way or the other. I'll have the photos by noon, but they won't be releasable till after five P.M. tonight, so come by and check with me then. I'll get this down in my reports so you get the credit you deserve."

I told him, "I don't need credit. But I want you to pursue it for my crew. I want it in their records at promotion time."

I started to get up to leave when Harvard asked one last question. "How'd you ever think of this? It's so simple, yet beautiful. This is warfare from hundreds of years ago when people stormed castles and the defenders inside tossed hot oil over barricades."

I answered, "I don't know. It was spur-of-the-moment. I made it up."

I tried leaving again, but Harvard pressed, "Look, JT, there's only you and me here. What was this *really* about?"

I pointed to my *Sehorn* ID bracelet and said seriously, "See this? Paybacks are hell."

I felt pumped. I had to share the good news with Jack. I found him—where else?—at the Quiet Bar.

I told him the story.

He blew smoke rings and listened quietly.

When I finished, he patted my back and said, "Congratulations, JT. You've broken through. You *understand*. It will never be the same. You've made it. I'm proud of you. You don't need me any longer . . . you'll get better and better on your own from here. How about that Lucky now? You've earned it."

I answered, "Jack, you were with me in spirit. I'll always need your advice, but I will take that Lucky."

I took a deep drag and held the smoke in my lungs without choking.

Gawd, it was wonderful!

I tossed and turned that whole day, anxious to see the reconnaissance photos. I wasn't on the flying schedule, so just after 5 P.M. I raced over to TUOC. I was out of breath when I stormed into the room and found Harvard sitting at the debrief table.

I drew up a metal folding chair and sat down. I asked anxiously, catching my breath, "Did we get him! Did they give us credit?"

Harvard kept his eyes on the photos he was shuffling and did not look up.

I got a clammy feeling.

I figured I must have destroyed friendly forces. I'd gone off half-cocked and now there'd be serious trouble . . . formal charges . . . loss of rank . . . lose my wings . . . full Church sanctions for killing our own guys . . . I'd screwed up big-time.

I gathered my courage and asked, "What's wrong? Did we get him or not?"

Harvard answered, "You want the good news or the bad news?" but did not look up at me.

My stomach churned. "I'll take the good news first."

"You got him, all right. These photos confirm your kill. Here; see for yourself." He handed me the pictures along with a magnifying glass. "Look at this." He pointed with his gold Cross pen. "You can clearly see the large chopper over on its side like some dead insect. You can see your chain wrapped tightly around his front rotor. There's *no question* . . . you got him. It's an incredible achievement . . . one of a kind.

"But there's more." He flipped over several eight-by-ten, black-and-white glossies. "This one shows where Navy A-4s zipped in this afternoon, pulverized the area to smithereens and then"—he selected another photo—"this shot shows the *whole mountainside* exploding. See this? It looks like an

erupting volcano. When it blew, it covered your mantis under tons of rock . . . there's no trace left. The guy must have
been building or servicing a previously unknown under-
ground weapons storage area . . . that's a whole lot of shells
that won't land on our guys in the South . . . you should feel
real good about this, JT."

I felt proud and relieved, yet confused. "So how can there
be any bad news? If the photo confirms the kill, what's the
problem?"

He kept his eyes on the photos. "Sir, I hate to tell you this,
but they gave your credit to one of our A-l squadrons."

I went ballistic. *"They did WHAT!"* I bolted upright,
sending my metal folding chair careening across the concrete floor. I pounded my fist on the table, BAM!

Harvard flinched, but did not look up at me.

"Why? A 1s don't even carry tie-down chains. How do
they explain *that*? Huh? I *told* you . . . all I cared about was
credit. What the hell's going on, Harvard?"

The man spoke into the debriefing table, "I'm sorry to tell
you this, but Saigon said you're 'just a forward air controller,' and that FACs aren't authorized to take down enemy
planes. They ripped me up one side and down the other and
warned me to remind you you're just a support aircraft. A
couple guys in the Pentagon office were even talking about
bringing you up on formal charges, but I talked them out of
it because we have the pictures to prove what you did. They
backed off, but I had to go to bat for you to keep them from
chopping your head off."

"But *WE DID IT!*"

"I know that and you know that . . . but . . . I'm sorry. I
know how you must feel."

I gripped the table edge with both hands, leaned over
him, and snapped, "No, you don't!"

"Hey! I fought like hell for you."

"And just what do you suggest I tell my crew? What's *really* going on here, Harvard?"

He shook his head. "Sir, I'm so sorry. You can tell them
this: Saigon said the main problem is they don't have a col-

umn in their computer program to assign a kill to a C-123, so they logged it in an A-1 column. It was easier for them. That's why you're not getting credit."

I blew up. "Then reprogram the computer!"

Harvard finally looked up at me. His eyes were red. "Look. I had to fight like hell just to keep them from court-martialing you. I'm on your side. I brought up reprogramming, but they said they wouldn't waste the money."

"Can we appeal?"

"No. I'm sorry. I pleaded, but Saigon said their ruling is final. They said, 'Tell Halliday, "Get over it." ' "

"Can I have a copy so I can prove it to somebody someday?"

"No, sir. This photo is classified top secret NoForn and isn't allowed to leave the building."

I said dejectedly, "But without that, nobody will ever believe me."

"I'm sorry."

I left the building stunned, confused, depressed, and angry.

I heard the bird of prey *screeeeeech!*

I staggered over to Wiley's trailer.

We spent the night getting shit-faced.

I watch Rich roll a six and Charles begins a perfectly coordinated turn.

Our greatest glory is not in never falling, but in rising every time we fall. What did we agree you'd do when they knock you down?

I answer Jack, Get back up.

No matter how many times they knock you down, get back up and keep going.

I look around the airplane . . . everyone is quiet.

My instrument panel clock ahead of Charles's right knee says 11:34 . . . twenty-six minutes to go, then a few minutes waiting for Candle 25 to show up . . .

. . . it's desk cleanup time.

Feeling sleepy now. My mind gets rubbery this late in the

flight. Important information hits and bounces off if I'm not careful.

Maybe if . . . for just a couple secs . . . I recharge my batteries.

I hit the swivel control on Charles's chair and rotate ninety degrees right so I face his desk, then lock the lever down . . . wish I could carry a pillow for times like this, but it wouldn't do much for my image. I cross my arms on Charles's desk into a makeshift pillow and lay my head down . . . rest my eyes . . . nothing left to do but wait for midnight . . .

CHAPTER *TWENTY-FIVE*

I'*m back on the dark beach with no horizon where the sand morphs into black ocean that merges with the velvet Philippine-painting black sky. The pressure and temperature plunge again, as always.*

I turn again to the two-dimensional black silhouette on my right and ask, "Did you feel that?"

He never answers.

The incoming tide I still can't see laps at our feet, warning us to move up the beach before we become part of the ocean.

I hear something come alive in the dark water.

I turn to the left shadow and ask, "Did you hear that?"

He answers, "Hear what?"

I turn back to the right shadow . . . but he's gone.

I search the length of the pitch-black beach, but he's disappeared again without a trace . . . nowhere.

I turn to ask the left shadow where the other went, but he's gone, too . . . obliterated.

I'm alone on the beach . . . again.

The pressure drops and a wall of cold air hits me like every time.

It's coming.

I won't be able to stop it any more this time than all the others.

I hear the animal pant behind me. I sense it without looking.

I slowly turn and confront the familiar golden-eyed timber wolf staring at me, sizing me up for the kill.

I freeze in place as always, paralyzed by fear.

The dark waters of the incoming tide grab my ankles . . . nowhere to run.

The wolf steps forward gingerly, asking once again for approval to come closer.

Now he places both front paws on my flight boot, as is his habit.

He jumps up against my chest and sneezes a plea for help, burying his face in my chest for protection.

I instinctively know what he fears.

We've been through this together too many times.

The wolf looks me in the eye as always and then stares over my shoulder in horror at something large rising in the waters. I don't have to turn and look to know. I can see its evil reflection in the wolf's golden eye . . . the same towering, five-hundred-foot green tidal wave that will consume us once again.

I wake up on Charles's desk . . . that same nightmare again. How long was I out? I try reading my watch, but it's a blur.

I rub both fists into my itchy eyes . . . still can't focus.

I unzip my left-sleeve cigarette pocket and extract my Visine. I unscrew the cap, tilt my head back, force my eyes wide open, brace, take aim, and squeeze . . .

Nothing? Nothing! I shake the bottle . . . empty. Great . . . just fucking great. I toss the empty bottle in our trash bag. What else can go wrong?

I stick my fingers in my *J* cup, tilt my head back, and tinkle ice water into my eyes . . . better.

I refocus on my Worldtimer . . . 11:36. I was only gone *two minutes*?

I'm worried; I've been having that same nightmare these past two weeks.

But, hey. I'll be all right. Dreams are just dreams, after all. I'll be okay . . . nothing to worry about. I'm stronger than that . . . at the top of my game.

I have to stop beating myself up, so I throw the dream into an imaginary steel box, rivet the top shut, toss it into a mental vault, close the heavy door, and throw away the combination . . . good riddance.

But I can still hear its muffled cries.

I should tell you now about the Bangkok dinner party. We're at a jumping-off point for more recent events anyway, and maybe I can use the comforting memory to rid the tsunami nightmare from my mind.

CHAPTER *TWENTY-SIX*

To cheer myself up, I grab two pencils off Charles's desk and drum out:

> *Day after day I'm more confused*
> *And I look for the light through the pouring rain*
> *You know that's a game that I hate to lose*
> *And I'm feeling the strain*
> *Ain't it a shame?*
> *Oh, give me the beat, boys, and free my soul*
> *I want to get lost in your rock and roll*
> *And drift away . . .*

Whew! Better now . . . a little music works magic.

I guess events started taking on a life of their own Halloween night after our Bangkok farewell dinner party for Jack. It was his last CTO. We were losing the oldest brother from our makeshift family. We all knew we'd never see him again.

Jack had only three days left at NKP. He was scheduled

for one final flight . . . primarily to get the traditional cele-
bratory hose-down by the fire truck brigade. The next day,
he'd board the shuttle back down to Bangkok and climb on
that Boeing 707 freedom bird. He'd been reassigned to a
KC-135 tanker outfit in Kansas, where he and his wife
would stay until he retires in eighteen months.

The evening was bittersweet. There were the six of us.
There was Ben, a young Thai gentleman who makes his living as a guide for several military wives. He exchanges dollars for baht, cuts red tape with passport officials . . . even
teaches rudimentary language lessons. And if the women
ever get in trouble, they can call Ben . . . day or night. But
most of all, he's a trusted member of our little family. Ben is
not his real name, of course. His Thai name contains eighteen hieroglyphic characters none of us can read, much less
pronounce, so he lets us call him Ben.

The rest of the guys at the party included the guest of
honor—Jack—me, and Ralph Doby, another forward air
controller, who lives in the trailer across from me. Ralph
flies the same missions we do, but in the tiny Rockwell OV-
10 Bronco.

Ginger Berano . . . you remember her . . . Rod's wife . . .
was our hostess. And the second wife? For the life of me, I
can't remember who she was. I can picture everything about
the evening except her face. Odd . . . it's blanked out like
those TV exposés. Like my dad, I generally have a knack for
remembering names and faces. But hers? A total blank.

Anyways, the six of us started celebrating in the late afternoon at the Beatles film *Help!* The ladies cried during
Lennon's haunting "You've Got to Hide Your Love Away."

After the movie, we went to Ginger and Rod's shoebox-
small apartment. The six of us crowded ourselves around her
tiny, round kitchen table. We were squeezed in shoulder to
shoulder, thigh to thigh, butt to butt, and cheek to cheek . . .
intimate, to say the least.

Ben boiled up a dozen Thai lobsters—more like large
crawdads than real U.S. lobsters—for which we three guys

donated ten dollars apiece, and the six of us whacked our way into them with a vengeance. Drawn butter sloshed everywhere.

I can still picture the six of us sitting around Ginger's dollhouse-size kitchen table with six straws stuck in the bowl of that knock-you-on-your-ass rice wine Ben procured for the occasion. Rice wine comes in brown ceramic bowls large enough to hold a houseplant. Huge! Americans *have to know somebody* to get rice wine. It's a part of Thai culture most Thais hold back from Americans, so we felt honored by Ben's gesture.

The six of us crammed into that tiny, un-air-conditioned room made for a sultry atmosphere. Honks of taxis and diesel-truck fumes from the busy city boulevard seven stories below seeped in through the open windows.

Ben stuck six straws in the rice-wine planter and demonstrated the Thai custom to commemorate a friend's departure—lean forward so all six heads touch to sip *together*. According to their centuries-old custom, no one is permitted to drink alone. If one sips, *all* must sip. And out of the same container? . . . Well, you get the idea . . . like Indian blood brothers.

Ben warned us to drink slowly because the concoction could knock us silly.

We teased him, "Yeah, right."

We finished off the first planter and then Ben produced a *second*. We dove in.

Then we got the giggles . . . *everything* seemed funny.

Ralph told Ginger she looked real sexy with that drop of sweat at the end of her nose she kept wiping off. Everybody froze.

I thought, Uh-oh . . . you crossed the line, buddy. Ginger'll ask us to leave.

I tried to think of something appropriate to smooth things over, but Ginger beat me to it. She tossed her ponytail, batted her baby blues, and gave us her best Scarlett O'Hara impression: "Why, Mr. Rhett Butler, I do declare. You know very well we Southern belles don't sweat. We *glisten*."

We roared with laughter. Ralph looked embarrassed and told Ginger he was sorry.

We polished off the second rice-wine planter and Ben produced a *third*! We moaned, "Oh, no! No more!" and then dove in again, our six foreheads touching.

I lost track of time, but sometime during the third planter the city streets outside the window turned quiet. When we finally drained it, everyone was disappointed our forehead-to-forehead tickling session was over.

Then Ben produced a *fourth*. Everybody jumped in gleefully and drained that one, too.

We reminisced into the predawn hours. We told Jack how much we would miss him. We told white lies about seeing each other back in the States. The sun started coming up. None of us wanted the occasion to end. Something special was dying that none of us had the power to stop, and we wanted to hold on to whatever it was as long as possible.

Ginger and the other woman whose face I can't recall cried and hugged Jack good-bye at the door. Jack was standing right there, but pieces of him were disappearing before our eyes.

When us four guys got on the elevator, the two teary-eyed ladies rushed the closing doors and reached fingers through to touch Jack one last time.

I got misty-eyed, too.

Ben poured the three of us into a Thai taxi with no seat belts, slammed the doors, paid the driver the Thai rate so the driver wouldn't charge the American fare, and told him to deliver us to the Chao Phia military hotel across town. I waved to Ben—"See you next month!"—as the cabbie pulled out onto the empty city street.

I rode shotgun.

We all must have fallen asleep, because without warning I was hurled against the dashboard. Tires *SCREECHED* as we skidded out of control toward another taxi COMING RIGHT AT US!

The second taxi loomed larger and larger! He was

RIGHT THERE! *SCREEECH!* We were gonna *HIT!* I braced my feet against the floorboard, locked my arms and elbows against the dash, closed my eyes, and waited for the IMPACT, the busted glass and the injuries. How would we explain being drunk, severely injured, and hospitalized to Growler?

Our taxi skidded out of control and shuddered to a stop . . . *inches* from the other cab . . . in the middle of an empty, predawn intersection.

I looked in the back to check on Jack and Ralph.

They were picking themselves off the floor. They looked badly frightened and rubbed new bruises, but mumbled that nothing seemed broken. Then our driver flung open his door and jumped out into the street just as the other driver did the same. The two drivers ran headlong toward each other. I thought, Oh, boy, here comes a fistfight with the Thai police breaking it up, the three of us going to jail, and Growler screaming.

The drivers started laughing. That's right. They *laughed* about our near-death experience as if it were some big joke. They hugged like long-lost friends, smiled, laughed some more, waved a cheery good-bye, jumped back in the cabs, backed up, and raced away at their original breakneck speeds.

I must have look frightened, because our driver looked over at me, smiled, and pointed to the plastic figure on his dash. "Buddha save . . . you no worry . . . Buddha save."

The Thais believe Buddha watches over and protects them against *everything* until their time here is over. Until then, they can race around like maniacs and Buddha will save.

Jack remarked how ironic it would have been for the three of us to be wiped out together on the streets of Bangkok after surviving months of shelling.

Buddha and I both watched the driver the rest of the way to the hotel.

The three of us took the shuttle up to NKP that afternoon and were eating dinner at the club that evening when Rod Berano rushed in looking petrified.

"Guys! Guys! You're not gonna believe it!" Rod grabbed the back of my chair, catching his breath. "Where's Ralph? I gotta tell him, too."

"Tell him what?" we asked, and pointed to Ralph at one of the OV-10 tables.

"I just got off the phone with Ginger. She said Ben was killed this morning!"

Jack and I stopped eating, stood up, and put our arms around Rod. "That's awful. Is Ginger okay? What in the world happened? We saw Ben just twelve hours ago! He was fine!"

"Ginger's okay. She told me that right after Ben left you guys, a moving van ran a red light and hit Ben on his Vespa. He was thrown thirty yards, hit a telephone pole headfirst, and was killed on impact. Ginger's really torn up. Ben was . . ."

We told Rod how much Ben meant to us, too. Then Jack told Rod about our taxi near-collision and mused how the four guys from the party almost died the same instant.

Four little Indians attended a dinner party . . . then there were three.

We had that night off to grieve Ben's loss, but it was right back to work the following night.

As luck would have it, I was Ralph's relief out over the Steel Tiger. Ralph had the eight-to-midnight coverage. I was his replacement for the graveyard shift . . . midnight to four. He radioed me he'd been working on a large convoy.

I flew us in at 11,000 feet as Ralph circled the burning carcasses at ten thousand . . . both our planes blacked out so gunners couldn't locate us.

I could see with the naked eye Ralph had already done a massive amount of damage. At least a hundred hulks were burning over a two-mile stretch.

I remember Ralph being so excited. "JT! This is the big one, buddy. I've been working this three hours. Take a look . . . we're gettin' secondary explosions all over the place! I blocked off the front and the back trucks, so take your time . . . the drivers are long gone. I've got six sets of fighters stacked up in the holding pattern rarin' to go and more on the way. Isn't this *great*!"

Then he listed the dozen fighters in the holding stack, each of them running out of fuel . . . information I'd need to take over and mop up. I wrote his information on the back of my hand with a black felt-tip pen so I wouldn't lose track.

Ralph was so excited; he kept *talking* and *talking* and *talking* . . . nonstop.

I kept thinking, Take a break, man. You're making yourself vulnerable.

One of the first things you learn as a FAC is to make radio calls in short bursts. Our radios work like the ones you find in police cars. Only one person can talk at a time. So if you ever have to do this, I caution you, talk in five-second bursts, then release your mike switch and *listen,* for chrissakes. That way, you'll open the frequency and let someone warn you about any threat they see but you can't. If you *ever* talk for fifteen seconds straight, you're putting yourself in an aural blind spot where no one can warn you.

But old Ralph was so elated by his accomplishment, he kept talking. *On and on.* "JT, I'm going Christmas tree so you can see me. I don't want that monster airplane of yours running into me. Go Christmas tree with me, please."

I thought, Don't do that! You'll telegraph your position to every gunner for miles around. Our standard one-thousand-foot altitude separation is all you need!

I watched him flick all his exterior lights on, then back off, but he forgot to turn off his leading-edge lights . . . one stupid switch.

I prayed, Ralph, shut up! They can *see* you! Turn those lights off! Let *me* get a word in to warn you. That's an FNG mistake! But he kept yammering, tying up the frequency.

I went Christmas tree as he requested, but flashed my lights on and off and on and off wildly to get his attention so he'd ask, "What?" and release his mike button so I could talk. But poor Ralph kept blabbering.

Then I saw the tracers.

Some fucking gunner on a mountainside *miles away* fired a volley of thirty-seven-millimeter tracers at Ralph when he was belly-up blind to the gun.

He was going to get blindsided and there was nothing I could do but watch.

I mean, Ralph wasn't even bothering that gunner. The boob should have kept his gun quiet. That's the way we play the game.

People back home think war is a no-holds-barred, I'll-do-anything-to-kill-you event, but it's not that way at all. While the Church has its published rules of engagement, those of us who actually fight subscribe to our own. You won't find them printed anywhere, but one that both sides understand clearly is, don't mess with me for just doing my job if I'm not bothering you, and I won't go out of my way to kill you.

Simple codes of behavior that likely predate recorded history and a code that even mortal enemies never break.

Except for this one, lousy, asshole gunner. He just couldn't keep his itchy finger off the goddamned trigger. It was a sucker punch.

Ralph looked like a Christmas tree as those tracers headed *straight for* his belly.

I smashed my mike key to try to break through. "RALPH! BREAK RIGHT! BREAK RIGHT! BREAK RIGHT!"

His own words blocked my rescue attempt.

I watched in silent horror as the shells found their mark. His little Rockwell OV-10 Bronco stuffed with high explosives turned into a white starburst explosion.

And Ralph was gone. Right before my eyes.

Rage consumed me. I thought, YOU GODDAMNED BASTARD! Nobody was after you! You could've kept your fuckin' gun quiet and nobody would have known you were even there. Everybody'd be happy. Your own truck drivers got to escape during the pause. The only thing at stake here was a bunch of lousy, burned-out truck carcasses. Nobody had to get hurt. But *NOOOOO!* You had to go and pull an asshole stunt like that.

I checked my wrist notes and called the next pair of fighters. "Gunfighter 22 Lead, did you see that?"

The pilot answered in shocked disbelief, "Yeah, Candle. We saw. Too bad."

I explained deliberately, "That was a good friend of mine. Will you help me take out that gun?"

He answered unhesitatingly, "No problem, Candle. He's toast. But how're we gonna find him? All he's gotta do is keep quiet and we'll never pick him out against that dark mountainside."

"You'll see. Just be ready. When you see his tracers, you're automatically cleared in hot. Don't wait for me to clear you. Just take him out for me, okay?"

His puzzled voice answered, "Roger."

I flew over to about the spot I saw the tracers originate and went full, blazing Christmas tree. I turned on *everything*: my landing lights, taxi lights, anticollision lights, wing lights, position lights . . . interior cargo lights . . . the whole schlemiel.

From the ground, we must have looked like a blazing Roman candle against the black sky . . . an irresistible target.

I taunted that gunner, "Here we are, you bastard! All lit up . . . just for you! Take your best shot, asshole! See if you can hit *this,* you sum'bitch!"

I circled his suspected position once. Nothing.

A second time, lights ablazing. Nothing. Did I miscalculate? Had he figured out the game and not taken the bait?

The third circle was the charm. He couldn't stand it any longer . . . his trigger finger got itchy again.

A volley of tracers came *right at us*.

Gunfighter Lead chuckled, "Sierra Hotel, Candle. I'm in hot."

I yanked us over on the left wing, turned into the tracers, wiggled through, and the shells whizzed by and exploded harmlessly overhead. I watched that F-4 pilot ride those tracers like a locomotive on train tracks right back down to their source.

Then the black mountainside erupted in a Vesuvius of flames.

Like I said before: paybacks are hell.

In tribute to Ralph, I finished off the rest of his convoy for him. Then I told Moonbeam that the FAC shot down was my good friend and requested permission to RTB. They approved returning to base three hours early, but I'd have left no matter what.

I fired up both jets, ran them up to 100 percent, and screamed back to NKP at max cruise speed—180 knots. I had to warn Jack.

Only thirty-six hours had passed since our Halloween dinner party and already two of the four men were dead. And the two still alive had already dodged a bullet on the streets of Bangkok. What were the odds?

All I could think on the flight back was, Something is up. Something is definitely up. I've got to warn Jack.

Four little Indians; then there were two.

CHAPTER TWENTY-SEVEN

Back on the ground, I quickly stripped out of my survival gear. I tossed my holster and gun onto the armory table and told the technician, "No inventory."

I charged the half block to the auditorium/chapel, flung open a side door, and interrupted Ralph's memorial . . . standing room only.

The mourners were grieving in silence as the chaplain circulated up and down the aisles. I scanned the crowd from the doorway, but couldn't find Jack. The chaplain wove his way through the aisles, giving it his best:

"'Yea, though I walk through the valley of the shadow of death, I shall fear no evil . . .'"

I jogged up and down my side of the room . . . peering down each row of men holding their faces in their hands.

The chaplain was relentless:

"'For thou art with me, thy rod and thy staff, they comfort me . . .'"

He passed through each aisle, laying his hands on those most affected.

I ran up and down and up and down, combating the urge to yell, *"Jack!"*

The chaplain shot me a dirty look and continued:

" 'Thou preparest a table before me in the presence of mine enemies: . . . Surely goodness and mercy shall follow me . . .' "

Some of the mourners started glaring at me.

I realized Jack would have noticed *me*. There could be only one other place . . .

I bolted back outside and raced the three blocks to the club, the sloshing water flasks I'd forgotten to empty grabbing at my ankles, slowing my progress. I nearly ripped the Quiet Bar side door off its hinges, stepped into complete darkness, and stood motionless waiting for my eyes to adjust.

There was Jack . . . on a barstool . . . alone in the dark . . . blowing smoke rings . . . hunched over a long-neck San Miguel. A second opened long-neck stood at the ready beside him.

I shuffled over, sat down, and drained half the bottle.

I could see from his reflection he'd been weeping. He wouldn't look at me, so I knew it was bad. I put my right hand on his shoulder and squeezed.

Not a word was spoken.

I reached across the bar, slid open a rolltop cooler, pulled out two six-packs, and plopped them on the bar . . . this was going to take a while.

Jack extracted a fresh Lucky, lit it against his own, and passed it over.

I nodded thanks and started blowing smoke rings with him.

After a long while he asked wistfully, "What took you so long?"

I sighed. "I got lost on the way."

He joked, "Still need your ol' nav to point the way, huh?"

I chuckled, "Always."

"So what happened out there?"

I opened two more bottles and recapped the story.

Jack asked, "Did you get that gun?"

I described how I made myself an easy target.

He smiled and patted my back. "Atta boy."

After a while I worked up the courage to address the key issue. "Jack, I want you to do me one last favor."

"Sure. What?"

I said hesitantly, "I know this might sound stupid and it's probably none of my business, but I don't want you to take your final flight tomorrow night."

"What are you talking about? Of course I'm going."

I explained, "Because there's only the two of us left alive out of the four guys from your party."

He shook his head. "You and I both know everybody looks forward to getting hosed down after their last flight," he objected. "I've been waiting three hundred and sixty-three days for that. There's no way I'm not going."

I proceeded cautiously. "But you admitted yourself our accident could have meant all four guys getting wiped out the same instant. It's not worth tempting fate."

Jack countered, "You're overreacting. Things like that only happen in the movies. Don't worry. I'll be fine."

I pleaded, "What's the big deal, Jack? *Please* . . . let it go . . . for me."

His voice hardened. "I can't do that."

I squeezed his forearm. "Jack, *please*. We've got lots of new navs who need the experience. Just take tomorrow night off, ride the shuttle out the next morning, and get the hell out of here before something happens to you, too."

He made a face. "What's this all about, John?"

I answered evasively, "I have bad feelings about it."

Jack said firmly, "You're going to have to do better than that."

I took a deep breath and let it out. "Okay; here goes . . . but don't laugh. Can't you *see*? It's like we're characters in that Agatha Christie play *Ten Little Indians*. The one based on that children's rhyme where all the characters are killed off one by one until 'and then there were none.' First Ben. Now Ralph again a day later? Can't you see the pattern?"

"So you're saying fate is coming after *me*?"

"*Exactly*. This reminds me of that movie *Fate Is the Hunter*. The star was Glenn Ford. Remember?"

Jack shook his head.

"Oh, sure you do," I insisted. "Ford played an NTSB accident investigator charged with finding out why *both* engines of a DC-6 airliner caught fire *at the same time*. The pilot tried to dead-stick his plane onto a deserted beach north of L.A., and it looked like they were gonna make it . . . until . . . at the last second . . . a deserted pier . . . the only obstacle for *miles* . . . loomed up out of the dark and they crashed right into it. It was fate . . . they were doomed no matter what they did."

Jack's face lit up with recognition. "Oh, yeah. I *do* remember!"

Thinking I might be close to convincing him, I surged ahead. "And after a yearlong investigation, Ford's character couldn't figure out why *both engines* caught fire *at the exact same moment* because the odds against that happening *and* that deserted pier looming in *exactly the wrong place* were astronomical. The only way Ford could figure out to solve the riddle was to fly the same profile again himself. Remember that?"

Jack chimed in, "Yeah, and the sole survivor—a stewardess—was in the cockpit helping him duplicate everything when *both engines* caught fire *again* and they were gonna crash into the *same* pier *again*. What a movie!"

"Yeah. That scene has haunted me. As strange as it sounds, that's the feeling I have now. I don't want you tempting fate like Ford."

Jack looked skeptical. "So you're making a case for predeterminism?"

"Prede-*what*?"

"You don't remember? I'm sure we talked about it."

I answered no.

"This is off the top of my head, but here goes: Predeterminists believe our lives are preordained—that fate is running the show. They say what we think of as free will is a mirage . . . that the die is cast and we're just going through the motions."

"So what you're saying is, this conversation . . . was always *guaranteed* to happen?"

"No," he said abruptly. "I don't believe it. But what *they're* saying is—"

"Let me try. That would mean . . . no matter whether or not you fly your last flight—"

Jack jumped in, "—the results will be the same."

"I don't believe that, Jack."

"Me neither."

I told him politely, "I still don't want you taking your last flight."

Jack was silent, but I sensed he was close to honoring my request.

To push him over the edge, I offered, "Suppose I do this? I know some of the guys at the fire department. Suppose I get a bunch of our crewmembers together tomorrow afternoon and we get you hosed down out by one of the airplanes? We'll spray you with champagne . . . take pictures . . . have the party . . . the whole deal."

Jack studied my face for a moment. "You're serious about this, aren't you?"

"Deadly."

He scratched his chin. "All right, all right. I'm not admitting I believe in inexorable fate, but if you feel that strongly, I won't fly again if you'll do me one favor in return."

I jumped at the chance. "Shoot. You name it. Anything."

His tone turned serious. "I want you to be the keeper of the ledgers."

I protested, "No way. Give them to Wiley. I'm not ready for that kind of responsibility."

"Nonsense," Jack lectured. "Besides, Wiley's leaving in a couple weeks. You're the only one I'd trust with the material besides him. It's time for you to grow up, John, and *share it with others*."

I said hesitantly, "I don't know, Jack." But realizing I was backed into a corner, I reluctantly agreed.

Jack closed with, "Assuming you're right about fate targeting us, you're forgetting one key issue."

"What's that?"

He stared at me gravely. "What about *you*?"

Oh . . . oh . . . here comes more "American Pie" . . .

> *Ohhhh, and there we were all in one place*
> *A generation lost in space*
> *With no time left to start again*
> *So come on, Jack be nimble, Jack be quick*
> *Jack Flash sat on a candlestick*
> *'Cause fire is the devil's only friend . . .*

So what's up with Tonto? I haven't heard from him in a while.

Dammit, Halliday! You were supposed to tell him the light might go out.

I call my friend now. "Tonto, Candle 23."

No answer.

I try again, "Tonto, Candlestick 23."

Trouble.

I raise my voice, *"Tonto, Candle 23. Do you read? Over!"*

CHAPTER *TWENTY-EIGHT*

Still no answer from Tonto . . . not good. He *always* answers right away.

I start worrying. I yell, "TONTO, CANDLESTICK 23! DO YOU READ?"

I hear the sounds of a radio dragged across stones. A sleepy-voiced Tonto yawns, "Candle, Tonto. Wha . . . ?"

Damn! I forgot the poor man was going to sleep. This guy fights off bad guys all day and night, and when he gets the rare opportunity to sleep under the security of our candlelight, I go and wake him up.

Stupid, stupid, stupid.

"Sorry, Tonto. Go back to sleep."

"Roger . . . Tonto sleep."

I see Rich turn around to smirk at my public mistake. He sees me looking at him and turns back to continue to monitor Charles's flying.

Jack thought Rich was reachable, but I don't think so. He'll never hear me.

Now Tyrone silently materializes on the back porch, pats me on the back, and leans into the cockpit to lean 'em out again. Beautiful.

Charles! I forgot about Charles. Shoot! He's been flying for . . . what? . . . more than an hour? . . . right through Rich's turn. Maybe Charles needs a break.

I call him now to check. "Charles, I'm sorry . . . I completely lost track of the time. You want me to come up and take my turn?"

"Are you kidding, JT? This is great!" Charles says joyfully. "I can't believe how fast time is flying by. Back there at the table, time drags on and on when I have nothing to do on nights like this. Heck, I'm having a ball. I'll fly us back down to the Mekong and then you can jump in . . . if that's okay with you, of course," he hurries to add. "Not many guys let me fly. Wiley's the only other and he's leaving. So if it's all the same to you, I'd love to keep going."

"Make yourself happy, Charles. I could use the break, anyway. I get tired of having to hand-fly this thing, so go for it. I'll be back here if you need me."

"Thanks, JT."

Jack kept his word and didn't fly again. We got him hosed down and had that squadron going-away party. He grinned ear to ear the entire afternoon.

The next morning I chauffeured Jack out to the flightline in that blue pickup truck Wiley'd picked me up in six months before. I was nervous about how to say good-bye. Jack cut through all that nonsense by giving me a big bear hug.

I wanted to say something brilliant, but all that came out was "I . . . I . . ." I choked on my words as I fought back tears.

He stepped back, held my shoulders at arm's length, and smiled. He said wistfully, "Me, too. Don't worry. You'll be fine. See you later." Then he turned, walked over to the C-130, climbed the stairs, turned, smiled, and waved.

I waved back.

Then he disappeared inside. I tried spotting him through one of the dark porthole windows, but he must have taken a seat on the far side.

I breathed a sigh of relief when I saw his airplane taxi out and take off safely. I watched them climb out until the airplane was a tiny black dot.

And then my friend was gone . . . safe. No fireball crash. No augering in after takeoff like those C-133s I flew . . . nothing.

I drove back to the squadron feeling depressed and relieved. I knew that by the next morning, Jack would be safely away on that freedom bird and the danger would be over. He had escaped. And in his escape, he rescued me from our mutual destiny. Fate couldn't get all four of us now that he was gone. Both of us were safe. We'd broken the chain of events . . . beaten fate.

It was over, thank God.

Oh! Here comes more now:

> *Oh, and as I watched him on the stage*
> *My hands were clenched in fists of rage*
> *No angel born in hell*
> *Could break that Satan's spell*

. . . the rest slips away. How does it go?

CHAPTER *TWENTY-NINE*

G ot it now! The rest plays in my head:

> *And as the flames climbed high into the night*
> *To . . . light the sacrificial rite*
> *I saw . . . Satan laughing with delight*
> *The day . . . the muuusic . . . died*

A week went by after Jack's escape. For some reason I found myself walking through the squadron in broad daylight. To avoid Desktop's and Growler's wrath, my habit was to enter that dangerous turf only in the middle of the night. So I don't know what drew me there that afternoon, a moth drawn to a flame.

A large group stirred noisily around the bulletin board where they post the latest hot news. Unusual, I thought . . . the squadron is normally deserted during the day.

The crowd was standing ten deep. They were staring at *something,* but what? At first I hoped maybe those Paris peace talks had succeeded and we'd all be going home soon!

I jumped up and down in anticipation at the back of the pack, like a kid trying to watch a parade over taller adults. What was so riveting everyone was reading again and again? It had to be a peace agreement! We were all going home! Glory hallelujah!

I watched men at the front turn around and pick their way out through the sea of bodies anxiously waiting their turn.

Then I noticed everyone weeping as they left. Not a word was spoken.

I urgently asked one departing dazed friend, "What's *going on*? What's *happened*?" But he just shook his head and walked away.

Everyone followed the identical routine . . . work your way up to the bulletin board, read, stare, read, shake the head, stare, turn, and stagger away in tears.

What the hell was *going on*!

I finally worked my way to the front. The object of their attention was a single piece of feminine stationery . . . the words written in a woman's delicate hand. I smelled Jungle Gardenia wafting off the yellow paper, the posting was so fresh:

Dear Candlestick Squadron,
It is with deep sorrow I inform you of the death of my loving husband and your friend, Jack Ward. Jack wrote and talked about all of you so fondly, I wanted to let you personally know of our mutual loss. Jack said you were his family for a year and told me how much he loved you all.

My dear Jack was killed during a training accident on his first flight aboard his new plane, the KC-135. They tell me the crash happened during a touch-and-go landing. Everyone aboard was killed instantly. A memorial service will be held at the base chapel on . . . flowers may be sent to . . .

Mrs. Jack Ward

I couldn't finish her letter . . . something in my eyes. I turned
and staggered away.

> *Oh, I met a girl who sang the blues*
> *And I asked her for some . . . happy news*
> *But she just smiled and turned away*
>
> *I went down to the sacred store*
> *Where I'd heard the music years before*
> *But the man there . . . said the music . . . wouldn't*
>   *plaaaaay*
>
> *And in the streets the children screamed*
> *The lovers cried and the poets dreamed*
> *But not a word was spoken*
> *The church bells all were broken*
>
> *And the three men I admire most*
> *The Father, Son and the Holy Ghost*
> *They caught the last train for . . . the coast*
> *The day . . . the muuusic . . . died*

I got out of there and raced as fast as I could for Wiley's
trailer. I must have looked like some crazed madman to people on the sidewalk I nearly knocked down. But I had to get
to Wiley . . . fast!

Then from a block away, I faintly heard those soothing
words:

> *All my sorrows, sad tomorrows . . .*

I ran faster toward the comforting sound . . .

> *Take me back . . . to my own home . . .*

I pounded my fist on his door. BAM! BAM! BAM! I hit it
so hard I thought I might break some bones . . . no matter.

BAM! BAM! BAM!

I hollered, "LET ME IN! LET ME IN!" so he'd hear me over the music. A stumbling, red-eyed Wiley finally opened the door. The blast hit me . . .

ALL MY CRYINGS, FEEL I'M DYING, DYING . . .

Wiley handed me a San Miguel, a mike, and then closed and locked the door. Not a word was spoken.

We sat on the floor the rest of the afternoon and night getting shit-faced and screaming along with Marmalade . . . over and over and over and over . . .

Four little Indians attended a dinner party. Then there was one . . .

Me.

CHAPTER *THIRTY*

Mrs. Ward's letter arrived a week ago, which brings you up-to-date.

I've had to stop talking about the four little Indians aspect of this story. It's hard keeping it bottled up without telling *someone,* but when I share it with people, they give me their best Rod Serling impression: "Ladies and gentlemen, you have entered . . . the Twilight Zone."

Then they'll make that creepy "Dee . . . dee . . . dee . . . dee . . . dee . . . dee . . . dee" theme music and laugh.

Some guys are calling the events the Bangkok Curse.

Some even make a cross with their index fingers, hold it in front of their faces, and back away as if I were some vampire. Then they laugh.

I'm not laughing.

Either they don't take the situation seriously, or maybe they *do* and that's their way of dealing with their fears. I don't know. I do know it's spooky being the only man left alive from the dinner party.

And remember I talked about those strange looks I've been getting from across the dining room? Remember that?

And remember back when I said I keep getting paired with pilots scraped off the bottom of the barrel, or guys who don't have better sense not to fly with me?

I have become a pariah.

It's looking more and more as if after Wiley leaves, I'll spend the next six months in solitary confinement.

I can't shake this feeling of being stalked . . . sized up for the kill. It's the *worrying,* the *anticipation* that's wearing me down . . . why I was short-tempered with Tyrone earlier.

Something horrific is definitely going to happen.

It's just a matter of time.

So let's get it on . . . helter-skelter . . .

> *Helter skelter in a summer swelter*
> *The birds flew off with a fallout shelter*
> *Eight miles high and falling faaaaaaaast!*
>
> *It landed foul out on the grass*
> *The players tried for a forward pass*
> *With the jester . . . on the sidelines . . . in a cast*

I'm wondering more and more what form my tsunami will take. I've spent hours in the tomblike base library researching ancient tidal waves, obsessed with the image.

Fossil records indicate a wall of water *fifteen hundred feet* tall rose up off the Yucatán Peninsula thousands of years ago and consumed everything in its path as far inland as Oklahoma. You can find shells of ancient sea creatures in Tulsa.

Tidal waves suck dry entire bays. Their force approaches silently . . . deadly. Observers on high ground report watching people on beaches below staring in stupefied wonder at the onrushing wall of water. They appeared frozen; transfixed.

I can identify with those beach people.

But on the other hand, maybe this is just a bizarre string of coincidences. Maybe my imagination is running wild. Bangkok Curse. Hah! Who are they kidding? Let's get real. Everybody knows there's no such thing as curses.

Right?

> *Now the half-time air was . . . sweet perfume*
> *While the sergeants played a marching tune*
> *We all got up to dance*
> *Ohhh . . . but we never got the chance*
> *'Cause the players tried to take the field*
> *The marching band refused to yield*
> *Do you recall what was revealed?*
> *The day . . . the muuuuuusic died*

Whew! Feeling better again.

You've probably been wondering what business all these songs have in this story. Here's the reason: I stumbled onto the study of mantras during my library research and have been experimenting with music as my mantra. The lyrics and melodies are *supposed* to transport the mind to a higher plane of inner peace and tranquillity; help you peer inside your mind and release your fears . . . if only for a few moments.

Mantras evidently help one perceive the true nature of the mind and achieve rising power. I could use some rising power right about now.

One reference I hold on to quoted Govinda. This may not be an exact quote, but it's close: "Mantras are tools for thinking, thought that creates mental pictures. A mantra . . . is knowledge, a truth beyond right and wrong, a reality beyond thinking and reflecting. Whatever the mantra expresses exists and comes to pass."

Whatever the mantra expresses exists and comes to pass.

I have no idea if mantras work, but I'll try *anything* at this point to help loosen the barbed wire wrapped around my mind.

• • •

Now where was I?

Oh, yeah . . . Wiley and I have talked about worst-case scenarios. "A runaway prop would be the worst," Wiley suggested. "The prop could rip up to thirty-four hundred rpm before you could stop it. That flat blade angle would stick out like a barn door and produce so much drag you wouldn't be going anywhere but down. To overcome the drag, you'd have to run *both* jets at max power. But that configuration's never been flight-tested . . . too dangerous. You'd be ass-holes and elbows.

"But for the two-jet solution to work to any purpose," he continued, "the runaway prop would have to happen in the middle of the flight. I mean, those jets suck so much fuel. You might reach the northern Thai rice paddies before you have to bail out. But that wouldn't be so bad. You'd spend the night cold and wet waiting for rescue in the morning, and the aircraft would be a total loss, but everybody'd survive. That scenario *might* work, unless . . . now get this . . . *unless* you were at the very end of a mission and didn't have much gas left. With those gobbling jets, you'd flame out before you reached Thailand. You'd wind up . . . well . . . bailing out deep over bad-guy territory. That would be the worst. What'd you come up with?"

"I'm picturing flak incapacitating both me and the copilot," I answered. "That's why I've talked Charles into buddy-bidding with me in return for flying lessons. I think he could belly her in back here. It wouldn't be pretty, but we'd prob'ly survive if—"

"Oh! I almost forgot," Wiley interjected. "Twin thirty-seven-millimeter hits could destroy *both* props. You'd be a glider until you shut down *both* recips, started *both* jets, and limped home that way. But that's never been flight-tested, either. That's assuming again, of course, you had enough gas.

"If you didn't . . . well . . . there you are again bailing out over the bad guys. You might as well bend over and kiss your ass good-bye. If it happened early—and you had *beaucoup* fuel—attempting an approach solely with the jets would be a dicey proposition. It's those damned toggle-switch throttles instead of conventional ones. You get max power or idle . . . nothing in between. But since jet-only approaches are prohibited, you'd be back to being a test pilot."

I've been practicing jet-only approaches for the past week. For safety's sake, I power up the recips for landing. I may be crazy, but I'm not stupid.

Growler will have me for lunch if he finds out. I don't care. He's the least of my worries.

Something horrible is just around the corner. It's a matter of time.

I suppose at this point someone could ask, "If you're that concerned, why not *get the hell out of there!*" And my answer would be, "The Church won't let me. So I'll just have to come back up here tomorrow night and the night after that and the night after that."

See? There is no escape.

Aside from that, I admit to a certain morbid curiosity. I feel like a moth drawn uncontrollably toward a burning candle, flittering in and out of the fire, tempting the flame to burn its wings.

And another reason I don't turn tail and head home? Plain old American arrogance; I'll admit to that. Hey! I'm at the top of my game. I'll never be better than I am right now.

So take your best shot. Bring it on, baby. *Bring it on*.

Let's get it *on* . . . you and me.

> *Hope you . . . have got your things together*
> *Hope you . . . are quite prepared to die*
> *Looks like we're in for nasty weather*
> *One eye is taken for an eye . . .*

Ever wonder what happened to that naïve FNG Wiley met six months back?

Dead and buried.

I have become aggressive, arrogant, and overconfident. I have become dangerous to myself and others. I go out of my way to pick a fight. I thrive on uncertainty. I have jettisoned any shred of self-preservation. I can't wait to race back up here each night and raise holy hell.

I can relate to prowling, knife-wielding, big-city street gangs looking for trouble. Violence has become a way of life. Not violence for violence's sake, but focused, surgical violence like a powerful laser beam. Violence where it does some good.

I go out of my way to create dangerous situations to sharpen my fighting skills, the way a heavyweight contender pummels his sparring partner to warm up for the championship fight. Crazy stuff, I know. But there it is. I'm not making any apologies.

I'm so far over the line, I can't even *see* the line. If I ever venture so far across the line I might not return, I'm hoping Charles yanks me back. My chief concern is Charles may not know enough about piloting to know where the line is.

I scare myself with my increasing viciousness. I may have become my own foe . . . creating some self-fulfilling prophecy . . . maybe . . . I just don't know.

But here's an alternative explanation: I may be nuts.

Even so, I feel like a homicide detective searching for clues to a murder that hasn't happened yet . . . my own.

Well, what do you know! I am looking down into the stream of memories and . . . by golly . . . looks as if I covered everything before my midnight deadline. Now you know everything.

Now I can call in that fleet of cement trucks and bury these memories, once and for all. Good riddance. I can see the lead truck coming over the hill.

I check my Seiko: 11:49 and two seconds. We head home in what? Twenty-five minutes, give or take. This one's over . . . not gonna happen tonight. I stretch and yawn. Maybe tomorrow night.

Tonto's terrified voice screams in my headset, "CANDLE 23, TONTO! MAYDAY! MAYDAY! MAYDAY!"

CHAPTER *THIRTY-ONE*

I bolt upright to answer, but before I can press my mike switch, Tonto's bloodcurdling screams rip into my ears.

"MAYDAY! MAYDAY! MAYDAY! CANDLE 23 . . . CANDLE 23 . . . HELP TONTO . . . BAD GUYS . . . *THEY COME!*"

I try to calm him down by keeping my voice composed. "Tonto, Candle 23. What's wrong? Do you need more light?"

His terrified voice screams, "NEGATIVE! NEGATIVE! LIGHT NUMBER ONE! Bad guys come! Light no work! Light no work! THEY COME! *HELP TONTO!*"

Frustration hits. I don't understand his situation, so I can't understand how to help him. I try again, "*Slow down.* What do you *see*? How can I help?"

Rips of automatic-weapons fire blanket his voice. "Many, many bad guys. Tonto see many bad guys across road! Tonto need bombs! Tonto see FACES! *HELP TONTO!*"

My mind's eye pictures an overwhelming enemy force across the narrow dirt road launching an all-out attack, ignoring our candlelight. I check my watch. 11:49:27 . . . 28 . . . 29 . . . tick . . . tick . . . tick . . .

I radio back, "Tonto . . . hold on . . . I get fighters . . . *hold on!* . . . I get bombs." Now I rotate my interphone switch to our second radio to call Moonbeam.

Charles turns around and gawks at me wild-eyed. His shaky voice asks, "You want back in here, JT?" He points at my left seat.

I shake my head and tell him, "Not until I get things set up with Moonbeam." I key the mike. "Moonbeam, Candle 23. I've got a Mayday from Tonto."

Moonbeam answers calmly, "Go ahead."

"I've got a life-and-death situation. Tonto is being overrun and I'm at bingo fuel. There's no time for messin' around. I need two things from you immediately. I need a flight of slow-mover fighters . . . I repeat . . . *slow-movers* NOW and I need Candle 25 to get his butt up here. What fighters you got on tap?"

"Not much, Candle . . . been a slow night . . . stand by . . . checking."

I talk rapidly, "Moonbeam, while you're checking . . . I need *good* fighters with bomblets or daisy cutters . . . some sort of antipersonnel ordnance. I'll take hard bombs as a last resort. And no nape. I repeat . . . no nape. This is a TIC . . . I repeat . . . a troops-in-contact situation . . . I need Navy A-4s or A-6s off the carrier . . . . or Air Force A-1s . . . something that can go in *low and slow* and make a surgical, pinpoint drop the first time. There's no second chances on this one. Do you copy?"

The voice answers more urgently, "Moonbeam copies. Stand by, stand by. Get right back to you."

I lean back in Charles's seat to await their answer and gather my thoughts.

Translation: Don't send me any Air Force F-4s, and in particular, don't send me any armed with napalm. I couldn't say that over the airways, but the Moonbeam controller can read between the lines . . . he knows the F-4's rotten reputation as well. The airplane wasn't built for close air support.

To ask an F-4 to rescue Tonto would be like asking an Olympic weight lifter to perform the ballet.

I close my eyes and silently pray, *please* . . . no napalm! That stuff splatters *all over*. The canisters tumble out of control and can wind up anywhere . . . even on the good guys. It's rare to see a load of nape, but it shows up every once in a while.

I check on Tonto. "Tonto, Candle 23. You okay?"

No answer. Not good.

Rich bows his head and says sorrowfully, "He's gone, John."

I hope maybe Tonto is busy shooting back. Or maybe his radio got shot up, or the battery died. But what if Rich is right and my friend is dead? He was the only English speaker in his unit. What if a surviving buddy answers in Laotian . . . I could never get final approval for the final bomb run.

What the hell's taking Moonbeam so long? Where are my slow-movers?

I call them angrily, "Moonbeam, how's it coming? We're running out of time."

"I *said STAND BY,* Candle," a voice answers sternly. "We're doing the best we can. You'll have to be patient."

I take a deep breath and tell myself, relax . . . don't rush . . . one step at a time.

I remember the last time I worked an F-4. His radio calls came across weak. I hollered, "I can barely hear you . . . have maintenance check your radio. But if you see me and my ground markers, you're cleared in hot." The pilot reported seeing us and the marks, dive-bombed, but we didn't see any explosion.

I advised the pilot, "Nothing . . . must've been a dud . . . try again . . . I'm going Christmas tree . . . when you've got me in sight, you're cleared in hot."

He came through faintly, "Got you . . . sight . . . Cand . . . hot."

I looked down for an explosion, but the jungle remained dark.

Finally I asked the fighter pilot what TACAN channel he was using for navigation. When he answered, "Channel 98," I groaned inside. I scolded him, "I *told you* channel 89 . . . I don't know whose ground marks you've supposedly been seeing or whose Christmas tree you've reported seeing, but my nav tells me you're out over the South China Sea. You're dropping in the fucking ocean! You're a *whole country* away from our position," I told him disgustedly. "Just wrap it up and go home."

Please . . . anything but F-4s.

I hear, "Candle 23, Moonbeam. Still working. Stand by." I don't answer.

I switch back to interphone, start to signal Charles to get out of my seat, but see him already halfway through the doorway to make room for me to get by.

I announce, "Battle stations, everybody. Battle stations . . . let's get to work!"

I take one last look back in the cargo compartment. I see Tyrone run across the cargo compartment and wake up Eddie . . . good. I swing Charles's seat around to face forward and lock it in position. Then I unplug my headset from the interphone cord, zip up my flightsuit, tighten my chute chest strap, cinch down both crotch straps good and hard, slam down both calf zippers, unbuckle the seat belt, and launch myself onto the back porch. Hurry! Now I bend over and shove my white-socked feet into my boots. Zip, zip, and they're back on . . . good old zippers.

I stand and hold up Charles's interphone cord. I wiggle it in his face so we don't lose it in the dark. He yanks it twice to let me know he's got it. Good old Charles . . . glad he's here for this one. I race up the two steps into the cockpit, slam myself down into the left seat, buckle my lap belt, and plug in my interphone cord. Fifteen seconds lost . . . tops. And no white shooting stars this time . . . doing good. I tell Rich seriously, "I've got the airplane," and shake the control column to confirm.

I tell the scope, "I'm gonna set up our standard left-hand orbit over the scene. Keep dropping flares so Tonto's guys

can see to shoot. As soon as you acquire the target area, I
want you to drop three ground-burning markers *right on the
road*. Then give me the drop heading . . . no need to answer . . . Ramp . . . load three ground marks for deployment
on the scope's command . . . no need to answer . . . just do
it. Hurry!"

I check my right-knee windup clock. 11:51:09 . . . got a
lot done in ninety seconds. Midnight shoulda been bingo
fuel, but the way we've been saving gas with the engines
leaned out, I should have enough time to pull this off . . .
gotta be careful, though . . . no margin for error.

Tyrone appears in the doorway. I tell him, "Tyrone . . .
gimme the mixtures full rich, props to twenty-four hundred
rpm, ignitions to 'both,' and I've got the throttles."

"Yes, sir!"

Out of the corner of my eyes, I watch him adjust the
throttle quadrant and feel this sleepy old warhorse come
back to life as we transform it from simple care provider to
avenger capable of kicking some serious bad-guy ass. As
Tyrone moves the fuel mixtures to full rich, I imagine hearing a giant sucking *slurrrrrrrrrrrp!* of the little fuel we have
left rush through the carburetors into the intake manifolds.

If this old machine had that new, automated Caution—
Low Fuel warning-light system, it would be blinking like
crazy.

"Okay, guys, here's the way I see the situation," I begin,
laying out the basics of my plan. "Tonto's not gonna last
long if we don't help soon." I scan the two fuel gauges on the
overhead panel . . . three thousand pounds per tank . . . six
thousand total . . . bingo fuel.

Damn!

I select our second radio and holler at Moonbeam in frustration. "Moonbeam, I'm at bingo *right now*. Where're those
damned fighters? And where the hell's Candle 25? I gotta
wrap this up in"—I check my knee clock—"fifteen minutes
to get back to NKP with emergency fuel . . . over."

"Stand by, Candle. We're working on your fighters . . .
bad news on your replacement, though. Two-five says he

can't be on station until three zero after the hour . . . half
past. Can you remain on station that long?"

I answer angrily, "Are you crazy! Not unless you want us
running out of gas, bailing out, and losing this fuckin' airplane. No way . . . that would put us back at NKP with . . .
what? . . . fifteen minutes' gas? That's *fumes,* man."

Rich shoots me a suspicious look I ignore.

Moonbeam responds, "Do the best you can. Get back to
you on your fighter situation ASAP . . . Moonbeam out." As
an afterthought, the NCO controller adds apologetically,
"Sir, I'm sorry, but the capsule commander standing behind
me advises to remind you of the regulation against the use of
profanity over the radio."

I switch back to interphone and announce, "Okay, guys. I
was reviewing the big picture. The weather's good back
home . . . the plane's working good . . . we can get this strike
done, lean 'em out all the way home, and *not* start the jets for
landing. I'll make a falling-leaves descent and approach . . .
so we'll land with thirty minutes' gas . . . maybe as little as
twenty-five . . . not the forty-five minutes' we're *supposed* to
have, but . . ."

I see Rich waving his arms wildly. Now he points up rapidly at the fuel gauges, flashes me the thumbs-down sign,
and then repeatedly jerks his thumb over his shoulder in the
direction of NKP.

I shake my head and signal, *Wait for me to finish.*

I continue, "As I was saying, we've got three thousand
pounds in each tank right now . . . normal bingo . . . that's
six thousand total . . . so this plan should put us landing with
an easy thirty minutes' gas . . . twelve hundred pounds per
tank . . . piece of cake. Now if we *don't stay* the extra fifteen
minutes, Tonto is toast. It's still a few minutes before midnight . . . we should be done with this airstrike by quarter after if Moonbeam'll ever get us those fighters."

Out of habit I add, "Anybody see anything I forgot?" As
the words leave my mouth, I wish I could grab them back.

Rich abruptly says, "Pilot from Copilot."

I roll my eyes and answer irritably, "Rich, for chrissakes.

Cut the formality. There's only the two of us here. I *know* it's you. What do you want?"

Rich nags, "You don't have the authority to go below bingo. And *not* start the jets! Under whose authority? The regs require the jets for every approach. What're you gonna do if we lose a recip? This is exactly what the regs are for . . . so guys like you don't go off half-cocked. Tonto'll be just fine until Two-five shows up. We need to close this thing up and head home *right now*."

I turn around to check my bellwether and see Charles flashing me a silent thumbs-up "I'm with *you*, JT" message out of Rich's sight.

I smile inside. Good old Charles . . . I haven't crossed that line yet.

I turn my voice to gravel and address Rich seriously. "Thanks for your input, but we're staying. First off, we won't need the jets for landing. We'll weigh so little, even if a recip quits, the remaining engine could handle the weight. Remember, they flew these airplanes for two decades with no jets. And on top of that, I have all the authority I need. As of this moment, I am exercising my captain's emergency authority. I'll break any rule I deem necessary. I am *not* leaving Tonto alone to die, so get going home out of your head. It's not open for discussion. Now let's get to work."

Rich won't give it up. "Pilot from Copilot. The rules *clearly state* we must be *on the ground* at NKP with fifteen hundred pounds per tank. You're talking about *starting an approach* with only twelve hundred? Not even *on the ground*? You'll burn another two hundred . . . maybe three hundred pounds during the approach . . . so we'll be landing with . . . what? Nine hundred pounds! And that could be only *five hundred pounds* because you're forgetting about *gauge error*. You and I both know these old gauges are only certified accurate plus or minus four hundred pounds. Four hundred pounds could actually be *zero*."

Rich drones on, "So you're planning on landing with five hundred pounds per side? That's what? Twenty? . . . No . . .

fifteen minutes . . . *fumes,* Halliday! If anything went wrong . . . we . . . we . . . we gotta head home *now.* I'll call Moonbeam, tell them we can't stay, and cancel the fighter request."

I stare at him in disbelief. I order, "Don't do that, Rich."

In my mind, I launch myself across the cockpit, grab his throat, and squeeze.

But I pull my punch, aware I still need his help to pull off this attack.

I try a different approach. "Rich, you're so wrapped up in the trees you can't see the forest. It took me a long time to come to grips with the concept the airplane is *always* running out of fuel. If we left for home at three thousand pounds per tank like normal, we'd get back with the required forty-five minutes' fuel, right?"

Rich shakes his head as if he's already rejected every word before I finish.

I charge ahead. "All I'm doing is staying an extra fifteen minutes. Do the math, Rich. Forty-five minus fifteen is . . . guess what! Thirty minutes! Not your fifteen!"

Rich opens his mouth to interrupt, but I tell him, "Be *quiet* and let me finish. On top of that, watch this." I reach up to the overhead panel and push the eraser-size press-to-test button between the two fuel gauges. We watch both pocket-watch-size fuel gauges drive counterclockwise down to zero. Then I release the button and we watch the needles drive back up to a needle's width below three thousand.

"See?" I tell him. "Both gauges just passed the authorized flight-manual test. Your gauge-error argument doesn't hold water. Now let's get to work."

Rich drones on, "But that's just an electrical continuity check from these gauges to the fuel probes. It proves nothing about how much fuel's in the tanks."

I counter, "But the fuel burn has been perfect since take-off. You have absolutely no evidence the gauges are wrong."

Rich counterattacks, "But what if rice fog rolls in and shuts down the airport? We won't have enough gas to divert to an alternate. What if we encounter a headwind going home and it takes longer?"

I sigh. "I'm well aware of those things, Rich. They're risks I'm willing to accept."

He bellows, "Well, I'm not!"

A voice chimes in. "Pilot, Scope. I'm with you . . . no problem."

Tyrone squeezes my right shoulder. He says seriously, "Sir, speaking for the enlisted guys as the senior man . . . there's *no question*. Just tell us what you want."

As Tyrone speaks, I watch Rich point repeatedly at his watch and jerk his thumb over his shoulder in the direction of NKP. Next he repeatedly draws his hand across his throat like a blade. I stare at him. It comes to me he's been holding this back for months. All social pretenses are now out the window. His utter contempt for me has finally shown its ugly face.

I ask incredulously, "So you'd rather let Tonto *die* than chance landing with emergency fuel? Do I have to remind you our basic mission is keeping guys like Tonto from being wiped out?"

"No, it's not," Rich snaps. "Our mission is killing trucks and dropping flares. A TIC is outside our charter. We don't even have procedures for a TIC. Tonto is toast. We've got to save ourselves. There's nothing you can do to save him. Give it up."

"We'll see about that, Rich."

"But if you screw this up, you could wipe out the rest of Tonto's men right along with the bad guys. They'll blame you back home."

"I am very aware of that, Rich."

Rich's face turns to a scowl. "If you don't turn south right now, I'll be submitting a hazard report when we get back," he warns me self-righteously. I watch him triumphantly fold his arms across his chest as his eyes bore in for my reaction.

My Irish temper erupts. I lean across the radio console, lower my voice two octaves, and address him ferociously. "Don't you *threaten* me, *Dick*."

His eyes get big as saucers.

"Do what you have to, *Dick,* but don't you *dare* threaten me. I'm in command—not *you.* We're *staying.* I'll be *damned* if I'm gonna let the light go out. Now I don't have time to argue. So *shut up* and let's get to work."

Rich's eyes burn with hatred.

I need to buy some quiet mental time, so to get him off my back, I overload him with things to do. "You fly the plane . . . work with the scope and the rampers . . . then call Moonbeam . . . update the current and forecast NKP weather for the next two hours . . . and get an ETA on those fighters. Move!"

Rich shakes the controls violently to register his disagreement. I watch him switch radios and begin coordinating with Moonbeam.

That should keep him out of my hair awhile.

Rich charges back. "But you're well aware regulations prohibit Air Force weathermen from forecasting fog. What if—"

I shout, "Enough!"

Rich looks startled and turns quiet.

Now I turn to Charles and tell him, "Back me up. Be my timekeeper in case I get busy and lose track. Our fighters'll prob'ly be here by twelve oh seven or so, so we'll only have eight minutes to pull this off."

"No problem," Charles answers. "It's eleven fifty-three and counting . . . should work out okay."

I order, "Scope and Ramp . . . work with Rich . . . I want those three ground marks laid right *on the road* for a clear line of demarcation between the two forces. I know it's hard pinpointing where they land, Scope, but can you make that happen?"

"Tall order, JT. You know these markers have a mind of their own, but I'll give it my best shot."

I sit back and listen as they set up for the drop.

I glance over at Rich. My anger at him turns to sorrow for his having lost his humanity. He's looking for an organizational justification for staying. He could look all night and won't find one.

Don't let . . . the light go out
It's lasted for so many yearrrrrrs
Don't let . . . the light go out
Let it shine through our love and our tears . . .

I recline my seat and force my mind to think about the upcoming battle. The enemy leader must think I don't give a damn about Tonto's unit. And somehow he's figured 25 is late. He figures he has a window of opportunity to wipe out Tonto's little band once and for all . . .

"Drop mark . . . drop mark . . . drop mark."

"Marks away!"

The ground marks plummeting down, I order Rich to reestablish our left-hand orbit. I watch him comply and now anxiously await to see if our marks landed on the road and for our slow-movers to check in on frequency.

Maybe the enemy leader thinks somebody like Rich is in command. He must figure it's a quiet night, so Moonbeam won't have fighter assets to challenge his attack. He *thinks* I won't risk losing this airplane for some little Laotian guy I've never met. He *thinks* I'll fold my weaker hand and not challenge his overwhelming advantage.

But he's wrong. Dead wrong.

We're not leaving. We're staying.

But if anything goes wrong from here on out, we'll be in serious trouble. I get a sudden twinge of stage fright, but now it fades. Funny; not like me to feel that these days.

I study Jim's ID bracelet and jiggle it against my wrist. Yep, I'm right. We're staying.

Heavy automatic-weapons fire buzzes again, mixed with Tonto's terrified screams, "CANDLE 23. MAYDAY! TONTO NEED BOMBS!"

CHAPTER THIRTY-TWO

I smile and sit up straight. I tell Rich, "See? I *told* you."

I radio my friend back. "Tonto . . . are you okay?"

Heavy machine-gun fire covers his answer. "TONTO SEE MANY BAD GUYS. TONTO NEED BOMBS *NOW* . . . HURRY!"

"Hold on, Tonto! I check on fighters!"

I tell Moonbeam urgently, "Moonbeam, Candle 23. Where the *hell* are my fighters? I needed them five minutes ago, not tomorrow. Tonto's not gonna last much longer."

Moonbeam answers, "Candle, I have good news and bad news. The good news is, the time is now . . . eleven fifty-four, straight-up. Your fighters are only ten minutes away . . . coming to you right off the tanker at full afterburner . . . they've been advised of your situation. And the bad news?" His voice turns apologetic. "I warned you we don't have many resources tonight . . . rainy season and all, ya know . . . all we've got is two F-4s armed with napalm. Sorry."

I blow up. "Ten minutes! Are you shittin' me? Tonto's not

gonna last *five*. And I *told you*: no F-4s or napalm! You gotta have something else . . . I'll take *anything*!"

The mature, baritone voice of the full colonel capsule commander interjects authoritatively, "Yes, I know *exactly* what that means . . . Tonto is going to lose some men . . . Sorry, but this F-4 flight is all we have . . . everything else is parked with the night off . . . rainy season. You'll have to work with these F-4s . . . you're lucky we have anything . . . Just do the best you can . . . Moonbeam out. Oh . . . one more thing . . . I admonish you once again against using profanity on the radio. Clean it up, Candle. Moonbeam out."

I tell myself there's no sense arguing. The prick just admitted he knows some of Tonto's men are going to burn to death along with the bad guys.

Charles cautions me, "Remember, we're not supposed to use nape on troops unless absolutely necessary . . . those new rules of engagement from the protests back home."

"I know," I answer seriously. "But they've left me no choice. You see any other options?"

I turn and see him shake his head sadly.

Rich looks astonished.

"CANDLE 23 . . . HELP TONTO *NOW*!" Amidst heavier firing.

I answer, "Tonto . . . can you hold on ten minutes? Bombs come."

Silence.

I repeat the question.

No answer back from him.

Finally his hollow voice answers, "Negative . . . ten minute bad . . . Tonto die."

I check my knee clock: 11:54:28 . . . 29 . . . tick . . . tick . . .

I think to myself, Ten lousy minutes out of an entire year and all I can do is circle helplessly and listen to my friend and his small band meet a violent death. If only the Church had armed us with that new side-firing cannon we've been asking for, we could cover Tonto until those F-4s get here.

I hear, "Pilot, Scope. Great news! All three marks landed right on the stupid trail! My best shot ever!"

I tell him congratulations, but find it hard to let go of this losing feeling of having only benign markers and flares for weapons. If only . . .

Tyrone pats my shoulder. He says sadly, "It's okay, JT. You did your best. We're gonna lose him, sir."

I shake my head and tell him firmly, "I am not giving up. There's always a solution. You just have to find it."

I lean forward, grab Jack's die, and roll it around my palm. I close my fist around the red cube and close my eyes. *Let it wash over you.*

I get excited. Of course! That's it! I toss Jack's die back to its resting spot below the engine instruments.

"Ramp, Pilot! How many flares you got left?"

"Enough, sir."

"Correct me if I'm wrong, but don't we have a *timer* on those flare canisters?"

"Right."

"Well, can you set up the flare chutes to deploy at a much *lower* altitude so the canisters fall a *long way* before the flare ignites?"

"Yes, sir. No problem . . . a twist of the dial. Never done it before . . . they come preset to go off a thousand feet below us. What'cha got in mind?"

"Can you set the timers so the canisters fall quickly to . . . let's say, two thousand feet above the surface, ignite there, and then be ready to throw out a whole barrage of flares in rapid succession?"

"Yes, sir. How many'd you have in mind?"

"Just keep droppin' till I tell you to stop."

"*Yes, sir!* But I'll need some extra hands back here. Can you send Tyrone and Eddie back to help yank flares out of the pallet box and haul them back to us?"

I whip around to tell Ty, but see he's already grabbed Ed-

die. I watch them squeeze their way between the flare pallets and the right-hand fuselage wall and then disappear in
the dark.

Good, good, good. We can still do this.

I call Tonto. "Tonto. Hold on! Hold on! I make guns
stop."

No answer back.

"Ramp, Pilot. Ty and Eddie are on their way back. Advise
me as soon as you guys are ready to go."

His answer arrives between deep breaths. "*Yes, sir!* But
these canisters are pretty heavy . . . in progress."

"Pilot, Scope. I don't get it. What do you want me to do?"

"No time to explain, but I want you to start dropping
flares at fifteen-second intervals and keep going until I tell
you to stop . . . you'll see . . . but you won't need that
starlight scope much longer."

He answers hesitantly, "I'll do it, but *why*?"

"Just do it. You'll see in a second. And, oh! You'd better
open the nuclear protection kit and find that stupid
monocle . . . no . . . make it *two*. Strap on two patches so
you'll be bifocal. You may be our only pair of eyes."

I warn Tonto. "Tonto, tell your men to protect their
eyes . . . cover eyes. Do you copy?"

Continuous machine-gun fire punctuates his shaky voice.
"Roger, Tonto copy. Bad guys close."

To make the interphone available for coordinating the
flare drops, I hold up my right hand, make an airfoil symbol,
and begin silently signaling Rich how much bank I need to
stay over the target area.

"Pilot and Scope from Ramp. Ready back here, sirs!"

I announce urgently, "Scope, Pilot. Let 'em rip."

"Ramp, Scope. Drop flare!"

I watch the first flare ignite close to the ground on the east
side of the trail behind the bad guys' position.

Perfect . . . that'll make 'em pause and wonder.

"Ramp, Pilot. That timer setting worked great. Keep it
up!"

"Drop flare!"

The second flare joins the first and lights up the enemy's backside.

I tell the crew, "It's working!"

Charles sounds bewildered. "What are you doing?"

"Shoving the power of the sun right in their goddamned faces. I'm gonna blind 'em till those F-4s get here. We're gonna make it so bright the bad guys'll have to drop their weapons or be permanently blinded. I figure we drop maybe fifteen flares around our orbit . . . so let's see . . . four million candlepower per flare . . . that's sixty million candles jammed right in their faces. I want their retinas to turn to dust if they don't cover their eyes."

I continue, "Break. Scope. Did you get those monocles on?"

"Got 'em on, JT."

"Drop flare!"

A muffled oxygen-mask voice enters my headset. "Candle 23, this is Gunfighter 56 Lead . . . flight of two F-4s checking in. Confirm your position and stand by for our information."

"Drop flare!"

I check my knee clock: 11:56 . . . tick . . . tick . . .

"Gunfighter, Candle. Moonbeam relayed your information."

"Stand by. I'll get right back to you . . . busy on this end. But you don't need our position. Do you see the bright light?"

"Affirmative. What *is* that!"

"Drop flare!"

"Just come to the light. We're right over the PDJ. You can't miss us. Say ETA."

"ETA your location is zero four . . . I say again . . . four minutes after . . . coming at you in full 'burner. We bingo at quarter past . . . won't have much play time . . . two passes apiece max."

I get the feeling I'm juggling too many balls, yet can't afford to let a single one drop . . . gotta juggle faster.

I check my knee clock: 11:56:23 . . . 24 . . . tick . . . tick. I confirm the time with my Seiko. That'd be all we need at this point . . . the seven-day windup clock to run down or stick. If that should happen, I'd lose track of time, maybe hang around too long, and run out of gas.

I lean forward and wind it tight . . . tick . . . tick . . . time's running out . . . gotta pick up the pace and not drop any balls.

"Drop flare!"

Our flares make a half-circle starting on the eastern flank, arc through north, and now curve through west behind Tonto's position.

Beautiful. The light blossoms so bright I have to squint.

I reach for my sunglasses in my helmet bag and put them on. Out of the corner of my eye I see Charles looking excited. He hops off his director's chair, lands on the back porch, and leans into the cockpit. Now I watch him wedge himself into the tight space between my seatback and the main circuit-breaker panel.

I slide my seat forward to give him more room. I think of cautioning him, "Be careful your chute doesn't pop any circuit breakers back there," but he seems so enthusiastic I decide not to spoil the moment.

Charles studies the growing circle of flares as they arc through southeast and now crawl back toward the first flare.

We watch together as the circle of light becomes complete. Charles looks at me and grins. I smile back.

I call Tonto. "Tonto, Candle. Is the light working?"

No answer. Too little too late?

I try again. "Tonto, Candle. Are you okay? Light okay?"

We hear the sound of a radio dragged across pebbles. Tonto is evidently blinded, but has keyed his mike, because the only sound we detect is beautiful, dead silence. No weapons fire.

Glory hallelujah!

I tear up. Well, I'll be go to hell, Jack . . . it worked . . . it actually worked. I look at Charles and see he is crying, too.

My Laotian friend sounds confused. "Tonto no see . . . bad guys no shoot. Number one light. Light number one."

I wipe away the tears.

I counsel myself, Don't go there, John . . . we have a long way to go before this one's over. I struggle to keep my voice composed.

"Ramp, Pi . . . Pilot," my voice cracks. "It's *working*! Keep it up, guys!"

"Drop flare!"

Now I call the F-4s. "Gunfighter, for your protection, I recommend you lower your sun visors. We're dropping a ton of flares . . . you should see our light by now."

"Roger, wilco," he chuckles. "Holy moly! We were *wondering* what the heck that is . . . looks like a nuclear blast. Standing by for your brief so we can get to work as soon as we arrive . . . this AB burn is makin' us short on gas . . . our play time will be next to nothing."

"Ours, too, but we're gonna pull this thing off . . . together," I answer.

Charles looks at me and says, "Congratulations, JT."

"We're not out of the woods yet," I answer. "We still have to pull off this airstrike and not burn up Tonto in the process."

CHAPTER *THIRTY-THREE*

Rich's voice scratches like a needle across a record. "Pilot from Copilot."

I groan to myself, *Oh, no.* Not again. I *knew* he couldn't keep his mouth shut.

Charles looks me in the eye and slowly shakes his head.

I call the F-4s. "Gunfighter, I'll brief as you fly in, but I got a problem here. Get right back to you."

He answers suspiciously at my lack of preparation, "Okay, but hustle . . . we won't have much time on target."

I study Rich. Then I address him harshly, "What do you want now? Can't you see we're busy? This had better be good. And I *told* you, drop the military crap. Just talk to me, but be quick about it. There isn't time to mess around."

"Roger, Pilot. We need to balance up these fuel tanks." He points up at the overhead fuel gauges. I look at them with him. The left tank gauge is down to 2,600 pounds while the right indicates a hair below 3,000.

"Rich, there's no way that can be right. Just a couple minutes ago they were evenly matched at three thousand. There's *no way* the left engine could burn an extra four hundred pounds . . . that twenty-six hundred *has* to be a false indication . . . prob'ly green goo. Remember that?"

He shakes his head no.

"Oh, sure you do," I remind him. "Maintenance tries getting rid of it, but can't, and it'll make a fuel gauge drop *just like this*? Surely you've seen this before."

Rich charges ahead as though I've said nothing. "Still, Pilot, we should balance before it gets out of control. The published cross-tank limit is five hundred pounds, so request permission to cross-feed to even 'em up."

"Drop flare!"

I lecture him, "Rich, didn't you *hear* me? There's *no way* that indication can be real. It's the green goo. Don't touch that cross feed valve. Just *leave it alone* and that left side'll come back up to three thousand all by itself."

"Candle 23, Gunfighter. You still there? We need your drop information pretty quick. Time's running out, buddy," the fighter pilot chastises me.

I check my knee clock: . . . 11:58:06 . . . tick . . . tick . . .

They'll be here in six minutes . . . gotta get Rich out of my hair.

Rich goes into his Disney's Abe impression again. "But, Pilot, the rules clearly state: 'The flight crew shall balance fuel when the lateral imbalance reaches four hundred pounds.' Request permission to begin cross-feed operations."

Rich has me in a Church-sanctioned headlock I need to free myself from and get on with business. Knowing Rich, he'll sneak that valve open as soon as I look away, and then I'll have a fuel-imbalance ball to juggle along with all the others.

"Drop flare!"

I decide to stop him before he gets out of control.

"Rich, I'm gonna tell you one last time. Permission *denied*," I order sternly. "Don't touch that damned valve. Your four-hundred-pound figure isn't even a structural limit. It's only there to remind us not to let any imbalance get too far out of control. The actual limit is one thousand pounds, but again, that's not structural. We could let that tank go completely dry and it wouldn't hurt the airplane one bit; so drop it."

Rich raises a finger and argues, "Yes, but—"

I cut him off. "Look, I gotta start working with these fast-movers. You and I tested both gauges a couple minutes ago. You saw that yourself. So we know they're working okay. Besides, if you cross-feed, you'd prob'ly lose track of the fuel while you're concentrating on flying. That *left* side'll recover shortly. But if you cross-fed, you'd've *created* your own artificial imbalance you'd have to fix. You'd be a dog chasing its tail."

Rich opens his mouth, but I blow him out of the water. "*If* fuel balance *is* a problem, and I don't think it is, we'll balance up on the way home when we have more time to pay attention. We'll have an hour down to the river and then another twenty-five minutes down to NKP, and you can fiddle with it all you want. So just fly the damned airplane for me and let's get back to work."

Rich answers defiantly, "You're wrong, Pilot. I can fly and cross-feed at the same time. Since you've decided to utterly disregard the regs and land on fumes, we gotta balance fuel early to stay on top of the problem. Request permission—"

"Candle, this is Gunfighter Lead . . . *look* . . . we need your instructions pretty soon, buddy, or this isn't gonna work."

I apologize, "Look, Gunfighter, I've got an internal problem . . . be right back to you . . . sorry . . . please stand by."

I suddenly realize Rich's argument has nothing to do with fuel. This is another boot-zippers argument. Rich is using the issue as a wedge to assert authority in a situation where he has none. Balancing fuel is well within his copilot job description, so he's carefully crafted a Church-sanctioned argument I'll likely lose and waste precious seconds.

"Drop flare!"

I go over the consequences: If I let him cross-feed, he'll

get busy flying, forget to check the gauges, and create a self-inflicted imbalance. The *left* gauge'll recover to 3,000, but then the *right* tank'll be down to 2,700 because it'll have been feeding *both* engines. Then he'll have to start the process all over in reverse for a problem of his own making . . . right, then left, then right again, then back left . . . a dog chasing its tail.

But the biggest danger is this: the ancient cross-feed valve might not close when he tells it to. A C-123 pilot with any common sense never trusts these rusty old valves to open or close on command. We keep our hands off them. If that valve ever sticks *open* when he goes to *close* it, we'd be in even worse trouble I don't have time to think through right now.

But if I *don't* let him cross-feed, he'll nag and piss and moan and whine until I can't concentrate. But . . . if I give him his cross-feed tail to chase, at least he'll be out of my hair.

I keep my voice composed and tell him, "Okay. Go ahead and cross-feed, but keep an eye on it."

"Roger, Pilot. No problem. Cross-feeding now."

I watch him grasp his Cadnica rechargeable flashlight off the radio console and shine it on the black fuel panel. He turns the silver dollar–size rotary valve ninety degrees left to "open." Now he turns off the left-tank fuel-boost pumps to start burning both engines from the right tank. We quickly look down at the left-engine instruments to check if the ancient valve actually opened.

They look normal . . . no coughing or sputtering from fuel starvation.

Whew! At least that's one ball I can drop and not worry about until we head home.

I scan the overhead tank gauges. Left: 2,600. Right: 2,900 . . . maybe a whisker below. To keep track, I take my felt-tip pen and scribble the readings on the back of my left hand.

"Drop flare!"

I leave Rich chasing his tail and look out my left window to get back to work.

I key the radio. "Gunfighter, back with you now. What idiot loaded you guys with nape? You know what that *means*?"

"We know," he explains. "We told them it was a stupid load, but they put it on, anyway. Sorry . . . the supply channel is screwed up. You know the rest . . . can't say it on the radio."

I think to myself, that damned bomb shortage just bit us in the ass.

Suddenly I get a creepy-crawly feeling about the way this is going. Events should be folding together naturally, but I'm jamming things together. Something feels wrong, but as I try concentrating on whatever it is, the feeling slips away.

I shrug it off and get back to work. "Stand by, Gunfighter. I have to check with my ground FAC to get final approval. He's not aware all you got is nape."

"Roger, Candle."

"Tonto, Candle 23. Bad news. Fighters have napalm . . . I repeat . . . napalm. I'm sorry. You still want bomb?"

"Drop flare!"

Tonto's voice sounds depressed. "Stand by . . . Tonto check."

My friend knows some of his people will likely burn to death in the firestorm or drown when the fireball sucks up all the available oxygen.

I sit back and wait for Tonto to translate for his commander to get a final decision.

Tonto answers solemnly, "Candle 23 . . . go ahead . . . drop bombs."

I pause to gather my thoughts. What I say next to the F-4s will have much to do with Tonto's survival.

I lecture sternly, "Gunfighters, I want you guys to listen up. I know your airplane wasn't built for this kind of close air support. And I am well aware nape is near impossible to control . . . but I'm not giving out excuses tonight. This one has to be perfect. This one *matters*. That guy down there is a personal friend of mine and . . . stand by."

Out of the corner of my eye I see Rich waving frantically.

Now what!

"Drop flare!"

I ask harshly, "What, *Dick*!"

"You can't talk to a fighter pilot like that! You know the pecking order. You piss him off, he'll leave!"

I continue my lecture. "Gunfighter, as I was saying . . . Tonto's my friend and I don't want him burned up. So I don't want you doing any of that new toss-bombing crap where you lob ordnance like slow-pitch softball and *hope* it hits somewhere inside Laos. *That's not gonna cut it.* I want your best work ever. Do you copy?"

He answers seriously, "Roger, Candle . . . just tell us what you want."

"Great, thanks. The trail runs south to north in the target area. The good guys are on the west . . . I repeat . . . *west . . . left* side of the road. The bad guys are on the east . . . I repeat . . . *east . . . right* side. Don't get it mixed up. I'm timing our flare drops so they'll burn out right as you arrive. When it turns dark, you're gonna see my three ground marks *right on the road*. I recommend a south-to-north drop to the *right* of my marks . . . I say again . . . *east . . . right* of my marks. Now as soon as you see my marks and you've got me in sight, you're cleared in hot. The first drop is the one that counts. Any questions?"

He answers, "Just one favor . . . keep droppin' those flares. Don't stop."

His request makes no sense. I ask incredulously, "You want us to *keep flaring*? But you won't be able to see my ground marks and the target area in this blinding sunlight."

He answers confidently, "Yes, I will . . . you'll see . . . just keep on flaring."

I answer hesitantly, "Okay, but I hope you know what you're doing."

I check my knee clock: 12:03:11 . . . tick . . . tick . . . time's running out.

"Drop flare!"

I hear, "Candle, Gunfighter. We're in the area now. I have

you, the road, and your marks in sight. I confirm . . . I will drop south-to-north on the east side. Tell your ground guy to take cover. I'm in hot."

I switch radios and yell, "TONTO! TAKE COVER! TAKE COVER!"

I cross my fingers and peer out the top of my window to catch the lead F-4 slicing through our altitude . . .

Nothing.

I lower my scan to the horizon . . .

Nada.

So where the heck is he? His giant, jungle-camouflaged fighter-bomber silhouetted against all this light should be easy to spot.

Charles taps my left shoulder and points repeatedly *down*. Down?

Charles yells at me off interphone, "Look down . . . No . . . *all the way down* . . . he's right on the deck . . . *below the flares*. Look! You can see his *shadow* on the road . . . then look just above that."

I yelp, "I see him! Looks like he's flying formation with his own shadow! Holy cow! He's way below treetop level. He's gotta be seeing their faces. They could throw a rock and knock him down. He's really hangin' his ass out."

My eyes water and the scene becomes blurred. I wipe them clear and turn back to watch.

Charles hollers, "Look out! Oh my God! He's headed right for two of our flare chutes! If he sucks those into his engines . . ." At the last possible second, we watch the fighter pilot roll up on his right wing, jink between the flares, and continue his bomb run.

Charles exclaims, "Did you see *that*? He almost bought the farm!"

To myself, I think, just an hour ago I figured the minute-man spirit of the American fighting man was dead. I was wrong. That spirit is alive and well, after all. I've found it over this remote jungle in this gunfighter pilot risking his life for a faceless ally he'll never meet.

I watch him fly right down the fucking road as a rooster

tail of flames engulfs the east side and now chases him. I watch scarlet, black, and orange flames mushroom like an oil refinery blaze. The half-mile firestorm behind him now gathers a life of its own and races up from behind, trying to catch him! It's gaining! Yards behind now and racing up his ass faster and faster!

I switch my radio to emergency guard and yell, "Gunfighter, this is Candle on guard. Get out! Pull up! Pull up! Fire! Fire! Fire!" I watch him and his shadow continue dropping nape canisters with that flaming rooster tail gaining ground.

My eyeballs wince from the combined flare and fire light. I reluctantly turn away, look back inside, and catch Rich looking transfixed by the devastation.

My eyes recover. Now I look back down and see the gunfighter pull straight up, showboat a four-point victory roll, and finally level off just above our flares. He asks proudly, "How's *that*, Candle? I think I got most of them, but I'm ready for my second pass . . . then my wingman'll follow up with two more. How's your ground guy doin'? Did I miss him?"

I holler, "Unbefuckinlievable! Stand by . . . I'll check how he's doing and try to get you some BDA."

"Roger. Standing by bomb damage assessment. Won't make my second pass till I hear from you."

I radio apprehensively, "Tonto, Candle 23?" Silence.

"Tonto, Candle 23. Are you okay?" No answer from him. My forearm goose bumps return.

I call urgently, "Tonto, Candle 23 . . . are you there!" Nothing.

Oh, shit.

CHAPTER *THIRTY-FOUR*

I panic. Have I killed my friend?

I try one more time. "Tonto, Candle 23 . . . are you okay?"

Tonto's excited voice crackles in my headset, "OOOOOOOO-OOOOOOOH! NUMBER ONE BOMB-BBBBBBBB! I CAN HEAR THEM *SCREEEAMING*!!! DO SAME, SAME!!!"

I feel his words permanently branding my brain as an electric current zips beneath my skin. Like I said, paybacks are hell.

Charles squeezes my left shoulder. He says sadly, "They left you no choice."

I tell Gunfighter, "Great job. Sierra Hotel, guys. Tonto says, 'Number one bomb. Do same, same.' You are cleared in hot at your discretion. Go get 'em. We'll just sit back and enjoy the show."

"Roger, Candle . . . no problem, big boy . . . glad to help . . . I'm in hot."

Ty's voice intrudes, "Pilot, Engineer."

Strange—Ty knows not to interrupt an airstrike.

I answer abruptly, "Ty, can it wait? We're busy up here, ya know?"

His serious voice responds, "No, Captain Halliday, it can't. We got ourselves a real problem back here."

A twang of fear wets the back of my neck. I wipe it off.

Jammed flare in the deployment chute? I ask apprehensively, "Ty, say your location. You still back on the ramp?"

"No, Captain Halliday," Ty addresses me formally a second time . . . uh-oh . . . I feel my stomach cramp.

Ty's baritone voice continues, "I'm back at my normal station by the number one engine, and, well . . . I never seen anything like this before . . . not sure how to describe it."

I prod, "Just tell me what you see."

His tone is drop-dead serious. "Sir, we got ourselves a pretty good fuel leak coming off this left engine. I think you better come back and look for yourself."

I recall it's guys like Ty who taught me this old warhorse is nothing but one continuous hydraulic, oil, and fuel leak. Between constant prop oil leaks and what? . . . eighteen gallons of engine oil . . . it's normal to have all kinds of crud sheeting across the cowling. I remember Ty explaining a pint-size oil leak can look like a gusher. He taught me, "Start worrying when this old beast *stops* leaking."

I answer, "Look, Ty, I'm real busy. Can it wait five minutes? You sure it's not just your standard C-123 leak?"

"No, Captain Halliday, it's not," he says firmly. "This can't wait. You'd better come back and look at this thing."

Thing? I am suddenly frightened.

I look up and check the overhead fuel gauges. The left tank reads the same old 2,600, but the *right* gauge indicates 1,200.

Twelve hundred on the *right*?

Confused, I ask Ty, "You sure you didn't get turned around? We're showing the *right* side low, not the left."

He answers firmly, "No, sir. This leak's definitely off the *left* engine."

"Then we've got two problems. There's something wrong

with the right fuel gauge, too. I'll come back after I troubleshoot this other problem."

No answer back from him.

I stare at the gauge and tell myself, no way . . . it read much higher a couple minutes ago . . . didn't it? I check my hand note . . . yep . . . 2,900 . . . maybe we've burned down to 2,700 . . . but 1,200? Fifteen hundred pounds? No way . . . must be the green goo . . . or . . . what?

Oh, I get it! Charles's chute must've popped a circuit breaker when he squeezed in behind me . . . should've told him not to do that . . . my fault.

I turn and tell Charles calmly, "Hey, do me a favor. We're showing a bad right fuel gauge. I think your chute popped a circuit breaker. If I remember correctly, the rule on losing power is 'AC lies and DC dies.' Since our fuel gauges are AC-powered, this low indication's prob'ly just a loss of power."

I grab my Cadnica rechargeable off the center radio console and pass it back to him. "Why don't you back out of there slowly and then look for what CB popped."

Charles answers apologetically, "Jeez, sorry. I'm on it."

As he crawls out, just in case I'm wrong, I reach overhead and push the fuel press-to-test button.

Oops . . . both gauges drive counterclockwise toward zero . . . not an electrical problem . . . must be the green goo as I first thought.

I see a concerned-looking Charles scanning for popped CBs and tell him, "Forget it. I was wrong. Sorry . . . must be a green goo problem . . . the gauge'll return to normal after this test."

Charles looks relieved.

I release the test button, hoping in my heart of hearts the test will kick the green goo where it hurts and the gauge will come back up to 2,700.

I release the test button and . . .

Twelve hundred.

Uh-oh.

This could be real trouble.

I glance at Rich and ask, "You got any ideas?"

A brush of fear crosses his face, but then he regains his deadpan composure. He shrugs. "Not a clue."

"Hey, Ty, this doesn't make sense. We're showing twenty-six hundred on the left and *twelve hundred* on the *right* . . . you're on the *left* side? . . . You absolutely sure you didn't get turned around . . . confirm you're looking at the *left* engine . . . I—"

Ty cuts me off and says seriously, "Captain Halliday, you'd better come back and look at this *thing* right now. I never seen anything like it in the twenty years I been flyin'."

I get that state-trooper-materializing-in-your-rearview-mirror-with-sirens-blaring-and-lights-flashing feeling, a dual twinge of heat and fear. My heart pounds in my ears.

I look at Rich for advice, but he looks back perplexed. Now he throws his hands up. His expression says, "I don't have a clue, but don't blame me . . . I told you something like this would happen."

I tell Ty, "On my way back right now."

I check my knee clock: . . . 12:04:34 . . . tick . . . tick . . .

I order Rich, "Confirm with Gunfighter Lead he's cleared in hot. Tell him we're RTBing and to finish up on his own. Just in case this is a serious problem, get turned around for NKP while I go back and get this straightened out with Ty."

I repeat the irritating disconnecting drill. I slide my seat back, unplug my interphone cord, unbuckle my lap belt, and leave my headset on to protect my ears from the lumber-mill howl of props and engines. I spin around to straddle the radio console and come face-to-face with a frightened-looking Charles occupying the doorway.

He steps down to the back porch to let me by.

I stand up, smack my head hard against the overhead panel, feel for a wet spot . . . yep . . . bloodied it again . . . move through the door, and land on the back porch beside Charles.

My heartbeat echoes in my headset, *da-boom, da-boom.*

I look left, expecting to see Ty on the *right* side.

No Ty there.

I look right to the *left* side and see him waving frantically. "Hurry up!"

I struggle down the stairs under the tonnage of my survival gear. I stop in my tracks as my boots hit the metal floor . . . more dancing white stars . . . low oxygen . . . hypoxic . . . not good for the brain . . . go slow . . . no need to rush . . . can't be much of a problem, anyway . . . Ty must be exaggerating . . . doesn't make sense . . . *left* side leak; *right* tank low?

Ty keeps waving. "Come on! Faster!"

Da-boom, da-boom.

I tell myself, easy does it . . . slow down . . . plenty of time . . . don't panic . . . more shooting stars . . . they say never rush in an airplane . . . when something happens, sit on your hands . . . don't touch anything . . . light a cigarette . . . think about it . . . I'll take a sec to ease Tyrone's concerns and then get back up and catch the rest of the show . . . missing the best action of the year, dammit!

Da-boom, da-boom.

I lumber over to the still frantically waving Ty one step at a time like some large, green, prehistoric turtle standing upright for the first time . . . left foot . . . now the right . . . left . . . now right . . . one slow step at a time . . . straighten out Ty on this simple fuel-sheeting problem, then get back to the cockpit . . . can't leave Rich by himself long . . . no telling what he'll do . . . something stupid . . . hurry . . . heartbeat jackhammering in my headset, *da-boom, da-boom.*

I see Ty still waving. *"Come on! Come on!"*

I think, Yeah, yeah, yeah. Hold your horses; I'm coming.

I reach Ty.

We are standing less than two feet from the combined engine and prop lumber-mill-ripsaw HOWLS . . . hard to hear myself think.

Ty looks terrified and points out the porthole. He cups his hands and megaphones, "LOOK AT THAT! LOOK AT THAT!" and points again.

I put my left boot on the wooden catwalk to climb up to see the problem, but my chute pulls me back down . . . aft center of gravity. I motion Ty I need a boost.

I launch myself at the elevated catwalk. Ty shoves from behind and pins me against the fuselage wall.

I peer out.

Da-boom, da-boom, da-boom.

I draw in my breath at the horrific sight. I gasp aloud, "Ahhhhhh!" An electric charge races down my spine.

That can't be!

My exclamation has fogged the window so I can't see. I shake my head to blow out the low-oxygen cobwebs. I tell myself, No, that *can't be* . . . eyes playing tricks . . . nightmare images like that only happen in old black-and-white Saturday-morning serials . . . not real life.

DA-BOOM, DA-BOOM, DA-BOOM.

I use my sleeve to wipe off my breath fog . . . howling ripsaw sounds and whirling propeller *inches* away make it hard to concentrate.

I hold my breath so I don't refog the window.

I smash my nose against the crazed glass for a good look.

I discover the phrase *his blood turned cold* is real. It's one hundred-plus degrees in here, yet I feel I'm standing on the Chicago lakefront in an ice storm.

Oh, sweet Jesus!

DA-BOOM, DA-BOOM, DA-BOOM, DA-BOOM, DA-BOOM.

This is the type of thing you don't recover from.

It's a death sentence. Fuel is *gushing* out the bottom of the engine like out of a fire hose.

CHAPTER *THIRTY-FIVE*

I turn to Ty and yell over the lumber-mill howls, "WHAT HAPPENED!?"

"MUST . . . E   OUT . . . SIDE . . . LING . . . WH . . . CAN . . . SEE!"

I bellow, "WHAT? CAN'T HEAR YOU!"

I hop down so we are standing chest to chest. He shakes his head, turns, and points to his left earcup.

I place my lips against the blue plastic and holler, "WHAT? SAY AGAIN!"

Ty turns and faces me. His lips and mustache shout, "MUST BE ON THE OUTBOARD SIDE OF THE COWL-ING WHERE WE CAN'T SEE!" He turns away.

I yell, "BUT WHAT HAPPENED!?"

He turns to me and shakes his head. His mustache shouts, "DON'T KNOW! MUST'VE TAKEN A THIRTY-SEVEN HIT AND IT TOOK OUT THE MAIN FUEL LINE!" I see his eyes stuffed with fear, and then he turns away again.

I holler, "DON'T SEE DAMAGE! SHOULD BE RIPPED-UP METAL!"

Ty faces me and shakes his head vigorously. His mustache howls, "MUST BE OUTBOARD WHERE WE CAN'T SEE IT!"

I stand on tiptoes and peer out the porthole, hoping the vision will have disappeared . . . but the fire-hose gusher remains.

I stare at it in horror. This isn't your everyday, run-of-the-mill problem. This is *real* trouble.

I suddenly feel akin to those tsunami beach people, transfixed by the vision of approaching death.

I force myself to study the leak . . . focus on the details. While most of the fuel is harmlessly atomizing away in the slipstream, some is rippling *up the side of the engine cowl*. I watch in terror as it creeps along and up the cowl and now ripples its way *forward* toward the inboard red-hot exhaust stack.

Forward and up? How is that possible going into a 130 mph wind? And if that fuel reaches that cherry-red exhaust stack, with 2,600 pounds of gas in that wing tank?

Oh, my God . . . we're a ticking time bomb.

I turn to Ty and bellow against his earcup, "HOW COME IT'S NOT ON FIRE?"

His mustache roars, "JUST LUCKY SO FAR! SHE COULD BLOW ANY SECOND!"

Every fiber in my body screams to race back to the cockpit to do *something,* but I command myself to stay to find out *what's going on* so I'll know what to do when I get back up there.

I shout, "HOW'S THE ENGINE STILL RUNNING WITH THAT MASSIVE A LEAK?"

"DON'T KNOW . . . SHOULDN'T BE . . . COULD QUIT ANYTIME!"

"HOW DO WE STOP IT?"

Ty bows his head and looks down like someone staring into his own grave.

I shake his shoulders. "HOW DO WE STOP IT!?"

He does not look up.

His voice trembles. "DON'T . . . DON'T . . . THINK WE CAN!"

I repeat, "TY, WHAT CAN WE DO!"

He looks up sorrowfully. "NOTHING!"

"LIKE HELL." I tug his sleeve. "COME ON."

I spin around and spot Charles frantically waving from the end of a football-field-length sewer pipe. "Get back up here!"

How'd he get so far away? It'll take me *forever* to get there.

I feel Ty's boots reverberate on the metal floor behind me . . . careful . . . prob'ly hypoxic . . . not too fast . . . good . . . hey . . . maybe this is just another nightmare and I'll wake up . . . but Ty saw it, too . . . no nightmare.

Charles stares bug-eyed at Ty and me charging him.

Somehow I gather speed, fly up the steps, and zip past an apprehensive-looking Charles shouting, "WHAT'S GOING ON? ARE WE IN TROUBLE?"

I holler, "NO TIME!"

I blast through the doorway and see Rich pointing up repeatedly at the fuel gauges. His face shows extreme panic.

I slam into the left seat, strap on my lap belt, plug in my headset, and hear Rich finishing excitedly, ". . . dropping like a rock! What's going on back there?"

I check my knee clock: 12:06:08 . . . 09 . . . tick . . . tick . . . tick . . .

I was only gone *ninety seconds*? Seemed like an hour!

I sit, hoping; maybe that gusher was in my mind. Nothing could be *that* bad.

I force myself to look up at the fuel panel, not wanting to know. The left gauge still shows 2,600 . . . good.

The right side is down to 1,000.

Holy Christ! How can that *be*? I was only gone over a minute and we've pumped *two hundred more pounds* of precious, life-sustaining fuel overboard?

What the hell's going on?

If I don't do something fast, in five minutes, that right tank's gonna be empty and one of these engines is gonna quit!

But which one?

Wrong . . . *three* minutes . . . if Rich is right about gauge error.

I check our heading . . . 165 . . . good . . . a beeline for NKP . . . at least Rich got us turned around . . . we can still make NKP if we get the leak stopped.

I check the right gauge pointer . . . now halfway between the 1,000 and 800 marks . . . still falling.

Shit!

Tyrone appears in the doorway and leans over the throttles to check the fuel gauges. Charles's frightened face crowds through the doorway, and now he piggybacks our flight engineer.

I announce, "Okay, guys, listen up. Here's our situation: We've got a massive fuel leak on the *left* engine Ty thinks came from a thirty-seven hit. The leak is getting close to the exhaust stack, so we could catch fire or explode at any moment. On top of that, the *right* fuel tank is dropping like a rock . . . we're losing two hundred pounds a minute. We're headed south to try to make it to NKP. Does *anybody* see what the problem is?"

Rich says, "Maybe it's—" but stops. He tries again, "No . . . maybe it's—" but this also fails.

I look at Charles. He shakes his head no.

I check the right gauge and see the pointer indicate a whisker above 800. My mind visualizes that rippling fuel creeping up toward the glowing-red exhaust manifold. I look at three pairs of eyes staring at me, waiting for me to do something.

I ask myself, And exactly what would that be?

Ty breaks the silence. "Sir, maybe they cross-wired the gauges when they worked on 'em last. They could've wired the left tank to the right gauge and the right tank to the left gauge. It's happened before. Crews have pulled a fire handle for a bad engine, but it's the opposite *good* engine that shuts down, leavin' 'em flying on the engine on fire. Lots of crews haven't figured it out before . . . well. Anyway, if it's a cross-wire situation, it could've been hiding for months since the last overhaul and nobody'd ever know until something like this happened."

I confirm, "Correct me if I'm wrong, what you're saying is the *left* engine'll stop when the *right* gauge gets to zero, and then we'll be able to fly home on the *right* engine with the twenty-six hundred pounds in the *left* tank? Is that *right*? I mean, 'correct'? You're saying, all we gotta do is sit on our hands and do nothing?"

Rich says authoritatively, "Ty is right. The operating manual also recommends a precautionary shutdown for any fuel leak. We gotta pull the number one fire handle right now to shut off fuel to prevent a fire."

I watch his left arm snake out of the dark to pull it. I smack his arm away and growl, "Try that again and I'll break your fuckin' arm. It's working fine, so just leave it alone. We got enough problems without being down to one engine."

Rich exclaims, "But it's gonna catch fire!"

I tell him, "If it does, we'll let it burn. At least it'll be giving us power."

I check the pointer . . . between the 8 and 6 marks . . . 700. Ninety seconds to Rich's 400. And we're still *guessing*.

I ask, "But, Ty, if you're wrong about the cross-wire . . . Wait a minute . . . let me figure this out . . . shit . . . I can't . . . anybody jump in here . . . What happens if that's not it?"

"If Ty's wrong," Charles fills in, "then we're in for some real surprises. One of these engines'll die, but you won't know which. Then the other motor'll run until the leak drains all the gas off this airplane, and then it'll get real dark and real quiet in here. You don't *know* the condition inside that wing. That thirty-seven hit could've ripped the entire leading-edge plumbing apart and you won't stop it no matter what."

Ty chimes in, "The man is right."

I rub my forehead.

"Pilot from Ramp. Would it help save fuel if I closed up the back?"

The answer bolts from my lips. "*No! Absolutely* not! We might need it soon."

It comes to me we're not going to make it home, but maybe we can make the river. If we get that far, we'll get out of this alive . . . *if* we can find a way to isolate the leak . . .

I tell Charles firmly, "Gimme a new heading for the closest part of the Mekong. It runs north to south, so pick the closest point . . . wait . . . maybe we could even make Vientiane . . . there's an American consulate there . . . I think it's only about one hundred thirty miles away . . . check 'em both."

Charles exclaims, "Right! Stand by, I'll check," and disappears to his desk to plot the new course.

But what if, when the right tank gets down to 400 and one engine stops, the other continues to run, but the *left tank continues to drop* from Charles's idea of a fuel plumbing catastrophe?

"Come right to a new heading of two two zero," Charles answers, his voice sounding discouraged. "Still too far . . . at least forty-five minutes."

I turn to Ty and ask, "Do the jets come off a separate fuel line? I'm thinking if they do, maybe we start the left jet, maybe shut down the left engine, work around the leak and retain what gas we've got left. Would that work?"

Ty answers dejectedly, "No. Same plumbing. You want me to start the jets?"

I answer firmly, "Negative. We'd burn even more gas. And if the left jet and recip died together at full power, she could flip over."

Charles says authoritatively, "Hey, look. I may only be a lowly navigator, but I'm also the senior officer onboard, so I'm gonna say it: You guys are grabbing at straws. You don't *know* what's wrong. And I, for one, am not willing to bet my life on your whims. So nail it down."

Silence.

I go back to the beginning: We started with 3,000 pounds per tank before the attack. Then . . . the left side went down to what? Twenty-six hundred? While the right side stayed up at 2,900. So far, so good. So . . . what that means is . . . the left side leak must've started *right then*. Then . . . Rich whined about the fuel imbalance and wanted to open the cross-feed . . . so, it's . . . it *has* to be . . . Y*es! That's it! The damned cross-feed valve! It must be open! It's been open the whole time!*

I shout, "I've got it! It's the cross-feed!"

Rich looks stunned.

I check the fuel panel to confirm my theory, but can't find the black rotary valve. Except for the two lit gauges, the panel is pitch-black. Where is that damned thing?

I guess at the valve's location, but jam my fingers into the dark panel. Hurry!

I check the tank . . . 400.

Shit.

Too late?

Ty shines his Cadnica onto the black panel. He groans, "Oh, no," and hangs his head. Charles looks confused.

But there it is . . . the source of the problem . . . hiding in the dark.

The cross-feed valve is *wide open*. I reach up, turn the left boost pump back on, and close the cross-feed.

I glare at Rich. My voice rings with disgust: "What the hell've you done, *Dick*?"

Rich's face changes from bewilderment to astonishment to horror in less than a second. Now he covers his face with his hands, shakes his head violently, and cries out, "I'm sorry, I'm sorry, I'm sorry . . . I'm *so* sorry . . . I didn't mean . . . I thought . . ."

Charles asks apprehensively, "What's going on?"

I explain dejectedly, "Charles, I'm not sure, but I think we've been pumping gas from the good right tank *through* the open cross-feed manifold, through the damaged left engine, and pumped it overboard. But I gotta prove it. I could still be guessing."

Charles sounds bewildered. "How do you do that?"

"If I'm right, the *left* gauge'll start dropping at the same rate now and the right tank'll stabilize at four hundred . . . stand by."

I push my face against the glass to detect any drop.

Nothing. No movement.

Stuck at 2,600. Maybe I got it wrong.

Suddenly I remember fuel pointers move like watch hands, so I tear my eyes away and focus on my knee clock second hand as it ticks off fifteen seconds . . . tick . . . tick . . .

At two hundred pounds a minute . . . that's one hundred in thirty seconds . . . so . . . that's fifty pounds in fifteen seconds . . . so when I look back up . . . I should see a small, black fifty-pound space between the white pointer and the white 2,600 mark . . . yeah, that's it . . . look for the black space . . .

The second hand stumbles in slow motion . . . tick . . . tick . . . tick. I warn myself, don't look up, or you'll have to do this all over again . . . fourteen . . . fifteen.

Now! Look!

There it is, a tiny black space between the needle and mark. Relief! Mystery solved!

"We got it, guys!" I announce. "The leak was out of the left tank the whole time . . . now we just have to figure out what to do next . . . Wait a sec . . ."

I talk the situation through. "Help me out . . . the right side's at four hundred . . . maybe ten minutes' fuel at cruise power, and then the right engine'll quit, but now the twenty-six hundred pounds in the *left* tank'll finish gushing overboard in about . . . thirteen minutes from now . . . so our options are . . . what?"

I watch the left pointer fall toward 2,400.

Our predicament finally dawns on me. It's obvious now what's wrong and what's going to happen.

I tell Charles, "Gimme a new heading for the absolutely *worst terrain* you can find . . . as rugged, remote, and as far off the trail as possible."

Charles fires back, "Come further right to new heading of two four oh." Then he appears beside me and asks privately, "What are you doing?"

I answer off interphone, "Putting as many ridgelines between us and the remaining bad guys as possible. Hopefully that'll buy us enough time for the Jolly Greens to reach us at first light before we're hunted down."

"But most of us won't survive that, John."

I face him and answer sadly, "I know . . . last resort."

We're not going anywhere. We're not going to make the river. We're not going to make Vientiane. We're not even going to make it across enough protective ridgelines.

We're staying *right here*.

Even if I start the jets and crank the speed up to 180 . . . three miles a minute . . . for maybe twelve minutes . . . thirty-six miles . . . we'll be . . . where?

Right here with the remaining bad guys we just bombed to hell. My plan to save Tonto has blown up in my face.

We are doomed.

Rage consumes me. I explode over the party-line interphone, "DICK, you stupid bastard! You stupid, anal, fucking asshole! Look what you've done! You've *killed* us! If you'd left your hands off the goddamned cross-feed like I told you, we'd have enough gas to make the river, but *noooooo* . . . you had to go and screw with it!"

Rich's torso deflates to half-size. Now he looks at me with shock, fear, and embarrassment. Finally he bows his head and pleads, "I'm sorry . . . I'm so sorry . . . I didn't mean . . ."

I stare at him with disgust and continue the attack. "Now just sit there and don't touch another goddamned thing unless I tell you, or I'll have your ass hauled out of that seat and put Charles in." I shake the controls violently to telegraph my furor. "Now, I've got the airplane back."

Rich collapses like a punctured Thanksgiving Day balloon.

Now I ask myself, What's next? I draw a complete blank.

I finally answer myself, Nothing. There is nothing next.

A wave of nausea rolls over me. I was in complete control just minutes ago. We were on top of the world. Now nothing I do is working.

One way or another, this is going to end in disaster.

My rage against Rich morphs into a feeling of inevitability coupled with a sense of despair. My disembodied voice reverberates in my head as I announce, "Crew. This is the pilot. I want each of you to prepare for imminent bailout. Now hear this: I don't want anyone jumping off this plane until I give the final command. But I say again . . . I want everyone to prepare for imminent bailout."

No one answers. There isn't much else I can do.

I check my Worldtimer. It's 12:08:53 . . . tick . . . tick . . . tick. By 12:22, most of us will be in some form of dying.

The only thing left is to wait for death to come.

CHAPTER *THIRTY-SIX*

We tumble onward, head over heels into deeper levels of disorientation and confusion, adrift in increasing levels of darkness as that black inkwell feeling returns.

I tell Rich, "Give Moonbeam our Mayday information and tell them we're going to be bailing out."

He nods weakly and radios, "Moonbeam, Candle 23. MAYDAY. MAYDAY. MAYDAY. We've been hit. We have a massive fuel leak. Crew will be bailing out. I repeat, crew will be bailing out."

No answer back from them.

After a while we hear the capsule commander, sounding like a priest issuing last rites. "Moonbeam copies. We'll send rescue at first light. Good luck and Godspeed." It comes to me that's the last outside human voice I'll ever hear.

We're on our own from here on out.

I check my watch: 12:09:17 . . . tick . . . tick. In thirteen minutes, one of these engines will sputter to a stop. Shortly after that, the second will die. Once they stop running, we'll begin to run down, too. The cockpit will turn dark and quiet as we transform into that unpowered WWII glider. And we'll drop like an anvil if I don't feather the props before the engines stop turning.

I realize now my control of the situation was as precarious as a house of cards. Those fifty-two cards now lie scattered helter-skelter across my mind.

If I could just pull over and set the parking brake, I could rebuild my house of cards, but that damned left gauge keeps dropping . . . no choice . . . have to play with a partial deck.

Ty pipes up, "Sir, I been thinking . . . maybe we could slow down the *rate* of loss and buy ourselves time if we turned off the left-tank boost pump. I'm thinking that engine-driven pump is so powerful that it's likely been sucking enough fuel *through the leak* to keep the engine running. So maybe if we turn the boost pump off, maybe we'd pump gas overboard at a slower rate."

I tell him skeptically, "I'm not sure that's a good idea, but it's worth a shot. Go ahead; try it. But have your finger on the switch if the engine rolls back."

I watch him switch the pump off, then I check the left instruments.

Winding down! Nose yawing!

I yell, "Turn it back on!" The four of us watch the engine cough and sputter back to life.

I review our bailout options: I could order a mass bailout right now while we have both engines. But we'd land beside the battle scene . . . gotta get as far away as possible . . . at two miles a minute . . . in thirteen minutes . . . twenty-six miles away tops . . . order a group bailout there . . . but the surviving bad guys would come after us with a vengeance . . . we'd be easy to find in one bunch . . . everyone tortured and killed.

Or, I could order one man out starting five minutes from now and space them one minute apart . . . singles more difficult to find . . . but then each man would be a trail of bread crumbs leading to the others.

Or, I could order a bailout in *pairs* and stretch out the distance between bread crumbs . . . four pairs . . . two minutes between jumpers . . . pairs four miles apart . . . Rich and I jump when the engines quit in . . . thirteen minutes . . . figure back . . . eleven . . . nine . . . seven . . . first pair jumps in seven minutes . . . two miles a minute . . . fourteen miles . . . crap . . . still too close to the carnage behind us . . . need more separation . . . more speed. I jam both throttles up to max cruise power.

"*Sir!* What are you *doing*!" Ty's terrified voice yelps. "You can't do that!"

I watch the speed build . . . 130 . . . 140 . . . 150 . . .

Bewildered, I ask, "Why not?"

"Have you forgotten that fuel rippling near that exhaust stack? Sir, I gotta warn you," Ty says sternly, "you shouldn't move those throttles again. We're lucky it isn't on fire right now. But you go changing the airflow across that cowl like that . . . she'll torch and blow." His harsh tone says he's losing confidence in me.

"Sorry," I answer. "So you think we're stuck with the throttles where they are for the rest of the flight?"

"Yes, sir. Unless you want a fireball . . . and then if that oil tank blows . . ."

I yank my Nomex gloves out of my thigh pocket and shove them on.

Ty clamps his giant left paw around the throttles. "If you don't mind, sir," he says testily, "I'm gonna guard these guys the rest of the flight. Don't want you goin' movin' 'em again."

"That's fine," I reassure him, "I won't need to. All we gotta do is fly straight ahead."

He answers firmly, "All the same, sir. I'll guard 'em from here on out in case you forget."

I watch the speed stabilize at 180 . . . good.

I force my thoughts back to the bailout issue: Our options just got better. Now when the first pair jumps in seven minutes . . . at our new three miles a minute . . . the first pair will jump twenty-one miles from the ground action . . . 50 percent increase . . . worth that fire risk.

I conclude we'll jump in pairs. No one should die alone.

I will not allow myself to be tortured . . . maybe I'll stay in my seat and ride her in . . . honorable thing to do . . . unafraid . . . like Nemo accepting his watery grave . . . just ride her straight into a mountain . . . won't see it coming.

I announce, "Okay, everybody, listen up. We're bailing out in pairs starting seven minutes from right now. I want the rampers to jump first. Two minutes later, Ty and Eddie will go. Two minutes after that, both navs . . . then Rich and me."

Rich says, "The rules say we're supposed to bail out as individuals; not pairs like you said. Harder to find."

I explain, "Yeah, well, I'm breaking that rule. Nobody should face this alone." I continue, "So I want you guys to buddy up, check out each other's chute and then silently review your bailout procedures. And remember, I don't want anybody jumping out until I give the final order and you see the green jump light come on. Now, Charles, I want you to open the 'secrets' and give everyone the escape-and-evasion letters."

Charles announces, "Guys, the rescue letter today is delta, and the letter of the month is foxtrot. Remember, you can't write them down because they could be compromised. But you gotta remember, or the Jolly Greens won't pick you up, worried you're bad guys working a scam."

The plane turns quiet . . . everyone making private mental preparations to meet his end. I look over at Rich and watch the gray mask of death settle over his face.

How could I have screwed up so bad? I must have felt what I was doing was right, but it was *so wrong*. Just a few minutes ago, we were on top of the world; then, *Wham! Bam!* Things are spinning out of control.

It's obvious now what's wrong: I've blown it.

This isn't Rich's fault. It's *mine*. *I'm* in command . . . not him. If only I'd told him not to touch that cross-feed valve, we'd still have a good right tank . . . might've made the river . . . everything would be different . . . my fault . . . not Rich's . . . tell him now while there's time . . .

I reach over, rub his shoulder, and publicly admit on interphone, "It's okay, Rich . . . not your fault. This is *my* mistake . . . sorry I yelled at you."

Rich shakes his head, does not look at me, and says nothing.

I force myself to review standard bailout procedures . . . let's see . . . hand on the D-ring . . . jump out into oblivion . . . close my eyes . . . tuck like a turtle . . . count to ten . . . pull the D-ring . . . brace for the opening shock . . . open my eyes, look up, check the canopy . . . watch our abandoned airplane sail away . . . bend over, grab my chute knife out of my inner-thigh pouch, reach overhead, make the four-line cut to slow the descent . . . feet and knees together . . . toes pointed . . . knees bent to absorb the landing shock . . . cross my arms and cover my face to protect my eyes from being poked out by tree branches . . . hope one doesn't skewer a thigh . . . human shish kebab . . . gooey branch sap invading my leg . . . infection setting in as I bleed to death in horrific pain . . .

Or if I get lucky and make it through the trees down to the jungle floor, there'll be those fifty-foot pythons to swallow me whole . . . man-squeezing boas squeezing my breath out to save me for breakfast . . . packs of speed-demon Komodo dragons running me down . . .

Or if I get real lucky and land softly into some broad limbs, maybe I could sleep till sunrise . . . and wake up to a flesh-eating beetle gnawing my finger . . . I'll fling him off . . . awaken slowly . . . and realize *thousands* of his friends are zeroing in for breakfast.

I pull my opera-length flight gloves *over* my sleeves . . . less exposed skin.

Or if I'm especially lucky, Rich and I will wind up hanging in adjacent trees. I'll make him promise if we hear the bad guys coming, we'll shoot each other on the count of *three* . . .

I'll bet you dollars to doughnuts he won't break *that* rule . . . I'll fire on *three,* but he won't . . . I'll be swinging in my harness, watching him die . . . what if I have to shoot him a second time? . . . After that the bad guys'll come, they'll peel me like a grape . . . expose my organs . . . and leave me that way while I beg them to kill me.

No way I'll let that happen. I suddenly understand the hidden purpose for my revolver. Suicide. I'll eat my gun.

So every way you look at it, we lose.

Fear consumes me . . . the fear that comes from knowing there's nowhere to run. I feel myself being sucked into mental collapse . . . it would be so easy to just let go. No need to hurry now . . . all that running and shouting and raving was futile.

No need to rush and thrash about now.

Don't know what . . . maybe just let go . . . doesn't matter . . . scared . . . so dark.

Is this the right heading? Would another be better?

No . . . doesn't matter . . . they all lead to the same place.

My father's voice reaches me. "Say your prayers, Johnny."

I whisper, "Now I lay me down to sleep, I pray the Lord my soul to keep . . ."

"Stop it! Stop it! Stop that right now!" Sharon's voice scolds, transporting me back to the cockpit. "Stop wallowing in self-pity! You still have time! Do something!"

The cockpit rematerializes around me. How long was I gone? Must be time to bail out. Some guys have probably already jumped. Must almost be out of gas.

My knee clock says 12:10 and eleven seconds . . . tick . . . tick . . .

That *can't* be! It felt as if ten minutes passed!

So what that means is . . . I shake cobwebs out . . . I wasted a minute wallowing in self-pity I could have spent doing something productive . . . we had twelve minutes' gas . . . eleven now . . . to do . . . something.

I ask myself, Exactly what would that be?

I look at Rich and Ty to see if they noticed my meltdown. Rich is staring straight ahead at nothing. Ty is focused on the fuel gauges. Charles is standing behind Ty studying his map by flashlight.

I hope maybe they're stuck in their own meltdowns and didn't see mine. Or maybe they've been in one, come out, and are hoping *I* didn't notice theirs.

I check the fuel. The left pointer indicates twenty-one hundred. The right side still shows four hundred.

The three men stare at me now . . . waiting for a decision.

They'll wait forever. I don't have a clue what comes next.

I ask, "Does anybod—?" but my voice breaks. I clear my throat and concentrate on each word to shove out the question I know has no answer. My voice quivers: "Does . . . does anybody have any ideas?"

Silence.

CHAPTER THIRTY-SEVEN

Charles's voice breaks the silence. "How about going into our emergency alternate, Long Tien? They swear it's impossible, but . . . under the circumstances . . ."

I spin around to see Charles smiling broadly.

I tell him, "Charles, if you were closer, I'd kiss you. Long Tien has gotta be close. How far is it?"

"Twelve miles due west."

It's as if Charles has thrown me a rope and, with one mighty yank, pulled me out of quicksand onto solid ground.

New life! My confidence soars!

I tell him, "Gimme an initial heading."

"Roger, come right to heading two seven five."

I glance over at Rich to see if he's going to start another fight. He looks startled, but keeps his mouth shut.

I roll out on the new heading and peer out my bug-covered windscreen to try to see our new destination . . .

Nothing but pitch-black darkness.

I swallow hard. I sure hope Charles knows what he's doing.

Now I lean forward, draw my face up to the windscreen, straining to catch any glimpse of Long Tien and see . . . Charles's reflection at his desk studying a map.

I spin around. "Charles, I can't see out front! Turn your lights down!"

"Sorry. Turning 'em down."

I whirl around, lean forward, put my eyes up to the glass, and stare. Nothing but blackness.

Who am I kidding? A foot closer to see something *twelve miles* away? Besides, who'd light a field closed at night?

This is another mistake. I lean back and lecture myself, You idiot. You're gonna have to be a lot smarter than that.

I check the time: 12:10:45 . . . 46 . . . tick . . .

I check the fuel gauges. Left: 2,000. Right: Just under 400. Ten minutes to dry tanks.

I see Rich begin to reinflate. He stammers, "Wha . . . what're you guys doin'?"

I think about lying, but decide he deserves the truth. I answer seriously, "I'm going to try to land at Long Tien."

Rich explodes on cue. "Are you *insane*! Everybody *knows* Long Tien's impossible at night! You'll crack up and kill us all!"

I explain, "I know it's a long shot. But at least we have a place to go. The best we can prob'ly hope for is finding the canyon and bailing out overhead."

He thinks about this, relaxes back in his seat, and says, "I guess that's okay." Then he argues, "But even *finding* the damned place is a needle in a haystack! There's not gonna be any lights and there's no nav aids. We'll sail by one side or the other and won't even *see* it. You're talkin' about a fuckin' crapshoot, man!"

"I'm well aware of that. We'll have to put our faith in Charles's dead-reckoning skills and take the rest as it comes." I add, "But I want to make it clear: If I see the runway, I'm gonna take a shot. If it doesn't look good, I'll order a bailout inside the canyon. You got a better idea?"

No answer back from him. There were no rules for this.

I focus on how to use the time ahead. The field was

twelve miles . . . at three miles a minute . . . four minutes. We'll have six minutes' gas to make two circling, slam-dunk descents . . . three minutes per turn . . . so that means . . . we'll run out of gas before landing . . . damn! If I hadn't wasted that minute back in that mental quicksand pit.

Gotta get that minute back, but how?

I call Charles. "I don't see a thing ahead. You got a map so I know what to look for?"

"Sure. Unbuckling . . . bring my map up."

Charles squeezes beside Ty, wrestling a monster-size three-foot map he spreads across the radio console. The cockpit instruments reflect off his thick glasses. He shines his flashlight at the middle and points at one spot. "That's it right there."

I glance down from flying, but see nothing like a canyon. "Charles, all I see are splotches of green and brown. Point it out."

"It's right *here*," he says defiantly, and jabs at the same spot.

I am looking right where he's pointing. "I don't see a thing."

"It's *right here* under my finger." He pokes repeatedly. "See all those black contour lines forming an oval? That's Long Tien."

As his finger moves aside between jabs, my heart skips a beat. The entire canyon was hidden *under* his fingertip.

The canyon isobars jam together, forming a solid black oval indicating great vertical steepness. Charles's map is useless for an approach.

I try to stay calm and explain the problem. "Charles, I can't possibly find my way into the canyon with *that*. Take a look in those two Volkswagen-size map cases and see if you can't find a larger-scale map. And try finding that 'Laos airfield directory' or anything that looks like an approach procedure."

"Right . . . let me check."

"Hurry. We're running out of time." I watch him disappear into the darkness.

I add, "Wait! What altitude can I go down to between here and there? I gotta start down soon, or we'll run out of gas up here *talking*."

"Oh, right . . . of course." Charles studies the map. "Nine thousand should clear everything . . . higher terrain close on both sides though, so make sure you don't drift off this heading."

"Good. I'm gonna start her down to nine while you get me those charts."

I reach to pull the throttles back, but my palm hits Ty's bear paw.

I jerk my hand back.

Ty cautions, "Sir, you're in command . . . do what you want . . . but you go movin' these throttles again, you'll change the airflow and the whole wing could fireball."

Trapped! What else can go wrong?

I explain, "Ty, this old glider won't descend if I can't pull the power off. If we don't start down right away, we'll never have a shot at landing."

Ty says seriously, "I don't know what to tell you, sir. Do what you think best," but now wraps his bear-paw hand even tighter around both throttles.

I think about this, leave the throttles set, roll the nose over, watch my altimeter unwind from 12,000, and watch the speed build from the descent . . . 190 . . . 200 . . .

Rich asks apprehensively, "Wha . . . what're you doing?"

"Takin' her up to redline," I tell him seriously.

"But this old tub's never been over one eighty. You don't know what'll happen."

I answer matter-of-factly, "We're gonna find out real soon."

My airspeed pointer rises through 220 . . . 240 . . . redline.

Not a shimmy, not a whine, not a shake, as this old war-horse hums along.

I smile. Beautiful . . . just fuckin' beautiful.

I check my altimeter: passing 11,500. My confidence soars. It's working!

Rich doesn't like it. "What're you *doing*? This old piece of shit won't take this speed. And you've still got the ramp open. You've damaged the airplane!"

I tell him firmly, "I don't care. I've got bigger fish to fry. I need to make up one minute and this is the only way to do it. Think it through . . . Long Tien was twelve miles away . . . *four* minutes at one eighty. But at two forty, we'll get there in *three* minutes, and getting that minute back just might make the difference. And I'm betting the extra airflow'll blow that fuel leak back away from that exhaust stack."

Rich answers, "Oh . . . good idea," but I feel his feet start tap-dancing through the rudder-pedal connection.

Ty says, "Sir, that oughta work for now. It's when you slow down and go changing that airflow that worries me. That's when she'll torch."

Another mistake . . . I am piling mistake upon mistake that will soon become a self-stoking avalanche of snowballing errors unless I break the cycle.

So what that means is, everything has to be perfect from here on out.

I coach myself, Calm down. You can do this. You're at the top of your game. All you gotta do is find the canyon, the runway, figure out the landing pattern, avoid the mile-high karst, find the keyhole entrance in the next nine minutes, and not run out of gas or fireball. Just take it one step at a time.

The pallets! If Rich and I have to run back and jump out at the last second, we'll never squeeze by the pallets in time!

I call the loadmasters. "How fast can you guys jettison the pallets?"

An excited voice answers, "You give the word, sir, and they're gone."

I tell them seriously, "Jettison both pallets."

"*Yes, sir!* In progress."

Rich looks shocked. He opens his mouth to complain about getting higher headquarters approval, but I shoot him a hard look and he keeps his mouth shut.

I ask Charles, "Where's those charts I asked for? I need time to study them."

"Stand by . . . still looking."

"Well, hurry. I need 'em *now*, not five minutes from now."

I review my options: First, I fly over the canyon, circle a couple times, and order a mass bailout *inside* the valley. But that would turn half of us into red smears running down those karst stalagmites.

If only we had some light, maybe we could steer our chutes clear.

Our flares!

I call the loadmasters. "Wait! Did you guys jettison the pallets yet?"

"Negative. We were just gonna call you for final approval."

"How many flares we got left?"

"Stand by . . . counting . . . four . . . five. We only got five . . . what'r'ya gonna do with 'em?"

"I'm not sure yet. Just pull 'em out of the box and set 'em aside."

"*Yes, sir!* In progress."

I check my instruments . . . passing 11,000 feet . . . 240 knots . . . good, good, good.

And my second option is: Attempt a landing. But the trouble with that is, if I screw up, I'll kill everybody.

I hear, "Pilot, Ramp. We put the flares aside . . . standing by your order."

I hesitate saying the next words because hearing them will underscore how truly desperate our situation is. "Jettison the pallets."

I whip around to watch. How many times do you get to see something like this? I bet they'll fly along with us like Wiley's limo, confused, before dropping out of sight.

I scold myself, What the *hell* are you doing! You're running out of gas, about to catch fire, and you're playing games? This isn't some dress rehearsal. Get back to business! Do the next thing!

I face forward and silently coach myself, Okay, the pallets are gone. That was good. Build on that. Saving those flares was good, too. All you gotta do is put another hundred more decisions together in perfect order with no mistakes, not skip anything, and we should be okay. That jettison was a nice parlor trick, but pretty soon you're going to have to come up with something more substantial.

I ask irritably, "Charles, how're those maps coming? I don't have all night. We'll be on top of it soon."

"Stand by . . . still looking."

"Okay, Rich," I begin briefing, "I remember it's an east-west runway and they land west—"

"Nope, you're wrong," he interrupts. "It's a north-south runway and they land north."

I ignore him. "If we *find* the damned place, I plan a couple southeast descending left turns. I remember the lowest terrain is over—"

Charles interrupts, "Can't find another map. They stopped putting the better ones on last month . . . budget cuts, ya know . . . that one I showed you's all we got. I dug around and found a booklet labeled 'Laos Approaches and Enroute Supplement.' It's got narratives, approach procedures, and runway diagrams."

I get excited. "That's perfect . . . everything I need. I'm kinda busy, so read it to me for starters."

"Just a sec . . . dropped my glasses."

I bite the index fingers of my Nomex gloves between my teeth, jerk, and spit them on the floor.

Rich notices this. "You have no intention of jumping out, do you?"

I lie, "I don't know. I'm just making this up as I go."

As we wait for Charles, I'm thinking that the approach booklet is the hiking map I need. It'll have a detailed drawing, show all the contour lines, the elevations, the keyhole entrance . . . everything I need to build a mental picture to land.

And the "Enroute Supplement" portion should say something like:

> The field elevation is 2,000 feet. The dirt runway is 2,000 feet long. Rapidly rising mile-high karst all quads surround runway within one-quarter mile. DO NOT land short. Extreme drop-off at approach end shaped like the back of an aircraft carrier. Approach the field from *xxx* direction. Canyon opening is from *xxx* direction through keyhole. Go-arounds prohibited due to mile-high karst wall located end of runway. Airfield closed and unmanned during hours of darkness. Nobody here. No nav aids. No radar. No runway or approach lights. No communications. No air traffic control. No fuel. No oil. No maintenance. No nothing. GO AWAY. Airfield security in question . . . confirm with Intell prior to entry. Arrivals must provide self-contained security forces. U.S. military use restricted to daylight emergency ops. Night operations STRICTLY PROHIBITED, so don't even *think* about it, or you'll bust your ass.

I look out ahead and my mind's eye sees a mile-high, neon skull-and-crossbones sign flashing:

WARNING

DO NOT ENTER

CHAPTER THIRTY-EIGHT

I aim for the middle of the skull, smash through it, and watch it shatter into a million pieces.

To hell with that.

Charles calls, "Found my glasses . . . but you're not gonna like this approach plate . . . not much here."

I get a sinking feeling. "What'd'ya mean?"

"It only shows a runway stick drawing. All it says is, 'Land thirty-two *to* fourteen.' So the runway heading is 320 and 140 . . . northwest-southeast . . . not east-west like you thought, JT. But I don't understand this 'Land thirty-two to fourteen' . . . guess we're supposed to fly in *from* the north-west, slip through the keyhole, and land *toward* the southeast on runway fourteen. And this other note . . . *well* . . . you don't want to know."

I answer, "That doesn't make sense. I *clearly* remember it's the *opposite* direction; land northwest heading 320."

Charles argues, "Yeah, but remember, this is published by the Laotian government, so something prob'ly got lost in translation . . . happens all the time . . . I'm *positive* this means we land on runway fourteen. I—"

I cut him off. "That's gobbledygook. Pass it up to Rich and let him have a look."

I watch as Charles passes the flip chart over Ty and now wait anxiously as Rich studies the document. Out on the horizon I see something the others don't notice. Far to the west, the dark sky has a wavy, eerie, luminescent glow.

Not understanding this sighting, I keep it to myself.

Come on, Rich! We don't have all night!

Rich announces confidently, "Charles is right. The procedure is, 'Land three-two *toward* one-four.' We fly *beyond* the runway out to the northwest, make a one-eighty back to a heading of 140, fly through the keyhole, and land on runway one-four."

Shocked, I ask, "Are you *sure*? I'd bet my life it's the *opposite* way . . . pass that over . . . lemme look."

I grab the document and study the page.

Anger and confusion run over me.

There's nothing on the page but a third-grader's stick drawing of a runway with the cryptic inscription:

NIGHT OPERATIONS PROHIBITED
LAND32TO14

No contour lines, no ridgelines, no spot elevations, no depiction of the keyhole . . . nothing about how to fly an approach.

I toss the useless document on the floor.

I check my altimeter . . . passing 10,000 feet for 9,000.

Any approach attempt will be done mapless.

The dancing green luminescence reappears in my windscreen—larger this time, but now disappears again. Unsettling . . . maybe I *am* losing my marbles.

I say, "Rich, landing on fourteen *can't* be right. Are you guys *sure*?"

Rich says confidently, "I don't remember much about this place, but *even you* can't argue with a published procedure."

"But, Rich, are you *sure*?"

All his old arrogance comes roaring back. "*Absolutely. No question.* It's right there in black and white."

I spin around and ask Charles, "What do you think?"

He answers reluctantly, "I'm gonna have to go with Rich on this one."

I feel suddenly unsure of my footing. I counter, "But if you guys are wrong, we'd smack into the back wall—"

Rich breaks in, "The answer's right in front of your eyes . . . land *from* three-two *to* one-four . . . a no-brainer."

I don't answer and shake my head to get the cobwebs out. I was *so sure*.

That green glow reappears and now mushrooms in my window.

Northern lights, or am I seeing things?

I rub my eyes, look again, but the northern lights keep dancing.

Not understanding, I keep this third sighting to myself. The Church beat it into us: "Don't trust your own judgment . . . use your crew . . . defer to more experienced people."

Reluctantly, I conclude *I* must be wrong.

Their answer *feels so wrong*; yet I have no way to disprove it.

I leave it as a hanging question as I descend into the blackness. I look over at Rich and say, "Maybe we can tell better when we're closer in, but landing on fourteen feels wrong."

He says seriously, "You can't bet our lives on a feeling."

Out of the corner of my eye, I catch a faint glimmer of light.

I look ahead, but the light disappears as though someone had opened a curtain and then closed it.

I yell, "Rich, look! There was a light out there. It must be Long Tien."

He peers ahead, shakes his head, and now looks at me suspiciously. "You're losing it, man."

I think to myself, Maybe he's right . . . the northern lights now fill my windscreen, but if he can't see them . . . and all these mistakes . . . wrong runway . . . seeing things now . . . must be back in that quicksand . . . Charles is so positive . . . he got me this far . . . go with Charles.

I glance over at Rich and . . .

There it is again!

An opened curtain exposes the faintest of lights, but stronger this time.

I whip around to look at it again, but the curtain closes.

I keep this sighting to myself, also . . . don't need to confirm their suspicions about being Looney Tunes . . . all Rich needs is an excuse to take over . . . over my dead body . . . but who'd leave lights on at a closed airport . . . doesn't make sense.

Wait! I know what it is!

I look over at Rich to test my theory . . .

The light reappears.

I was *right*! I'm not nuts, after all! It's the rods and the cones!

I plead with Rich, "The light's *there,* I *swear.* You gotta believe me. It's that rods-and-cones thing from pilot training, remember? Turn your head to one side, look out the corner of your eye, and you'll see it, too!"

Rich looks dubious, but turns his head. Then he yells, "You're right! There *is* something there!"

The light becomes strong enough now I can stare straight at it.

It *must be* Long Tien! I was right! I'm not nuts!

I count . . . one . . . two . . . three faint lights.

Rich says, "Those don't look like runway lights . . . they're . . . *triangular* . . . weird-looking."

I study them closer and see what he means.

They *don't* look like standard rectangular runway lights.

❁

❁

❁

The lights form a sideways *V*. Two on the right and a single one between them on the left.

Rich shoots down my discovery. "You can't tell that's a runway. That could be a warehouse or anything."

I say nothing.

It's clear we aren't going to agree on any issue, but now I don't know what to do next. Just fly along, I suppose, and hope I'll come up with something.

I check my clock . . . 12:13:03 . . . tick . . . tick . . . we'll be over the lights in a minute.

I check the tanks: Left: a whisker above 1,600. Right: a skosh under 400.

Rich notices this, too, and says solemnly, "That right engine could roll back any moment."

I say nothing.

I tell Charles, "I don't want to level at nine. We gotta get as low as possible . . . every foot counts. How low can we go and have five-hundred-foot clearance over the highest peak?"

"Way ahead of you," Charles answers. "Counting contour lines with my calipers and magnifying glass . . . stand by . . . five . . . six . . . seven . . . that's it . . . no eight-thousand-foot contour ring, I think . . . can't tell for sure . . . having to interpolate . . . eighty-five hundred's pushing it . . . not one foot lower."

Rich looks shocked. "Five hundred feet? Are you guys nuts! You know damned well we're required two-thousand-foot clearance in mountainous terrain. We gotta climb back up to ten, or we'll hit something."

I ignore him and watch my altimeter unwind through

8,700. "I trust you, Charles . . . continuing down to eighty-five hundred."

Ty warns, "If she's gonna torch, this is where it'll happen . . . when you slow down and change that airflow."

I pull back on the controls, roll in a couple handfuls of nose-up pitch trim, and settle in at 8,500. The four of us watch the speed bleed off . . . 220 . . . 200. I see Charles staring at the fire handle . . . back to 180 mph.

My mind's eye pictures that fuel creeping toward that red-hot exhaust. I hold my breath . . . one thousand one, one thousand two . . .

Nothing. Whew!

Ty says, "You was lucky. I wouldn't go tryin' that again if I was you."

I let out my breath and nod yes.

Charles points ahead and shouts enthusiastically, "There it is! Long Tien! We're gonna make it!" An unseen hand draws the curtain aside and we get our first full look.

No one echoes Charles's cheer.

The sight jolts me. The view is deadly. The image ice-picks my eyes.

I turn away and see Rich looking terrified. He gasps, "Hoo-ly shit."

I order myself to turn back and stare at the karst-ringed, saw-toothed canyon . . . a world without hope or faith. A death force. Pure, unconscious evil . . . something seen, but not understood . . . smoky nothingness changing shape as I stare . . . blind . . . sinister . . . a world devoid of life . . . too narrow to maneuver once inside . . . the keyhole obscured in a pit of bottomless darkness.

I realize my mistake too late. If I order a bailout now, we'll be cut to ribbons. I look at Rich and watch his face turn to stone.

My pulse races as the image moves closer . . . an oval ring of jagged peaks shimmering in green, neon light; the rest of the mile-deep hole obscured in moving shadows.

Light? What light?

I lean forward, put my face against the windscreen, tilt

my head to look straight up, and see . . . that sliver crescent moon from an hour ago. Any approach attempt will be guided solely by faint moonlight.

Half-blind and mapless.

I spot the keyhole at the southeast rim.

I was right! They were wrong!

But as I stare, that opening closes.

Now a passageway appears at the northwest end, but as I study it, it, too, closes.

Mind games.

How do I grab hold of something that has no handles? Where do I begin?

As I continue staring, the canyon *comes alive*.

The view is a large-scale version of the old-maid/fair-maiden visual perception test in which the line drawing of an old maid dissolves into that of a maiden; then the images shift back and forth . . . old maid . . . maiden . . . until your mind locks on to one of the images and the second disappears . . . no matter how hard you try to see that maiden again, your mind is stuck on old maid, old maid, old maid.

So it is with me now.

The canyon Rorschachs into open dragon jaws . . . stalagmite teeth . . . back to canyon . . . back to open jaws awaiting our arrival . . . a midnight snack.

I squeeze my eyes shut and rub them. Now I open them and see the dark canyon return.

Relief!

Now it Rorschachs back to open jaws!

Stop that! I order my mind. No such thing as dragons.

I see canyon . . . jaws . . . canyon . . . jaws . . . jaws . . . JAWS . . . JAWS!!!

I want to turn away, but know my only hope is to stare it down. I tell myself, it's all in your mind . . . no dragons, but the image hits harder and harder, pummeling me back in my seat. The jaws gape wider and wider, rushing closer and CLOSER!

HERE HE COMES! JAWS WIDE OPEN! RIGHT AT US!

You're doing fine. Don't be scared.

The saber-toothed canyon peaks Rorschach back into view . . . for the moment.

There's no place to begin. Nothing that tells me what to do next, where to go, or where *not* to go. I suppose I could accept Charles's and Rich's idea of landing southeast on runway fourteen. That would be the easy way out . . . go with the flow.

But that leaves one tiny problem: I think they're both wrong.

I fly us ahead.

My knee clock is relentless . . . tick . . . tick . . . tick . . . coming up on seven minutes left . . . the damned thing *keeps ticking*! I have an urge to haul back, stomp my bootheel through the face, and smash it to pieces to *MAKE IT STOP!*

Tick . . . tick . . . tick . . . tick . . . tick . . .

The facts change as I stare, but it's the facts I *can't* see that'll kill us and . . .

I still have to make a decision!

Any decision about keying on the lights will be pure conjecture, a leap of faith.

We fly in closer. I make a shallow left turn, watch the mysterious *V* lights—our only hope—slide across to Rich's window. Now I turn right and roll out heading northwest . . . 320 degrees . . . straight into the lights . . . overhead in fifteen seconds, and *I still don't know which direction to try to land!*

Here come the lights! Tick . . . tick . . . tick . . . tick . . .

Which way?

I'll only get one shot . . . no fuel to change to *my* pattern if *theirs* is wrong . . . but we'll crack up if I take my way over theirs and *I'm wrong* . . . no way of testing without killing us from the *wrong* choice. Logic is out of the picture.

Which way? Choose one, dammit! Choose!

I tell myself: the question has no answer.

The choice comes down to personal preference . . . a whim.

Here come those *V* lights . . . passing right under the nose! Time's up.

Do I follow my intuition, turn left, corkscrew down to the

V lights, and hope I find the canyon entrance at the southeast corner? Or do I fly straight ahead northwest, make a 180-turn back in, try to find the keyhole, and land heading southeast as Charles and Rich say?

WHICH WAY?

CHAPTER *THIRTY-NINE*

Nothing jells.

Here comes that third and final light in the *V* . . . disappearing UNDER THE NOSE!

I gotta keep the lights in sight as long as possible, or I won't be able to hit them. So to check if they're truly runway lights or Rich's warehouse, I stand her up on her left wing and gaze six thousand feet *straight down* into the dark abyss.

YIKES!

That Jimmy Stewart spinning vertigo feeling grabs me again.

I snap the wings back to level and stare at my instruments . . . don't let Rich see . . . mind control . . . deep breaths . . . Oooh! . . . better . . . don't do *that* again.

WHICH WAY? CHOOSE!

STRAIGHT AHEAD, OR CORKSCREW LEFT?

I choose *both*, fly straight ahead and leave both options open. Finally: I reject the burning urge to descend before we run out of gas. I stay level at 8,500 and fly us into another dimension made of both options, yet independent from them.

I check the fuel. Left: 1,400 pounds. Right: 300. Time for two descending, three-minute racetrack patterns and be on the ground with a minute's gas . . . should work.

I hack my clock and decide to fly straight ahead for forty-five seconds. Seeing me continue out northwest, Rich *thinks* he's won the argument to land heading southeast. I say nothing to correct his false impression.

The moonlight shows us whizzing over the dragon's teeth. Rich says, "You can start down now."

I remain level, do not answer him, and stare ahead into a complete void . . . a black velvet canvas . . . no stars . . . no ground . . . no horizon . . . an absence of everything.

I swallow hard. We have flown right off the chart.

Rich tries again. "Didn't you *hear* me? We need to start down *now,* or we'll run outta gas!"

I tell him firmly, "Not going down yet."

His old belligerence reignites. "*But you got to!* We passed the rim . . . you saw it . . . you gotta start down *now*."

I answer calmly, "I'm staying up here awhile."

Rich flashes me a tormented look and bellows, "Have you lost your fucking mind?! We'll run out of gas!"

"I heard you, but I'm not convinced you guys are right. I'm gonna fly northwest for forty-five seconds. That's only a couple miles. Then I'll make a one-eighty back, and *if* we see the lights again, that'll prove the keyhole is where you guys say and I'll drop her in like a sledgehammer."

Rich looks at me with amazement. He explodes, "*What the hell is wrong with you?* Of course we're right! You read the procedure: 'Land *from* three-two—northwest—*TO* one-four'—*toward* the southeast . . . you can't go making up more crap—"

I counter, "But if you guys are *wrong* and I start down now, we'd be trapped behind the northwest rim, never spot those lights again, and never have enough power or gas left to climb up over the rim to start looking for them to come in the *opposite* direction."

Rich leans across the radio console and yells in my face,

"You're outta your mind! You're gonna kill us all," and throws himself back in his seat.

I say nothing, trying desperately to hold both options in suspended animation.

I check my clock . . . ten seconds left of the forty-five . . . now five . . . three . . . we'll know soon who's right . . . one . . .

TURN! GET BACK TO THOSE LIGHTS!

I make a sixty-degree bank right turn, yank the controls into my lap, and stomp in full right rudder.

Oh, no! *Another* mistake! I should have turned *left*!

I begin rolling out to turn back left, but see the heading already passing 350. I realize too late if I turn back left, I'll be making a 210-degree turn instead of the 150 degrees left in this direction . . . can't waste that much time.

"Damn!" I blurt aloud, and reluctantly roll right.

Rich asks, "What now?"

"I wanted to turn *left* so I could see the lights for myself as early as possible."

"*I'll* find them and guide you around the turn," he answers arrogantly, then looks out his side window so all I see is the back of his head. He makes his left hand into the airfoil I used earlier and jerks it steeper. "You'll see," he says sarcastically. "We'll see 'em any second . . . they're gonna be *right there*."

This is yet *another* mistake. I have painted myself into a corner of being Rich-dependent. He *should* spot them halfway around, but with this mistake, I won't see them until almost rolling out.

Dumb, dumb, dumb.

I watch the speed bleed off . . . 170 . . . 150 . . . 130 . . . 120 . . .

G forces.

If this keeps up, she'll stall.

I instinctively reach to firewall the throttles to stop the speed decay and to wrap us around the corner tighter so we hurry up and get back to those lights, but my hand hits Ty's paw again.

Ty says, "This is the part I warned you about. That fuel's crawling farther up that cowl . . . she could torch anytime." His free hand reaches under the glare shield for the left fire T-handle.

I order, "Like I said before, don't T-handle it."

He asks incredulously, "Sir?"

"You heard me," I tell him seriously. "If it torches, fire both extinguisher bottles, but leave it running. We're not gonna be in this thing long after that anyway, and I'll need symmetrical power for bailout."

He draws his hand back.

The airframe shudders.

Rich shouts, "She's stalling!"

I check the speed . . . 115! . . . shit . . . got distracted.

I reluctantly shallow out to a mere thirty degrees of bank and relax some back pressure . . . speed 120 . . . controls mushy . . . losing   precious   seconds . . . more   Rich-dependent . . . the hairpin turn I planned has become a goose egg taking us farther north than I wanted . . . which means . . . gotta compensate by turning *through* 140 over to . . . 155 . . . maybe even 160 degrees to get back to the canyon.

I check my heading indicator . . . passing 050 . . . halfway through the turn . . . Rich should pick up the triangle lights any second. I crane my neck forward to see around him, but his torso fills the window.

I yell in frustration, "Can you see them! They should be *right there*."

"Not yet." His bald spot shakes. "Any second . . . keep the turn tight."

I yell, "This is the max!"

Something is terribly wrong. Rich should have spotted them by now.

Those three lights should stand out like a lighthouse beacon.

If only I'd turned *left*, *I* would be seeing them by now.

I watch the heading spin through east . . . only fifty degrees to go.

I ask, "Do you *see* them yet?"

His bald spot shakes. "Not yet . . . keep 'er coming." Uh-oh.

My skin temperature drops. I plead, "Are you *sure*? They gotta be staring you right in the face."

He says belligerently, "Nothing yet. Just keep the turn coming tight as you can . . . they'll be there . . . you'll see."

I glare at his bald spot and think, You pompous asshole. How'd I get stuck in this mess with *you*, of all people? But why can't he see them!

I tell him, "Forget the lights . . . look for those karst tops . . . we saw those first . . . they can guide us back."

"Roger . . . good idea."

I tell him, "Compensating for this goose egg . . . coming all the way over to a one-sixty heading. Look farther right . . . they must be over there!"

He nods all right.

I roll out heading 160, hack a new forty-five second clock to time this inbound leg so I'll know when we're close, and Rich and I stare out the front windows. Nothing.

No *V* lights . . . no karst tops . . . no stars . . . no horizon . . . once again, a complete absence of *everything*.

What happened to our moonlight?

I lean forward, peer out the top of my window, and discover the terrifying answer . . . the moon has drifted behind an upper cloud deck. My approach-by-moonlight plan just imploded.

I'm *right back where we started* . . . a ship without a port.

Except I've made the situation worse. Now we're not only mapless, we're totally blind.

A flash of terror crosses Rich's face. He screams, "Where'd the lights go! They should be *right in front* of us!"

I panic with him. "The headings must be wrong! They must've got screwed up in the turn . . . we're on the wrong heading! Cross-check our headings!"

Rich and I cross-check our two independent systems, but find they agree.

So that means . . . what?

They *both* precessed the same amount! They're *both* screwed up!

We're headed the wrong way!

No, wait! Cross-check the whiskey compass! That'll tell us what the heading *really* is and then I can apply a correction! Hurry!

I flash up to the standby mag compass at the top middle of the windscreen. The instrument is spinning wildly; the numbers are a blur. The instrument is useless.

Rich looks badly frightened. He cries out, "Maybe we slipped too far north and need to come farther right!"

I explain, "Rich, these headings are so screwed up, I wouldn't know which way to turn . . . right *or* left. We could be way off *either* direction. We could be heading east, or even south, for all we know!"

Rich exclaims, "Maybe they turned the lights off! Maybe they heard us fly over, somebody turned 'em off, and we'll never find 'em again!"

Failure. A feeling of complete and utter failure overwhelms me. I thought back there, even if Rich and Charles are wrong, I'm good enough to compensate and come up with a plan B. I was wrong.

Dead wrong.

I check my clock . . . thirty seconds left on this inbound leg and still no sign of the lights . . . tick . . . tick . . . tick . . .

Fear ripples across Rich's face as I watch him deflate again.

Good riddance . . . could've done better by myself . . . hope he realizes what he's done. His blind faith in rules has condemned us to death a *second* time and I fell for it again.

If only I'd had faith in my own judgment and turned southeast, I'd have kept the lights in sight and we'd be halfway through the first of two sledgehammering left turns down to landing.

Now I don't know what to do.

The canyon could be way over to our right, or way off to the left . . . no way of telling. It was so deep and narrow; we could slip by a quarter mile north *or* south and never see it.

I could try turning, but any turn would be a crapshoot with these messed-up headings . . . or maybe this 160 indication *is* correct and they *did* turn out the lights. But who is "they," and why would they do such a monstrous thing?

So what's it gonna be, JT? Left? Right? Straight? Bail out?

I announce to the crew, "Okay, guys . . . we've lost the lights. I want a face in every window on both sides. Scope . . . stay right where you are in case we're directly overhead. Ramp . . . one of you guys stay back there and scan behind . . . maybe we passed it already. Number two Ramper . . . grab a window and start looking." Ty disappears back into the darkness.

I suddenly realize what has happened. I have managed to fly us *inside* the dragon. He has swallowed us whole.

This is it.

This is how we die. There's no getting out of this one.

Seventeen seconds left on my knee clock and ticking . . . tick . . . tick . . . tick . . .

If only we had more fuel, I could set up a search pattern and maybe stumble upon it, but the tanks show a smidgen over a thousand pounds in the left and two hundred in the right . . . *maybe* five minutes, and that right engine could quit any second.

If I keep wandering aimlessly like this, all will die. I tell myself, At least have the guts to admit you're beaten. Order a bailout *right now* while you've still got power and lights . . . a couple guys might make it till morning . . . you don't have the right to kill everyone stumbling around in the dark.

I reach overhead, break the copper safety wire off the red bailout horn guard, uncap it, expose the switch, and silently review the signals: three short blasts to prepare for bailout, then one long blast to jump.

I fly on, but don't know why . . . nothing else to do. My mind feels full of old oil sludge. I push it for a new solution, or what to do next; but nothing comes. It would be so easy to let go . . . weary of fighting . . . maybe give up . . . accept the inevitable.

I gave it a good shot, but it didn't work out.

Eight seconds! I try one last time. "Does *anybody* see those lights!"

No answer.

I look at Rich and see the blood drain from his face, revealing the gray mask of death. The mask gasps, "We're not gonna make it."

My knee clock ticks down. I reach overhead and grab the bailout switch.

One long blast in . . . five . . . four . . . three . . . two . . .

NO! NO! NO! Not yet!

Remember, we flew out at 180 knots and inbound we've only been averaging 140. Yes! That would explain it! The valley could still be ahead!

So add . . . what? . . . fifteen seconds? I hack my clock one last time and peer out into the black abyss . . .

Nothing.

Ten seconds . . . nothing.

Seven . . . still nothing . . . tick . . .

Four . . . oh, shit . . . tick . . . two . . .

This whole struggle's been worthless!

IT'S OVER! EVERYTHING! SHARON! GONE!

My mind silently screams, NOOOOOOOOOOOOOOOOO-OOOOOOOOOOOOOO! NOOOOOOOOOOOOOOOOOOO-OOOOOOOOOOO!

CHAPTER *FORTY*

Blink! In my front window . . . one faint light a mile straight down as we whiz over a karst pinnacle *a few feet below*. Close!

Blink!

A second light!

Blink!

All three!

Salvation! Hope!

I announce, "Guys, I got 'em back in sight!"

Back where we started! I was dead-on! The lights were there the whole time—hidden behind the canyon wall!

I was right! The approach *is* from the southeast!

My confidence soars! We've still got a shot!

I vow to myself, Never lose those lights again . . . whatever it takes.

My newfound exhilaration blends with the uncertainty of what lies ahead as something comes alive in my mind. The ridgeline of dragon's teeth must be right *over there,* then the ridge must fall away gradually southeast . . . *it must*.

I begin a shallow right turn and aim directly for it.

I tell Charles, "Confirm the south ridge falls off southeast."

He stutters, "I . . . I . . . can't . . . the map scale."

I tell him firmly, "Yes, you can. I'm guessing south, but I need your twenty years of reading maps to make sure."

He answers hesitantly, "Okay . . . I think . . . I don't know . . . yeah."

I answer exuberantly, "Thanks. That's all I needed."

Don't go down yet. Rocks below.

I envision three descent-path options. First, I could descend within the safety of the open valley, but then I couldn't turn back around tight enough between the walls to land.

So I reject that option.

Second, if I take what seems the easiest path, descending into the adjoining valley south . . . we'd avoid the karst, but lose the lights again as we sank.

I reject that option, too, and choose the deadliest route: straight down the saber-toothed ridge . . . flying by braille.

I make a shallow left turn, roll out heading 140, and aim where I imagine the crest to be.

You're clear of the terrain.

This is it. I take a deep breath . . . no turning back from here.

I reach to pull the throttles back, but Ty warns, "She's gonna torch when that prop stops blowing the gas away from that stack."

I hesitate, losing precious seconds we should be going down.

Let it wash over you.

Prop wash! I could use prop wash to slap that leak back where it belongs!

"Ty, gimme twenty-eight hundred rpm. Hurry!"

"Sir?"

"No time . . . just *do it*!"

As Ty resets the props, I yank the throttles to idle, take a leap of faith, slam the nose forward, get falling-elevator feelings, and plunge us into the black abyss.

We are falling out of the sky.

This is the whole shebang. We'll know in seconds if I've guessed right.

Rich flashes me a tormented look. "What're you doing! You can't see a goddamned thing out there!" I ignore him as Ty and I stare at the red fire T-handle.

The red fire warning light flickers on . . . off . . . on . . . off . . . on . . .

. . . and stays off. The prop-wash trick worked!

Ty whistles and exclaims, "Oooo-ee! You was lucky."

I reassure Rich, "It's okay . . . I know the way now."

"How? It's pitch-black out there!"

"I don't know *how*," I answer calmly. "I just *know*."

Except for those three dim lights that now slide across the front portion of my side window, we are engulfed in darkness.

I watch the speed build . . . 150 . . . 170 . . . 190 . . . 200 . . . and hold her there as we rappel down the ridgeline, more mountain climbers now than fliers.

I check the vertical velocity . . . not enough . . . need more drag.

I holler, "Ty, gimme the cowl flaps full open."

"But, sir, that'll make the cylinder head temps too cold. The engines'll—"

I snap, "Just do it!"

I watch him toggle the cowl flap switches full open, and now the descent rate increases . . . good.

Ty announces warily, "Cowl flaps full open, but I gotta remind you, the time limit at twenty-eight hundred rpm's only five minutes."

I explain, "Ty, these engines won't be running that long."

I picture the pattern . . . one minute straight ahead . . . three miles past the entrance . . . not too far, or I'll lose the lights . . . a one-minute hairpin left turn back . . . find the keyhole . . . zip through . . . a sixty-second final approach . . . land on fumes.

Should work.

As my altimeter passes 8,000, I shift my attention to the altitude-loss problem: Okay, we started at 8,500. The runway's at 2,000 . . . which means . . . we gotta drop 6,500 feet in two minutes to establish a stabilized final approach.

Yikes! Over three thousand feet a minute? Never been done and I'm already behind!

I watch the lights slip across the center of my side window and conclude I have to turn this soaring glider into an anvil. I make the standard thumb-down signal and order Rich, "Gear down."

He responds, "Negative . . . way too fast. The gear doors'll rip off."

Ty nods.

I growl, "Put the goddamned gear down, *Dick*, or I will."

He lowers the handle and the airframe begins shaking violently as the gear doors open into hurricane-speed airflow. My mind's eye sees the right door ripping back along the hinge line, then flying off into space. I imagine the left door fighting the 200 mph wind, but then peeling back and ripping down the fuselage like a can opener. It finally loses the battle, flies off, and bangs into the tail controls.

I check the gear indicators. Only the right main indicates green.

The left main and nose show red.

I check the vertical velocity . . . better, but still not good enough.

I order Rich, "Gimme full flaps."

"Too fast! They'll rip off!"

I reach across the throttle quadrant, slam the handle full down, and feel the aircraft shudder as the flaps struggle against forces they were never designed to withstand. I picture rivets popping, monster jack drive screws stalling as they try to extend the wing panels. As the screws push harder and harder, pushrods warp and bend, cotter pins explode, and panels flap around like broken screen doors.

I watch the flap indicator get halfway down, stop, and vibrate . . . the needle a blur. No way of telling if they've stalled, forever jammed, or if the sensor flew off like the gear doors.

I'm no longer flying the airplane; I'm destroying it.

This old warhorse will never fly again.

I watch our descent rate increase . . . good.

I wait to see how this is working out before doing any more damage.

Altitude?

Approaching 7,500 feet, my new start point.

Suddenly the impossible complexity of this descent hits me in the face. To get down to the runway at 2,000 feet, I must first reach the next halfway mark of . . . what? . . . 4,750?

We can never land without going *through* that 4,750-foot halfway mark.

But to reach that 4,750-foot halfway mark, we'll have to fly halfway to *that* halfway mark, because, again, we can't get to the 4,750-foot halfway mark without flying through the quarter mark of . . . what? . . . 5,950? But we can never fly through that quarter mark without flying halfway to *that* quarter mark of . . . what? . . . 6,650?

I check my altimeter . . . passing a new starting point of 7,200 . . . almost a minute into the pattern . . . two minutes from touchdown.

It dawns on me there are an *infinite number* of halfway points to traverse. And for each foot lower, the process starts *all over*.

So what that means is . . . each foot lower is a major obstacle.

Every ten feet lower an act of faith.

Every hundred, an act of devotion.

Every thousand, a miracle.

I consider shoving the nose over to 250 mph again to get down faster, but two new horrifying dimensions of the problem pop into view. First, 250 would carry us so far ahead I could lose the lights or plow into a mountainside I'd never see until . . .

Second, I gotta make that hairpin turn soon, but at 250, the turn would be yet another goose egg. We'd overshoot the keyhole, fly *outside* the north wall, and become lost and blind again.

But even if I keep the speed at 200 for now, I'll still have to pull the nose up in the turn back and slow, to say . . . 160 . . . to give us a shot at slipping through the keyhole.

So what that means is . . . we can never get down before we run out of gas.

The maneuver's impossible . . . can't be done. I am locked in a performance straitjacket.

Either we'll smash into something dead ahead, fly beyond the north rim, or be stranded up here, too high to land.

Every way you look at it, we lose.

I fly ahead . . . it's all I can do. I spot the triangle of lights moving toward the rear portion of my side window.

I check my clock . . . tick . . . tick . . . time's running out . . . only one option left.

I bite my lip and reluctantly order, "Ty, set thirty-two hundred rpm."

"But the prop tips'll nearly be supersonic. I don't know what'll hap—"

I firewall the levers and hear the propellers scream in protest.

Ty says seriously, "Sir, you can't do that. They could seize."

I say nothing.

I watch the vertical velocity increase as it turns darker and darker outside. I'm still here, breathing; so this *must* be the right way. Still . . . wish I could see something.

Our wing landing lights! You idiot, why didn't you think of them before?

I slap on the powerful beams, scan ahead for rocks, and see . . .

Nothing . . . pure black. This darkness is so perverse; the powerful beams shoot out a mere few feet, where they stop dead . . . gobbled up by the darkness.

Nose veering left! What now?

Ty announces, "We're losing the left engine." I check the fuel gauge . . . 600 pounds . . . enough . . . why's it stopping?

I yell, "Rich! Do something! I gotta have that engine!"

Out of the corner of my eye, I see him fiddle with the fuel panel and now feel the engine rumble back to life.

My three lights! I got distracted. Where are they?

I spin, look out my side window, and find them . . .

. . . gone.

I smash my face up against the glass and catch them slipping from sight. Turn!

I flip her up on the left wing, jam full left rudder, and aim for them.

I check the speed . . . 200 . . . too fast . . . goose egg!

We'll whiz *outside* the north rim! No choice . . . slow down!

Reluctantly, I yank the nose up to level on my attitude indicator and watch the speed bleed off . . . 190 . . . in horror . . . as the vertical velocity drops to zero . . . 180 mph. Come on, come on! Slow down! Finally 160 mph . . . I let the nose fall and start down again.

Rich announces, "The left main gear's down and the flaps came all the way down when you slowed, but the nose gear's still showing unsafe."

I ignore this minor irritant as I watch those three gorgeous lights slide back to the center of my front window.

Things are falling into place.

Rollout! I take a wild stab at the keyhole and head directly at the lights that now grow brighter and larger.

We're GONNA MAKE IT!

LIGHTS DEAD AHEAD NOW!

OH, MY GOD! I'VE DONE IT!

Rich yells excitedly, "You sonofabitch! I don't believe it! You did it!"

I check the fuel. Left: just above 400. Right side: 50 pounds.

Two minutes, maybe . . . tick . . . tick . . . tick . . .

I tell myself, You gotta land outta this one . . . no more second chances. The lights grow brighter and larger.

We've made it!

But now I watch the lights move lower on my windscreen. To land, they should be staying in the *middle*.

I watch in silent horror as the lights slip lower and lower. The cockpit turns dead quiet.

It's obvious what's wrong . . . we're way too high.

By slowing up in the turn, I wasn't aggressive enough in getting down. If only I'd cross-controlled and skidded around the corner, maybe . . .

But I didn't think of it and now it's too late. We're *way too high* . . . they'd have to shoot us down from here.

I check my altimeter . . . 4,000 . . . the runway's still two thousand feet below. So close, yet so far away.

No time left to start again.

It's over. The only part left is the dying.

CHAPTER *FORTY-ONE*

We're back where we started—again. I've been flying a death spiral and now we're thousands of feet down between the dragon's gaping jaws. Despair consumes me as I feel the canyon walls close in from both sides as they narrow to a blank wall a few thousand feet ahead.

I was kidding myself I could make it.

No sense in diving for the runway this high, so I level off at 4,000 and watch the speed bleed off . . . 160 . . . 150 . . .

Rich cries out, "You better do something, or we're gonna hit pretty soon!"

I say nothing and watch the speed bleed back to 130, then add power to hold that speed as I imagine the engines making empty-glass straw-sucking sounds.

Slurrrrrrrrrrrp!

Ty blurts, "Sir, the fire—" but breaks that off as he realizes fire is the least of our worries.

I check the gauges. Left: 400. Right: a needle width above 0.

An overwhelming sense of defeat comes over me.

Eddie calls, "Don't come any more right . . . mountain-side."

The only way he would see that is by our rotating beacon reflecting off the canyon . . . wish this thing had curb-feelers.

I watch the first light disappear under the nose and feel the walls closing in.

It won't be long now.

I check my knee clock . . . 12:19:47 . . . tick . . . tick . . .

Guess they were right. This was impossible, after all.

I consider sounding the bailout horn. The rampers could jump before we crash . . . too far back to the ramp for the rest of us to make it out. But even if the rampers get out, thousands of pounds of aircraft wreckage will rain down and consume them after we hit.

There is no escape.

I came sooooooo close . . . the lights are *right there*. I watch the second light disappear.

The scope's voice booms, "You were right! It *is* a runway!"

Keep going. I believe in you. You can do it.

HARD LEFT TURN!

FULL LEFT RUDDER!

FIREWALL THE THROTTLES!

PULL BACK, PULL BACK, BACK, BACK, BACK . . . PULL LIKE CRAZY!

GET AWAY FROM THAT DEAD END!

Every second counts!

Rich yells over the screaming props, "What're you *doing*?"

I yell back, "Circling around for another try."

"She's gonna stall again if you keep pulling this hard!"

"No, she won't!"

"Why not?"

"Thirty-two hundred rpms of prop wash!"

"Oh."

He checks the fuel panel and hollers, "Fumes, man! We're gonna run out!"

I holler back, "I'm counting on it!"

"What!"

"Later!"

I check the heading . . . passing 230 . . . halfway through the 180-degree turn. Oh, my God! We didn't hit!

If I can still hear Rich's voice, that means . . . *we're not dead!* There's still hope!

Instantaneous, out-of-nowhere knowledge pours through me as I watch the remaining jigsaw pieces merge.

Yes, I tell myself, this is *exactly* how they fly the pattern during the day. It *can't be* any other way . . . only this . . . straight up the blind canyon, two corkscrew 360-degree left turns, slip through the keyhole, and land on thirty-two. Halliday, you idiot! I can't believe it took you this long to figure it out.

I shallow out to thirty degrees of bank.

Rich shouts, "Why're you shallowing! You gotta keep it steep and get back!"

"No!" I holler. "We'd pick up too much speed in the descent and overshoot the north rim. We gotta get spacing on the runway, go back out where we were, and start over."

"But we're lower now. We could hit!"

"No, we won't," I say confidently.

He yells, "How do you know!"

I answer simply, "I just know."

I roll out over the ridge heading 140 and check the clock . . . tick . . . tick . . .

Maybe ninety seconds left.

I check the lights . . . back in the middle of my side window again . . . perfect.

Rich says apprehensively, "You better start down."

I explain quietly, "No, we'd hit."

He yells, "How can you possibly know that! You can't see a damned thing!"

I answer solemnly, "I don't know. I just do."

I stay level at 4,000 feet, leave the throttles firewalled, and watch the speed build . . . 140 . . . 160 . . . 180 . . . good.

Rich erupts, "What're you doing!"

"Turning this thing back into a glider. I'm storing what

fumes we've got left in the airframe, you, me . . . everything. If the engines quit, we're gonna glide in."

"But how're you gonna get rid of all this energy? We'll scream off the end of the runway and smash into the canyon!"

I admit, "I haven't figured that part out yet."

I check the triangle lights . . . just over my shoulder.

Clear below now.

I yank the throttles to idle and shove the nose over.

Nose veering!

Ty hollers, "Number one's rolling back again!"

I yell, "Rich! Help!" and see him reach up to the fuel panel, fiddle with something, and now feel the engine rumble back to life for the last time.

Tick . . . tick . . . tick . . . tick . . . seconds remain.

Turn back. Offset thirty degrees southeast to slip through the keyhole.

I turn, aim for the invisible entrance, hope for the best, and keep descending . . . passing through 060 . . . halfway through the turn . . . the triangle lights moving back toward my center window.

We're gonna make it!

FREEZE FRAME

We stop, suspended midair as the wing lights pick up a tower of green karst filling the front windows.

There you are, you bastard. *You* are the reason Long Tien's impossible at night. You've been quietly hiding in the dark all this time, knowing we'd be drawn here like a moth to a flame.

It takes me a moment to realize the cockpit is dead quiet . . . not a sound.

I check my knee clock . . . frozen.

I tap it to make sure it's not stuck and discover the second hand has stopped.

I check the engine instruments . . . all frozen.

Suddenly I have all the time in the world.

I stare at the edifice . . . craggy chunks of limestone . . . individual rocks . . . small bushes . . . hanging green moss. I lean forward, peer out the top of my window, and see this single green stalagmite thrust up in the dark and out of sight.

I marvel at my mistake. The jagged peaks . . . the saber-toothed ridge . . . the narrow walls . . . were mere red herrings.

You are the true killer.

I relax back in my seat and look around the cockpit.

Everyone else is frozen.

Rich's mouth and eyes are wide-open as he gawks at the tower.

Ty is bowed in silent prayer, his eyes squeezed shut.

Charles is checking his watch like a commuter waiting for the evening train.

Looking back out front at the green tower, I realize what I'm seeing is already in the past. It's too late to avoid smacking into it. Think about it: the light from our landing lights had to travel *to* the tower, reflect *back* to my retina, and then be processed by the brain.

By the time my brain computes the danger, signals my hands and feet to do something, and those muscles and tendons eventually contract to move the controls, and that energy is finally transmitted through *two hundred feet* of worn-out cables across a tired system of pulleys and trunnions, and the ailerons and rudder finally *move* and slooowly change our trajectory from hurtling into the tower, toward the lights, while part of the airplane keeps slipping sideways even though the lights are in my front window . . .

We'll be dead.

Most of us don't think of this time lag as important, but for us, it means . . .

. . . we're already history.

That grimy green tower filling my window is already part of the past because you can't be aware of something until *after* you've seen it, and that means the tower is therefore unreal . . . a ghost from the past.

I fill with rage and tell the green image, "Go fuck yourself."

RESUME ACTION

Rich yells, "Look out!"
STAND HER UP ON THE WING!
LEFT FULL RUDDER!
PULL! PULL, PULL, PULL . . . HARD AS YOU CAN!
I half-expect the control column to break off in my lap.
HOLD ON, JT! HOLD ON!
I search for the *V* lights and spot them in my front window:

※

※   ※

Holy moly! We're *vertical*!

The speed bleeds back . . . 180 . . . 160 . . . 140 . . . skidding sideways into the tower.

I wait to hear the first impact sounding like a simple car crash. Next the speed will drop to 100 as the fuselage pancakes against the tower, followed quickly by a monstrous oil-canning sound of junkyard cars being crushed.

The ribbings won't withstand the collision, so the airframe skeleton will collapse upon itself like the *Hindenburg*. Soon after, both windscreens will shatter and launch a thousand glass missiles that, powered by a 100 mph wind, will blind us and turn our faces to hamburger.

I hold my breath and wait for the first innocent bump of our tires against the tower . . . hope it doesn't hurt long.

CHAPTER *FORTY-TWO*

I roll out and see the runway lights dead ahead on a normal glide path.

We didn't hit?

How?

The left engine sputters and the instruments roll toward zero.

I yell at Rich, "Do whatever you did again!"

Ty explains, "The tank's empty. She's gone for good and I have no idea how number two's still running."

I holler, "Feather number one!" and watch as Ty punches the electric feather push-button and see the rpms drop to zero.

Down to one engine now . . . any idea of a last-second pull-up to save the rampers just flew out the window.

That's okay, though, because the lights are *right there* . . .

Thirty seconds ahead, tops. All I gotta do is point us right at the lights.

I get chills of excitement. I relax my shoulders and begin celebrating.

Rich screams, "PULL UP!"

The landing lights pick up a perpendicular, razor-sharp ridge just below—poised to tear the gear off, stall the wing, and send us tumbling head over heels.

I yank back as hard as I can and wait for the impact . . . one . . . two . . . three . . .

Nothing.

Whew! Can't take another one like that.

But now we're too high! I shove the nose over and figure, that's gotta be the last one of those, or nobody'd ever—

Rich hollers, "LOOK OUT! ANOTHER ONE!" as another killer ridge jumps out of the dark. I yank back as hard as I dare and not stall, suck in a breath, and . . .

Here it comes!

I feel the tires bounce on the ridge, but . . . we're still flying.

I breathe out and shove the nose back down at the lights.

I check the speed . . . 160! Too damned fast!

Any more than 100 and we'll zip off the end and smack into the dead end.

The lights are brighter and closer now . . . seconds away . . . the lights pick up the rocky surface . . . going too fast!

Make something up.

I lock my legs against the brake pedals and tell Rich to do the same.

I expect to hear him lecture, "Landing with locked brakes is prohibited. We don't have an antiskid system," but feel my brake pedals depress farther from his extra pressure.

He didn't have to say a word. We're both aware the brakes' temps will peak at six hundred centigrade twenty minutes after touchdown. The discs will glow cherry-red, the fuse plugs will blow, and the rims will melt. Then the tires will catch fire. We'll get out, *if* we can stop from ramming headfirst into that wall, but with no fire equipment, we'll watch helplessly as she burns to the ground.

We're over the end! I slam us down!

Touchdown!

I check the speed: still 160!

The nose gear *KA-WHAMS* down from our prelocked brakes.

Rich and I hurl forward into our shoulder harnesses like car-crash test dummies. The inertial reel finally senses the rapid deceleration and locks our nylon straps. My shoulders sear with pain as the webbing pile-drives the bones.

The speed comes down . . . 140 . . . 100 . . . 80 . . .

Come on, come on! Slow down!

. . . 60 and stops . . . the indicator unusable any slower.

Rich and I stare ahead; we expect to see the canyon wall charge out of the dark as we hurtle off the end.

Even as slow as *twenty,* Rich and I will be crushed.

Please, please, please stop . . . *please* . . . wait.

What's going on?

Are we stopped? Is it over?

I hesitantly turn and look out my side window to check for movement.

We're not moving! Oh, dear God! We're not *moving*!

I start to cry. I don't believe it!

We made it!

I tell myself, Celebrate later . . . keep going . . . things to do.

So we don't roll around, I set the parking brake. I turn the landing lights off and check the fuel gauges.

Left: zip . . . nada . . . empty.

Right: needle touching the top of 0.

Time was up.

How could things have possibly worked out this way?

I tell myself, Worry about that later . . . shut her down.

I shove the right fuel lever down to "cutoff," listen to the prop wind down, reach overhead, uncap the red battery switch's safety guard, turn it off, yank my headset off, toss it on the dash, unbuckle my lap belt, throw off my shoulder straps, hit my recline lever, and collapse backward as silence engulfs the cockpit.

CHAPTER *FORTY-THREE*

Dark silence. A sarcophagus feeling.

I must be dead. We crashed and this is what comes next as only the soul survives . . . that's the only logical explanation. Funny, it didn't hurt much.

My eyes are open, but see nothing, so this must be death.

"Tick . . . tick . . . tick . . . tick . . ." breaks the silence. How *rude*!

But this death thing isn't as bad as I'd imagined.

"Tick . . . tick . . . tick . . ?" Louder.

I wonder if . . . nah . . . makes no sense. We're dead, all right, and the aircraft wreckage our mausoleum.

Part of me says, "Okay, if you're dead, go ahead and prove it." And another part of me answers self-righteously, "Okay, I will. Watch. I'll try raising my arm off this armrest and nothing will happen."

I watch in disbelief as the disembodied limb levitates with a mind of its own. I study the hand and fingers with the wonder of a newborn.

I tell this floating apparition, "Twist left," and it does!

I wonder if it can close its fingers in sequence and make a fist? I watch each digit close seemingly on its own, then fan open to five fingers again. It still works!

We're alive!

But how?

I command the arm to lower and the fingers to pick up my Cadnica, flick it on, and point it at my knee clock.

The pinpoint light confirms it: 12:24 . . . tick . . . tick . . . alive two minutes more than we have any right to be.

Rich! I have only enough energy to roll my head across my headrest to check on him, and what I see frightens me: Rich imitating a cadaver on a slab . . . his face chalky white.

I ask him, "You okay?"

He struggles to mumble, "Uh-huh. I think so."

My mind searches for suitably momentous words to commemorate our achievement, but comes up blank. All I can think to say is an embarrassingly simple "Thanks, Rich."

After a while his corpse groans another "Uh-huh."

I try to stand, but collapse back in my seat. Lying here in this dark quiet, it comes to me how ridiculous and wrong movies depict this moment—people full of energy, jumping up and down, yelling, smiling, high-fiving their success.

Real life isn't like that. Rich and I are just lying here breathing heavily, trying to recover.

I summon all my energy, unbuckle my chute's vise grip on my chest and thighs, wiggle out, and shed its weight so maybe I might actually stand the next time I try. Now I unbuckle my leather lap belt, unzip my survival vest, and collapse back in my seat again. Part of me wants to lie *right here* and never move.

I tell myself, "What's the rush . . . this plane's no longer airworthy. I doubt we could even call this wreckage an airplane. And besides, it's out of gas and I didn't see any Shell stations during the approach. Relax; we're not going anywhere soon."

I realize that this moment—right here, right now—is the defining moment of my life. I'll never have another moment this large if I live to be a hundred . . . never. What could *ever* top this?

So I lie here, drinking in the moment.

I watch the last wild twenty-five minutes play over and over on a closed-loop mental videotape, each replay lasting mere seconds. I lie here watching so I never forget.

My Cadnica catches a flash of red below the engine instruments . . . doesn't make sense . . . I killed the battery, didn't I? I look overhead and check the switch . . . yep . . . off.

I struggle to lean forward to find the source of the red glow.

I smile to find it's Jack's red die. I pick it up, roll it around my palm, close my fingers around it, and zipper·it away for safekeeping beside my extra chest bullets.

It's time to go. With great effort, I push up off the armrests, stand, turn, straddle the radio console, and look down at my seat.

What I see rocks me.

Right there, in front of my eyes, still recovering, is the ghostly image of *me*. For this moment, there are *two* of us: that old, worn-out, frightened version and this new, revitalized edition.

In my mind, I tell this spent image of myself, "Thanks, old friend, but this is good-bye. I'll take over from here."

This fresh version turns to Rich, offers an arm, says, "Come on, partner. Let's get outta here," and yanks him to his feet.

I move through the open doorway to make room for Rich, take a tentative step down to the back porch, turn on rubbery legs, and see Rich coming through the doorway, chuteless.

We stand side by side on the back porch, peering around the empty cargo compartment, trying to get our bearings.

Empty? Where'd everybody go? Not a soul in sight. No Charles. No Scope. No Ty.

Oh, no! I hope they didn't panic, jump out, and are somewhere *out there*. How the hell will we find them?

Rich whispers, "Maybe they're out back."

I whisper back, "I hope so."

Rich and I hold on to each other so we don't tumble off and now gingerly move our boot tips around to feel for the first step. We repeat these tentative baby steps on still-rubbery legs down to the cargo floor and are now standing on it, waiting for our sea legs to quit wobbling and our eyes to adjust before moving ahead.

The cargo compartment slowly rematerializes from the darkness, so we take a step.

CLANG!

I squeeze Rich's arm as we stop, startled. I whisper, "What was *that*?"

Rich whispers, also frightened, "Dunno . . . never heard anything like that."

We pause and listen . . . nothing. We shake our heads, shrug, and take another step.

CLANG!

We halt.

I chuckle and whisper, "It's our footsteps on the metal floor," and see him smile. I say to him, "That's weird. I've walked across this floor hundreds of times and never heard it clang." I tell myself it was always there, just covered by engines, props, and screaming hydraulic pumps. We just couldn't hear it till now.

To avoid a symphony of clangs, we shuffle ahead slowly. Rich whispers, "Watch out for the roller-skate pallet rollers. You could bust your ass."

We shuffle *right through* where the pallets were . . . too bad I missed seeing them go. Farther back, I spot the five flares the guys saved. Now a breeze hits my face, so I know we must be close to being outside.

We shuffle to what *appears* to be the ramp edge, but unsure, we feel around for the knife edge with our boot tips . . .

Got it.

We stop.

We'd normally jump the five feet to the ground, but can't see that far. We could pratfall and sprain an ankle or break a bone. Knowing even the slightest injury could be fatal, we tickle around for the ramp edge, squat, scoot along on our butts, and now dangle our legs over the edge like kids on a fishing dock.

We swing our legs back and forth, back and forth.

We are just looking around.

As my eyes adjust, I make out two-dimensional shadows staggering around like train-wreck survivors. I try counting the moving shadows to make sure no one bailed out, but find it impossible. I see one shadow move away and disappear, only to rematerialize yards away a moment later.

What the . . . ?

Oh, I get it . . . *two* shadows . . . *two* different people . . . disappearing and reappearing.

Uh-oh . . . now *all* the shadows start disappearing. Assuming everybody's still here, we could lose somebody if they wander away more than a few feet.

I nudge Rich's arm and whisper, "Come on, let's go."

We shinny down the ramp and gingerly plant our boots on good ol' Mother Earth.

I stomp my boot on the rocky surface. *STOMP! STOMP! STOMP!*

Rich does the same. *STOMP! STOMP! STOMP!*

I thought I'd never again feel the planet beneath my feet! I promise myself to never again take this exquisite feeling for granted.

I turn to Rich and whisper, "Go out there, count noses, make sure nobody's hurt, corral 'em, and bring 'em back here. And don't go too far out yourself, or you might not find your way back."

His shadow whispers, "Okay."

I watch him move away and disappear in the blackness.

The shadow three feet ahead looks pickle-shaped and has an outline of horn-rimmed glasses. I whisper at the pickle, "Charles, is that you?"

The pickle whispers back, "Yes, it's me."

"You okay?"

"Yeah."

"How's everybody else?"

"I'm not sure."

"Why are we whispering? If anyone *is* here, it's no secret *we* are."

The horn-rimmed pickle shakes his head. "Feels deserted."

It comes to me why we're whispering: there's a reverence to this scene and any spoken word would be like shouting in church on Christmas Eve.

The pickle shadow and I just stand here—looking around. Thirsty!

I bend over, unzip my right calf pocket, slip out my flask, unscrew the top, tilt *way back,* and feel the water rush down the open channel. No swallowing, no chugalugging, no choking. Just straight down the old pipe.

I screw the top back on, bend over, secure the flask, and spot my plastic rings lying on the dirt runway. I scoop them up and tuck them away before Charles sees.

You have to understand; we're now facing an unresolved organizational issue about who is in command: me or Charles. With the plane out of commission, Charles could argue, as senior officer he should take over; and we don't need that conflict on top of everything else.

I look up at Charles for any sign he wants to take command, but notice nothing different . . . good.

I unzip my left calf pocket, extract my second flask, unscrew the top, tilt back, and let 'er rip. Then I replace the flask . . . no telling how long we'll be here, so we'll need to save all available water containers.

I hold my hand and open fingers up to my eyes to check I'm still okay. The digits are vibrating like a struck tuning fork . . . a blur.

I command them, "STOP!" but they keep shaking. Can't let the others, *especially* Charles, see me frightened. So I kneel down, raise my hand over my head, and SMACK! the palm on the rocky surface. I hold the fingers up to my eyes to check for results . . . still a blur.

I raise my hand high again and CRACK! the palm on the rocks and bring it up to my eyes again. No good . . . fingers still a tuning-fork blur . . . gotta make it stop before Charles sees and tries to take over . . . do it again!

I raise my arm, but a hand grabs my wrist. The unseen grabber yanks me to my feet, puts a protective arm around my shoulders, and pulls me tight beside him.

I turn to see who my rescuer is and see horn-rimmed glasses.

So that he doesn't notice my fears, I cross my arms, shove my hands under them, and clamp down. Charles notices this and whispers, "You cold?"

I lie, "Yeah, a little." We say nothing, but it's obvious he saw my fruitcake performance.

Embarrassing.

The plane! What shape's the plane in?

The brake fuse plugs must be ready to blow!

Afraid of losing sight of Charles, I tentatively sidestep over to the left side of the aircraft. I look back and see his shadow merging with the darkness . . . but just a couple more sidesteps and I'll *see*.

Shuffle . . . shuffle . . . there it is . . . the fuselage's left side silhouetted . . . look back for Charles . . . nearly gone.

Just a couple more shuffles . . . lean *way* over . . . I see . . .

The gear door? Still attached? Impossible. How?

And the flaps look fully extended. Amazing! How? They should be in shreds.

But what I really want to see is how much battle damage the engine took. The outboard cowling should be twisted metal from that artillery shell. I shuffle one more side step.

Damn! The extended flap silhouette blocks my view of the damaged cowl.

Silhouette? From what light source *ahead* of the aircraft?

I look back for Charles and find him gone, but just a couple more side shuffles and I'll see the damage! I teeter *way over*. I can *almost* see that cowling!

Someone grabs my sleeve and yanks me back behind the plane.

Dammit! I didn't get to *see*! Who the hell *did* that!

I search the featureless face and see horn-rimmed glasses. Charles puts his arm around me again, pulls me close, points up at the sky, and whispers, "Look!"

I look up and whisper back, "I don't see anything."

"Wait a second," he whispers. "Keep staring while your eyes adjust."

Slowly, as if by magic, a single star appears. I ask, "What's that?"

"Polaris."

"The North Star."

"Yeah."

A few twinkling stars appear. Then a few more. Now more and more twinkle as the towering canyon walls frame the starry carpet of the Milky Way.

Charles whispers, "Fantastic, isn't it? A real-life planetarium." He explains, "It's always there, but you don't normally see it behind all our man-made lights." Charles turns my shoulders and points me back in the direction we landed. "Look."

"I don't see anything."

The navigator whispers, "Just wait," and suddenly a monolithic shadow looms up out of the darkness. "You must've flown through solid rock."

Charles turns my shoulders north and we gaze up at the Milky Way. I get chills that make me shake all over.

Charles notices this and holds me tighter. We say nothing.

Now the camera in my mind soars overhead and pictures our tiny band of survivors huddled at the back of our crippled aircraft at the bottom of the mile-deep canyon deep in enemy-controlled territory.

As the camera flies higher, we become an insignificant dot, swallowed by hundreds of miles of ridgelines wrapped around us like tentacles, as my elation over being alive blends with the understanding we might as well be stranded on the dark side of the moon.

We have jumped from the frying pan into the fire.

How will I get us home?

CHAPTER *FORTY-FOUR*

Out of the corner of my eye, I see Rich and five shadows emerge from the darkness. He whispers, "Everybody's here and they're fine."

They are all staring at me for what to do next.

They can stare all night. I don't have a clue.

The Intell officer's words from that first night reach me: *We don't even know who owns the damn place, our reports are so bad. If you did manage to land, the welcoming party'd kill you outright.*

I suddenly feel the crosshairs of a high-powered rifle burning a hole in the back of my neck. Guard hairs on the back of my hands stand up like a frightened cat's.

Somebody knows we're here.

Move! Fast!

I grab Charles's sleeve and whisper to the crew, "Come on! Let's find some cover." To make us a smaller target, I demonstrate crouching forward. They are just standing there gawking at me as if I were crazy.

Charles finally crouches with me and now everyone else follows suit.

We scurry forward single file under the right wing, past the still-attached right gear door . . . amazing . . . how? I see the silhouette of our three-bladed prop ahead, stop, turn to Charles, point out the sharp blades, and whisper, "Don't anybody cut their head open . . . pass it back." I wait until I see the last shadow nod and then scurry forward half-bent at the waist.

As we pass the nose, I spot a gully ahead on the right, head for it, and hear seven pairs of boots behind me scuffle along the rocky runway.

I scamper down into the gully, spin around to face the plane, get on my hands and knees, and stretch out prone on the shallow slope. I watch some shadows race by me while the rest stop short on my left. They all join me in the gully. I am in the middle of the pack, I guess . . . hard telling in the dark.

Next I scrunch back down the gully to get my head below the runway surface so we're hidden better.

I am looking right along the runway surface.

But your head's exposed, you idiot!

Some James Bond you'd make! Get down! I scramble backward farther down the angled wall of the gully and . . .

Shit!

My boot tips fall off a ledge that could be a six-inch drop—or a thousand-foot one. I feel over the edge with my toes for a bottom . . . nothing . . . not a gully!

A precipice!

I scramble forward on bare elbows through sharp rocks until my toes land on solid ground again. I scan left and right to make sure we didn't lose anybody and see them all scrambling back up. I see Charles's horn-rims on my right and *someone's* shadow on my left. I whisper, "Rich, is that you?"

The shadow answers, "Yes."

We're stuck. This is it. This is where we make our stand. If we move forward, our heads'll poke up in the light. If we back down to hide better, we could plummet who knows how far.

We're trapped.

I look up at the aircraft and the image gives me goose bumps.

The old glider looms over us, seemingly extending its wings over us like a bird of prey guarding its young. Steam rises off the fuselage as individual rivulets of water stream down the side and off the nose . . . condensation . . . we must've descended so fast in this humidity, the water vapor chilled rapidly and turned to water and steam.

There's not a mark on the plane. It looks like the first production model rolled out under promotional spotlights for flashing photographers' lightbulbs.

Wait a sec . . . how's it being lit?

I trace the beam back to its source . . . a light directly across the runway . . .

. . . the middle light of the *V*.

Impossible. We stopped *halfway* down? A *thousand* feet? We're *not* at the end? The charts say that's impossible. How'd we stop so fast?

Rich pokes my ribs, points far up the mountain, and whispers, *"Look!"*

High up on the ridge down which we just rappelled wind six narrow headlights, lazily S-turning down what seems a series of switchbacks. They *know* we're here and they're coming for us.

I whisper to Rich, "Tell everybody to release their safeties and get ready to fire. But tell 'em not to shoot until they hear me fire first." He turns away.

I turn to Charles, repeat the instruction, watch him nod and turn away to pass it on.

The headlights make another switchback in the sky, so I have only moments left . . . let's see . . . six vehicles . . . at least two men per jeep . . . a force of . . . twelve . . . against the eight of us . . . maybe even twenty-four of them. That's what I'd do . . . show up with overwhelming force—twenty-

four guys toting AK-47s against our eight P38
peashooters . . . so arrogant, showing themselves this
boldly . . . as if they *own* the place . . . knowing they can
easily wipe us out . . . no contest.

My extra bullets! Hurry! Now's the time!

I raise up on my bare elbows and drive rocks and gravel
into my skin but ignore their intrusion. I unzip both chest
pockets, dig in, pull out my extra bullets, and make a pile on
the rocky runway. I try standing each on its base as we did
on the firing range, but each one falls over on the uneven
surface. I try to stand two up again so I can reload quickly;
but these, too, topple. I finally leave them lying in the pebbles and line them all up like a machine-gun clip.

I look up at the mountainside and see the six headlights
make another S-turn. It won't be long now.

I unbuckle my holster, draw out my P38, unlock the
cylinder, check each chamber is full, snap the cylinder
closed, hear a click, release the safety, and get ready.

I *will not* allow them to torture me. I'll go down
blazing . . . take out as many of 'em as I can before . . .

The vehicles are lining up six abreast . . . *right across the
runway!* Thirty yards!

Growling diesel engines. Not U.S. inventory. I recognize
U.S. jeep headlight patterns and these are too close together.

Enemy jeeps!

I hear yelling and shouting as they see the plane for the
first time, realizing someone has invaded their sanctuary. I
strain to hear English amongst the racket.

Someone yells a phrase in Laotian.

Laotian! Crap!

Now a pair of uniformed legs paces back and forth in the
exhaust behind the growling lights. It won't be long till they
discover our scant hiding place . . . only so many spots we
could be.

I plant my gunstock on the rocks, bring my eyes down to
runway level, focus on the front sight, line it up with the rear
sight, cock the hammer, wiggle my finger onto the trigger,
and take aim. My hand is rock-steady . . . all the shakes gone.

My plan is that the legs straight across from me go down first. Dammit! I should've told the guys to aim straight across so we don't wind up shooting the same target.

Too late now.

The legs are still partly hidden behind those headlights in foggy exhaust . . . can't get off a clear shot. I squeeeeeeze the trigger tighter . . . as soon as they step out front in the light and I get a good target . . .

A lone silhouette steps out front. A perfect target . . . dead-on in my gunsight . . . can't miss.

I squeeeeze . . .

CHAPTER FORTY-FIVE

Bathed in a deep, Texas drawl, a voice above the legs calls out, "WHAT THE *HA-IL* YOU-ALL DOIN' HERE?"

HALLELUJAH!

WE'RE NOT GONNA DIE!

Nobody could fake *that*!

WE'RE SAVED!

I take my hand off the trigger and lower the hammer. We scramble to our feet in loose gravel, clamber up the rocky slope, slip, catch our footing, and charge across the runway toward the headlights. We stop short and shield our eyes against the beams.

I guess from our rescuers' perspective we look like invaders, because now a dozen angry-looking young Americans materialize to defend their drawling friend.

I tell myself, Whoa! This ain't over yet. Somebody could still get shot. But *Americans*? Why?

Now I notice two Laotians on my left next to the plane: one young, one middle-aged . . . the older dressed in some phony-baloney uniform complete with silly fringy shoulder boards you only see on egomaniacal South American dictators.

In the exhaust-fumed shadows of their headlights, all the faces seem ghoulish, misshapen. None of our hosts appears armed, so while it's clear they're not going to kill us, they're none too happy to see us, either. I get the feeling we've stumbled onto something forbidden.

No one on either side says a word. We all just stand here in the foggy headlights, sizing each other up like rival street gangs before a knife fight. The atmosphere is explosive.

No one knows what to do; there's no script to follow.

Tex glares at the pistol I discover I'm still holding, so I thumb the safety on and holster it. The rest of my crew does the same, but Tex's face remains aggressive.

I have the feeling he could make our lives miserable, so decide to be careful about what I say and do next.

Tex says sternly, "This place is off-limits. Who the hell are you guys and who authorized you to land here?"

I notice he's lost his Texas drawl . . . curious.

I explain firmly we're an Air Force crew out of NKP, Thailand, that we were shot down and this was the only place we could land.

He studies the plane. Then he says, "Bullshit. I don't see anything wrong."

I explain I couldn't see it either since it's so dark.

Tex asks accusingly, "Who authorized you to come in here?"

I defend myself. "*I* did. I used my captain's emergency authority."

He says authoritatively, "You can't do that."

"Actually, I can," I lie firmly. "The 'Laos Enroute Supplement' lists Long Tien as an emergency alternate, and that's all the authorization I needed."

This surprises him. "Oh, I didn't know that. That makes it different."

I raise my hand to cover a smirk. My bluff worked!

Tex and the others relax, but remain wary. No one

makes a move to cross the line between our two gangs. Then Tex steps closer and eyeballs me up and down until I feel uncomfortable.

I try to break the tension by introducing our crew, but he interrupts, "How'd you . . ."

This sentence fails as he stares at the plane and shakes his head as if it were a ghost ship that might suddenly disappear.

I say, "Wait a minute. I'll show you my ID card," and reach for my absent wallet, only to realize we're sanitized . . . no ID . . . no patches . . . no rank . . . no name tags . . . nothing to verify my claim. No wonder he's suspicious. We could be *anybody*.

As Tex gawks at the plane, I explain sanitization protocol, but I can see from his expression he's not buying it.

My blood chit! The stupid blood chit! I unzip my thigh pocket, pull out the silk hankie, unfold it, show Tex the American flag, and say, "See!" and watch his face relax.

As Tex turns back to me, his aggressive expression changes to wonder. He gawks at me, too, as if I were a ghost. He asks incredulously, "So *you* landed this thing?"

I tell him yes, but the way he keeps gawking and asking the same stupid questions makes me start to snicker. I tighten my face muscles.

"So you *intended* on coming here?" Tex asks incredulously.

He and the others are staring at us as if we were men from Mars.

I shake my head and repeat firmly, "No. We were shot down, ran out of gas, and I flew us in here."

Tex turns and gawks at the sweating airplane. I look with him, and I have to admit, in these headlights, it *does* look like a ghost ship.

Tex says, "You *couldn't* have landed here. I mean . . . we fly in and out of here all day, but we're not crazy enough to try it at night . . . you're . . . you're insane." His hard expression turns to awe.

"Or desperate," I add.

"So *what happened*? *Who* are—" but this attempt is cut off by "How'd you—" but this, too, fails.

I help him along. "Maybe I could explain better if we got off this runway. I'm freezing and we're dying of thirst and starving. You got a place we can go and I'll tell you the whole story."

Tex answers, "Oh, sure." But once again he looks back at the ghost ship he seems sure will disappear.

We don't seem to be getting anywhere, so to break the impasse, I introduce the rest of the crew.

I finish and Tex introduces his companions, using one-word nicknames.

Both sides step forward uneasily, make perfunctory handshakes, and lie, "Nice to meet you," then jump back to their side of this Maginot Line. You could cut the tension with a knife.

Tex concludes his introductions by waving a hand toward the stern-looking, middle-aged Laotian in the dictator's costume. Mimicking a master of ceremonies, he announces, "It is my distinct honor and privilege to present to you the commanding general of the Royal Laotian Army, General Bang-Pow."

I say nothing, stunned.

Bang-Pow! I thought he was a myth, but here he is. What else can happen tonight?

I remember my manners, pop to attention, salute, and say formally, "General, it's an honor to meet a hero such as yourself."

Everyone remains quiet, shuffling their feet in the rocks, waiting for someone to make the next move.

Bang-Pow leans over and whispers terse words to the young Laotian I conclude must be his aide. The aide nods and translates in a serious tone, "Bang-Pow say, 'First time you fly over Bang-Pow house, you wake up Bang-Pow. Make Bang-Pow vely, vely angly.' "

The aide runs out of words and turns to the general to reload.

I get that waiting-for-the-dentist-to-start-drilling feeling.

I woke up their George Washington! I start apologizing, but the aide waves me off as Bang-Pow continues in an angry tone.

The aide nods and translates, "Bang-Pow say, 'Second time you tly to land on Bang-Pow loof . . .' " There's a pause as the aide scans his memory for the proper translation. "Bang-Pow say he have to get out of bed, get dlessed, come down, and see what clazy asshole tly stupid tlick.' " Tex looks shocked. Everyone else is looking for a cue how to react.

One thousand one . . . thousand two . . . thousand three . . . Bang-Pow grins wide and belly laughs. A Laotian Don Rickles!

Everybody laughs and the two gangs fall together like long-lost relatives.

Questions start flying: "What happened?" and "Where're you guys from?" and "How'd you manage to miss the karst?" and "How'd you get shot?"

I answer for us, "Tell you what. You get us something to eat and drink and we'll tell you the whole story. How's that?"

Tex nods. "That's a deal. Come on . . . have your guys jump in"—he points to their jeeps—"and we'll go find a couple of beers."

Our newly merged groups jump into jeeps unlike any I've seen. As Rich and Charles jump in the backseat of Tex's jeep, I ask, "What *are* these things?"

Tex laughs. "Captured enemy booty . . . not sure if they're Chinese- or Russian-made . . . that's why they look so funky." He jumps in the driver's seat.

The front passenger seat looks like a rusted-out lawn-chair frame.

Tex prods, "Come on. Get in and *hold on* tight."

I gingerly get in and try to sit without falling through to the ground. Tex grinds the gears several times, gives up, smashes them together, hits the gas, and we rocket away. My lawn chair rears like a bucking bronco so I wind up in Charles's lap looking up at the stars. He shoves me forward and I grab the smashed-out windshield frame as we barrel off to . . . somewhere.

Tex laughs. "I *told you*. We don't have parts. The clutch went out years ago, so we have to jam the gears . . . beats walking." He laughs more to himself.

I holler, "I didn't get your name."

"That's right," he yells back, and says nothing more as we race northwest down the remaining runway.

Our survival radios! I forgot them! Damn!

I yell, "Stop!"

Tex keeps driving and, although I know he heard me, hollers, *"What?"*

"I forgot our emergency radios. Turn around and go back. I need 'em to call Moonbeam and let 'em know we're okay."

Our host shakes his head and says firmly, "Too late."

I shift tactics and argue, "But they're accountable items. I can't afford to pay for 'em if they're stolen."

"Don't worry, they'll—"

"But, it's *right there*." I point behind. "It'll only take a second."

Tex says officiously, "You can use the radio at our communications shack."

I answer hesitantly, "Well . . . I guess that'd be okay."

Feeling I'm abandoning my best friend, I turn for one last look at our disabled aircraft, then watch it blend into the darkness.

I shout over the jeep's screaming engine, "Shouldn't we post a guard at the plane? I could leave one of my guys in rotating shifts to make sure nothing happens."

"Nah. It'll be fine."

"But couldn't the bad guys do something to it? Maybe I should move it off the middle of your runway."

Tex stares at me as if I said something stupid. "Nobody's gonna bother it. We'll check on it in the morning."

Figuring Tex might say more now that we're away from the others, I ask, "What's your job here and who are those other guys?"

Tex ponders what he can divulge, then finally explains

he's the sole Air Force officer here, strictly a noncombat adviser. He says everyone else is a "soldier of fortune" or "civilian volunteer."

I ask what that means and he says harshly, "I could tell you, but then I'd have to kill you," and chuckles.

I force a laugh, but part of me thinks he might be serious. After all, as far as the Church knows, we're dead men. Until I contact Moonbeam, these "volunteers" could do pretty much anything they want with us and nobody'd ever know the difference. We're not out of the woods yet.

I prod, "Your friends are obviously Americans; so who are they exactly?"

No answer back from Tex.

Figuring he's another officer like me, I try again. "I just saw Nixon on TV swearing we have no ground forces in Laos, but that's obviously not true. I just saw some."

"You are mistaken." Tex lowers his voice and glares at me. "There are no U.S. ground forces in Laos."

That dentist-chair feeling returns, so I stop talking.

The headlights pick up a structure that reminds me of Boy Scout campground buildings. Tex aims the jeep for an Old West hitching post out front. From twenty feet away, he shuts off the engine, coasts to a stop, and cranks on the emergency.

"No brakes," he explains.

Ahead I see heavy gangplank steps that lead up to the porch of a dilapidated shack. The other five jeeps pull up and park alongside.

Tex announces, "This is it . . . our communications shack . . . everybody out. The rest of you guys," he shouts at the other jeeps, "wait *right here*. Don't go wandering around on your own. We'll be right out."

My stomach flip-flops. We can't wander around? And Moonbeam will have a ton of questions. So why does he think we'll be "right out"?

I tell Rich and Charles to relax in the jeep while I call Moonbeam because it might take a while, but Tex repeats authoritatively, "I *said,* everybody out. *Please,* I insist."

This confirms it: Tex is our "handler."

I begin to wonder, are we prisoners, or what?

Charles and Rich climb out, walk over, and shoot me looks of concern that say, "The sooner we get out of here, the better."

The four of us climb six cupped wood steps up to a large wood porch.

Tex produces a ring of maybe fifty keys, searches for the proper one with his Cadnica, unlocks the door, *creeeaks* it open, and in a sweeping gesture proudly announces, "Our communications room. Knock your socks off."

I step into the dark room, get a face full of spiderwebs, and brush them out of my hair and eyes.

Tex says, "Oops, sorry . . . shoulda warned ya," and chuckles to himself. "As you can see, we don't use this place much." He gropes for the light switch and flicks it on.

The place looks as if a bomb went off. Papers surrounding a dilapidated desk and strewn across the floor bear the date 1968. A single wooden swivel chair lies cockeyed. Dust of the ages over everything.

I walk to what must pass as their radio. French name. Missing case . . . exposed vacuum tubes . . . 1940 technology. I ask if this is all they have since I can't reach Moonbeam on it.

He answers yes and explains they don't use it much because they don't have much need to contact the outside world, but I can "give it a try" if I want. He says my best bet is to try reaching the American embassy down at Vientiane, but there's probably nobody there this time of night. I check my Seiko . . . a few minutes after one.

I ask Tex, "Do you know how to operate this antique?"

He responds, "Not a clue."

I flick a switch labeled in French to what I guess is ON, and watch three-quarters of the tubes come to life. I take a dark one out and hold it up to the bare overhead bulb . . .

. . . completely black. A dead soldier. I place the tube back . . . no sense checking the others.

It dawns on me this has been a charade . . . not turning back for our radios . . . don't go wandering . . . now this . . .

Tex is here to make certain we *don't* contact the outside world.

I spot an old phone with no dial. With growing anger, I ask Tex if I can try it.

He answers easily, "Sure, but I don't think it works."

I pick up the handset, bring it toward my ear, but a foot away I hear a cacophony of electronic pops, cracks, and whizzes. I hold it away from my ear and hear a female operator say something in Laotian. Knowing very well any officer sent here was required to attend the Navy foreign-language cram course at Monterey, I ask Tex if he can translate.

He closes his eyes and slowly shakes his head no.

I ask, "Maybe we could get Bang-Pow's aide in here."

He grins, shrugs, and in a singsong tone says, *"Sorr-eee,"* but his expression says he isn't. Weasel.

I tell the operator, "No speak Laotian. Speak English?"

She hollers back gibberish.

Knowing it won't work, like an idiot I shout slowly, "DOES ANYONE THERE SPEAK ENGLISH? AMERICAN EMBASSY? VIENTIANE?"

She *yells* back angrily in Laotian, then I hear a click. I slowly replace the receiver.

Tex lies, "Maybe you can try again in the morning. Come on; let's go find those drinks." We are being herded like cattle.

I feel my Irish temper taking over. In my mind I draw my revolver, point it at Tex, and tell him, "Look, asshole. Take me back to the aircraft. *Now*." But I breathe deeply, cool off, and caution myself, "Not now. Bide your time. There'll be a better opportunity down the road."

Instead, I tell Tex cheerfully, "Sounds good. Let's go." There's nothing else I can do.

I walk out to the porch, down the wooden steps, and over to the awaiting jeeps as Tex locks the door. I start to climb onto my lawn chair, but Tex orders, "Not the jeeps . . . we walk from here." More herding.

I figure he must have a path in mind to keep our prying eyes covered like horse blinders. Charles and Rich look at me apprehensively, but we join Tex, who now leads our group of maybe eighteen, I guess, up a beaten footpath onto the mountainside we'd watched them S-turn down.

"Where're we going?" I ask.

"You'll see." He starts hiking up the mountainside.

I check with Rich and Charles and see them looking as bewildered as I feel. We fall in behind Tex.

We hike in silence along a footpath that periodically crosses that switchback road. I think about Wiley and how I wish I'd been able to call Moonbeam to let him know we're okay. It won't be long before Moonbeam alerts Saigon, who'll call NKP, who'll alert the chaplain, and everybody will attend one of those impromptu memorials for *us*.

Everybody but Wiley, that is. Tonight Wiley will sing for *me*

Poor Wiley.

Our climbing group is making such a racket that porch lights start flicking on in a long row of shed buildings to our right . . . the same kind I lived in with Crazy Mark. Except these are far grander . . . like upper-Michigan logging camps. The lodges jut *right out* of the mountainside like Sierra Nevada train trestles, suspended midair on stilts to compensate for the increasingly steep mountain slope we continue to climb.

As we pass each lodge, sleepy-eyed men wearing shorts, T-shirts, and sleep-tousled hair stumble onto their porches, see our parade, rub their eyes in shock, and yell at us, "What's going on?"

Each time Tex yells back, "These guys just landed a C-123 in here! Can you *believe* it? Come on; we're headed for the bar to hear the whole story!" and waves them to join us.

The mountainside turns steeper.

More lodge porch lights flick on, more sleepy-eyed men repeat the exchange with Tex, hop-skip-run and jump in alongside anyone in a flightsuit. "You're the navigator! *Wow!*" and "So what happened?" and "No way!" and "You gotta be *shittin'* me!"

Mingled between, I hear, "How'd you get a plane that

huge in here?" and "Which one's the pilot? I gotta meet that guy and shake his hand."

As the growing number of lodge lights illuminates a complex of large buildings on the left, it becomes obvious this is no small, remote site. No; somebody has invested a lot of money in this place. We have stumbled onto a major, top-secret U.S. operation.

I turn to Tex and say, "They briefed us this is a no-man's-land. It doesn't look that way."

"Been the cover story for years," he finally admits to something. "It keeps snooping eyes away, at least until *you* showed up."

I explain, "Well, your cover story almost got you shot."

"Why'd'ya think I started with that Texas drawl?" He laughs.

I laugh with him.

I turn around and see my crew having the time of their lives. I tell myself, Why rain on their parade? For *one day* in their whole lives, these guys are heroes. Who am I to spoil their fun? Just lean back and enjoy.

So I drop my concerns about Tex and his hidden agenda and the anxiety over how to fix the plane and refuel it and what's going to happen next and how we're going to get home and all the other crap I should be thinking of and start enjoying *this* moment. We have nothing but time on our hands and this night has all the earmarks it might turn into one rockin' good party.

Now the mountainside rises so steeply I have to lean forward to keep from falling backward. I dig my heels into the hillside, thigh muscles burning. I plant one heel in, *push,* lean forward, *swing* the back leg ahead, plant that heel, and *push up* again.

It comes to me there's something symbolic about climbing the mountain that nearly killed us, but when I can't figure out what, let it slip away.

I turn around again and see our parade has grown huge.

I tell myself, First things first. First we party; then we figure how to get home.

CHAPTER *FORTY-SIX*

We climb a while longer and reach a plateau.

Tex announces, "We're here," and points up to a wooden structure, seemingly hovering in the sky, built atop a rocky cave dead ahead. Off to the cave's right, worn stone stairs rise right, curve left up and around, and finally disappear en route to the wooden edifice.

"Our bar is built over a natural cave," he explains. "Come on over. I'll show you something before we go up." He leads us to prison bars that cover the thirty-foot-wide opening. I stop a foot back from the twelve-foot-tall, weatherworn wrought-iron bars. *Is he going to jail us?* flicks across my mind.

No, I answer my fears . . . too many witnesses.

The surging crowd shoves me against the bars. I grab with both hands and shove back, but they've got me pinned.

I tell Tex nervously, "I don't see a thing."

"Just wait. You'll see."

A moaning hulk lumbers out of the darkness. A bear! Headed right for me!

I try to back up, but the crowd shoves me forward.

Two bears now! Standing up and leaning into the bars! Inches from my face! I can smell this one's breath!

He could reach through and grab me, but remains politely on his side.

Reassured he won't get me, I snap at Tex, "You scared the hell outta me." He chuckles.

I calm down and ask, "What kind of bears are they?"

"Asian brown bears."

"So . . . how come they're here?"

"They're Bang-Pow's pets."

"But they belong out in the wild."

"No, they don't. If they were out roaming around, they'd've been blown up by now. American bombs had already killed their parents when Bang-Pow adopted them as cubs. He hand-raised them, has kept them here since, and plans to release them after the war is over. In the meantime, they're safe."

Now the bear in front of me leans forward and looks me up and down.

Tex whispers, "Stay very still."

I freeze . . . and see a faint yellowish glow appear around the bear's head, like a halo in religious paintings. He leans closer, groans, and his eyes smolder from an inner illumination.

I whisper at Tex, "Do you see that?"

"See *what*?" he booms.

I whisper, "His *eyes* and that aura around his head."

Tex booms sarcastically, "I don't see a damned thing."

I hold a finger to my lips. "*Shhhhh* . . . quiet. We're talking here." I stare in wonder as the creature reaches his mind into mine: "I *know,* but don't try explaining to *them.* They'll never hear you."

From behind, I hear the crowd leaving, stomping up the stairs.

Tex tugs at my sleeve and says anxiously, "Come on; let's go."

I yank my sleeve away. "Not yet."

"Why not?"

"Because we're not through talking."

Tex stares at me curiously, then at the bear, back at me, the bear, back at me again, and apparently sees nothing because he says, "You musta got whacked in the head back there. You've lost it, man."

"No, actually, just the opposite," I start to explain, but knowing he won't understand, I say seriously, "I think I'm getting it for the first time in my life."

Tex says, "Let's go. The beer's getting warm," and tugs me away midconversation, pulling me backpedaling up the stone stairs. The bear leans into the bars to keep eye contact with me until Tex and I disappear around the curve.

I make a mental note to finish our conversation later.

We stop in front of two massive, carved teakwood doors. Tex grins and says proudly, "It ain't much, but we call it home," opens the right door, makes a sweeping gesture, and ushers me in. My mouth drops open as we step into a posh Fifth Avenue pub. Huge thirty-by-forty-foot room. Mahogany paneling. Deep-pile Oriental carpets. Heavy leather couches and chairs. Hand-carved teakwood bar. High-back barstools. Massive stone fireplace. Five-by-six open hearth. Wurlitzer jukebox in the far corner. A $3,500, four-foot carved wooden water buffalo opposite. Original-looking oil paintings. Tiffany lamps throughout. Twin picture windows overlooking the valley.

A real palace.

Tex says, "You can close your mouth now; you're catching flies," and laughs.

The place smells of *money*; it's reminiscent of those Wisconsin "logging camps" restricted for congressional use. *Somebody* is taking very good care of these people.

The crowded room is abuzz in conversation. Everyone has a drink. Our parade has broken into groups of seven or eight locals surrounding each of my guys.

Tex and I walk over to the only space left—the bar. I lean against the teakwood bar and look around.

The bartender strolls over and asks, "What'll you have, gents?"

Knowing he won't have much of a selection, I hesitantly ask, "You got *anything* besides San Miguel?"

He makes a face. "We don't allow that swill in here." I ask him what he does have.

"Anything you want . . . Heineken, Dos Equis, dark Beck's, Singha, Guinness stout, Sapporo, Tsing Tao, Elephant, Moosehead, Labatt's, Corona, Coors—"

I get excited. "Whoa! Stop right there. Coors! You can't get Coors east of the Mississippi. How'd you manage to get it at this godforsaken place?"

"Connections," he answers obliquely, produces a chilled schooner, pours a perfect head, and slides it across the bar. I take a sip, close my eyes, swish it around, and swallow. Pure heaven!

Tex points to a stool. "Have a seat."

I explain I've been sitting for hours and want to enjoy the simple pleasure of standing. I reach for my wallet, but remember it's back at NKP in the little green bag. I apologize, "They won't let us fly with any money."

Tex says, "No problem. Your money wouldn't be any good in here tonight. You can pay by telling us your story." Hearing this, eight or nine guys my age migrate over and form a tight semicircle around us.

I answer, "Okay. Thanks." I raise my schooner and begin chugalugging while I think where to begin. I tip my glass for the last chug, but Tex grabs my wrist and says, "Don't."

Puzzled, I ask why not.

"We have a tradition that's *never* been broken," he answers. Everyone nods. "Step over a couple feet and I'll show you."

Confused, I move aside.

Tex bends down, pulls up the floorboard I was just standing on, and lays it on the bar, producing a gaping hole larger than my boot.

What the . . . ?

He whistles down the hole. I ask him what he's doing and he answers, "Wait a sec . . . you'll see."

I bend over to see and . . . *yikes!*

I jump back and knock over a barstool as the hole fills with *jaws* . . . lapping pink tongue . . . white *fangs* . . . black nose! *Inches* below where my boot was a second ago!

I tell Tex, "I could've lost a foot! I *told you* to stop that crap."

Tex ignores this and scolds me, "Stop teasing him."

"What?"

"We *never* finish a beer. That's the tradition. We always share the last swallow. It brings good luck."

I blurt out, "But you're turning them into alcoholics! What happens when the war's over?" but wish I could stuff the words back in my mouth because I can see from his expression he's offended.

Oops.

Tex squints at me. "We live by combat rules . . . there are none."

I watch the bear dry-swallowing in anticipation.

"Stop teasing him," Tex says impatiently.

I shrug and with an "Oh, well, when in Rome . . ." finality bend down and pour the last swallow . . . down the old hatch. Now Tex and the others share their beers as I watch the second bear shove the first bear away.

With everyone finished, I grab the plank to cover the hole, but Tex grabs my wrist and orders, "Leave it open."

"But somebody could lose a foot down there."

He answers sharply, "I *told* you, combat rules. Leave it open."

I think about this, hop on a stool, and hook my heels in the lower rung.

Tex suggests, "How about taking off that survival vest and gun belt?" and points across the room at the hearth big enough to roast a cow. "You can pile them over there."

I stand, take my gun and vest off, walk to the fireplace, start a pile, signal my guys to join me, watch them toss the now useless gear into a messy pile, weave my way back through the crowd to my stool, pick up an awaiting Coors, and discover a round of yellow cheese eighteen inches thick and two feet across.

Tex sticks a foot-long bowie knife in the middle and says, "Help yourself."

I whack off a wedge, sip my second Coors, and start the story.

I tell them about Tonto's Mayday, our deciding to stay though we'd be low on fuel, the fuel imbalance, cross-feeding, calling Moonbeam for fighter support, how I reluctantly had to use napalm, the hydrofoil of flames, "Oooooh! Number one bomb . . . I can hear them *screaming*!" and watch my audience's faces turn wild.

Then I tell them about Ty reporting the leak I first ignored as an indication problem. "Bad on me," I say. "I should have listened. Maybe we'd've isolated the leak and made it to the river; but I ignored him and let the situation get worse. So in a way," I admit, "this is all my fault. If I'd headed home when Rich wanted, none of this would've happened."

They nod seriously but say nothing. Finally a man wearing a Stanford T-shirt adds, "And Tonto'd be dead."

A man in a Syracuse T-shirt asks how we got hit. Did the bad guys get off a lucky shot, or did our flares make us more visible?

I sigh, "We'll never know. I thought our flares would blind him. So it must've been a lucky shot."

They nod agreement.

They are all gawking at me as if I were some sort of hero, so I decide not to tell them about my meltdowns . . . no sense spoiling the moment.

"How'd it feel when you thought you were gonna have to bail out? Were you scared?" Syracuse wants to know.

I think a moment. "I was *way past* scared. I went places in my mind you *never* want to go. I think Thomas Jefferson came close when he said of slavery, 'It was like holding a snarling wolf by the ears. I could neither hold on, nor let go.' That may not be an exact quote, but it's close."

While they picture that image, I down the rest of my second Coors, slip off my stool, bend down, and pour the last swallow into the awaiting pink jaws. Then I shinny back onto my stool and, feeling guilty about the bears, decide to switch to hard stuff.

Pushing my luck, I ask the bartender, "You got any Scotch?"

He answers gleefully, "What kind would ya like? We got Johnnie Walker Red, Glenlivet, Cutty Sark, Chivas Regal, Royal Salute—"

"Royal Salute? How old is that?"

"Twenty-eight years."

"That's three years older than me! It must've cost a fortune." I ask politely, "Could I please try just a smidgen?" holding my thumb and forefinger a half-inch apart.

He reaches behind the bar, opens a locked cabinet, pulls something off a shelf, and presents a purple velvet pouch secured with a gold-braided drawstring. He loosens the drawstring and, in sort of a striptease act, s-l-o-w-l-y unveils a bulbous crystal bottle. Then he twists open the stopper, slides the whole shebang across the bar at me, and says, "On the house . . . enjoy."

I tell him thank you very, very much and cradle it in my arms.

Now I realize I skipped a part, so I back up and tell them about getting out of the seat to see the leak for myself.

A Georgetown T-shirt remarks, "Not many pilots would've done that. That . . . right there . . . saved your life. That was the turning point."

I tell him, "Maybe, but to me the key point was Ty finding the leak. Without that, we wouldn't have known till the engine quit. We'd have been assholes and elbows."

They look over at Ty with his group and nod.

I check my watch . . . 2:14 . . . and I've barely scratched the surface.

A man sporting a Yale T-shirt wants to know the extent of the damage.

I explain, "We're not sure. The shell hit the outboard

cowl, so there's prob'ly a bunch of twisted metal out there that'll have to be cut away and replaced. I tried checking after we landed, but it was too dark."

Syracuse wants to know if the airplane is flyable.

I answer dejectedly, "Probably not. It'll need major structural repairs before it flies again. I'll radio Moonbeam in the morning and arrange for a team of Air Force mechanics to fly in. A maintenance officer will have to sign off the logbook to approve an emergency, onetime flight back to NKP. I don't have the authority."

They look as if I just said the dumbest thing they ever heard, but with the glow of Scotch running through my veins, I let it pass and get back to the story.

I am talking about discovering the cross-feed *wide-open* when Yale cuts in, "Wait a minute . . . that doesn't make sense. If it's like most fuel panels, your cross-feed valve is *right between* the fuel gauges four of you were looking at. It was *right in* your faces. How could you *not* see it?"

I shake my head, take a deep breath, and admit, "I don't know. I should've spotted it earlier. But I do understand why Ty spotted the leak first."

"Why's that?" they want to know.

"It's where they hid the fuel panel . . . *way up* on the overhead panel . . . out of sight, out of mind . . . especially when your attention's focused on an airstrike. Now, if they'd have put it in front of the copilot's knee like Boeing did on the newer B-52, we might've caught it earlier. So thank God for Ty."

I skip over my thoughts of shooting Rich and suicide as too personal.

"But my point is, I had given up when I asked, 'Does anybody have any ideas?' I'd be out hanging in some tree right now if it weren't for that guy over there doing a good Clark Kent impression." I point at Charles.

Charles notices them staring and walks over. I point out the bear hole and he steps around it. I announce, "Gentlemen, I want you to meet tonight's true hero, Major George Keene."

I tell him, "Charles, you saved my life and I'll never forget you as long as I live."

"As you saved mine," he says seriously.

I ask, "How'd you find Long Tien in the first place? When you brought that map up, I couldn't see a thing. How'd you know we were so close?"

"I didn't. I used an old navigator trick they stopped teaching twenty years ago because it's so primitive. The new kids don't learn it. You see, that three-by-four-foot map was way too big. An image that large overpowers the senses, so I cut it down to size. We were headed south when I started looking for an emergency field. I computed we only had a thirty-mile range, so I stuck the point of my compass in our position and drew a thirty-mile arc starting east, all the way through west."

He sips his beer and clears his throat. "I knew you wouldn't want to go north, so that cut the search pattern in half. Next I cut the southern half-pie into six thirty-degree sectors. Then I started looking inside each sector, focusing between the ten to twenty miles I thought you might reach. I didn't find anything in the 180-to-210-degree, nor in the 210-to-240 sector. I was just about to throw in the towel when I took one last shot at the 240-to-270-degree sector and *bingo*! It jumped off the chart."

I tell him, "Well, thank God for old navigators."

A man in a Penn State T-shirt remarks, "I can't believe they don't give you guys better maps. We've got plenty, so it's not like they're not available."

I explain, "We've asked, but they told us we're not budgeted for them."

Penn State's face turns red. "So there's some pencil-necked, draft-dodging geek in D.C. driving home safely on the beltway every night making life-and-death decisions about something he doesn't understand, half a world away?"

I sigh, "I guess."

The group starts discussing how to use Charles's technique for their own flying, so I lean over and whisper to Charles, "Why'd you believe I could get us in here?"

"I just thought you could do it," he whispers back. "Of the

other pilots in the squadron, there's only one other I'd have even *told.*"

"Who? Wiley?"

"Yeah. Now if Desktop or"—he jerks his thumb at Rich, leaning against the fireplace—"or your 'friend' over there had been in command . . . well . . . I'd be out there hanging in a tree right now." Then he adds, "But, John, just between you and me, how *did* you do it? I couldn't see a thing during the approach."

"I don't think I'll ever understand," I answer mournfully. "There was . . . this voice . . . coaching me."

His expression says he thinks I'm not telling the truth. But he nods and says, "Well, thanks for saving my life," turns, and walks over to the jukebox. He leans against the rainbow case, searches, makes a selection, smiles, points at me, and mimes, "This one's for you."

> *Lean on me, when you're not strong*
> *And I'll be your friend*
> *I'll help you . . . carrrry . . . on*
> *For . . . it won't be long*
> *Till I'm gonna need*
> *Somebody to lean on . . .*

I nod, smile, and mouth back, "Me, too."

As the Scotch warms me, I think to myself, I could sit here on this barstool forever. Why not keep the fact we're alive secret and hide out here the next few months? They've had our memorial. So what's the rush? We could hang out here, drink free liquor, and then call Moonbeam in about . . . when . . . May? Wouldn't that be a hoot! Six months of not getting our asses shot off?

Sounds good to me.

Tex and the others are still arguing about the map-scale issue, so I excuse myself and walk over to one of the rampers.

He notices me approach and looks up. "Yes, sir?"

"Sorry to interrupt . . . one question . . . what'd the pallets look like when you guys tossed 'em out?"

His face lights up. "You shoulda seen it, sir! It was like those old Road Runner cartoons where Wile E. Coyote'd run off a cliff, look bug-eyed, and then drop out of sight. Those pallets, they flew along in space right behind us like they was confused about what they was supposed to do, then dropped straight down."

"I knew it," I say enthusiastically. *"I just knew it."*

I turn to go and hear, "But, sir, how'd you ever think of tossin' 'em out?"

"A friend taught me." Then I add, "Thanks . . . great job," and weave my way through the crowd back to my stool.

"So what happened next?" Tex prods as I sit down.

I describe turning toward Long Tien, jettisoning the pallets, having the rampers save the remaining flares, managing the fire threat, and then I bring up the issue of their wrong-way approach plate.

"What nearly got us killed was confusion over which way to land. Your approach chart says to 'land from thirty-two to fourteen,' but clearly that's wrong."

They look confused and are quiet. Then Yale says cryptically, "You'd bust your ass if you tried to land on fourteen."

"Yeah, we sorta figured that out," I say wearily. "Maybe you could message whoever publishes that thing and get it changed."

Yale explains he's tried to submit several changes, but by the time his request makes it all the way back to their people in the States, gets forwarded to the Pentagon, then the State Department, then to the Laotian government at Vientiane, and maybe a year later *finally* reaches some Laotian translator better at French than English who actually writes the damned thing, the meaning gets lost.

He concludes, "It's a shame, because that last guy in the chain? He's only one hundred and forty miles from where we're standing."

I ask sarcastically, "Did you ever think of picking up the phone and calling him?"

"Oh, they'd *never* let us do that," he explains sadly.

I nod and change the subject. "Your triangle runway

lights threw us a curve, too. What the hell kind of lights are those and why do you leave them on at night?"

"We don't get much sun at the bottom of the canyon," Tex explains. "It sets by two P.M. and leaves the field obscured in deep shadows. Sometimes the lights are the only way we can spot the runway. As to why they were still on . . ." Tex looks around the room, spots someone, and yells, "Hey, Harry! Did you forget to disconnect the batteries?"

Harry looks embarrassed. "Yeah . . . sorry . . . guess I forgot."

I ask incredulously, "You mean we're alive because Harry *forgot*?"

Syracuse says, "Your getting in here is even weirder than that. Remember now, this is the rainy season. Most nights? You'd've been on top of an overcast and never seen the lights. You should be dead. You really shouldn't be here."

"He's right," Tex agrees. "And the lights? They're just battery-powered sixty-watt patio lights Harry ordered out of the Sears catalog and jury-rigged to run off jeep batteries. That's why he's *supposed* to disconnect them . . . so the batteries don't run down. If he hadn't forgotten, you'd have been . . ."

"Toast," I fill in, and take a swig of Scotch.

We're alive because of *whims* . . . pure chance.

Out of the corner of my eye, I spot a beet-red face over in Rich's group.

Beet-face sees me looking, charges through the crowd, and pokes his finger in my face. *"You shouldn't be here! You were just lucky!"* He stammers, *"You . . . you . . . you . . . you broke all the rules. You should be . . . dead,"* storms out, and SLAMS the door.

I stand up to go after him, but Tex grabs my shoulder and pushes me back down on my stool.

Bewildered, I ask, "What set him off?"

"You better get used to that. He knows he couldn't have possibly done what you did. When you get back, there's gonna be lots of guys who'll tell you they admire what you did, but hate you for it behind your back. You might not want to share this with too many people. They'll think you're either bragging or lying."

"But it's the truth!"

"Hey, look; I wouldn't have believed it myself if I hadn't seen it with my own eyes."

I think to myself, My guys need some real food and rest before morning, but it's clear I'll have to finish before those things can happen; so I rush ahead.

I talk about the disastrous flight northwest, turning back, the moon going behind the clouds, losing the *V* lights, being lost a second time, almost ordering a bailout, and finally finding their lights again.

Now they begin arguing how they would have flown the approach, so my attention wanders. I am looking around the room and see a completely different-looking Rich leaning against the stone hearth.

The old Rich looked like an overstarched shirt. This new Rich looks as relaxed as a golf pro.

I realize I am looking at a completely new person.

He notices me staring, and this new Arnold Palmer version of Rich saunters over, picking his way through the crowd. I think, uh-oh. Here comes trouble.

I point at the bear hole and say, "Watch out." He notices it and steps around.

I launch a preemptive strike. "Rich, I'm sorry I yelled at you. I was out of line. It wasn't your fault—"

This new Rich waves me off. "No; this is my fault. If I hadn't insisted on cross-feeding . . . I'm . . . I'm . . . just so sorry. And that 'land from three-two to one-four' . . . you were right on that one, too. We'd be twice dead if you'd done what I said. Peggy'd've had the baby alone and he'd never have known his father. I'm so grateful."

"The baby!" I exclaim. "I forgot. No wonder you wanted out of there."

He lets me off the hook. "It's okay. Staying was the right thing."

We turn quiet and listen to the end of Charles's song.

So just call on me brother, when you need a hand
We all need . . . somebody . . . to lean on
I just might have a problem that you'd understand
We all need . . . somebody . . . to lean on

I ask, "But how'd you manage to get that left engine relit? That was like getting water from a stone. If you hadn't got it running, I'd have had to order a bailout."

Rich looks sheepish. "I'm not sure you want to know."

"Sure I do. Just tell me."

"Well . . ." He hesitates. "I . . . I opened the cross-feed."

I laugh and exclaim, "You did *what*?"

"It was our last shot. I figured it might add enough fuel pressure from the right tank *across* the leak . . . and it did." He rushes to add, "But I closed it as soon as the engine relit."

I stare at him and ask incredulously, "So you took what little fuel we had and squirted some overboard?"

"Yeah, but there wasn't time to tell you. I hope it was okay." He looks down.

I think to myself, Jack was right. Pinocchio has become a real boy.

I tell him, "Rich, it was perfect. How'd you ever think of that?"

This new Rich looks up and smiles. "Well, I guess . . . I sort of . . . made it up."

"Perfect." I grin. "Absolutely perfect."

He nods, turns, and shuffles back to his group by the hearth.

Tex tugs my sleeve. "But even when you picked up the lights the second time, how did you manage? You can't see a hand in front of your face out there."

I begin to answer, but he adds, "And how come you didn't use the flares you saved? That was a major mistake on your part. You could've used 'em to find your way around."

I shake my head and say simply, "I didn't need them."

Their blank expressions tell me they don't understand.

I explain, "I could see *without* them. It was like . . . looking at . . . a moving X-ray. And the flares? Their shadows would have made the situation worse."

Penn State says bluntly, "You're fulla shit. Nobody can see in the dark. Come on; don't hold back. Tell us. Your secret won't leave this place."

"I'm *not* holding back. It was a sense different than seeing. It was like someone was whispering what to do and where to go. I doubted it at first, but the more I listened, the more I realized it was right, and in the end, I gave myself over to it completely."

They say nothing, so I continue, "It was like . . . stepping into another dimension . . . the feeling migrating whales must have . . . or swallows coming back to Capistrano . . . or salmon returning to the *same spot* in the *same stream* they were spawned. It was a feeling of . . . coming home."

A Budweiser T-shirt attacks, "Aha! Then you *have* been here before."

"No," I answer quietly, "I've never seen this place."

"But that's impossible!"

I chuckle, "Tell me about it!"

Budweiser says, "Well . . . you must've flown over during the day."

"That'd never happen. We're down at the Mekong by sunrise. Otherwise, we'd be too easy a target."

They stare, giving no sign they understand, so I take a sip of Scotch and try another approach. "There is one other possibility."

"What's that?" Georgetown asks.

"The 'many worlds' theory of quantum physics."

They look even more puzzled.

" 'Many worlds' says that at the point when we nearly crashed, the universe split into two potential worlds. In one, we crashed and died. In the other, we landed safely. In other words, we were trapped in a state of suspended animation where *both* outcomes were possible. The question is which would become reality, and many worlds says there was no way of knowing until you guys showed up."

Budweiser looks surprised. "What did *we* have to do with it?"

"Everything. Until you drove down and *looked at us,* we both crashed *and* landed, frozen in limbo. It could have gone either way. If you'd heard our crash, rolled over, and gone back to sleep . . . well . . . you'd wake up in the morning, discover our wreckage, and wonder what damned fool tried landing here at night because *everybody knows* it's impossible."

I take another swig of Scotch while I gather my thoughts.

"But as soon as you *looked at us,* the crash potential collapsed. So what the scientists are saying, if I have it right, is the universe generates countless potential realities that exist in suspended animation until *we* observe *one,* which then becomes reality and all the others vanish."

Yale asks, "So you're saying *we* saved your lives?"

"Exactly. And the next question is, how do we know which version was going to become 'real'? And the answer is, we don't. We can say the two possibilities were life or death, but there's no way of determining which reality was going to be selected. Nobody knows what causes one possibility to become reality and the other to collapse. So what determined our fate was a matter of . . . I hate to admit . . . pure chance . . . a roll of the dice."

I drain my Scotch.

"But there's this other part of many worlds that's *really* wild," I continue. "Some scientists claim *all* the potentials are real and that they are *all* happening and all *at the same time*—just in different worlds that coexist with ours. So . . . when we nearly smacked into that karst stalagmite, the entire universe split in two, creating *two different versions* in which we are both dead *and* alive. In this reality, we are partying with you, but in the other, you sleep in and discover our wreckage. Neither version is aware of the other, and each of those versions goes on producing endless versions of reality."

They all stare at me as if I were nuts.

I tell myself, This is getting spooky.

Syracuse asks, "So where are those guys?"

"Right here; right now."

"Why can't I see them?"

I explain, "They're in another dimension we can't sense. We're like two-dimensional movie-screen characters who can't 'see' the audience 'out there.' "

Penn State says, "That's plain crazy. We're the only reality."

I counter, "How do you know your twins in the other realities aren't saying the same about you?"

He looks startled and says nothing.

Yale asks, "How can you prove this parallel universe exists?"

"I can't," I reply. "They say it's impossible for us to picture it."

Now on a roll, I keep going. "There is one other possibility: superdeterminism. The superdeterminists believe ever since the big bang, reality couldn't be any other way. That Jack Ward was *always* going to die in a plane crash and Harry was *always* going to forget to disconnect the light batteries. You see, *no matter what I did,* they're saying we were destined to take that hit and wind up here with you . . . that the universe *couldn't be any other way* . . . that being here with you was always *the only thing ever possible*. There was no stopping it."

Yale asks, "So what you're saying is I have no free will? That I can't choose what I'm going to do tomorrow?"

"No. I'm not saying that at all. I'm just telling you what some of the best minds on the planet are thinking."

Syracuse scratches his head. "Where did you come up with these wild ideas?"

"I read a lot."

The Notre Dame T-shirt asks cynically, "What crackpot came up with this junk?"

"Disciples of that crackpot Albert Einstein. And the ideas aren't so wild. They've been widely accepted science for forty years. Just because you haven't heard of them doesn't make them any less real."

I explain, "I've been studying this 'junk' to help me understand things I've been seeing recently." I tell them about the Bangkok dinner party, the Four Little Indians angle, the taxi ride near-disaster, Ben's death the same moment, Ray's being killed as I watched, and Jack's widow's letter.

I finish with "So you see . . . I felt something was coming. I just didn't think it would be this bad," and laugh.

Stanford asks, "Who were the ladies at the party? You gotta warn them."

"No, I don't. For some reason, I've beaten the curse. It's over; I can feel it. But to answer your question, let's see, there was Ginger Berano . . . Rod's wife. And the other woman?" I shake my head. "I've always had trouble picturing her face. Oh, yes! I can see her now . . . it was Peg . . . Oh my God."

I collapse against the back of my stool, feeling queasy.

Tex exclaims, "What!"

"It was Rich's wife, Peggy! Out of *all the other* pilots, I wind up flying with her husband? What were the odds! See what I mean?"

Silence. They are all staring at me frog-eyed. No one knows what to say next.

Now a curious thing begins to happen.

You see, men aren't comfortable touching each other. Women do all the time; but not men. If we accidentally brush hands reaching for the same cockpit switch, we jerk back as though struck by lightning and apologize, "Oops . . . sorry."

Homophobic fears, maybe . . . I guess . . . I don't know. But not tonight. Not here.

As I've talked, my group has drawn closer and closer, "accidentally" bumping into me. For example, Notre Dame is now pressing against my thigh far too long. Next, Georgetown repeatedly pounds my shoulder and says, "You lucky sonofabitch! You used up all the luck anybody should have in a whole lifetime!"

I tell him, "I hope not."

Now another puts his arm around me uncomfortably long. Another reaches out and tousles my hair as if I were a human rabbit's foot. They seem to be having a great time, so I don't object.

Georgetown remarks, "You had a guardian angel tonight."

"Maybe so," I respond.

"So how'd it *feel* coming *that* close to dying?" another T-shirt asks.

I scan my memory, then answer seriously, "I think Charles Lindbergh said it best after landing in Paris: 'I know how the dead would feel to live again.'"

More silence from them.

I tell them, "The end. You saw us and here we are."

Georgetown says, "You gotta write a book. That's the best story I've heard to come out of this war."

I shake my head. "I wouldn't know where to begin. The story's so . . . huge."

"Still . . . you should write it down."

Tex says, "He'd have to wait thirty years before they'd allow him to publish it." Then he adds, "Now . . . start over . . . from the top."

"Kind of you to ask," I answer, "but I'm sure you guys'll want to get some sleep. It's already"—I fake a yawn and check my Seiko—"after four."

"Tell it *again*," he says firmly. "Start at Tonto's Mayday and don't leave anything out. Besides, some guys came in late and didn't hear the whole thing. We're still trying to figure out what we'd have done."

I rub my itchy eyes. "It's your lost sleep, not mine."

The bartender refills my glass and I start all over.

As I talk, I notice them spending much of the time debating what *they* would have done, but aren't asking *me*. So what do they think I am? Chopped liver?

To myself I think, This is what's wrong with accident boards. The members whine they have to *guess* what the dead pilot was thinking. This "board" has the live pilot right in front of them, but all they seem interested in is their own stale opinions. No wonder the same accidents happen over and over.

I fight my way through my group's interruptions and fin-

ish the second telling just as the bartender flicks the house-
lights and announces, "Last call!"

Feeling I've done enough male-bonding shtick, I tiptoe
up to the issue of their identity again. I joke, "Okay. I've
shown you mine; now you show me yours," and chuckle.
"Who *are* you guys?" Silence. They look at each other, then
at Tex.

I prod, "Come on . . . your secret's safe with me."

More silence and concerned looks. Tex finally says with a
straight face, "Like I said: if I told you, I'd have to kill you,"
and does not laugh.

I laugh nervously, but he adds, "Don't laugh . . . I really
might have to."

I try a different approach. "Okay, but you can't send me
home empty-handed. Nobody's gonna believe me if I don't
have *some* proof. How about this? Any of you guys got a
camera?"

Tex says sharply, "No pictures."

I plead, "Oh, *come on*! I promise not to show them to
anyone."

Tex says seriously, "No cameras allowed."

I shift subjects. "All right, all right, but something's been
bothering me all night. You said you fly in and out of here all
day, right? So where are your planes?"

Syracuse explains, "They're flown out to a secure location."

"What do mean 'secure'? It looks to me like you guys
own this place."

"Oh, we do," Tex assures me. "But if we kept our planes
overnight, the bad guys'd eventually shell 'em. That's why
we weren't exactly thrilled when we saw your machine show
up. You see, we had this nice little stalemate going until you
came along and upset the applecart. You painted a big red
bull's-eye on us that will remain as long as your plane's out
there. It won't take more than a couple days before word
gets out and the bad guys start shelling it *and* us. Not to
mention the fact you shut down our airport."

"I'm sorry . . . I had no idea . . ."

"Well, you should have thought of that before coming here. Now, if I know Bang-Pow, he won't put his people at risk for something he places no value in. So . . ."

I get edgy. "So *what*?"

"So . . . we talked it over . . . and . . . well . . . you're not gonna like it."

"What!"

"Unless I miss my guess . . . unless you find a way to get your plane outta here by tomorrow night . . . well . . . I don't know how to tell you."

I stand up and get in his face. *"What? Say it!"*

"For his own protection, Bang-Pow will prob'ly have his men turn that piece of shit of yours around, roll it down the runway, and shove it off the cliff. I figure it should break up pretty good and look like just another unidentifiable pile of scrap."

CHAPTER FORTY-SEVEN

He can't do that!" I protest. "That old piece of shit, as you call it, saved our lives!"

Tex snaps, "Hey! I *told* you: combat rules. He *can* and he probably *will*. You gotta remember . . . this is *his* country. His house, his rules. You are *not* in control here. These people don't give a rat's ass if your Air Force has one less C-123. You're in this country as a guest of the Royal Laotian government; you have no legal standing and zero authority . . . zero. You got it?!"

I think that over and then ask, "But how do we get back to NKP?"

"I don't have a clue, but you might be here awhile. My guess is you've turned into a political football. The bad guys don't have to shell us for your plane to be a serious problem. Don't you remember President Nixon on TV swearing we *absolutely, positively* have no U.S. forces in Laos or Cambodia?"

I answer yes.

"Well, you've gone and made the president of the United States a liar. All the bad guys have to do is take a *picture* of your plane, distribute it to the world press, and this could turn into an international embarrassment for the administration. So by the time I tell my people in D.C.—oh, shit. I wasn't supposed to say that. Oh, well." He shrugs. "Anyway, they're not gonna be happy. By the time they cool off, contact the Pentagon, and together they try to work something out with State . . . well . . . it could take . . . weeks . . . *months* for you to get out of here."

I plead, "But my commander will extend our assignments by however long we're stuck here!"

Tex shrugs. "Hey, that's your problem. You should've thought of that before you came in here."

Asshole! I should've shot you when I had the chance.

I feel my temper rise like lava. But realizing intelligence is what's required instead of rage, I try to schmooze him. "Hey, come on. Throw me a bone here, Tex. Give me *something*. What if I go down, call Moonbeam, and arrange for a C-123 to fly in this afternoon with a full repair team? We'd be out of your hair by sundown."

They say nothing, look at each other, then back at me as if there's something I don't understand.

I prod them, "So what's the problem?"

More silence from them.

"Tell me!"

Tex explains, "Not gonna happen. Remember, as far as anyone's concerned, this place doesn't exist. Our people won't like even *you* being here, much less approve inviting more people. And second, there's no way a C-123 could land. The runway's way too short."

I look at him and say nothing.

"The largest planes we ever get are STOLs. You know, those short-takeoff-and-landing jobs. Everybody knows it's impossible to stop a C-123 that short."

I remind him, "But there's one parked out there right now."

He thinks about this, then says, "I know. That's what doesn't make sense."

I ask, "So the Air Force was *always wrong* listing Long Tien as an emergency alternate?"

"Yep."

Grasping at straws, I say, "Let's try a different approach. You must have your own mechanics. Maybe one of them could help us bang it back into flyable shape. Maybe all we'd have to do is cut off some twisted metal and hope for the best on the rest. It flew in; so I'll find a way to fly it out."

"You don't have the authority. You'd be in a monster amount of trouble with the Air Force."

"In the words of Ted Kennedy, we'll cross that bridge when we come to it."

He thinks about this; then laughs. Good. Now we're getting somewhere.

I remind him, "That mechanic?"

"Well . . . there is one guy . . . but . . . well . . . he's right over there." Tex points to a bedraggled-looking person sitting Indian-style against the hearth.

I look across the room and study the image. Yearlong, untrimmed beard . . . shoulder-length, uncombed hair . . . filthy Korean War fatigues . . . torn, black high-top tennies . . . midfortyish . . . obviously hasn't bathed in a month . . . nursing a Coors.

"That guy?" I ask incredulously. "I wouldn't trust him to fix a lawn mower. Who else you got?"

"He's *it*. I told you, planes fly in and fly right back out, so there's no need for a whole staff of mechanics."

I let that sink in. "What's his name?"

"Toothless. He's a loner. Nobody knows his real name. They say that since Korea he's been making his way around the world as a freelance mechanic anywhere there's a war."

"You can make a living doing that?"

"Oh, sure. There's lots of guys like Toothless who drop off the human radar screen. But the downside at spots like this? We don't see many dentists. You'll see."

I ask, "Do you think he'd help?"

"Hard telling. He's a cantankerous sort; but you could ask." Tex chuckles to himself.

The morning sun now pours in through the picture windows, making everyone squint. Tex yawns, stretches, and says, "Well, thanks for a great story. I'm bushed. We're all headed for bed. Good night," then turns and walks out with the rest of the locals in tow.

I look for someone—*anyone*—to offer us a soft spot to sleep.

When no one does, I look around and conclude we're supposed to sleep on the floor. There's only the nine of us left in the bar . . . us and Toothless. Having told our story, we've become as useful as yesterday's newspaper.

I take a last swig of Salute, tuck the bottle under my arm, scoot down off my stool, dance around the bear hole, move across the Oriental carpets, and squat in front of Toothless to look him in the eye. The man ignores my presence and keeps gazing into his Coors bottle.

I try getting his attention. "Excuse me . . . Mr. . . . Toothless?"

He raises his head, looks at me through beer-stained eyes, and snarls, "What do *you* want?"

Surly bastard. Any idea I had of leveraging my newfound hero status just flew out the window.

The man growls, "Don't you go insultin' me, *sonny boy.* It's just *Toothless*. They ain't no *Mister*. Just *Toothless*, s*onny boy.*" He takes a swig of Coors.

"Okay, 'Just Toothless,'" I joke, and offer a handshake. "But my name's John . . . not 'sonny boy.'"

He waves an oil-stained hand and says sarcastically, "Whatever, s*onny boy.*"

Next I try appealing to his natural mechanic's curiosity. I ask, "I was wondering if you could maybe help us fix our plane."

"What's in it fur me?" he snaps. "How much money you got?"

I explain about sanitization and that I have no money.

"Too bad for you. Like they say, 'No money, no washee.'"

I think about this, then reluctantly shove my Royal Salute under his nose.

He cradles it in both hands, scans the room like a dog guarding a bone, tucks it under his fatigue jacket, then asks, "What's wrong with it?"

"We're not sure." I explain the hit, the fuel leak, and that I overstressed every major component, then finish, "But the main thing's the fuel leak. I'm thinking we could chop off the damaged parts, jury-rig a repair on the fuel lines, and limp home."

He complains, "Ain't got no good tools. All mine's worn-out."

"They don't provide you new ones?"

"Nah . . . goddamned outfit makes you buy yur own. If you ain't noticed, they ain't many hardware stores round these parts."

"You can use ours. We've got a flyaway kit stuffed with brand-new tools for situations like this. We have enough tools to change an engine."

"Don't got no parts."

"I'm thinking we can cannibalize parts off another system . . . maybe cut out a hydraulic line we don't need, tap off that system, and make a battlefield repair. *Please* . . . it's the only way we're going to get home."

He starts to stand up; but struggles.

I offer a hand, but he knocks it away. He snaps, "Don't need no help, *sonny boy*," then stands and walks toward the door.

I motion my guys. "Let's go."

We pick up random gun belts and vests from the messy pile, throw them over our shoulders, and scramble to catch our benefactor, already out the door.

I run ahead to walk beside our only ticket out of here and catch up with him at the bottom of the stone stairs.

Brrrrrrr! *Cold!* I can see my breath! I shove my hands under my arms and eye with envy Toothless's Salvation Army field jacket.

"Is it always this cold?" I ask, trying to break the conversational ice. "This feels like winter . . . must be in the thirties!" My teeth are chattering.

"This ain't no Thailand, *sonny boy*. You're way up north. We get snow."

We begin hiking down the mountainside. Sunlight glistens on blue, pink, and yellow wildflowers on both sides. The morning light twinkles on frost along the path, turning it into a sparkling carpet of diamonds along which we hike in silence.

Broad-leafed jungle trees are nonexistent here. The only trees are stunted, twisted pines struggling to eke a living from the four or five hours of direct sunlight they must capture before the sun disappears beyond the canyon walls.

Pine-tree shadows slice across the carpet of diamonds. From somewhere above, a lone songbird warbles; and now his melody echoes around the canyon.

I lose my footing, slip, and begin falling backward.

Toothless catches me and shoves me to my feet. "Watch it," he says, "or you'll bust yur ass."

I say thanks and we continue down the mountain in silence. I turn around to make sure everyone is keeping up.

I casually ask Toothless, "So how long's it been since you worked on a one twenty-three?"

"Never."

I stop, grab his sleeve, and spin him toward me, halting us so quick we get rear-ended. "What! Tex said you'd worked on 'em before."

Toothless stares at my hand like a dog ready to bite; so I let go. "Look, *sonny boy* . . . take it or leave it. I don't give a damn 'bout you or yur fuckin' plane. I should be in bed sleepin' off this hangover. I don't owe you *nothin'*. So what's it gonna be? You gonna keep whinin' or shut up? S'all the same to me."

I backpedal like crazy.

I smooth his sleeve, apologize profusely, promise to keep quiet, and then we continue down the mountain in silence.

After a while we round a bend where I catch glimpses of runway through the pines, but don't see our machine.

My stomach turns inside out.

I yell at Toothless, "Where the hell is it!" leave him behind, race ahead around a stand of pines, and find . . .

It's gone!

CHAPTER *FORTY-EIGHT*

I spin around and ask Toothless, "What the hell have they done with my plane?"

"Prob'ly towed that sucker off," he answers nonchalantly.

"How?"

"Hey!" he says sharply. "These people don't got time for messin' round. Yur plane was in their way . . . they prob'ly got fifty or sixty guys and a big ol' rope and just hauled that beauty off."

I laugh. "The Air Force would've waited a week for a tug and tow bar to be flown in."

"Yur plane's prob'ly over there at the base of the canyon in the shadows." He points northwest. "You'll see."

We reach runway level, I look beyond the end of the runway, and sure enough, there it is, *backed up* into an amphitheater-like depression.

Bewildered, I ask Toothless, "How'd they get it turned around?" I can't believe my eyes.

I can see only the right side as we walk, but the gear doors and flaps look normal. The damaged left engine remains hidden on the other side of the fuselage.

I run ahead to see how bad the damage is, stop, turn, drop my gear on the ramp, and stare in disbelief.

No damage. Clean as a whistle.

No bomb blast. No shredded metal. No gaping hole. No dangling, ruptured fuel lines.

As Toothless and the others approach, I begin worrying: Did I imagine it? Did I commit the largest aviation blunder of all time? Was there never anything wrong and we're the victims of an overactive imagination?

The group reaches me, turns, and sees the undamaged cowl. Their eyes get big, their mouths drop open, they drop their gear, and now turn and look at me suspiciously.

Toothless shakes his head in disgust.

"Toothless, I *swear*. Fuel was *gushing* off this engine." I look around for support. "You saw it, didn't you, Tyrone?" The flight engineer nods sheepishly, suddenly unsure.

"First things first," Toothless says, "let's take a look and see how much fuel you *really* got in this machine," eager to prove our bungling.

He wanders over to a toolshed the size of a three-hole outhouse, tucks his Royal Salute into a corner, rummages around, emerges proudly holding a three-foot screwdriver, and walks back. Now he reaches up to the bottom of the left wing and unscrews the yellow drip-stick thermometer-type probe that will confirm my horrendous blunder.

As the probe falls out, the mechanic runs off to avoid being splattered with fuel.

The rest of us stay put and look silently at the probe. Dry as a bone.

Toothless rejoins us.

"See! I told you so!" I tell him exuberantly. "So how'd we lose all that gas?"

"One step at a time, sonny boy. Next, let's see just what you got in the other tank . . . so we know what we're workin' with 'fore goin' off half-cocked."

The nine of us hustle over under the right wing and watch Toothless repeat the probe unscrewing process. As the probe wiggles down, we all scatter.

We stop and stare from ten feet away. Dry as the Sahara. We wander back in and circle the probe in wonder.

Toothless breaks the silence. "Ooooooo-eeee, sonny boy. I don't know what you was runnin' on last night, but it sure weren't fuel. They's not a drop of gas on this whole damned machine."

I tell him, "That can't be!" I turn to Rich. "That engine was running when we landed, wasn't it? I clearly remember shutting it down."

Rich says, "I *thought* it was running . . . but . . . now . . . I don't know."

Toothless is losing patience. "Watch this, I'll prove it." He takes the screwdriver handle, bangs it on the bottom of the fuel tank, and we hear the sound of an empty fifty-gallon drum. My head starts spinning.

I suddenly realize everyone is gaping at me with their mouths open.

Their stares are making me uncomfortable, so to break the moment I ask Toothless, "You got a maintenance stand we can use to reach that other cowling?"

"Sure, that's next, anyways."

He grabs Ty, they walk over, disappear behind Toothless's outhouse, and then reappear pushing a "high reach" stand that careens around like an out-of-control grocery cart. They wrestle it left, right, left, right. We all jump out of the way so they don't hit us, and they finally position it below the left outboard cowl. Next they lock the wheels in place, clamber up the ladder, and using Toothless's giant screwdriver, pop the cowl latches open, grab with both hands, give it the old heave-ho. It jams at an inch open.

Toothless hollers down at us, "We could use a hand up here," and I watch in surprise as the new Rich scrambles up the ladder.

"On my count," Toothless says. "One . . . two . . . *three*!"

The cowl sounds like an ancient crypt being pried open, but gives way, enabling the guys to prop it open like a car hood. They peer inside.

I holler up, "See anything?"

"Not yet . . . everything looks normal so far," our benefactor answers. Maybe it *was* all in my head; I stayed too long and ran us out of gas after I lost track of time.

Toothless announces, "Okay, here it is, sonny boy. Yur off the hook . . ."

Relief!

"Here's your culprit right here." Toothless points to a copper-colored metal casing the size and shape of an ostrich egg. "See . . . this here's your fuel strainer. All the gas from yur fuel tank boost pump goes through this to strain out impurities." Now he holds the two separate halves out for display, one in each hand. "See? The two halves come plumb apart, so all the fuel coming from your boost pump was going overboard."

"So how'd the engine keep running?" I ask.

"Can't figure . . . it shouldn't have . . . that's a miracle. Maybe, somehow, the engine-driven pump sucked enough gas by the leak . . . damndest thing I ever seen."

I holler up, "Can you fix it?"

"Don't need to. They's nothin' wrong with it."

I make a face. "What are you talking about? It nearly killed us."

"Ya see, whoever put these two halves back together after cleaning out yur fuel screens didn't put 'em back together right. Listen to this."

We watch him rotate the egg halves righty-tighty and hear *click!*

"Did'ja hear that click?" he asks. "That locks the two halves together so they don't come apart. Somebody back at yur base didn't *listen* for that click." He adds, "But they's more. See this little copper wire dangling here?" He points to a wire the size and shape of a woman's bobby pin dangling from the top half. We all nod.

"This here's your killer," he explains. "Even if these two

halves backed off like they did, this little two cents of safety wire is *supposed* to be twisted on *left*—counterclockwise, *opposite* from normal—so it tightens and keeps the two halves together if they separate. But whatever bozo did this work twisted this safety wire righty-tighty; so when the two halves backed off, they twisted the safety wire right off with them. You never had a chance."

I start getting angry. "Are we talking sabotage?"

"Nah, nothin' that sinister. All it takes to mess up this job is rushin' off shift to grab a cold one, or listenin' to music while you work, or just havin' some asshole yakkin' at you while you're tryin' to concentrate." Toothless shoots me a hard look.

I tell him I get the message, but does he have any replacement wire?

"Same answer . . . you can use this little guy. We just twist it on *left* this time. But now don't you go on some headhunting trip back home. Whoever did this work made a mess of it, but it's his supervisor's butt I'd like to kick."

"Why?"

"Because any critical component like this has to be inspected and signed off by a supervisor, and it obviously weren't. This screwup woulda been easy to catch, but that supervisor decided to sit on his fat butt, drinkin' coffee, and pencil-whip his inspection."

I tell him I'll track down who was responsible, work with the maintenance officer to have all our planes inspected, and have a priority message sent to all C-123 units to check for the problem before it happens again.

"You can forget that, sonny boy. Yur maintenance officer'll never let it off base that his guys screwed up so bad under his watch. You see, he wants his next promotion. It'll never see the light of day."

I protest, "But this could happen to somebody else."

Toothless nods and says simply, "Yep, prob'ly will."

Ty says he has some friends in maintenance and that he'll make some phone calls to get the word out.

Toothless looks at me. "Now if you'll stop yakkin', Ty and I here'll get yur airplane fixed."

We first need to address the fuel situation. I ask Tooth-less, "How can we get refueled?"

He asks how much we need and I tell him ten thousand pounds, to be on the safe side.

He looks surprised, whistles, rubs his whiskers, and finally says, "That'll plumb clean us outta gas. We'd have nothin' left." He thinks about this. "We got one old broken-down fuel truck. After that, somebody'd have to hand-pump outta fifty-gallon drums, but if you guys'll take turns, you can have it all." Then he laughs.

He adds, "But we better get you outta here 'fore Tex sobers up . . . 'bout noon or so . . . and finds out you stole all his gas. But fur now, what that asshole don't know won't hurt him," and laughs again.

I smile, turn, and wander down the runway, searching for the spot where we hid last night. I find my extra bullets in the dirt, scoop them up, and tuck them away.

I look beyond the embankment we hid on . . . only a ten-foot drop—not the thousand I feared, but enough to break an ankle.

I walk a ways farther south, find a grassy spot, squat down, wrap my arms around my knees, draw them to my chest, and wait for the first sun rays to appear and warm me.

I am just sitting here, looking around.

A green-and-yellow grasshopper flitters up and lands beside me. Yesterday I would have shooed him off, but today he is looking up at me and I am looking down at him and the two of us are sitting here, just looking around.

The sun rises through the canyon V-notch, hesitates there, and for a split second flashes bright green. Then it rises higher in the V, casting a sunbeam laser on me.

The orange ball continues to rise up the V and now triumphantly bathes the entire canyon floor in morning light. Songbirds begin singing about the morning's beauty, and their songs echo throughout the canyon.

From overhead, I hear a bird of prey *screeech*. My grasshopper and I are just sitting here, looking around.

After a while, from behind I hear, "Hut! Hut! Hut! Hut!" accompanied by a symphony of stomping boots.

I spin around and see the hut-hutting is a platoon of what must be Laotian marines jogging up from somewhere below. *Have they come for the airplane?*

The hut-hutters charge up the hill directly at the plane, turn left, hut-hut down the runway toward me, hut-hut past, and ignore me. I watch them hut-hut down the runway and then disappear around a bend to the right.

Now the sun reaches the top of the V, warming both me and the canyon.

My grasshopper flits off.

I get up, dust off my rear end, and hut-hut down the runway, reach the end, stop, and peer two thousand feet *straight down*.

Nothing. I smile . . . no Jimmy Stewart feeling. Like my airsick classmate, I've beaten my fears.

Exhilarated, I turn and jog back up the runway. Hut! Hut! Hut! Hut!

I hut-hut close enough to keep an eye on Toothless's repairs without being a pest and sit in some grass alongside the runway. Toothless has produced a 1930s fuel truck along with a fifty-foot hose and nozzle. I watch as Ty materializes out of the top hatch, walks across the left wing, and unscrews the overwing fuel cap. Toothless tosses the hose up to him and they start fueling.

Looks as if it's going to take a while.

I hear lawn mower sounds, turn, and watch an unmarked, small, white Porter plane materialize out of the mountainside and land. The pilot stops on a dime, taxis up across from me, and fishtails a 180-degree turn. Two men run over, open a rear door, throw in several lumpy laundry bags, slam the door, bang on the side twice, and the Porter takes off in the length of a house. Laotian pony express.

I am just sitting here watching the morning unfold. A squadron of blue-and-green dragonflies hovers two feet out, circles, hovers again, then zips off. After a while, a handful of women and children appear from nowhere and the children begin to play games on the runway. Soon several men appear and set up primitive storefronts that remind me of sidewalk Kool-Aid stands. More people appear, approach the kiosks, and pay for things the vendors have cooked and are selling for breakfast.

Now the entire runway comes alive . . . men . . . women . . . cats . . . dogs . . . a pet monkey. An old woman struggling with two sacks of laundry at the ends of a bamboo pole slung across her shoulders disappears into the crowd. No wonder they towed our plane off . . . we landed on Main Street, Long Tien!

I hear a commotion at the plane. Toothless is shouting up at Ty that the fuel truck is out of gas and they'll have to finish by hand-pumping from fifty-gallon barrels. He drives away, then reappears balancing the first barrel on a handcart. He parks the barrel behind the left wing, unscrews a cap, screws in what looks like a country well pump handle, connects the hose, and starts pumping like crazy. He motions to the others to take the hand truck, get more barrels, and start lining them up behind each wing.

Rich takes over pumping to give Toothless a break.

I holler to ask if I can take a turn, but my copilot grins and says they have everything under control. As I study him pumping and grinning, I realize I am looking at a brand-new person and wonder if Peggy will like this new Rich.

It's obvious we're not going anywhere right away, so I close my eyes and just sit here . . . enjoying the morning sun toasting me like an English muffin. After a while, I hear Charles call my name.

I come back to reality and see the navigator at the crew entry door waving a tablet, signaling Rich and me to come over. Ty notices this, takes over pumping from Rich, and I hut-hut over.

Rich and I stand beside Charles as he explains, "I went up to the cockpit and got that approach plate you threw on the floor. *See?*" He jabs his finger at the cryptic note,

LAND32TO14. "See this? It clearly says, 'Land *from* the direction of 320 *to* 140.' That's backwards. It should read, 'Land *from* direction 140 *to* 320.' We have *got* to get this changed. It's gonna kill somebody." I agree with him, but as I look, the words Rorschach into a different meaning.

I see the problem.

I chuckle to myself and ask them, "Can you see it?" They say no.

"Watch this. I can't believe I didn't see it before," I say, grab my black felt-tip, and add a dark diagonal line between the *T* and the *O*:

LAND32T/O14

They are shocked.

Rich exclaims, "So *TO* means 'take off'? Holy cow! So now it reads . . . what? 'Land on runway three-two, *turn around*, and *take off* one-four.' Oh, my God!"

Charles looks astonished. He stutters, "John, I'm . . . I'm . . . I'm . . . so sorry . . . I can't *believe* I made such a bonehead error. I nearly got us killed."

"Hey! Me, too, remember," I say cheerfully. "All three of us looked *right at it* and made the same mistake."

I remind them of the old-maid/maiden perception exercise. Then I explain, "Once our minds locked on the old maid, we couldn't see the maiden again no matter what . . . until the *V* lights reappeared as we zipped across the rim. That was like a pie in the face."

They laugh.

I continue, "It's a normal mistake. As human beings, we look for *confirming* evidence from the world around us that our view of reality is correct . . . even when we're dead wrong. We tend to disregard, or treat lightly, any discordant information that has the *audacity* to disagree with our view of reality. I think that's what happened last night."

They look relieved, nodding seriously.

I add, "But look at this, too," and put my pen tip on the

LAND32. "Even now, we just said, 'Land *from* three-two to one-four.' Right?"

Charles shrugs. "Sure, that's what it says."

I chuckle. "No, it doesn't. Look again . . . there's no *from* there at all! We *added* it."

Rich looks stunned and wants to know why.

"You can't beat it. It's the way we're hardwired as human beings. I've seen it in my readings, too. By the time I reread a chapter the fourth time, I'll find missing periods, misspelled words, or wrong quotation marks I missed the first time when my mind filled in the gaps, correcting the errors. So I think that's what happened: *all three of us* added *from* so it made sense. See . . . it should look like this." I draw the note in accordance with international standards:

LAND 32 T/O 14

They simultaneously slap their foreheads and exclaim, "Oh, no!"

Charles says, "So when they published it, the typist ran the words together like their much longer Laotian words, never understanding their true meaning?"

"Exactly," I answer.

Charles sums it up. "So we were nearly brought down by two cents of safety wire and a couple of printing errors?"

I answer, "Yep, that's about the size of it. And from the research I've been doing, that's completely normal. Experts are now saying it's the little things that crash airplanes, not big ones like engines blowing up that make the headlines. It's the little things the mind steps over, like ants, that are actually causing crashes.

"But there's still one thing I haven't figured out," I tell them. "How could the four of us look *right at* that open cross-feed valve several minutes and not see it *wide-open*?" They shake their heads.

Charles adds, "And how'd the right engine keep running with no fuel?" I tell him I'll wonder about that one as long as I live.

I look up and see the sun directly overhead, so guess it must be about noon . . . looks like less than an hour of direct sun remains. On top of that, Tex will likely wake up soon.

I gotta get us out of here. Now.

From behind, I hear Ty say the fueling is complete and he is going to start the exterior preflight. I meander over to the maintenance stand and look up at him and Toothless latching the cowling shut.

I holler up, "Did you guys check the *right side*? If they changed both strainers at the same time, we could lose the right tank the same way." They look stunned.

They latch the cowl, scramble down, unlock the wheels, race the wobbly stand over under the right engine, lock the wheels, charge up, pop the latches, shove the clamshell open, and peer inside.

"This one's okay," Toothless yells down. "Nice catch," he admits. "What'd you say your name was, sonny boy?" I answer, John. They close the cowl and climb down.

I walk up to Toothless and ask, "You got any silver aircraft repair paint and a small brush?" He says sure, he'll go get some. But what am I going to do with it?

I answer, "You'll see."

Now I ask Ty to check the wings, fuselage, and tail assembly for popped rivets and rippled skin.

He nods, hops up through the crew entry door, disappears inside, and then reappears through the top hatch. He begins walking down the length of the wing again.

I tell him to be careful and watch him tightrope-walk down the aircraft spine, arms extended. He peers around the tail, turns around, gingerly tightropes back, and hollers down, "I can't believe it, sir. Not one popped rivet. Far as I can tell, they's nothing wrong with this old warhorse. I'm going inside to start the interior preflight, so you guys might wrap it up down there."

I nod and think to myself, the true heroes last night were the men and women who designed this machine. They overbuilt it to take punishment, but that would never happen today. The Church is already having troubles with their shiny new C-141; the design is weak. Long after their new toy is in the boneyard, this old warhorse will still be flying.

Toothless reappears with the silver paint and brush.

I take it and say, "Thanks," turn, walk up to the fuselage below my window, and begin writing.

Everyone gathers around to peek at what I'm doing, but I cover my efforts to save it for an unveiling.

I finish . . . *I* . . . *E,* step back, and admire my work with everyone.

AMERICAN PIE

The old Rich would have said, "You can't do that! There's been a hard-and-fast rule against naming airplanes since WWII," but this new Rich gleefully says, "Gimme that . . . you forgot something," and takes the paint can and brush.

He saunters over and begins adding *something.* Now he steps back and we see:

MISS AMERICAN PIE

I put my arm around his shoulders, squeeze, and tell him, "That's perfect, Rich. Absolutely perfect."

"What's *that* mean?" Eddie wants to know.

"You're too young," Toothless explains. "*Miss American Pie* was the name of the plane that crashed and killed Buddy Holly, Ritchie Valens . . . you know . . . 'La Bamba' . . . and the Big Bopper . . . 'Chantilly Lace.' " Then Toothless looks at me and asks, "How'd you come up with that, John?"

To avoid a long-winded explanation of how the song has been playing over and over in my head, I answer, "Who knows where ideas come from?"

We hear Ty start the auxiliary power unit, followed by the whine of our hydraulic systems. The airplane is coming back to life. It's time to leave.

I watch my guys pick up their gun belts and vests and strap them on.

I think to myself, This is all wrong . . . not the way it's supposed to be. I tell them, "Stop . . . no gear today. You guys are heroes and you're going to arrive home looking the part."

Cheers and hollers and hoots and smiles from everybody. Even Rich. No, *especially* Rich.

They strip off their gear and take gleeful turns throwing it through the entry door into a heap.

Ty emerges from his preflight, walks over to our tool chest under the right engine, and with two hands *heaves* it through the door. He reaches to shove the chest farther inside when I tell him, "Give me that."

He looks puzzled, but his expression quickly turns to understanding. He cautions me, "Sir, that's an accountable item. They make me sign a hand receipt for it. They'll dock my pay if "

"Don't worry," I interrupt. "My report will say it was strapped to those pallets we chucked overboard." Ty nods and shows me a big grin.

I grab the chest in both hands and spin around to face Toothless. "Merry Christmas from the United States Air Force."

His mouth drops open, his eyes moisten, and his arms cradle the heavy container like a Christmas puppy. He chokes on his words. "I . . . I . . . I . . ." I think we should change his name to "Speechless."

Finally he manages, "My real name is Martin."

"Well, Martin, thanks for your help . . . enjoy."

A silence follows that neither of us wants to break. Finally Martin says, "You better skedaddle outta here 'fore Tex sobers up," and he scans the mountainside. "He could show up any minute."

I tell him, "Like the man said, combat rules."

Martin thinks about this, smiles, laughs, and says, "Serves the little bastard right."

"How do we get out of here?"

His expression says he doesn't know what I mean. "You flew in, didn't you?"

I point at the local carnival on the runway. "All those people. Can you get them to move?"

He makes a face. "Nah . . . they'll move when you start her up."

Unsure, I say, "Okay, if you say so."

"I'll clear the props. How many blades you guys use?"

"Six," I answer.

The sun drops behind the north rim. We are in shadows.

I shake Martin's hand, turn, jump in the plane, jog up the back porch, and plop down in my seat. Rich and I leave our chutes in our seatbacks for cushions, but do not strap them on.

I look over and see the new Rich is not wearing gloves. I think of teasing him about this, but decide not to spoil the moment.

He reaches to put his headset on and I say, "No headsets today . . . we'll talk like normal people."

He grins broadly, rips it off, and discards it behind his seat.

I look out my window and see Martin circling his index finger, signaling the area around the prop is clear for start.

I nod, throw the left-tank boost-pump switch on, turn the ignition switch to "both," and hack my clock to monitor the starter limit. Martin signals six blades of rotation, I wave my hand forward, Ty brings the left mixture lever up to "rich," and now we are waiting for the engine to fire off . . .

Nothing.

"Let's give it a few more seconds," I say, and cross my fingers. Nothing.

I exclaim, "Come on, baby! Come on!" Nothing.

Ty and I stop the start procedure and listen as the prop grinds to a halt.

Martin raises both palms skyward and mouths, "Beats me." Rich and Charles look at me apprehensively.

Now what?

CHAPTER *FORTY-NINE*

Ty suggests, "It's prob'ly just cavitated fuel lines. Let's leave the boost pump on a minute and then try her again."

I say okay and cross my fingers.

Now the cockpit begins filling with bodies. Two guys are squeezing in behind me and two more wedge in behind Rich. Then Charles crams his way through the doorway to stand over a kneeling Ty as we wait; the cockpit is stuffed like a Roaring Twenties phone booth.

I signal Martin we'll try another start. Ty and I repeat the sequence, and this time we hear the engine cough, backfire, sputter, kick, choke, and struggle back to life.

A voice shouts, *"Hooray!"*

Martin smiles, flashes me a thumbs-up, and saunters over to Rich's side to clear the right prop. It, too, struggles to come to life, but finally roars back.

Both engines running! Smiles and cheers and looks of relief all around the cockpit!

We're going home!

I start both jets, nudge the recips forward, and taxi ahead into direct sunlight at the start of the runway. Ty cautions me, "Sir, if we were gonna do this by the book, I'd need a half hour to compute the takeoff data."

"No time," I answer firmly. "She'll fly. I can tell."

Ty points at the runway and says apprehensively, "I don't know, sir. Looks awful short to me."

I explain, "Ty, it's now or six months from now," then glance around and see he really does look worried we might drop off the end.

Rich suggests, "I saw a documentary on Navy carrier pilots that showed them holding the stick back in their laps to get airborne as soon as possible. We could try that."

"Great idea," I tell him, and pull the control column against my chest.

Ty looks down and shakes his head.

We reach the start of the runway. I set the parking brake, scan ahead, and see Main Street still jammed with people and animals. Concerned Tex might show up any second, I run the recips up to max to warn the crowd.

RRRRRRRRRRRR! No one budges.

When they don't even glance our way, I idle the recips.

Rich says, "We can't run over those people. What are we gonna do?"

I shake my head, then look out Rich's window and see Martin frantically waving, GO! GO! GO! so I run the recips *plus* the jets up to max power.

RRRRRRRRRRRRRRRRRR!

The noise is deafening, but no one in the crowd looks in our direction.

I see Martin pointing hysterically up the mountainside. Here comes Tex! Running full bore! Arms waving!

Martin is bug-eyed, frantically waving, GO! GO! GO!

The new Rich raises his arm like a race starter flag. He swings it forward and exclaims, "Damn the torpedoes! Full speed ahead!"

I release the brakes, feel the airplane catapult forward,

and watch as we zip by an astonished-looking Tex. *So long, sucker.*

We race down the runway and watch a miracle happen. Like the parting of the Red Sea, just before we are about to strike a man, dog, or chicken, they scramble clear. I wait for an impact, but suddenly . . . we are past the crowd . . . and . . .

AIRBORNE!

We're FREE! We're FREE!

Rich remarks, "We shoulda named her *Lazarus.*"

We raise the gear and flaps. I aim straight for the mountainside ahead, then suddenly the V-notch appears out Rich's window. I head for it, hugging the right side in case someone comes through in the opposite direction.

I think, UP! UP! AND AWAY!

Strictly cornball, but it makes me feel good

The tops of the V tower above as we fly through the narrow pass and suddenly we pop out . . .

In the clear! Out in the open!

I begin a left turn. Rich notices this, looks confused, and points right toward NKP.

I shake my head no. "Let's take a tour first." I keep turning—outside the north wall now—and keep climbing as it towers above us. I think to myself, This is where we'd've become lost *again* had I overshot.

I roll out northwest, keep climbing, and then level off a hundred feet above the north ridge. I idle the jets and pull the recips back to cruise power. I turn left, then back to the right, jump on top of the ridgeline, and see Martin still standing there, watching, clutching his Christmas present.

I'll bet we're the first plane he's watched climb out in years.

The eight of us stare in silence at how impossible last night was.

An unseen hand squeezes my shoulder. A voice says solemnly, "Thanks, John."

We are halfway down the north rim and I stand her up

on her left wing until we are looking *straight down*. One
man behind me involuntarily grabs my seatback to avoid
falling out.

> *I can see clearly now*
> *The rain is gone*

There's our hiding spot as we waited for the jeeps.

> *I can see all obstacles in my way*
> *Gone are the dark clouds*
> *That had me blind . . .*

There's where we rode along in the jeeps and there's the
communications shack. Martin is shielding his eyes against
the sun to keep an eye on us.

> *It's gonna be a bright, bright*
> *Sunshiny day . . .*

I fly northwest beyond the canyon for a minute, now
make a left 180 back . . . for a look at what we couldn't see
last night—a mile-high wall of karst.

If I'd descended here last night, we'd just be a curious
spot of wreckage.

Now we pop out over the northwest rim and I roll her *way
up* on her left wing again so we are looking *straight
down* . . . to the center of the earth.

I glance around the cockpit and see every face spell-
bound. I smile.

I roll out and fly along the south rim we must have
skimmed by less than a hundred feet. I see Martin still looking at us, clutching his toolbox. I was right . . . there was no
way to turn around inside the canyon.

To the immediate south, we see the next valley I might
have safely descended into, only to lose sight of the lights.

White, puffy clouds surround us in picture-postcard
beauty.

I make another left 180 and fly smack-dab down the dragon's throat.

> *LOOK ALL AROUND!*
> *THERE'S NOTHING BUT BLUE SKY!*
> *LOOK STRAIGHT AHEAD!*
> *NOTHING BUT BLUE*
> *SKYYYYYYYYYYYYYYYYYYYYYYYYY!*

As we cross the north rim for the last time, I wing-rock Martin *So long,* then ask Charles to take us *way out* west before heading home. Dead ahead is one mountain range after another, as far as the eye can see. To the south rise more jagged peaks . . . the same to the north. Rich sees this and remarks, *"Jeez!"*

I shut down the jets, give Rich the airplane, and tell myself, happiness is Long Tien in the rearview mirror.

The guys behind our seats claw their way out and then disappear back into the cargo box. Show's over.

After a while I ask Charles to give Rich a heading to the closest point on the Mekong and watch Rich turn south. He wants to know if he should call Moonbeam to tell them we're alive.

I answer no. He nods.

The cockpit turns quiet. Rich and I watch mountain range after mountain range pass beneath.

I check the fuel gauges to make sure Martin got the repairs right and find the needles perfectly matched. Satisfied everything will be okay, I recline my seat to carve out some quiet mental space. It's an hour down to the river, so we have plenty of time.

I unclutch my mind and let it freewheel through the overnight images. With each quiet mile that passes, the events seem more a fantasy, and now a pang of depression washes over me. With every mile that passes behind us, we turn from heroes back into everyday people, the events fading like Civil War photos discovered in an attic trunk. In ninety minutes, all this will be over. Desktop will give us a couple days off to write a formal report, and then we'll be just like everybody else.

Heroes no more.

Every few minutes, a face appears in the doorway, stares up at the fuel gauges to make sure it's not happening *again,* nods, and then disappears to the back without saying a word.

Their faces tell me they feel it, too. Peggy Lee has it right: "Is that all there is?"

We fly along in silence.

After a while I turn around to see what Charles is doing and find him folding maps. The rest of the crew is untangling the fur ball of parachutes, gun belts, and survival vests; organizing them into personal piles. Everyone looks sad.

Is that all there is?

I answer myself, that can't be all there is. You can't let this end this way.

Then make something up.

I see Charles scribbling madly. I ask, "What're you doing?"

His voice is excited. "Writing it all down so I don't forget!"

"Why?"

"Well, if you remember, I'm the squadron awards-and-decs officer. This is my first draft to get you the Silver Star."

"What's the Silver Star? I don't pay much attention to military stuff."

"You're kidding!" he says incredulously. "You don't *know* what the *Silver Star* is?"

I answer no.

"*Well,* the Silver Star is a *rare* award given to individuals who, from their *own individual effort,* save lives and equipment from certain loss . . . and that's you. I can't believe you don't know about it . . . it's only two steps below the Medal of Honor . . . below that comes the Air Force Cross . . . you won't get that . . . but you're a shoo-in for a Silver Star."

Charles gets more jazzed up. "John, I read the top awards all the years I was the awards-and-decs officer back at Castle, and there's nothing . . . *nothing* . . . that holds a candle to what you did last night. Everything else pales in comparison."

I plead, "I wish you wouldn't, I'm not comfortable being the center of attention."

"That's poppycock, John, and a bit selfish if you don't mind me saying."

"*Selfish!* Why selfish?"

"Well, think about the rest of us who are making the Air Force a career. Historically, whatever award the pilot gets, the rest of the crew gets the next lower . . . in this case, the Distinguished Flying Cross for a onetime event—not that 'living and breathing' DFC everybody automatically gets. For the enlisted guys especially, a onetime DFC could ripple throughout their careers. Isn't that right?" Charles asks Ty, who has reappeared to check the fuel gauges.

"He's right, JT. If I get it, I might make Chief and get a better job back in the States. Without it, I'll prob'ly retire as a master sergeant and God knows where I'll get assigned."

"*See!*" Charles says. "So don't be selfish. Over the next couple days, I'll interview you to get the details right."

I think this over and reluctantly promise to help.

I turn forward, check the fuel gauges again, watch more white puffies go by, and listen to the silence. After a while I get an idea how to end this adventure on a high note. I smile, look behind Rich's seat, then my own, to make sure the equipment we'll need is still there, and tell Rich, "I'll be back . . . I'm gonna talk to Charles about those reports." He nods okay, so I step down to the back porch to begin laying out my plans.

As I tell Charles what I have in mind and the key role he's going to play in putting it all together, the smile on his face turns broader and broader. I finish with "Make sure they rehearse their parts, but let's keep the main show just between you and me. I want them to be surprised."

Charles agrees, motions everyone in back to gather around, and as I go back up to the cockpit, I hear Charles begin, "Okay, here's what we're going to do . . ."

As I sit down, Rich points ahead and hollers, "There it is! The Mekong!"

I look out my front window and see the Mekong River impersonating our own mighty Mississippi . . . a ribbon of yellow shimmering in the early afternoon sun, meandering its way southeast. The ancient border between Laos and Thailand.

I thought I'd never see it again.

I tear up, but quickly wipe the moisture away. Rich sees this, but says nothing.

As we pop over the last mountain range between us and the river, I tell Rich, "I've got her back." I yank the power off to idle, shove the nose over, and snow-ski down the last Laotian mountainside.

WHOOOOPEEE!

We reach the flatlands a few miles before the river and I level off five hundred feet up so we can see the river serpentine south. I can see trees lining both banks and the yellow ball of the sun reflecting off the surface as we fly closer. I reach the river, turn left, and jump on top of it.

Our own shadow appears on the river of gold out my front window, and now I play tag with it. The shadow is on my side, so that Rich is having trouble seeing it. Unbelievably, I watch him unstrap, do a push-up off his armrests, and let out a *"Wow!"*

As the river turns, our shadow races away, but now returns to us at the next bend. Our shadow slides across to Rich's side, so that now we zip along and catch it. I anticipate the old Rich's tap-dancing feet, but this new Rich is just looking around.

I shove the nose over and descend to our minimum "legal" altitude . . . two hundred feet . . . where we can pick out individual currents and eddies. Schools of fish sense our shadow and maneuver away en masse as we skim along at treetop level.

I tell myself, Lower still . . . give 'em a thrill they'll never forget.

I push the nose over and take her down to *one hundred feet.* I level off and take the next bend to the right. Trees on both banks are individual specimens rising above us. I look straight down . . . and see the muddy bottom.

I take us lower: *twenty feet.*

The river now races beneath like a continuous sheet of yellow steel. The trees tower above like Empire State Buildings. A woman wringing laundry on the Laotian side hears us approach, stops midwring, looks up, smiles, and waves. I see her face clearly and wave back.

Now more people on both banks come in view. Some are bathing; others are fishing. We pass children jumping off a tree limb who disappear underwater, then pop up wearing big smiles and waving. We wave back.

A white whooping crane leaps off a banyan tree branch and soars away as the river and trees cradle us in serenity. Smoky wisps of steam rise off the water. I turn and fly through two wisps.

Banyans on both sides now lean their branches *way out* over the water, drop, and drink from the Mekong.

Now we pass men on the Laotian side framing a house in expensive teakwood harvested nearby. Men on both banks fish with bamboo poles.

These people don't give a hoot about the war, or about us. All they want to do is to catch something for dinner.

I *smell* the river as Creedence blasts away in my head.

> *If you come down to the river*
> *Betcha gonna find some people who live*
> *You don't have to worry*
> *'Cause you have no money*
> *People on the river are happy to give . . .*

We're "lollin' on the liver" as individual shafts of sunlight beam down through white puffies on the Thai side while the winter rice crop pokes up from flooded fields to catch the rays. Shafts of direct sunlight pour in through our overhead eyebrow windows, toasting us like Campfire marshmallows. I focus on this feeling and silently vow to never again take it for granted.

Rich asks, "How high are we? The altimeter's useless this low."

"About twenty feet," I answer.

"But how can you tell? This isn't in any of the books."

"I've done it a couple times."

"But couldn't we nose in and sink?"

"No way. We'll do the math later, but at about half the length of the cord of the wing, water effect takes over. We're riding an invisible cushion of air beneath the entire aircraft."

Rich says he's never heard of this.

"Crawl under the fuselage sometime and you'll see the entire bottom is an airfoil . . . like those new NASA lifting-body concept drawings of the proposed space shuttle. Remember, they originally designed this as a glider, and it's those thirty-five-year-old designs keeping us safe above the water."

Rich nods.

I continue, "You couldn't poke us in the river if you tried. Watch . . . I'll prove it." I hit the yoke with my fist *twice,* yet we remain level. "See? You can't even *bang* your way through."

"Is this what you were doing down that ridgeline? Could you *feel* it?"

The question throws me. I think a moment, then answer, "Richey me boy . . . maybe . . . no . . . I don't know . . . as long as I live, I don't think I'll understand."

He nods, trusting I'm not holding anything back.

I ask, "You wanna try your hand?"

He nods, takes the controls bare-handed, and holds it like a newborn babe.

"Go ahead," I tell him. "*Try* going down . . . you can't . . . go ahead."

Hesitantly at first, then with gusto, this new Rich pushes forward.

"Can you *feel* it?" I holler.

"*Yes, I can! It's wonderful!* How'd you discover this?"

I think of explaining the ledgers, but shorten it to "I'll show you when we get back."

"But how can you make turns *this low*?" He points ahead. "I gotta turn right around that next bend, but if I bank at all, the wingtip'll be in the river!"

I tell him calmly, "*Rudder* . . . imagine we're a boat. *Rudder* your way around . . . but don't *move* the controls . . . just *think* about where you want the airplane to be and your feet will automatically do the rest."

Rich takes the turn gracefully and now grins even broader.

He sails us around a second graceful bend and then the river opens wider. Shafts of sunlight mix with the rising wisps of river fog, which glow luminescent. They race beneath us at 170 mph like a sheet of yellow gold. A reflection of the red ball of the sun shimmers on the golden river and we chase it south.

Now that Rich and I have water effect ironed out, I turn to Charles, standing in the doorway watching the show, and signal him it's time. He nods, turns, steps down to the back porch, and walks the length of the cargo compartment to where the guys are straightening out loose tie-down chains. He points at the ramp and tells them to open it. They look confused. "Why?" I lip-read.

"You'll see," Charles explains.

Ty shrugs and says, "Well, okay," walks over to the controls, throws a switch, and I feel the airframe shudder as the huge door drops open like a medieval drawbridge.

They won't see the surprise until the door is nearly level. Here it comes . . .

Mekong River . . . right in the old puss!

I gawk out this picture window and see nothing but blue water. Fantastic!

The men start jumping for joy like kids let out to play.

Ty flashes me a big grin and a thumbs-up. Charles walks *all the way back* to the cockpit, tries saying something, but his voice falters. He looks me in the eye, squeezes my shoulder, then pushes out a shaky "Great job. Better than any stuffy old award."

As Rich rudders us down the golden highway, Charles and I look out the back. I watch our lifting body smooth the river like water behind an ocean liner as twin ballerina water spouts formed by our prop wash rise thirty feet, pirouette, begin to collapse, but are now re-formed again and again from prop-wash energy . . . spinning, magical, twisting rainbows shepherding us down the river.

Incredible!

I suddenly realize the ballerinas were there all the other times I left the back door closed; I'd just never bothered to look.

I begin singing softly to myself so the others won't hear:

> *Cannon fire lingers in my mind*
> *I'm so glad that I'm still alive*
> *And I've been gone for such a long time*
> *From Yellow Liver*

Suddenly, I hear an echo.

I think, nah—too much Scotch, not enough sleep; so I keep singing:

> *Put my guns down the war is won*
> *Fill my glass high the time has come*

Now I hear the echo again, look over, and see—
Rich—humming along!

> *Yellow Liver, Yellow Liver*

He glances at me apprehensively, asking if it's okay. I look him in the eye, smile, wipe tears away, and nod yes.

> *Is in my blood, it's the place I love*

If Rich were Wiley, we'd be screaming at the top of our lungs. And while he's off-key and off-tempo, I get the feeling it's something we can work on.

The aircraft sails around each bend as though Rich had been doing this all his life. Cradled by the golden river, safely riding our cushion of air, I close my eyes and tell myself, never forget *any* of this . . . lock it all away to boost you through all the average days, months, and years ahead.

Charles reappears in the doorway with Ty.

They begin a series of involuntary *Ooooooh!*'s and *Oh, wow!*'s and tap one another's shoulder, point, laugh, and exclaim, "Look at *that one*!" I get the feeling the worst of this year may be behind us. From here on out, things are going to get better.

Charles points out the front window and yells, "LOOK OUT!"

OLD MAN STANDING IN A BOAT!

WE'RE GONNA FLY RIGHT OVER HIM!

TOO LATE TO TURN OR CLIMB!

IF I ADD POWER, OUR PROP WASH'LL CAPSIZE HIS BOAT!

HE TURNS AND STARES AT US IN SURPRISE AND HORROR!

HE DUCKS!

We fly *RIGHT OVER*!

Oh, no! What have I done?

I whip around, look out the back to make sure he's okay, and see his skiff rocking violently in our wake, the old man crouching, holding on to the sides for dear life.

He looks me in the eye as we fly off. He's smiling, laughing, waving good-bye!

He *liked* it!

I call myself Lucky, tell Rich I've got the airplane back, wiggle the wings, and climb her up to fifty feet. For a while longer we sail the Mekong, darting among rising wisps of fog until I recognize a landmark twenty miles northeast of NKP. Regretting this part is over, but hoping the best is yet to come, I pull her up to *just above* treetop level and now zip along the green carpet.

I tell Ty, "Start the jets," signal everyone to put their headsets back on, and I accelerate . . . 150 . . . 170 . . . 190 . . . 210 . . . 240 . . . and bring us in below radar coverage so they won't detect us, spoiling the surprise.

I stand her up on her right wing to practice for what lies ahead.

Yahoo!

I picture myself doing a victory roll *all the way over,* but decide not to push my luck and instead roll out wings level.

I turn and ask Charles, "Everybody ready back there? They get a chance to practice to get the timing right?"

Charles answers seriously, "They know what to do."

Rich looks puzzled. "What're'ya gonna do?"

"Surprise 'em. They think we're dead, right? Well, we're gonna give 'em a show they'll never forget."

He smiles.

I tell Charles, "Okay, show's all yours." The master navigator gives me a heading to line up with the runway twenty miles north, I climb to 1,500 feet and head in at a whopping 240 mph . . . not fast, but if you saw a box turtle racing around three times faster than normal, you'd think it was a pretty damned fast turtle . . . at least that's the effect I'm hoping for.

Rich notices we're not at our normal "slow-mover," I-don't-get-no-respect 1,000-foot-pattern altitude, and exclaims, "You're using fighter-only airspace! They'll freak out! *Great!*" and laughs.

I look ahead and see the runway! NKP!

We're home! We made it!

I radio, "Tower, this is Candle 23 . . . twenty-mile initial . . . fifteen hundred feet . . . requesting the overhead pattern."

I anticipate hearing an excited voice welcoming us back from the dead.

Silence. Rich and I check the radio is switched on and tuned to the proper frequency. It's okay.

"Try again," Rich says. "Somebody prob'ly blocked your transmission."

I nod, but begin feeling anxious. Ripping along, only twelve miles out now, we'll be on top of them in three minutes . . . if they don't answer soon, the surprise will be spoiled.

I try again. "Tower, Candle 23 . . . fifteen-mile initial . . . fifteen hundred feet . . . request the pitchout."

No answer back from them. Charles looks worried.

"Maybe that radio's dead," Rich suggests. "I'll switch us over to number two."

I nod, only eight miles out . . . two minutes . . . if they don't answer to the next call, it'll spoil all the fun. I am about to try one last call, but hear the tower controller key his mike.

Whew! I thought they were gonna blow it!

An angry voice scolds, "*All right!* Whoever that is . . . *knock it off . . . right now.* Everybody knows Candle 23 bought it last night, so that is *not* funny. Keep it up and I'll call the air police."

Charles exclaims, "Oh, no! He thinks it's some prankster!"

I plead, "Tower, you gotta *believe* me! It's *really* us! We're *back*! WE MADE IT! Put your binoculars on us . . . *PLEASE!*"

Silence. Five miles out! Too late?

I can't think of anything else to do, so tell myself, "Oh, well . . . would've been a nice ending . . . too bad."

We hear the beginnings of another transmission and now hear the controller's voice crackle with excitement. "Candle 23 . . . I'll be go to hell . . . I got you in sight . . . you guys are FUCKING . . . CLEARED . . . TO . . . LAND! WELCOME HOME!"

I can barely read my instruments through the tears.

Charles and Ty look excited and now move down to the back porch to get ready for the show.

HOORAY! IT'S GONNA WORK, AFTER ALL!

The runway is dead ahead now . . . four miles . . . one minute.

If I've guessed right, the tower controller will be picking up the red crash phone right now. Then all the major flight-line organizations will check in by prearranged sequence: "Wing Commander . . . Rescue . . . Hospital . . ." and so on, and he'll announce our return to the entire base.

At least I hope so.

Here comes the runway . . . under the nose!

I stand her up on her left wing and holler to Charles, "NOW!"

As we sailed south across Laos, Charles and I wrenched open our emergency flare-gun boxes. The ancient Very pistols inside are the original equipment signaling system, their design as old as the sinking of the *Titanic* . . . long since eclipsed by handheld radios.

The concept was to load the fist-size flares in the fat starter's pistols, lock them into gun ports overhead each pilot, and then fire them to signal "Rescue." No one ever uses them over here because you'd be signaling the enemy, too.

Ours have likely never been test-fired, so I am hoping these old babies work.

As senior man, I told Charles he could have the honor of firing first and running the show. He announces, "FIRING ONE!"

We hear *PHHHHHHHT!* as the flare ignites, races overhead, and . . .

We hear, *KA-POW!* and watch a yellow starburst explosion.

Rich starts laughing.

Hot damn! It's working!

I roll her up on her right wing, hear Charles command, "FIRE TWO!" and watch Ty fire over my head.

I duck, praying the ancient device doesn't explode in the cockpit.

PHHHHHHHT!
KA-POW!

This one's RED! Wow!

I look over at Rich and see him doubled over in laughter.

"FIRE THREE!"

"FIRING THREE!" the rampers report as they blast one out the back.

I start a series of victory wing rocks and watch masses of people pour out onto the flightline.

Good.

You have to understand . . . this isn't just hotdogging . . . I mean, it *is* . . . but it's far more . . . it's *their* celebration of *hope*, as well. I'm hoping they'll remember that one day *somebody* beat the odds, came back from the dead, and believe *maybe* . . . just *maybe* . . . they can, too.

At least I hope so.

But then that's the whole point of telling this story, isn't it?

Halfway down the runway, I relay to Charles, "NOW!"

"ROGER. FIRING ONE!"

Rich ducks.

PHHHHHHHT!

KA-POW!

This one's GREEN!

"FIRE TWO!"

PHHHHHHHHT!

More and more people are pouring out of the flightline buildings to catch the spectacle.

KA-POW!

A BLUE one!

"FIRE THREE!"

"FIRING THREE! Looks great back here, JT! What a *blast*, man!"

Rich yells, "How'd you ever think of this?"

I am about to explain when he says, "Wait . . . I know . . . you made it up."

Having lost the ability to talk, I just nod.

He chuckles, "You crazy sonofabitch!"

We reach the far end of the runway.

I make a right 180, roll out the opposite direction, idle the jets, and begin slowing to land. Halfway down the runway, I regain my composure and holler to Charles, *"Now!"*

They fire another round and I do more victory wing rocks.

Rich reports, "The place is ab-so-lute-ly *packed* . . . you won't be able to get into the parking area!"

Finally, regrettably, I idle the recips, configure her for landing, turn right, roll out on final, blast off a last round of flares, and touch down. I take the first turnoff, shut down the jets, head for the parking area, and stare in wonder as the crowd surges toward us.

I tell Ty and Eddie, *"Now!* Go for it!"

As we flew south over Laos, Charles and I prefolded my blood chit, located some string, our broom, and lashed the silk hankie on the broom head. As we worked, Charles asked me what we were doing.

I explained that as a kid, my dad told me stories of WWII submariners proudly sailing back into port with an inverted broom lashed to their conning towers—proclaiming to the crowds cheering their safe return they'd made a "clean sweep."

We repeat that tradition now.

Ty swings the ladder around from the bulkhead, locks it in place, and he and Eddie scamper up, open the top hatch, stand on the ladder, hang outside waist-high, and wave our old broom back and forth so most of what the crowd sees is the good old Stars and Stripes.

Rich sees this and I watch his face lose all composure.

Our broom flag works better than I expected, because now the crowd charges so fast I have to halt before the props hit anyone. I set the brakes, cut the mixture levers, and listen to the props wind down.

Out my window, I see the crowd form an arc around us. With the props still winding down, I watch my guys pile out the entry door and make their way to different parts of the crowd, shaking hands and getting hugs like presidential candidates, then moving on to more hugs, smiles, and handshakes.

Everyone is applauding . . . even the fighter pilots.

What a feeling!

Rich stands up to leave and tells me, "What're'ya waiting for? Come on, let's go."

I shake my head and choke. "You go ahead . . . I'll be along d'rectly . . . I just want to sit here and take it all in . . . to remember forever."

He nods, walks out, and then I see him emerge to a fresh round of cheers.

I look around the cockpit one last time, get up slowly, step down to the back porch, move through the entry door, and land on the ramp.

The crowd *cheers*!

I am just standing here, not knowing what to do . . . wishing someone would hand me a script. A giant bear of a man lumbers out from the crowd.

The Hawk.

I imagine the club curtains need to be washed.

The bear walks toward me . . . bloodshot eyes . . . Brillo-pad hair. In a gravelly voice, he says, "Welcome home, son." Now he comes right up to me, extends his paws, wraps both arms around me, and I become lost in the folds of his flight-suit until I can barely breathe.

I think to myself, they got his nickname wrong. It should be "Papa Bear."

Papa Bear releases me, holds me by both shoulders, and smiles. He is shielded from the crowd so only I see his tears.

Papa Bear says, "Son, we thought you were dead."

"So did I, sir. So did I."

He turns so we both face the cheering crowd. I feel self-conscious, unsure what to do next.

Wiley! Where's Wiley?

I scan the crowd and spot him at the front . . . unshaven . . . messed-up hair . . . weaving . . . drunk as a skunk.

I walk over.

He looks at me searchingly, as if I were someone he *used*

to know, but isn't quite sure I'm the same person. Now he says, "You look . . . *different,* man."

"I *am* different. I'm not the same person at all."

His voice rasps from the night of singing. "Where've you . . . how'd you . . . what hap . . . oh, crap." His sentences fail. He gives up, reaches out, and gives me another bear hug. As he holds me tight, I tell him, "It's a long story, but I'll tell you all about it."

From behind me, Papa Bear announces, "Okay, everybody . . . I'm officially shutting down operations the rest of the day. Now hear this . . . we're all going to the club for a mandatory formation and these guys are gonna tell us their story . . . and . . . the drinks are on me! So c'mon! Let's go!"

The crowd *cheers*!

Papa Bear puts one paw around Charles, the other around Rich, and begins marching up the street. I put one paw around Wiley, the other around Ty, and the whole mess of us head for the club, where I imagine we'll tell the story again and again and again . . .

CHAPTER *FIFTY*

NUMBER ONE BOMBBBB! I CAN HEAR THEM SCREEEAMING!

I'm in bed three nights later as my clock's red numerals laugh at me. It's 3:17 A.M. I watch it blink over . . . 3:18 . . . as the events kaleidoscope across my mind.

It's gonna be another toss-and-turn night.

I sit up, grab a fresh pack of Luckies, some matches, and my ashtray. Then I spin around, lean against the wall, and draw my knees up in the fetal position. I unwrap the cellophane, tear off the foil cover, tap the pack on my wrist, extract a single cancer stick between my teeth, and tuck the pack beside me. Then I one-hand the matchbook open, flick a single match to attention, strike it, smell sulfur as the flame ignites, light up, flick my wrist, and watch the room return to dark.

Blink! 3:19.

We partied till well after midnight that first night back, but to me everyone seemed like bug-eyed goldfish swimming in a bowl, ignorant of outside reality. How I envy their innocence.

The events of Long Tien have transported me into another dimension.

Wiley said I used up all the luck anyone gets in a lifetime. I hope not.

Sir, we got ourselves a pretty good fuel leak coming off this left engine. I think you better come back and look for yourself . . .

Desktop let me use his batphone to call Sharon. She said neighbors called the first night to tell her I'd been shot down, was missing in action and presumed dead. She said she didn't believe them and knew I was okay.

Must've taken a '37 hit and it took out the main fuel line!

I got word the next morning Growler wanted to see me in his office.

When I knocked on his closed door, he bellowed, *"Report!"*

I wondered, *Report?* Nobody does that military crap here. Blink! 3:21.

Damn you!

I lean forward, spin the clock, and shove its face to the wall. Better.

Anyways, I marched in, halted in front of his desk, came to attention, popped a crisp salute, and barked, "Captain Halliday reporting as ordered, sir!" He kept me at attention as he scowled through an open regulation and made notes on a legal pad.

I cleared my throat. "May I be at ease, sir?"

"Negative," he snapped. He finally frowned up at me and growled, "Holiday—"

"Sir, my name is Halliday."

"Are you aware you overflew your max duty day by *fourteen* minutes?"

"No, but—"

"You leave me no choice. I'm filing formal charges."

I pictured launching myself across his desk and grabbing his throat.

"But, sir . . . I saved the aircraft and—"

"My hands are tied. Rules are rules, Holiday. Dismissed."

A piranha in the goldfish bowl. Let him take his best shot; I don't give a rat's ass. I'll nail him if I ever get the chance.

I should've stayed up north with Tex and the boys.

I light another Lucky Strike.

Tick . . . tick . . . tick . . .

I expected the flight surgeon or shrink to bring us in for counseling, but we never heard from them.

How come it's not on fire?

Just lucky so far! She could blow any second!

I was on a two-day break, then ba-da boom! ba-da bing! Right back to work tonight. Just as well. When you're bucked off a horse, you gotta get right back on.

How can we stop it?!

We can't!

Tick . . . tick . . . tick . . .

I asked to be Candle 23 tonight to check on Tonto. My apprehensive radio call drew silence. Finally he exclaimed, "Candle 23! You no die!"

I told him I did.

He explained all his men survived the napalm.

Tonight's flight back was a nonevent. The entire Barrel Roll was undercast; so we just bored holes in the sky. It's the start of the rainy season, you know.

Tick . . . tick . . : tick . . .

Do you mind?!

Tick . . . tick . . . tick . . .

Eastwoods, you stupid bastard! Look what you've done! You've killed us! If you'd left your hands off the goddamned cross-feed . . .

Tick . . . tick . . . tick . . .

Dammit!

I reach over to my nightstand, grab my Westclox windup, rear back, hurl it against the wall, and hear it shatter in the dark.

Good riddance.

I light another Lucky.

Moonbeam, Candle 23. MAYDAY! MAYDAY! We've been hit!

Charles interviewed me for three days for my Silver Star narrative. He explained, "This is a big deal. If you get the Silver Star, you'll be a shoo-in for full-bird colonel someday, or maybe even general." When yesterday he told me security made him de-identify northern Laos as "the northern theater of operations" and list Long Tien as "a forward operating location," I blew up.

"But, Charles! That turns the event into *nothing*. That could be anywhere! Nobody'll ever understand, and you guys won't get your DFCs. What the hell's going on! Did they run out of silver?"

He hung his head and said sadly, "I'm sorry, sir. The best you'll get with what they'll let me write is a DFC, and the rest of us'll get routine Air Medals. With a DFC, I might've gotten promoted, but now I'll retire as an average major."

I put my arm around my friend and told him he'd always be my hero.

He said, "It's a crying shame, too, because this is the best flying story of this war, but it'll be buried in bureaucratic gobbledygook."

He added, "But they do have you trapped on a couple of technicalities."

I asked what technicalities.

"Well, if somebody'd died, you'd be a shoo-in for the Silver Star, but because you saved every—"

"Wait a minute." I rubbed my forehead. "You're telling me they'd've liked it better if I'd let someone die?"

Charles scratched the top of his head. "I never thought of it that way. And they've got you dead to rights on the second technicality. You see, the Silver Star is reserved for lifesaving events from *enemy action*. Now, if we'd've taken a thirty-seven hit like we first thought . . . but since this was just *maintenance malpractice . . .*"

I said dejectedly, "So it's a cover-up."

He pondered that, then admitted to himself, "I guess you're right." He added, "You're not even supposed to see the narrative, but I'll sneak you a copy for your personal records. That's the best I can do."

I realize now if I had that Silver Star in my pocket, I could have my pick of major airlines—maybe even TWA or Pan Am. But with just your everyday DFC? I won't get in their front doors.

Does . . . does anybody have any ideas?

How about going into Long Tien?

At least the assignments sergeants said as a hero they'll give me my pick of stateside assignments. When I told them I wanted to be assigned to the brand-spanking-new C-5 at Travis to get back home to Sharon, they said, "Sure . . . no problem."

I figure C-5 time will look good on my airline "apps."

Are you insane! Long Tien's impossible at night! You'll kill us all!

How many months do I have left? Let's see . . . December, January, February, March, April . . . oh, Christ . . . all of May . . . into June.

Six months!

I'm not even halfway home.

I light another Lucky.

You go movin' these throttles again, you'll change the airflow and the whole wing could fireball.

Tick . . . tick . . . tick . . .

This place feels deserted since Wiley left on yesterday morning's shuttle.

I bounce off my trampoline, open his fridge he left me, extract a San Miguel, bounce back up in bed, and pop it.

Tick . . . tick . . . tick . . .

I've started taking my meals at the off-limits-to-officers NCO club, where the people are nicer and they insist my money's no good.

Tick . . . tick . . . tick . . .

Peggy Eastwoods flew up on the morning shuttle after the party. She won't stop hugging me. She keeps looking up at me with dreamy eyes and gushing, "Oh, thank you, thank you, thank you for saving my Richie." She pulled me aside and whispered, "I don't know what you did to my Richie, but he's sooooo much nicer now!" Then she giggled.

Her nonstop hugging and giggling makes me uncomfortable, so I've been dodging her and Rich.

Tick . . . tick . . . tick . . .

Would you please hold the noise down!

Tick . . . tick . . . tick . . .

I bounce off my trampoline, grab my Worldtimer off the dresser top, open the bottom drawer, shove it under my socks and Jockeys, and then hop back up.

So . . . who were Tex and the boys? CIA? Air America? Soldiers of fortune? Your guess is as good as mine.

See those black contour lines forming an oval? That's Long Tien.

Maintenance impounded the aircraft and went over it with a fine-tooth comb for three days. They didn't find a single twisted screw.

How's that possible?

Charles is right. The procedure is, "Land thirty-two to fourteen."

Are you sure? I'd bet my life it's the opposite way.

Absolutely. No question. It's right there in black and white.

Ty and I sneaked out on the ramp our second night back and figured out why we couldn't see that cross-feed knob was wide-open: the yellow luminescent paint stripe that's supposed to show valve position had worn off from years of fingers turning it open and closed, open and closed, open and closed, over decades of preflight checks. A penny's worth of missing paint nearly killed us.

We knew it might take months of paperwork to fix the problem, so Ty and I commandeered a can of neon yellow spray paint, made a cardboard template, and went from aircraft to aircraft so it doesn't happen to someone else.

Didn't you hear me? We need to start down now.

Not yet, Rich, or we'll hit something.

Have you lost your mind! We're gonna run outta gas!

I feel something's been ripped out of my soul.

No matter; I'll get along.

I know one thing for sure: JT is dead and buried. I left

him for dead in the left seat up at Long Tien. Weak bastard couldn't cut the mustard. If I hadn't shown up in the nick of time, he'd still be up there wallowing in fear.

But I'm here now and he's not. I'm in control now and there's no way I'm ever going to be afraid again . . . of anything.

I gotta give JT credit, though. He's the reason I'm here, so I'll always have a soft spot in my heart for the old boy.

The headings are screwed up!

Rich, I don't know which way to turn. We could be way off either direction.

One thing's for sure. When I get back home, I'm not telling anybody about Long Tien . . . ever. They'll think I've lost my mind or was high on something.

What're you doing now?

Circling around for another try.

But we're gonna run outta gas!

I'm counting on it!

So . . . whose whispers guided JT into the canyon?

Was it Jack's spirit? Or did unseen beings rise up to guide the way?

Was it a miracle? Divine intervention?

Blind luck? Intuition?

Or, do we all have an animalistic sixth sense accessed only through abject terror? Like people who lift cars off victims under the power of adrenaline, is terror our passageway to long-forgotten animalistic senses? Even for me, there remains a dreamlike quality about the events.

But if it was a dream, what's that can of Coors doing on my dresser top? Huh? Answer me *that*.

NUMBER ONE BOMBBBB! I CAN HEAR THEM SCREEEEAMING!

Oh, no. Not *again*.

I bounce off, open Wiley's fridge, extract a San Miguel, and pop it. I pull out his candy-apple chair and sit down. Then I power up the equipment he left me: that Sansui 5000 amp and AKAI crossfield head tape deck. I crank up the dBs, flick on his mike, and hear his Pioneer CS99 fifteen-inch woofers come to electronic life as Marmalade whispers the opening bars:

> *I'm changing, arranging . . . everything*
> *Ahhhh . . . everything around me*

I volunteered to sponsor Ken Frazier, an FNG arriving on the afternoon shuttle.

Maybe I'll invite him over.

AFTERWORD

We interrupt the Lawrence Welk radio program to bring you this news flash from your WNKP news desk. Last midnight one of our own C-123K 'Candlestick' planes was shot down deep over the northern theater of operations. For those of you new to NKP, the C-123 is that plane on the ramp that looks like a Boeing 737 on steroids. The crew of the massive sixty-thousand-pound aircraft reported being hit by enemy artillery fire and preparing to bail out.

"Jolly Green Giant helicopters circling the crash site this morning spotted the wreckage splattered across a mountainside and estimate the pilot must have been making an ill-fated attempt to land at a forward operating location. Observers report the approach would be like weaving a Boeing 747 into Yosemite Valley using only last night's crescent moon for navigation and trying to land in the lodge parking lot.

"All aboard are listed as missing in action, presumed dead.

"The lead investigator concluded, 'The pilot must have been insane. We can't understand why he attempted such a foolhardy stunt.' Regardless of the battle damage, investigators say the pilot should have been able to limp south to neutral territory, bail out, and be rescued at first light. Local experts theorize the pilot lost his mind, was high on drugs, or even committed suicide; in his weakness he wiped out seven other lives.

"Investigators sealed the pilot's trailer as a crime scene and were observed carrying away several contraband items. When WNKP interviewed the pilot's squadron commander, he explained, 'No surprises with that one . . . Lieutenant Holiday was a renegade . . . I'm surprised he lasted this long.'

"In other local news, tonight's outdoor movie is *The High and the Mighty,* starring John Wayne . . ."

AUTHOR'S NOTE

My name is John Halliday. For many years, I resisted writing this book. Fact is, I kept it bottled up for twenty-five years. Then I had a chance layover in Columbus, Ohio, in April 1995, where US Airways captain Norm Komich, my best friend since 1968, was chairing a workshop at the International Symposium on Aviation Psychology.

Around 5 P.M., Norm, three friends, and I adjourned to the Hyatt bar where Norm asked us to share our most dramatic emergencies. He set the tone, explaining how he fondly looked back on his Vietnam flying. Norm asked me to go next, but I answered grimly, "I had an experience in Laos I'd rather not talk about."

Ever the gracious host, Norm skipped to our friends. When they finished, lubricated by good fellowship and dark Beck's, I gathered my courage and told the Long Tien story. The group looked flabbergasted. Norm was dumbfounded: "John, that is *the* air story of Vietnam. I've read every book on that air war, and your story's a quantum leap. You gotta write a book."

I refused. I explained that it would be hard, waste a

year—maybe two—plus the odds of a first-time writer getting published were a moon shot. Besides, I wanted my past left dead and buried.

That August, Norm and I addressed the Airline Pilot Safety Conference in Washington, D.C. Celebrating that evening with a dozen friends at the Old Europe German restaurant, Norm clinked his wineglass and announced, "Folks, you're in for a treat. We have among us an aviation hero of the highest order . . ."

I wanted to hide under the table, but self-consciously mumbled through a second telling. As we walked back to the Hilton, Norm exclaimed, "Did you see their reactions! They were mesmerized, especially the women. People'll be telling your story a hundred years from now. You *gotta* write a book."

I refused and begged him, "Please don't ever do that again. I've never even told Sharon."

Next year, Norm did it *again* at the Old Europe at the same table with different friends. I reluctantly repeated the tale, but again refused to write about it.

So Norm called in the big gun—my dad. In September 1997, one lone line of flying into Washington National magically appeared on our SFO bid sheet—our monthly schedule. It appeared that single month and never since. Anyway, I bid for it, and got it—way out of seniority. Mom had died three years before, so I wanted to spend the four Tuesday layovers at Dad's.

Norm flew down from Boston for my first Tuesday. The three of us went out to the Great Wall Chinese restaurant, where Norm insisted I tell Dad. I told only part of the story, but Dad was astonished. He said firmly, "Norm is right. You must write a book."

I steadfastly refused. "No way in hell."

I told Dad the rest of the story the second Tuesday. Again he said that I should write a book. I argued that to write the story, I'd have to unearth all my old demons, call them back to life, and invite them to once again howl in my face.

My father said ominously, "So be it."

◆ ◆ ◆

I was on a Boston layover at the Doubletree Guest Suites on the Charles River that same September. The leaves were turning. I walked the streets around Harvard. I watched as worried parents unpacked the family SUV, as daughters ran away for life with newfound best friends, leaving their parents wondering what thunderbolt had struck.

Back at the Doubletree, I hesitantly called John Nance, my longtime friend, bestselling author and ABC News commentator, to ask him to mentor my project. Aware that his policy was to never waste time helping new writers who'd never get published, I expected his kind rejection. But what I got was enthusiastic support and expert guidance over these past seven years. I still have those 1997 notes when he stressed three things: "Dialogue, dialogue, dialogue." When I was stuck on how to begin the last chapter, John donated the opening line, and I was off to the races. I will be forever grateful to him.

For three months, with my laptop's cursor blinking at me, daring me to write great, all I could think of was Snoopy atop his doghouse typing: "It was a dark and stormy night."

Then the nightmares returned.

I'd awaken in the middle of the night, my nightclothes and bedding drenched in sweat. I told myself, roll over, go back to sleep . . . jot it down in the morning, but found I couldn't remember most of it. So I bought a tape recorder to capture the ghostly images, then rolled over, and struggled back to sleep. I have more than a hundred hours of tape.

I stopped taping when I could no longer tolerate my voice sounding like that of a disemboweled corpse, so I shifted over to three-by-five cards that I kept on the nightstand. I transcribed nightmares throughout 1998 and 1999. Those tapes and three-by-five cards contain the words, paragraphs, and chapters of this book. Thousands of the rubber-banded cards now fill two dresser drawers, two fireproof safes, and a metal file box.

Sharon keeps urging me to chuck them, since I have everything backed up, but they're old friends. If the house ever catches fire, after Sharon and the cats, they're the next things I'd save.

I finished writing on Super Bowl Sunday, 2001. Unsure it was any good, I asked John Nance to read the five-hundred-page manuscript and give his opinion. Three years' work hung in the balance. I held my breath when John called a week later: "I've never seen anything within a light year with this much polish. This can stand up against anything since the Civil War. But it's not about Vietnam, is it?"

He answered his question. "No, it's not. This is the Eternal Battle that transcends time. With the country contemplating war with Iraq, your story should be required reading for *every citizen* to learn that when we go to war, these things happen."

Sharon had to peel me off the ceiling.

Supercharged, I knocked on New York agents' doors for two months, only to have them slammed in my face. So I reluctantly called John back. He graciously recommended me to an agent I'll call Sophie, who fell in love with the story and took me on. The project was filled with hope. Getting published just was a matter of time.

At our first meeting near New York's Greenwich Village, Sophie lectured me that before she'd submit my book, I'd have to cut three chapters that I loved, rewrite the first five, create a new chapter two, then write both an introduction and epilogue.

After picking the pieces of my shattered confidence off the floor, I told her, "Sure, no problem." But I was bewildered. How could Nance have been so wrong?

I rewrote through spring and summer. Then Sophie and I crossed our fingers as we submitted to five publishers on September 5, 2001.

Then 9/11 hit.

Sharon and I watched on TV at home as the second plane hit killing *my* friends, on *my* plane, on *my* airline, on *my* regular Boston trip. Friends I'd flown with for years turned to street dust. Sophie watched out her apartment window as both planes hit, and never recovered from the horror. I cried all day and was incapacitated by blinding migraines for a week.

All five publishers kicked the manuscript back. Sophie explained that the industry was in shock and was canceling books already under contract. One editor said the book showed promise, but I needed to hire a book doctor. Sophie agreed. It was clear that if I didn't hire a book doctor that I couldn't afford, she'd dump me. If I did, we'd wait a year and hope the country would heal.

I heard, *What'd we agree you'd do when they knock you down?*

I answered Jack, "Get back up." So I bought a dozen books on editing and started *all over* at page one.

A year later, in October 2002, Sophie pronounced that if I made *just a few more* changes, she'd resubmit in January. I proudly delivered the overhauled work to her on December 31, 2002, and then waited through three months of agonizing silence.

On April 1, 2003, sensing something wrong, I called and got her sledgehammer news that she'd decided to retire, having never resubmitted to anyone. I was devastated—two years' work together down the drain.

What'd we agree you'd do when they knock you down?

So I called John Nance again. He said he'd help me find new representation, but we searched all of 2003 and came up empty. By December, John advised that it might be time to throw in the towel. Then I had breakfast with my other best friend, Ken Frazier. When I told him it might be time to give up, Ken asked poignantly, "JT never gave up . . . so . . . why would *you*?"

I promised Ken I'd take one last shot, but set a deadline. If I didn't find an agent by April 1, I'd torch the documents, sick of years of watching the project crash and burn.

I learned the hard way that agents only accept written queries—a one-page overview. Having never written a query, I e-mailed six off and got back six rejections. Then I e-mailed off another batch of six and got four more rejections. Then Liza Dawson called and asked for the entire manuscript. She called back on March 3, 2004, and changed my life. She gushed, "I love your book! I was still turning pages after three A.M.!"

But my heart sank during our first meeting when she told me the book *still* needed editing. When I admitted that I couldn't afford a book doctor, I thought she might ask me to leave. But she volunteered her husband, Havis, a writer and editor.

That was the turning point.

Liza, you lassoed this project back from the brink of oblivion, and I will be eternally grateful. My greatest privilege in producing this work is my partnership with the incomparable, unsinkable, effervescent Liza Dawson. She solves complex problems with a smile and "Don't worry. We can fix that." This work remained frustratingly untitled until Liza conjured up the perfect *Flying Through Midnight*.

I also give thanks for Havis Dawson. Havis did light polishing throughout that made each page glisten. He unjumbled the critical opening four paragraphs that had been a nagging issue for years. That done, Liza was poised to submit last August, but she cautioned me that there were no guarantees: expect rejection, but then she'd try other publishers, likely get rejected, and keep trying until . . . well . . .

Then publishers started calling *me*. But I knew Liza'd found us the perfect publisher when Lisa Drew called. Lisa said that she'd nearly missed her subway stop reading it; she'd had to bolt through the closing doors. But she won me over with her understanding that the airplane and Jack's red die were major characters. Lisa polished Havis's fine work to a high sheen, epitomizing Stephen King's quote: "To write is human, to edit is divine."

I am thankful for Lisa's colleagues: associate publisher Roz Lippel, art director John Fulbrook for his stunning jacket, editorial assistant Samantha Martin, photographer Joyce Ravid, production editor Dan Cuddy, counselor Elisa

Rivlin, and copy editor Steve Boldt. I am also grateful for the talented people of the Scribner sales force.

The last part I want to tell you is about my dad and me on our third Tuesday in September 1997. Rather than driving from Washington National to the house, Dad detoured down Memorial Bridge. I watched the Jefferson Memorial and Tidal Basin whiz by.

Puzzled, I asked, "Where're we going?"

He answered cryptically, "On a trip down memory lane."

Dad circled the Lincoln Memorial in heavy traffic and then escaped onto the calm of Constitution Avenue. The Capitol dome was straight ahead. The Washington Monument was at two o'clock. Dad pulled over and parked along a wide, brown lawn. The sky turned gray and overcast.

I asked, "Why're we stopping?"

"You'll see. Let's walk over to the Reflection Pool."

I stepped out and got hit with an early autumn blast. *Brrrrr!* I folded my uniform collar around my neck. Dad saw me shivering, reached in the backseat, extracted a knee-length coat, hurried around, and helped me put it on. "You don't own a winter coat, do you, Son?"

Embarrassed, I admitted, "No, Dad, but it's Californ—"

"Take this one home with you."

I nodded sheepishly. Then my father wrapped his arm around me, I put mine around him, and he led us toward the Reflection Pool. We walked in silence and *shuuushed* through an inch-thick carpet of leaves. Then off to our left, I caught a glimpse of the black batwing edifice of the Vietnam Wall. My stomach cramped.

"Dad!" I snapped. "I *told* you I never wanted to see this place." I turned to escape. My father grabbed my coat sleeve, tugged me back, and said firmly, "It's time you faced your past, Son. Come on; we'll do it together."

I shrugged, Dad tugged me close, and we trudged down the left batwing. My shoes turned into bricks. Beads of sweat soaked my shirt. Dad said seriously, "Son, you need to face your demons right here and now. Otherwise, they'll torment you forever."

We stopped at the subterranean apex. Bouquets adorned both wings. To our left, a wind devil swirling a rainbow of leaves raced down the brown grass, encircled us, and then collapsed, sending the colors crashing to our feet.

I stared at the black granite wall and whispered, *How many?*

He answered solemnly, "Over fifty-eight thousand."

I said mournfully, "What were the politicians thinking?" Then I yanked my bent fifty-three-year-old frame erect and saluted them.

Dad: "You gotta write that book."

Get real. Airline pilot gets published? Not gonna happen, Dad.

"Look at Ernest Gann . . . *Fate Is the Hunter.* He was an American captain, too. And John Nance did it. Every once in a while, all the pieces fall into place."

What if I'm not good enough?

"Nonsense. You've been preparing your whole life."

But, Dad, I'm not a great writer.

"Don't try to write great. Just pretend you're telling me the story."

But the story's . . . huge! I wouldn't know where to start.

"At the beginning. And write from your heart."

Dad, I'm afraid.

"Fear is just a feeling. Don't let it run your life."

I said nothing.

"Your fears have all the power. Hold nothing back."

But what if I fail?

"The only failure would come from having never tried."

I wouldn't want to disappoint you.

"You could never disappoint me, Son."

But it could take years.

"Then you'd better get started."

It took me years to bury my nightmares. I don't want to unearth them.

"You must be willing to split your heart open, Son."

I shook my head.

"Johnny-me-boy," he said, echoing his father's Irish brogue, "years will pass. You can look back and say you wrote it, or regret having never tried."

It was a long time ago. What if nobody cares anymore?

"Look at all these people. You think *they* don't care?"

We'll see, Dad.

"But you *have to*! You kids were lambs at slaughter! They sent you out there with *nothing*! If you won't write it for me," he pleaded, and waved his arm across the 58,000 names, "write it for *them*."

I kissed Dad good-bye at Gate 28 the next afternoon. He waved, smiled, and hollered "Bye!" as I went down the jet-bridge. I waved back and shouted, "See ya Tuesday!"

The next Tuesday I attended his memorial service.

About 11:30 P.M. on September 25, 1998, while visiting friends on the Outer Banks of North Carolina, my father excused himself from their bridge game saying he wanted to sit on the porch steps and enjoy the full moon reflect off the incoming tide. When he failed to return, they went out to check on him. They found him leaning against the railing, apparently asleep. But when they nudged him and called softly, "*John*," he didn't respond.

A helicopter ambulance landed on the moonlit beach and life-flighted my father to a Norfolk, Virginia, hospital, where he died.

> *I wasn't there that morning*
> *When my father passed away*
> *I didn't get to tell him*
> *All the things I had to say*

My father's smiling photo at the back of my desk sustained me through seven years: "You can do it, Son."

Dad, you were right: Every once in a while, all the pieces fall into place.

*I know that I'm a prisoner to all my father held so
   dear
I know that I'm a hostage . . . to all his hopes and
   fears*

So, Dad, here it is. We did it.

*I just wish I could have told him
. . . In the living years*

J. T. HALLIDAY
November 2004

PERMISSIONS